Lilies of the Field

Studies in the Ethnographic Imagination
John Comaroff and Maurice Bloch, *Series Editors*

Lilies of the Field

Marginal People Who Live for the Moment

EDITED BY

Sophie Day, Evthymios Papataxiarchis, and Michael Stewart

Westview Press
A Member of the Perseus Books Group

Midwood

Studies in the Ethnographic Imagination

Published in 1999 in the United States of America by Westview Press, 5500 Central Avenue, Boulder, Colorado 80301-2877, and in the United Kingdom by Westview Press, 12 Hid's Copse Road, Cumnor Hill, Oxford OX2 9JJ

Library of Congress Cataloging-in-Publication Data
Lilies of the field : marginal people who live for the moment /
  edited by Sophie Day, Evthymios Papataxiarchēs, Michael Stewart.
    p.   cm. — (Studies in the ethnographic imagination)
  Includes bibliographical references (p.   ) and index.
  ISBN 0-8133-3531-0 (hc)
  1. Marginality, Social.   2. Social groups.   3. Hunting and
gathering societies.   4. Poverty.   I. Day, Sophie.
II. Papataxiarchis, E. (Evthymios), 1954–   .   III. Stewart,
Michael, 1959–   .   IV. Series.
HM136.L542   1999
305.5'6—dc21   98-30158
                                                                         CIP

10   9   8   7   6   5   4   3   2

2/26/01

Contents

Illustrations

Acknowledgments

The initial stimulus that eventually led to this volume came from a conference of Europeanist anthropologists organized at Le Creuseot by the Ministère du Patrimoine in 1992. Thanks to Christine Langlois and Claudie Voisennat in particular for the original invitations.

This volume grew more directly from the workshop on "Poverty and the Politics of Marginality," which was organized by the editors and by Rita Astuti at the London School of Economics in September 1996 with the generous financial support of the British Academy and the London School of Economics (STICERD). We would like to thank all the participants in this workshop, including Alexis Gardella, Dimitra Gefou-Madianou, Tom Gibson, David Lan, Tulsa Patel, Deborah Tooker, and James Woodburn—who do not appear as contributors in this volume. Melissa Llewelyn-Davies suggested our title. Participants at the anthropology research seminars at St. Andrew's, Edinburgh, and University College London made helpful comments and criticisms. Alexandra Bakalaki, Janet Carsten, Danny Miller, Olivia Harris, and James Woodburn kindly read and commented on the introduction. Maurice Bloch, David Lan, and Maria Phylactou read the entire book, and Maria in particular made countless editorial suggestions for each of the chapters. Many thanks for her help in the preparation of the manuscript. Hara Kavakli, Evi Kotsou, and Angela Zachariadou helped ease Greek-London links. Finally, we would like to thank Efi Avdela, Cornelia Sorabji, and Jonathan Weber for their help and patience.

Sophie Day
Evthymios Papataxiarchis
Michael Stewart

Consider the Lilies of the Field

Sophie Day, Evthymios Papataxiarchis,
and Michael Stewart

"Consider the lilies of the field, how they grow; they toil not, neither do they spin: And yet I say unto you, that even Solomon in all his glory was not arrayed like one of these. . . . Take therefore no thought for the morrow: for the morrow shall take thought for the things of itself. . . ."
—*Matthew 6:28–29, 34*

The Present

The original impulse for this book came from a sense that the ways of life of London prostitutes, Hungarian Gypsies, and Aegean Greek peasants—among whom we, the editors, carried out research—could be interestingly compared. These people live more or less in poverty at the margins of society, where they are often treated with contempt. Instead of adopting mainstream notions of work, productivity, and long-term economic planning, they appear to take a "natural" abundance for granted and to forage for their subsistence. Sex workers gather what they need from obliging markets, as Aegean Greek peasants and Rom Gypsies "harvest" money from state banks and the non-Gypsy world, respectively. In these cases foraging depends upon an idea of plenty; it is taken for granted that whatever you need is available more or less whenever you want it—there is no need to store, or to do without so as to hoard for the future.

This "anti-economic" stance is part and parcel of a specific set of attitudes towards time, person, and community, as indicated in this Introduction. This abundant world is celebrated in rituals that create a community of equal and autonomous individuals. Greek men drink and gamble themselves free from the mundane and oppressive world around them rather as the Gypsies drink and sing themselves into a brotherhood of equals. While London prostitutes do not create a corresponding community, they too achieve a satisfying individuality in their personal lives. In such ways, all three groups invert their socially marginal positions and claim a significant personal autonomy. Since these achievements are explicitly and systematically contrasted to the longer term orientation of their neighbors, it seems ethnographically accurate to say that they live in opposition to the mainstream. Certainly, at times, they are perceived as a threat to other, "respectable" ways of life.

This book deals with a much broader range of social groups and individuals than the European comparison that we had in mind originally. But the other people presented in this volume share the effort to live in the present, with little thought for the future and little interest in the past. Some chapters describe what are commonly known as "cultures," others deal with stages of the life cycle, and still others present individuals who are exceptional in their own settings. Some of these people work as wage laborers, some forage in the forest or on the sea, and still others trade or till the land. In the midst of this almost bewildering diversity, a common commitment to the present moment becomes all the more striking. These are people who live resolutely in the short term, and, in privileged moments, they transform this short term into a transcendent escape from time itself. In what follows, this quasi-ritual status outside durational time is called "the present." This term is intended to refer very generally both to the short term—to processes of foraging for example—and to a ritual transcendental moment outside durational time altogether (Bloch 1977). But, where relevant, the "short term" (durational time) is distinguished from "the present" (ritual time).

The achievement of a permanent, timeless present involves an exceptional inversion of mainstream practice, in which the present is seen as the location of suffering and deprivation that may—with luck, prayer, and effort—be overcome in the future. This view of the present can be found in nostalgic attempts to return to a previous golden age as well as in utopian theories or millenarian visions. The quote from Matthew's Gospel that opens this Introduction concludes, "Take therefore no thought for the morrow: for the morrow shall take thought for the things of itself; *sufficient unto the day is the evil thereof.*" For the early Christians, and for most of us, the ills of the world belong to the present. By contrast, the people found in this book imagine the present as other people imagine the future or the past: It is a source of joy and satisfaction. Through their fundamental commitment to living each day as it comes, these people invert their marginal status and put themselves at the center of their own moral universe. They also achieve a remarkable voluntarism in their sense of identity: the less you are concerned with past and future, the more true it is to say, "you are what you do."

This particular form of transcendence is achieved through activities that celebrate the evanescent nature of accomplishments. Freedom and autonomy, then, are defined precisely by their momentary characteristics—which refuse to be caught in any framework outside their fleeting performance. Freedom and autonomy stand in opposition to transcendental values associated with a variety of institutions that organize long-term social reproduction and, simultaneously, produce hierarchical relationships. Institutions associated with the long term come to be tainted by their associations with the state, with more powerful neighbors, and with processes of social control.

In response, people who live in the present try to disengage themselves from such institutions. Some of the people represented below have found that their sense of time or, indeed, timelessness constitutes a powerful tool of resistance and opposition to surrounding neighbors and institutions. In the mainstream, institutions such as the household—with its hierarchies and mechanisms of social control—appear to enable social reproduction through time and to connote a solid permanence. The people described in this book are prepared to try to do without such arrangements rather than enmesh themselves in a politically coercive world where they can find a place only as dependents.

Yet, the achievements discussed below are colored through and through by a sense of loss. In refusing to build a long term through conventional households, for example, some of these people find that they cannot reproduce themselves at all, nor easily pass on their values and achievements to a new generation. Hungarian Rom see themselves as "orphans" who live in homes without "parents." London prostitutes find themselves conceiving children only to lose them, and Japanese day laborers discover they will grow old without the prospect of becoming incorporated into the shrines of their natal families as ancestors, and so they will wander through the rest of time as rootless ghosts.

Plan of the Volume

In the course of this Introduction, the ethnographic material found in the book as a whole will be framed by various theoretical debates. We discuss the "culture of poverty" and the "encapsulation" of hunting-and-gathering populations. We then address briefly the ideological aspects of living in the present; and, through the single example of the household, we offer an example of the difficulties experienced by people who attempt to live in the here and now. Finally, we consider briefly the multiple political uses to which these cultural attitudes have been put, both by the people immediately concerned and also by more powerful others.

The book itself is divided into four parts, each prefaced by an introductory comment that locates the chapters with reference to our developing argument. Part One establishes the geographical and social diversity among cases in this volume, and the next two parts describe various strategies for living in the present. The final part raises questions about the academic and official discussion of marginality. This organization of the volume does not reflect any determinist argument about "living in the present." Rather, it represents one of the many ways a comparison could be made across our sample so as to highlight a common ethos. Part One moves from Michael Stewart's account of Rom (Gypsy) horse dealers in socialist Hungary to Frances Pine's chapter on Polish peasants and concludes with an essay by Laura Rival on Amazonian forest foragers. At first sight, no three groups could be farther apart in terms of social organization. Rom even self-consciously contrast themselves to peasants, including mountain people like the Górale. And the social/ecological setting of both these groups could not be more different from that of the Huaorani. And yet, we believe, it is possible to observe fundamental similarities that derive from a common orientation to the present moment. For instance, Stewart argues that the Rom representation of their subsistence activities is very similar to the Huaorani notion of gathering from a generous forest.[1] "Gypsy activity," *romani butji*, is described as scavenging, gathering, trading, begging, fortune telling. Such activities are united by an attempt to reap without sowing. Rom revel in the idea that it is possible to live without labor and production and to exist instead through the market and especially through trade in horses. As with the Huaorani and many of the examples presented subsequently, personal autonomy is achieved through gathering or tapping into abundant wealth, through sharing on demand, and through the immediate use of goods and resources.

The Górale constitute a limiting case. It would be perverse to suggest that these peasants in the Carpathian Mountains represent themselves as foragers. Like other peasants of the region, they reproduce themselves mostly in and through the medium of households—in the sense of a named building with associated land and a group of co-inheritors attached by descent, marriage, adoption, and joint labor on the family farm. In what sense, then, can the Górale be compared with the Gypsies and the Huaorani? The answer lies in their relationship with the outside world. Their houses symbolize "the inside" of the Górale community, which is pitted against all the various forces of "the outside" world that the Górale have confronted over the past few hundred years. And these apparently autonomous and self-sufficient households are sustained through activities in that outside world—through markets and migration— where the Górale do not behave like "proper peasants" at all. Inside their homes the Górale seem very different from the Huaorani or the Rom, but outside they become "tricksters" who behave in ways remarkably like the "Gypsies." And in these brief moments, the Górale see their own households in a less positive light, for they look more like other institutions of social control and hierarchy in that outside world.

The contrast between the Rom and the Górale introduces the volume because it indicates the extremes of a continuum that runs through the volume: whereas the Rom try and live exclusively in the present, these Polish peasants qualify for inclusion in the book only because they mark the limits of this orientation to the present. Resembling the example of other peasants in so many ways, the Górale example makes it clear that a commitment to the here and now can belong to mainstream values and behavior as well as to the margins; the difference is one of degree. This book is not, therefore, simply about other and more exotic folk, but about an *aspect* of many peoples' lives.[2]

The chapters in Part Two present strategies for living in the present on the part of two individuals: Rita Astuti describes a Vezo woman in Madagascar who sells fish in the market, and Yasushi Uchiyamada evokes an untouchable woman in South India who engages in quasi-marital, cross-caste relationships. The analysis of such strategies is developed in the context of social groups and "minorities" in the third part to the volume. These are single-sex groups. Tom Gill's study of day laborers segregated at the margins of big Japanese cities, Sophie Day's study of female prostitutes in London, and Evythmios Papataxiarchis's study of chronically indebted Aegean Greek peasants provide us with examples of an explicit *politics* of the present and of the self.

The fourth and final part juxtaposes Mark Harris's ethnographically based chapter on the *caboclos* of Brazil with Stephen Nugent's theoretical discussion, based on the same ethnographic case, of the misuses to which terms such as "marginal" can be put by anthropologists. Most of the people described in this book might be said to suffer marginality and what an earlier generation would have called "a culture of poverty." Nugent asks how best to present this kind of case material. An interview with an Egyptian doctor concludes the book with a life story in which an orientation to the present makes sense only in terms of the doctor's own perspective on place and history. Fanny Colonna's choice of an interview format was made specifically to avoid the reductionism inherent in explanation, and in this sense it provides a response to the anxieties Nugent articulates.

Accounting for the Present: The Issue of Marginality

It has not been always easy to persuade an audience that what is ethnographically recorded in this book actually exists. Yet, we are hardly the first to try to put this phenomenon on the ethnographic map and, more particularly, to point out connections between social disadvantage and a cultural commitment to the present.[3] In particular, this book will remind many of an earlier literature that implied that the very poor at the edges of capitalist expansion had a culture of their own: the culture of poverty as described by Oscar Lewis and others in the 1960s.

The Culture of Poverty

For Lewis, a culture of poverty emerged at points of proto-proletarianization, when already wretched peasants made the first moves into modernity. The main features of this "culture" were: gregarious behavior, informal credit among neighbors, alcoholism, the use of violence to settle quarrels, consensual unions, male desertion, a tendency to live in matrifocal families, and an abiding interest in short-term achievements over and above the long term.

Lewis's work was almost immediately attacked, and it is easy to see why. One problem, as Ulf Hannerz pointed out, was the addition of structural relationships to a list of cultural traits so that unemployment, for instance, became part of a learned culture (1969:180). This confusion rendered the model implausible, and offensive. Additionally, a methodological focus on the family divorced processes of socialization from the broader social and political context. Another problem was that the "marginal" was constructed as an object and reified so that it was not possible to appreciate the central role that these poor and disadvantaged people played in the reproduction of local and global capital (see Chapter 10). Lewis appeared to imply that the poor of Puerto Rico were "marginal" because their "deviant" culture made them so, thus reproducing the very ideology that sustained their oppression.

However, for all its limitations, Lewis's work did contain important insights into a widespread cultural syndrome. In a descriptive, non-theorized way, Lewis observed an important contrast between the people he was discussing and classic proletarians. In his foreword to the second edition of La Vida, in which he tried to elaborate the notion of a culture of poverty, he stated baldly that "when the poor become class conscious, or active members of trade union organizations, or when they adopt an internationalist outlook on the world, they are no longer part of the culture of poverty, although they may still be desperately poor" (1968:xliv). This particular insight has been lost in later writing because authors have mistakenly conflated Lewis' observations with studies of more traditional working-class communities.[4] They were helped in this confusion because Lewis himself considered ideas and ideologies to be mechanistic reflections of economic positions, such as poverty. His critics merely had to show that some poor people did not try to live in the present in order to undermine the correlation as a whole.[5] In reality, a range of identities may be found "at the margins," just as Hannerz found in a ghetto of Washington D.C. a number of overlapping and, in part, opposed lifestyles—"mainstream," "swinger," "street-corner"(1969:38–56).

Leo Howe's material on the long-term unemployed in Northern Ireland illustrates this point beautifully (1990, 1998). Howe describes communities where work is the foundation of most other statuses that married men hold. These were lost with long-term unemployment. In the face of an official discourse that aims to distinguish the "scrounger" and "cheat" from "real job-seekers," most unemployed men represent themselves as would-be and willing workers. Their dependence on welfare payments was presented as a means to sustain them in their search for productive activity. Howe worked in both Protestant and a Catholic communities, and he shows how unemployment among the latter is more readily seen as a structural feature of the system than as a failure of individuals. More Catholics than Protestants adopt an ambitious stance vis-à-vis potential payments from the social security office. Rather like the Polish and Greek peasants, the Catholics are less afraid to appear as "scroungers" before representatives of a state to which they have little attachment. In the Protestant community, better incorporated materially and ideologically within the British state, the rhetoric of the "deserving" and "undeserving" poor is more effective at preventing any activity that could be represented as "scrounging." Howe's data demonstrate clearly that historical relationships with the state (and thereby also with work providers) decisively differentiate activities among communities of the long-term unemployed that are similar in formal, structural terms.[6]

Another insight of Lewis's was to show that the very behaviors that enabled survival in a hostile world could have unintended effects, which themselves helped reproduce the relationships through which these people were disadvantaged. Paul Willis later provided an ethnography, better grounded in theoretical terms, showing "how working class kids get working class jobs" as a result of the very defensive strategies that they developed to cope with a school system from which they were excluded (Willis 1977).

Despite the very real problems in Lewis's approach, we have tried to recover these insights into the ethnographic phenomenon of "living in the present." However, a more recent debate on the distinctive traits of hunters and gatherers, and on the historical origins of this cultural adaptation, provides a broader theoretical framework.

Foraging: For Food, Wages, and Other Goods

Two links between the hunter-gatherer ethnography and the chapters in this book suggest themselves. First, there are similarities in cultural forms, including a common stress on mobility, gathering, sharing, and notions of affluence (see next section). Second, questions about the historical origin of these representations and practices are strangely similar. In both the hunter-gatherer debates and our own, a central question concerns whether living in the present is a phenomenon *sui generis*, a sort of cosmological choice, or whether it is a response to encapsulation. Encapsulation refers to a process of incorporation or domination within pre-modern, colonial, and, now, nation states, where hunter-gatherers live in enclaves because they do not participate in the ways of life practiced by more powerful neighbors—they do not till the land, breed animals, pay taxes, honor the dead, build houses, and so on (Woodburn 1988).

The ethnography included in this book throws light on processes of encapsulation in very different situations. It shows that living in the present is an active, not passive, response to conditions of marginalization and social exclusion, and that at times it constitutes an effective cultural and political critique. In this broader context, a comparison can be made between the strategies of avoidance that are classically associated with African foragers and the processes of confrontation and negotiation that are described by contributors to this book.

The French anthropologist, Claude Meillassoux extended Woodburn's description of the temporal orientation of African hunters and gatherers (Woodburn 1968). He described their economy as "tied to the present, without any duration or continuity" and hence as characterized by an "*almost* complete lack of concern for the past as for the future" (Meillassoux 1973:194, italics in the original). Meillassoux argued that this "offers opportunities for individual freedom which is revealed by the sexual attitudes, the weakness of marital ties, individual mobility, the fragility and instability of social institutions both within the band and the nuclear family" (1973:195). These general observations hold good not only for many foraging societies but also for many of the cases presented below and, indeed, for Lewis's poor.

As Bloch has pointed out, the problem with Meillassoux's technological determinism was that it ignored the variety among hunter-gatherers and failed to address the case of Australian Aborigines who combine foraging with an elaborate interest in a mythical past (1989:16–17). Woodburn's work among the Hadza of Tanzania contributed to a shift of emphasis (1979, 1982). He introduced the concept of "immediate return," which corresponds closely to what we are calling in this volume an "orientation to the present." He described Australian Aboriginal sociality in terms of a contrasting "delayed return."[7] Woodburn showed how immediate return was based on notions of an abundant natural world in which individuals could move freely and had independent access to resources as well as to the means of coercion. In this militantly egalitarian world, all forms of dependency and binding ties were avoided. Returns on labor were immediate, and there was little or no investment in either goods or particular social relations. In ensuing debates, the problem arose as to whether immediate return was constructed *sui generis* and produced through the foraging way of life or was a reaction to encapsulation by surrounding and more powerful social groups. In Woodburn's view, encapsulation may have encouraged immediate return by way of political opposition to outsiders, but it was equally intelligible as a choice of lifestyle that others would make if only they knew its benefits. In other words, "the present orientation" could be generated by opposition to authority and dependence *within* a society as much as in opposition to outsiders (1988:62–64).

Gibson's important study of the Philippine Buid (1986) brought these issues into focus, since the mountain Buid practice swidden farming and yet live in many ways like immediate return hunters and gatherers. Gibson attributed the egalitarian qualities of Buid social life, which involved a radical avoidance of all forms of dependency, to political relations with their predatory Christian neighbors.[8] These latter constantly tried to place the Buid in their debt, or to forge other long-term relationships in order to bind them into the political and economic hierarchies of the lowlands. Gibson's argument is rendered all the more powerful through the ethnographic demonstration of the revolutionary consequences of one Buid man's attempts to lead his followers into "conventional" politics (1986:101–21). Property relations began to emerge in kin groups, and sharing practices between Buid changed. As household ties came to mediate the relations between individual and group, a political leader representing the whole community emerged for the first time. The sense of Buid identity itself was radically challenged (1986:115).

The chapters on the Huaorani and the Vezo of Madagascar both illustrate that debates about origins may be misplaced in the absence of historical evidence. But Rival and Astuti also both argue that this should not preclude consideration of the current political uses and implications of living in the present. Rival argues that Huaorani culture is best understood as a social form *sui generis*, which arose in conditions as obscure as those that generated other cultures and societies within the Amazonian area. Huaorani lead their lives without past or future in an ever unfolding present because of a cosmological preference. At the same time, Rival shows how their way of life today constitutes an effective form of resistance to their neighbors and a strategy for dealing with encapsulation. Elsewhere, Rival has described how Huaorani children were kidnapped by Zaparo Indian rubber tappers, who turned them into bonded labor during the nineteenth century rubber boom (1992). In this book, she describes a sense of "absolute victimization" among the Huaorani, who live in constant flight from predatory outsiders, always under threat. The Huaorani consider that they are the only true humans in their environment, and they imagine all others as cannibals. These cannibals might snatch the vitality of the Huaorani to reproduce themselves.

Much the same historical uncertainty surrounds Vezo social forms. The Vezo, poor fisher people on the west coast of Madagascar, say that they were never subject to the Sakalava kings of the early modern era because they were always able to run away. If the king came to the coast, the Vezo would take to sea. By taking to their canoes, refusing to pay tribute and to be questioned about their past, the Vezo avoided incorporation within the kingdom. Astuti suggests that "by fleeing, the Vezo seem to have opted for an alternative mode of defining identity, a mode in which people are what they do in the present, rather than being determined by their own or someone else's past" (below, Chapter 4).

The encapsulation thesis also provides insight into relationships with the state in very different contexts. Gill shows how an identity fostered by the state is developed into a positive value in its own right. The Japanese state has historically marked out the category of day laborer as a particular type of person. In most industrial systems, day laboring is widespread, but it is just a type of work, even if it has a low status and is often associated with particular regional or ethnic groups. Partly as a result of state control, it seems that the categorical ascription is permanent in Japan: once a day laborer, always a day laborer. The return to their hometowns and to mainstream employment is more or less impossible. In big cities, day laborers provide a flexible workforce to the construction industry and are congregated into lodging houses *(doya)* that form large urban quarters around the *yoseba,* or labor markets, which are totally separate from the rest of the city. The conscious rejection of the bondage and long-term commitments of the white-collar worker, as well as the exclusive commitment to the present, can surely be seen as a response on the part of *yoseba* dwellers to this encapsulation.

Day discusses an analogous process among commercial sex workers who operate in a repressive environment, where they have to work in isolation through personal networks. London prostitutes find that their personal names are a means of state record keeping and legal control. Making a virtue of necessity, they adopt a variety of identities and, in general, possess at least two legal identities, using one as a private citizen and another for work. Some women develop different identities for different clients. This maneuver also enables them to sever ties temporarily with family and previous friends or colleagues. In these and other ways, prostitutes remove themselves from ascribed statuses, such as those associated with kinship, during the periods when they work, stressing that for the time being they are who they make themselves and no more.

Papataxiarchis discusses peasants of northern Lesbos and relates their experiences of political and economic dependency to late integration into the Greek state. These peasants often imagine themselves as a corporate unity of households aligned with the state. But experience of marginalization has also provoked them to construct an alternative social identity: *chorio*, "village, " is an imagined, egalitarian community of shared moods that in some way inheres in the place itself and exists outside time. The peasants of North Lesbos—particularly the more marginal ones, such as bachelors—have politicized this alternative identity in the form of protest against the state.

Although processes of exclusion and marginalization differ in these examples, ranging from continuous and extensive surveillance on the part of the British and Japanese states to occasional and minimal contact among Malagasy and Ecuadorian neighbors, the enclave reaction is similar. Before turning to the activities that anchor these people in the present moment, it is worth reiterating that this orientation to the present does not derive exclusively from social marginality or disadvantage. Note, for example, the Egyptian doctor who combines an active detachment from the world with an intellectual commitment and secular passion for his relatively high status and rewarding work. As noted earlier with reference to the Górale, most people live some of their lives in the here and now, but the chapters in this volume focus on a thoroughgoing marginality, where the difficulties of reproducing through time and the more or less self-conscious, explicit opposition to dominant groups and institutions are particularly clear.

Ideological Aspects of Living in the Present

The ethnographic study of hunter-gatherers has shown that a repertoire of practices exist through which durational time is transcended. These include gathering, sharing, and immediate consumption. In addition, obligations to other individuals—such as kin, as opposed to the wider social group—are denied. Irrespective of ecological and other differences, such practices construct a timeless present in conjunction with a sense of abundance. We consider that this involves an ideological commitment in the sense that these images of abundance and timelessness are a "representation of imaginary relations to the real conditions of existence" (Althusser 1971: 152).

The sense of ideology we employ is similar to the one Maurice Bloch developed in discussions of the representation of the life cycle and, particularly, of birth and death (1989, 1992a). Bloch is interested in images of the world created during rituals and the processes by which they are made to appear convincing. These deny or ignore durational time and the embedded processes of growth and decay, picturing instead a world outside that of daily experience—a world in which order is permanent and inscribed in the nature of things. In brief, Bloch argues that the formalization of communication found in ritual, but absent in everyday encounters, helps establish the truth of this view. One of the effects of formalization is to make each ritual communication seem identical to previous ones and thus to collapse the everyday experience of durational time into a special experience of transcendental, unchanging continuity, a kind of "non-durational time." Bloch links the amount of ritual found in a society with the degree of institutionalized hierarchy. It is through ritual that traditional authority, in Weber's sense, is constituted. This authority then appears to guarantee the long-term reproduction of the social order.[9]

It should be stressed at once that few of the people described in this book carry out much ritual, in the traditional sense of the term. However, ritual and secular activities may not be strongly demarcated. In these cases, the processes of foraging, sharing, and immediate consumption appear to be rooted in ideological representations that share qualities with Bloch's sense of ritual/ideology: They are symbolically marked; they constitute transformations of surrounding practices; and they deny the importance of durational time. It is therefore in a modified sense that we use the term ritual to describe such actions, which are performed often in a self-conscious style of explicit opposition to the rest of the world.[10]

A second point of contrast should also be clarified. Although we make extensive use of Bloch's insights, we are using his ideas on very different ethnographic material. Like the cases in the Pacific discussed by Brenneis and Myers, where formalized and ritualized speech acts appear to create a social space for egalitarian relationships (1984), in the chapters that follow, our authors show that a ritualized present can be thoroughly and self-consciously emptied of any associations with the past and with authority. And though we use the term "transcendence" to characterize this state, our use of the term refers to a very different relation to the world than that described by Bloch.

To talk of production as "gathering" implies the short term, since production thought of in this way negates notions of material transformation and of planning—ideas that are so characteristic of production processes that take time and that depend for their efficacy on the passage of time.[11] Gathering and gleaning provide a favorable context for the elision and transformation of the short term into a timeless present. Representations of foraging and associated concepts of natural abundance are antithetical to the very idea of economy, which relies on notions of scarcity, saving, delayed consumption, and planning. To speak of "economy" is to speak of a model of behavior according to which present actions should provide for the future. Gathering provides the opposite model, according to which there is no need for present action to provide for the future: The future is guaranteed instead by a generous, affluent, physical environment.

The denial of labor and effort in all these cases is exaggerated and buttressed by ideological means. The Vezo talk of fishing as a form of "gathering" and contrast it with agriculture.[12] They also forage in the market much as the Huaorani forage in the forest, or day laborers forage on the streets of Japanese cities. They treat the market as another resource like the sea, to be used each day without attending to seasonal fluctuations. But their rhetoric of market wealth is belied by their continuing poverty and dependence on the Masikuru agriculturalists for their staple food of rice. Likewise, the Hungarian Rom claim to be "boys of the market" but, in fact, subsidize their horse trading with money earned in factories.

Even the Huaorani could be said to put effort into appearing effortless. It is true that they make the Garden-of-Eden claim that the monkeys they hunt hand themselves over voluntarily. And they regard the gardening activities of their neighbors with ridicule, mocking the manioc drink that these people work so hard to produce. The Huaorani value *huentey* above all and in explicit opposition to the values of their neighbors. During these productive moments, you lie in complete tranquillity in a hammock, doing nothing at all. This is described as "an almost awe-inspiring state of grace by which a person feels so good that s/he does not feel any drive to spend energy or become restlessly active" (Rival 1992:161). Missionaries translated *huentey* as laziness; but this is a "creative laziness," for the Huaorani assert that the production of their own, prized, sweet manioc drink depends upon this *huentey*. Nonetheless, to the outsider it seems clear that this Huaorani drink is but a poor man's version of the beer their horticulturist neighbors make.

This process of reimagining the world is particularly apparent in the creation of images of abundance. Abundance "out there" is not simply a precondition for gathering; it is equally a symbolic product of such activities. Among Aegean Greeks, the Rom, and Japanese laborers—and even, though perhaps to a lesser extent, in London and Amazonia—a generous environment seems to be produced through ritualized activities that create a frame through which its prior and independent existence can be taken for granted.

Like gathering, sharing, too, can take activities out of time and relocate them in a timeless present. It is opposed in this way to reciprocity, which, as Bourdieu has demonstrated in his critique of Levi-Strauss's theory of exchange, is a temporal process governed by interested calculations (Bourdieu 1977).[13] Different forms of sharing can be distinguished. Woodburn, like Gibson, considered demand sharing to be particularly characteristic of a defensive reaction to encapsulation (see Woodburn 1998; Gibson 1986). Among the people described in this book, another type of sharing is elaborated even more extensively. In fact, it blurs the distinction between "exchange" and "use," for it involves the immediate consumption of goods in activities such as drinking, gambling, or singing. People share what they have in an expansive hospitality and sociality that bypasses *reciprocal* exchange. As Papataxiarchis has shown, in an analysis of the ritual etiquette that governs coffee shop hospitality, members of a drinking circle stop applying the code of reciprocity at a certain stage and come to treat drinking together as an expression of the heart, clearly demarcated from interested calculation (1991, 1992). Shared drinks make it possible to come together in true communion. This context is set apart by the etiquette and turned into a "ritual" where duration is transformed into a present without beginning or end.

In this book, Papataxiarchis describes an equally dramatic form of consumption that involves money. Men gamble away their wages and the European Union loans that pour into the local community through the Agricultural Bank; thereby they display their disdain of the obligations and self-interest associated with money and with working for bosses or answering to state officials. What is crucial in gambling is not skill but style. This is not a contest with another player but with money, whose standard meaning as a symbol of economic dependence is inverted and defeated.

The transcendental present insulates the ritualized space of the drinking or gambling table from the surrounding world of "dark" dependencies and "heavy" obligations that emerge in production and reproduction. Greek men, and particularly those who identify closely with the coffee shop, are momentarily able to recapture a "true" and "authentic" self that is governed from within by natural emotions and reach *kefi*—a state of lightness and good mood (Papataxiarchis 1994). Likewise, Huaorani men and women turn into playful children during their intensely gregarious feasts. As when Gypsy men sing together, the here and now becomes the only point in space and time that guarantees a sense of completion, of satisfaction, and, in this sense, of autonomy.

The ritualized, ideological nature of abundance based in sharing comes over particularly strongly in the case of the Japanese day laborers discussed by Gill. These men "come about as close as one can in an industrialized society to practicing 'immediate return'" for they consider their wages to be "present money" and quote a proverbial saying from the Edo period: *Yoigoshi no kane wa motanai*—"Money is not something you keep overnight." Many men do not work again until they have spent all their earnings gambling and drinking, without any thought to the future. In a comically futile gesture, the Japanese state encourages a saving mentality in the *yoseba* by opening banks in which laborers can deposit their daily wages. But these banks are hardly used, and Gill observed that deposits made in the afternoon were frequently withdrawn by the end of business on the same day.

In singing, drinking, and gambling, men "become" themselves. This exploration of the nature of "becoming" is taken in a different direction in the last chapter of the volume, where Fanny Colonna records a conversation with a middle-class medical practitioner in Upper Egypt, Dr. Nisseem. In one sense, this is a chapter about the history of Egypt since the 1950s. But, from another perspective, the conversation reveals the ways in which Dr. Nisseem strips away time and place. His form of individuality is explored over a whole adult life rather than in ritual moments such as those found in the Greek coffee shop. And, even though the story is a historical narrative, Dr. Nisseem plays down both past and future in favor of his commitment to the present moment and to the setting in which his individuality unfolds.

In his account of untouchables in Kerala, Uchiyamada shows how a similar process of becoming takes on specific meanings at the margins. He argues that cross-caste *bandham* relationships—which are conjugal as well as sexual unions, but neither fully marital nor commercial—create a particular sense of self. Uchiyamada's heroine is a split person who remains divided throughout her life, unlike upper caste women who gradually resolve the divisions between their sexuality (as single women) and fertility (as married women). Indian women are not supposed to enjoy erotic love outside the family or to cross caste boundaries. Thus the actions of untouchable women threaten the religious, dharmic order of the universe that keeps them subjugated, as Uchiyamada shows in the intensely moving concluding section to his chapter, where the reader is led to understand how one woman's anti-clockwise walk around a temple at midday "engulfed and erased the dharmic order."

Many of the people described below find themselves irredeemably divided between life in the present and the possibility of reproducing through time—building houses or tombs, tending family land, marrying and bringing up children. To participate in social reproduction is to compromise that present-oriented self, to become caught up in the long term and restricted by dominant, hierarchical relationships.

The Household, a World Divided

Few people manage to live wholly within the present and, for the majority, some aspect of the long term is reincorporated through the back door. Many of the people described in this book consequently experience a double identity, or even a divided world. Households provide settings in which this sense of division, often a juggling act between the short and the long term, is commonly located.[14] The household is readily reified as a badge of identity, emphatically distinguished from the surrounding world. Yet, its very permanence can be a source of mistrust. The household may look like an outpost of the state or of more powerful neighbors because of its hierarchies, explicitly recognized by many as a site—often the primary site—of commitments, responsibilities, and obligations in the long term: in brief, a trap.[15] For people who are so fundamentally committed to living in the present, it is difficult to reproduce in households, even when these are radically separated from the wider society. Indeed, taken to the extreme, an orientation to the present would preclude all social reproduction. A less extreme variant involves the construction of alternative models of the household. The effort to recuperate houses for people who live in the present is variously achieved by associating the long term with the other gender, with married as opposed to single people, with the dead rather than the living, and so forth.

The opposition between a male, public world and a female, domestic world is particularly familiar. It is true that women are associated with the household more often than men are and, in comparison with a ritualized present, they are often caught up more extensively in long-term processes of social reproduction. It is all the more striking then to come across the examples of Neny, Górale traders, and London prostitutes, all of whom contest the values with which they are (symbolically) associated.[16] The material in the book shows that women as well as men distrust the "household"–insofar as it stands for onerous duties and responsibilities–and can step outside it. Individual dealers in Poland or Madagascar as well as in London appear to become "themselves" when they leave home. These women lose themselves in the "magic of the market" and, even if they work alongside many others in bustling noisy marketplaces, they may act as though they were on their own. In Neny's case in Madagascar, her pleasure in dealing is so great that she can barely drag herself away from the chance to broker a deal in order to fulfill social obligations to other Vezo and their guests. For her, the emphasis is as much on her own skill and risk-taking as upon the collective nature of the market. Among the Górale, the equivalent moment, when women forget their ties and responsibilities to other people, appears to be so transitory that its poignancy is tangible. Pine shows how women hawk their wares in the marketplace with a distinctive, "trickster" manner, reminiscent of the way that Rom playfully dominate *gażos* on the horse markets of Hungary. While working on the land in cooperative teams, for instance, personal autonomy and equality are willingly limited, but a different, more individualist perspective emerges when dealing with outsiders.[17] From the perspective of the trickster, the house-based order is similar to the wider society, to which it is normally opposed, if only because both the household and state subsume the individual equally within a larger and long-term project of social reproduction and inequality.[18]

Single-sex celebrations of men have been discussed above in terms of a vision of the self where men harmonize their moods and their voices. In such contexts, these men consider themselves to have achieved an enhanced individuality; their identities are neither blurred nor merged. This state of being is similar to that achieved by some of the women as they cross various thresholds and shed their mundane obligations and commitments in favor of a heightened individuality. Therefore, this vision of the self cannot be tied exclusively to the realm of ostentatious consumption, and the settings in which autonomy is achieved appear to differ according to a number of characteristics, including gender. In this way, by moving beyond the standard opposition between a public male and a private female realm continuities between concepts of the self and living for the moment become more evident. This is not to suggest that the male and female selves are equivalent, nor, conversely, that they are invariably associated with alternative and oppositional models of the household.[19] Rather, the household provides an important example of the apparently inevitable contradictions inherent in an orientation to the present.

The material in this book also shows that multiple visions of the household can coexist. The communist state in Hungary saw in Rom houses a potent setting through which to encourage assimilation and a settled, sedentary life. "Successful" Gypsy households, led by respectable parents wisely accumulating resources to hand on to their children, were encouraged to abandon their fellow Rom and join mainstream, non-Gypsy society. State policy—organized around Hungarian officials' ideas of civilized, petty bourgeois domesticity—played upon a tension inherent in Rom life between the demands of reproduction in the household and an ideology of brotherhood that sustained Rom communities. The brotherhood was celebrated in a sphere of large-scale unisex celebrations in which women appeared to be relegated to the socially divisive and self-interested household. A similar opposition is described for Aegean Greeks. Yet, here an additional tension between men who identify with the value of *kefi* and householders is recorded (Papataxiarchis 1994). In both cases, women are represented at times as though they are compromised by their dealings with the outside world, by their commitment to saving for the long term and to planning, and by their opposition to some forms of conspicuous generosity and consumption.

However, as suggested above, this apparent association of a wholesale orientation to the present with "brotherly" men—who live for the moment (male/public), in opposition to "wifely" women in households wholly involved in reproduction (female/private)—is misleading both in ethnographic and theoretical terms, if taken as the whole picture. Stewart shows how this model coexists with another in which the Rom are "orphans." Rom counteract *gaźo* (that is, non-Gypsy) notions of the household by presenting themselves as though they were all children who perforce must depend upon the wider Rom community, the household writ large, for their nurture. Within this anti-authoritarian family, Rom grow up free to move from one house to another, to eat where they please, and to ignore demands made upon them by kin and non-Gypsies alike. This constitutes a particularly effective political method for dissolving standard connections between the long term and relationships of authority that were outlined above with reference to Bloch's approach to ritual. Rom, in other words, recuperate a notion of transcendent permanence without its associated hierarchies. The Hungarian state was therefore unable to delegate authority to household heads, who could govern the Rom on the state's behalf.

The difficulties in these efforts to redefine the household are particularly apparent in Day's chapter, where two perspectives emerge. The one is associated with acute divisions between work and home, or public and private, that can become highly problematic. For many of these women, the home is seen as a haven from the world of work, at least for some future time when they will have their own children and join mainstream society once more. However, most find it hard to build that future as they find themselves "addicted" to spending their money on trivia in the process of rejecting a "straight" lifestyle associated with the drudgery of ordinary jobs. Although freely spending earnings might seem similar to the practices of Gypsy or Greek men, to these women, it also appears lonely and restrictive. They feel coerced into a solitary and isolated existence where they experience little choice in what to do with their money.

This sense of coercion applied to other aspects of life as well. Reassuring themselves of their own fertility, which their work calls into question, many women repeatedly became pregnant. However, these pregnancies were often terminated because women were not ready to step into the mainstream future associated with childrearing. Partly in reaction to the problems of this divided self in a divided world, a minority of the women tried to live in a unitary here and now. Doing away with a putative, respectable, bourgeois future of children, home, and husband, they remained oriented to a present in which they constantly remade themselves through dealings with money and other forms of enterprise in all facets of their lives, including motherhood. In a sense, these women gradually achieved an individuality that was also a basis for social relations with other, like individuals, as they reintegrated different aspects of their lives and turned consumption into a constant source of pleasure and profit. The household was realized as an aspect of the here and now, rather than as a potential future. This permanent present seems to provide one radical solution to the problem of division.

Given the association between social reproduction and procreation, it is not surprising to find that single-sex gatherings recur again and again in this volume, since the business of social reproduction and procreation as a whole has been captured by the dominant ideologies to which these people are opposed.[20] Few people represented in this volume go so far as to abandon reproduction altogether, but some members of the single-sex groups described in Part Three do without households and without children. Japanese day laborers living in hostels, Greek bachelors, and many prostitutes do not have children. Others, like Dr. Nisseem, make use of other peoples' houses and enjoy "family" vicariously.

Although not necessarily images from inside the household, other examples in the book also describe split images of the world—images associated with marriage, parenting, or death—. Rival shows that a tension between dependency and autonomy emerges at the time of marriage. Although individual autonomy is celebrated in most matters from an early age among the Huaorani, couples are often forced into marriage. It is only in the context of cultivating a particular type of manioc for the marriage feast that Huaorani complain of having to do hard work. Once married, and for as long as they have dependent children, the couple lives out various forms of stylized mutual dependence that are not found in any other relationship in this society. In all these ways, marriage is a locus of binding ties and dependence that Huaorani life is otherwise organized to deny. On the other side of the world, Astuti shows that the Vezo dead impinge upon the living by demanding long-term plans and economies. Substantial sums are saved and then invested in tombs or are consumed by the living during death rites. Vezo "short-termism" is what differentiates the living from the dead, and yet the Vezo have to engage with a long term. The lightness and pleasure associated with market trade is incompatible with looking after the interests of the willful dead and of ancestors, who would like to dominate the living just as aggressive kings and royalty wished to do in the past. Vezo attempt to achieve a balance: They submit as little as possible to the long term by devoting themselves as much as they can to the freedoms of the present.

Cartoon representation of "Kamayan," an archetypal day
laborer, with nothing in his bag but freedom. The artist,
Arimura Sen, works at the Labour Welfare Center in
Kamagasaki, Osaka. (Originally published in Hotel New
Kamagasaki by Arimura Sen. Tokyo: Akita Shoten, 1992.)

The Politics of the Present

It is possible to look at how people use a present orientation without assuming that
it came into existence for and can be explained historically with reference to its
curent uses. The ritual construction of a present is not just an escape from the real
world but also changes the world. However, in the existing literature, the implications of this sort of action have not been adequately delineated because political
anthropology has focused on instrumental action oriented to the long term.[21]

Though the literature on hunter-gatherers and the culture of poverty address
these issues, from our perspective each of these traditions has its own problems.
Hunter and gatherer ethnographies are commonly too romantic in their celebration of the tenacity of this distinctive way of life and rarely sufficiently attuned to
the hardship and exploitation that follow from encapsulation. Conversely, the
culture of poverty model is too pessimistic since it implies a passive adaptation
by people who "can't help themselves."

Concepts of resistance have recently given an impetus to the anthropological
studies of politics.[22] In particular, they have encouraged the study of politics from
"below" and in the context of everyday life, an analytical strategy that is shared by

the contributors to this volume. Further, as they were inspired by a Gramscian interest in the contestation of hegemony, these concepts of resistance have put the processes of legitimation and consent into question.[23] Yet, many studies of resistance have suffered from essentialism and romanticism, particularly when it comes to describing the intentions of the poor (see Abu-Lughod 1990, Stoler 1986). The most serious limitation, however, has been aptly described in terms of an "ethnographic refusal," that is, the refusal of thick description: "Resistance studies are thin because they are ethnographically thin: thin on the internal politics of dominated groups, thin on the cultural richness of those groups, thin on the subjectivity—the intentions, desires, fears, projects—of the actors engaged in those dramas" (Ortner 1995: 190). A focus on resistance to domination has involved a curious assumption of internal homogeneity and even the backwardness of "culture" (with regard, for example, to religious beliefs), as well as a somewhat instrumental view of politics.[24]

The studies included in this volume display a willingness to engage with the ethnography and to confront unfamiliar forms of political practice, including its aesthetic dimensions. Terms like "pleasure" and "happiness" characterize these activities, which may have few points of contact with more mainstream, instrumental, planned action. Despite a lack of fit with conventional expectations—and in contrast to a view of resistance as "passive," "implicit," and "destructive"—the politics of the present is often constructive, politically effective, and in some cases obviously rewarding. The cases in this book illustrate, in varying degrees, combinations of all these three positive qualities.

In some we find a defensive stance of nonengagement, which aims to define an autonomous space through reducing contact with the dominant order to a minimum. It is interesting that the examples illustrating this form of politics most clearly belong to the two extremes of the world system: the Amazonian frontier and Japanese late capitalism. The Huaorani imagine themselves as the prey of their neighbors and therefore have to keep as far away as possible, and some of the *yoseba* dwellers reject attempts by the state and the unions to extend allowances that would implicate them in the state welfare system because this would compromise their masculine autonomy. This stance can be a politically effective position even though it is not aimed at transforming the overall context. At one time, it may have looked as though the Huaorani could be forced off their land, but Rival argues that they have managed to convert the oil companies into another feature of the ever-providing forest, since these companies now provide an endless supply of desired goods for the Huaorani.

A second form of resistant action seems to produce more conventional symbolic capital. The political success of Greek peasants in renegotiating their debts depended on the degree to which the government was attuned to the logic of their demands. In the course of the 1980s, when the socialist party (PASOK) came to power, the government became more responsive to peasant claims. In its populist practice, the PASOK government participated in a long-standing tradition of clientism, but it also pursued a cultural logic of anti-statist protest that existed at village level. It adopted a discourse that personified the state as a very rich and powerful patron who was expected, for example, to show a spendthrift attitude, of the kind that is admired in the coffee shop. In this context the state was required to model its relations with economic partners in the European Union on the coffee shop, somewhat to their bemusement, and then to generously redistribute its resources to its own disenfranchised citizens.

In a third type of political use, an openly aesthetic politics constructs a "whole" person in the present moment, whose active individuality rests on a balanced combination of emotion and self-interest. Day describes this lack of division as a radical individualism, and Papataxiarchis describes it as *kefi* fundamentalism. This too can provide an effective and pleasurable form of political action. Dr. Nisseem, too, represents a remarkable achievement. A sad historical comparison brings to mind all those who have gone to "share the lives of the rural poor" in Europe, including the Russian populists and so many others engaged in rural development. These revolutionaries and reformers often failed to achieve the political and social goals for which they set out. Nisseem, in contrast, by abandoning any future-oriented project of reforming and transforming the lives of others, has perhaps genuinely found a way of integrating the life-world of an intellectual with those he helps. As becomes clear in the interview—not by way of any boast or even an explicit claim, but simply by evocation of the conditions of existence today in Egypt—this project has also been politically successful in allowing the doctor to live as an "outsider," a Copt, in a place from which many would like to exclude him. Nisseem's transcendence of other forms of politics into a present of his own making is, in this sense, awe-inspiring.

Finally, Harris shows how these stances can be combined among the *caboclos*. Avoidance is possible in traditional spheres of domination by outsiders—such as god-parenthood. Through a performative sense of self, *caboclos* also evade the normal consequences of permanent migration to the city and treat it simply as a form of "walkabout." Yet in other spheres, such as the marketing of fish through brokers or the exchange of votes for gifts, a strategy of connection is preferred. *Caboclo* politics stress both separation and integration. Evasion, truculence, aesthetic and instrumental politics all coexist over time.

These marginal groups recognize that permanence is *ascribed* neither in nature nor in society but constitutes an image *inscribed* by more powerful people into the building blocks and institutions of their societies. They use the present as a source of empowerment and the means with which dependence can be translated into autonomy. Thus the denial of time in favor of the very opposite of the permanent, of that most fleeting moment in the marketplace or at the gambling table, remains to some extent self-conscious. By way of conclusion, a more troubling aspect to the politics of the present needs to be addressed.

In this Introduction, we have argued that the politics of foraging and of sharing (in a sense that excludes the reciprocal obligations associated with gift exchange) turn duration, or the short term, into a transcendent value through a sleight of hand. The pleasure of the markets in Hungary, Madagascar, London, and Poland, and of moving through the town in Brazil, the elevated spirit of Greek and Gypsy conviviality, and the happiness of the Huaorani siesta are all existential properties of the present. This achievement depends on displacing the present from its organic link to past and future within durational time. Through disconnecting the short from the long term, an "atemporal" present is constructed.

When the people described in this book deny durational time and transform it into a transcendental present in the many ritualistic and performative contexts described, they attempt to put themselves (with mixed success) beyond social intervention. Just as a concept of permanence locates authority beyond human will, so, too, the present is hard to contest (Bloch 1989). It is, quite simply, outside time and all those relationships of duration on which the authority relations inherent to states are built into the daily lives of their citizens. But this liberation is not complete since living in the present makes people, as emblems abstracted from all historical context and relations, peculiarly vulnerable to appropriation by others.

Living in the present often denies these people what Woodburn has called "the badges of success" by which mainstream society judges people. Like hunter-gatherers who "are all too easily identified with the incompetent and impoverished within their own societies," many of the people in this volume can seem feckless or irresponsible in the eyes of their neighbors (1997:352). But there is another way in which living in the present offers hostages to fortune. The alternative form of social life that is the present can be used by other people, including powerful elites, to build ideologies of society or nation. At best, these uses escape the attention or even the interest of marginal subjects, but having your image, your art, or your knowledge taken and used by others over whom you have little or no control is also a form of domination. During Stewart's stay in Hungary, erotic, soft-focused, "Gypsy romances"—a form of operetta with opera singers dressed up as Gypsies in the main parts—were occasionally transmitted on state television. These were loathed by the Rom. One, written by a man whom the Rom thought of as an assimilated Hungarian Gypsy, caused particular offense with its portrayal of Gypsies as free of all bourgeois cares and caught up in a libertarian sexual morality. (In fact, in sexual matters the Rom are studiedly puritanical.) A sense of domination was tangible to the ethnographer. The next day at work in factories, or shopping in the town, the Rom moved alongside non-Gypsies who now saw them through the images of television fantasy, and there was little or nothing the Rom could do to correct this false impression.

The ease with which cultural representations and social relationships were, and still are, reduced to objects—cultures, subcultures, marginals—in anthropology, *as in the wider world,* accounts for many of the problems in work like Oscar Lewis's. In his recent account of East Harlem street culture, some thirty years after *La Vida,* Bourgois is aware that survival-of-the-fittest, blame-the-victim theories of individual action in the United States make representations of poverty dangerous (1995). He is particularly worried about falling prey to a pornography of violence or a racist voyeurism in which Puerto Ricans come to represent a chaotic threat to the social order. Note, though, that this representation is also one of vitality. And, as the *caboclo* case indicates, it seems that an inner nature, an authenticity, and especially a vital quality may all be readily appropriated to stand for an organic sense of nation.[25] Hungarian Gypsies provide forms of what is almost a national music; the Górale can represent one version of true Polish ancestry; prostitution provides an image for a powerful and popular fantasy of sex without dependency; the *yoseba* laborers provide heroes for an extremely popular television series in Japan; and Amazonian people provide alternative images of South American states (past and future). Likewise, hunter-gatherers of Africa have long been seen as the true autochthons, with mystical links to the fertility of the land and animals (Woodburn 1997). All these people appear literally to provide emblems, for they remain quite dispensable as human beings: Amerindians can be killed off with deliberately introduced disease or forced off their land, but their ecological "secrets" provide a new global image for Latin American countries. Former hunter-gatherers in Rwanda can be slaughtered with impunity by Hutu and Tutsi alike, and few notice. Gypsies can be removed to ghettos or camps, leaving their music to be used by the nation state. At these times the constructed, liberating present offers no escape from the present others have the means to impose.

Notes

1. The term "forage" avoids overprivileging "hunting" in the more traditional term "hunters and gatherers" and creates a distance from more conventional notions of economic activity (however, see Ingold 1991:269–272). Although we prefer the term "foraging," the more conventional nomenclature is used where appropriate in reference to the classic literature.

2. The boundaries drawn around this volume are intended to be porous. Individuals and groups often orient themselves to the present for significant periods of time before returning to a mainstream. For example, young people in Europe become hippies and tourists and, in other ways, adopt what in eastern Europe might be glossed a "Gypsy lifestyle" before they marry and set up house (see, e.g., Fél and Hofer 1969).

3. In this sense our experience is reminiscent of Woodburn's, when, in the early 1960s, he returned from his research among the Hadza in Tanzania to be confronted by disbelief from his colleagues at Cambridge as he presented his findings on the absence of "social structure."

4. We distinguish ourselves from authors like Charles Valentine and, later, Janice Perlman who argued that the urban poor of Latin America were only different from their bourgeois countrymen in the level of their wealth. Such writers accused Lewis of taking situational responses to poverty as expressions of deep-seated cultural values. In contrast to Lewis, Perlman concludes her study by saying that residents of the *favelas* ("slums") in urban Brazil, "have the aspirations of the bourgeoisie, the perseverance of pioneers and the values of patriots. What they do not have is an opportunity to fulfill these aspirations"

(1976:213). This may have been true of some slum dwellers in urban Brazil, but the implication that there is no distinctive culture among any of the world's poor, just the mechanistic effects of poverty that wealth will remove, seems unwarranted.

5. This was a point that was made by David Lan early in the discussions that led to this book. His research in Zimbabwe demonstrated that Shona living in the northern Dande valley were marginal within their nation but did not live in the present, did not forage for their food, did not share their belongings, nor use up their resources all at once. During the war of independence from the postcolonial settler regime of Ian Smith, the Dande Shona found themselves near the symbolic center of a ritual ancestral domain (re-)constructed by the guerrillas and their aides, the spirit-mediums. Marginality inside the Rhodesian state predicated (briefly) centrality within the emergent Zimbabwean state. If today the Dande Shona find themselves once more marginal in their own land, they reproduce the imagery of the encompassing state in their rituals at least, placing themselves within the protective aura of the mainstream (Lan 1985).

6. Similarly diverse relations to "the center" are found in other parts of the world. Discussing household rituals of the Akha of Thailand during one of our workshops, Deborah Tooker demonstrated that even when these appear to invert those of the center, such ritual sustains the claim that the Akha are *a center just like the encompassing polity* from which they feel in some sense unjustly excluded (see Tooker 1996).

7. Australian aboriginal forms of sociality—predicated on and organized around the reproduction of a transcendental "dreaming," which established social hierarchies among men and between men and women, and which Woodburn characterized as "delayed return"—seemed to occur where hunter-gatherers had not been encapsulated.

8. For instance, in organizing agricultural labor Buid sat in a circle facing outwards, and when a person spoke s/he addressed no one in particular so that not even speech generated reciprocity. The emphasis was on the individual's relationships with the community as a whole, and no accounts were kept of labor exchanges between individuals (Gibson 1986:41).

9. See Bloch's collection of essays (1989).

10. This qualification applies also to other ideas and practices discussed in the Introduction, such as the households outlined below.

11. This is not to say that knowledge about the long term is lacking in these situations.

12. Astuti says that in fishing, a Vezo looks for food, going out each day and thereby collecting a little something every day (1995). Vezo notice how farmers have to wait to reap, and their land is fertile because of past work.

13. Woodburn, like Gibson, considers demand sharing to be particularly characteristic of a defensive reaction to encapsulation. See Woodburn (1998), Gibson (1986).

14. The terms house and household are used loosely and interchangeably. With their names, kin connections, land, and properties as architectural spaces, houses are much more than either buildings or families. See Carsten and Hugh-Jones (1995).

15. Harris demonstrated how easy it was for anthropologists to take the household for granted as a "natural unit" and to reproduce the very ideologies that underpin household arrangements in unwittingly normative descriptions (Harris 1981). Accordingly, many anthropologists have become more attuned to the continuities between households and other institutions—in particular, the state—so that it is possible to recognize the household as both a haven and a prison.

16. Thanks to Maria Phylactou for spelling this point out more clearly.

17. This is quite unlike some other peasants of the region who adopt a bored, phlegmatic air when engaged in market trades.

18. On the de-naturalization of the household and the anthropological study of cultural models of domestic life see also, among others, Yanagisako (1979, 1987) and Netting, Wilk, and Arnould (1984). See also Okely for an early discussion of the conflicting models of English Gypsy women's behavior (1975).

19. Whereas Gypsy men's devotion to their performances (and their subsequent oblivion to household obligations) is celebrated, Neny's neighbors among the Vezo note that she cannot "keep" a husband. Neny, the Górale, and the London women are not typically associated with large scale, single-sex celebrations and their transcendence of the world in a timeless present seems to be heavily qualified.

20. As Loizos and Papataxiarchis have noted, same-sex relatedness provides a context that favors the construction of alternatives to dominant models (1991:23–5).

21. In one sense, this whole volume could be read as a commentary on Marx's hugely influential description of the so-called "lumpen-proletariat" as "heterogeneous clusters of individuals who stand on the margins of the class system because they are not fully integrated into the division of labour, people who live on the crumbs of society, people without a definite trade, vagabonds, people without a hearth or home" (Marx and Engels 1958:55). While this may formally describe the position of these people within the social division of labor, we do not agree that the so-called "lumpen proletariat" cannot conceive of or embody the seed of an alternative social order.

22. See, for example, Scott (1985, 1990); Comaroff (1985); Ong (1987); Guha (1983).

23. The contemporary interest in resistance has been historically an aspect of a wider paradigmatic transition from structure to agency. Previous work on accommodation and reproduction tended to assume that actors are passive (for example, see Turner's (1974) treatment of marginals as actors mystified in the protective shield of the sacred).

24. A contrast may be found in Herzfeld whose description of the "contest between ambiguity and order" that emerges as "everyday usage continually subverts the official code" suggests that ambiguity is inherent to "discourse" and destabilizes it. This fact creates the possibility of what one might call an internal critique (1987:133).

25. As Bourgois notes: the "street culture of resistance is not a coherent, conscious universe of political opposition but, rather, a spontaneous set of rebellious practices that in the long term have emerged as an oppositional style. Ironically, mainstream society through fashion, music, film and television eventually recuperates and commercializes many of these oppositional street styles, recycling them as pop culture" (1995:8).

PART ONE

Life Without Thought
for the Morrow

These first three chapters establish the ethnographic focus of this volume by juxtaposing very diverse groups of people: "proletarian" Hungarian Rom, "hunting and gathering" Huaorani in Ecuadorian Amazonia, and Polish Górale farmers. As might be expected from discussions of the original affluent society (Sahlins 1968), the Huaorani assume an abundant world. What is surprising are the similarities between their outlook and the views of Central Europeans. All three groups assume that they can easily find what they need, indeed, even more than they need.

Clearly, this notion of abundance is as much an ideological construct as the more common view that there is not enough to go round: the vision of limited good. And, as with other ideologies, it fails to become all-encompassing; so, although the Huaorani make much of "natural abundance" in everyday life, this view is heavily qualified during preparations for their marriage feasts. At this time, they cultivate sweet manioc, and the work is said to be arduous and painful. It has to be planned several months in advance. Later success in making drinks for the feast depends on a sexual division of labor, the absence of sexual relations between spouses, and fasting—in great contrast to other social relationships of Huaorani "extraction" (Rival 1992:185). However, when they come to feast, the Huaorani symbolically assimilate the manioc to other features of the abundant forest on which the guests can feed, such as birds in a tree. Although prepared by gardening techniques, the manioc is now called a "fruit," as if it grew spontaneously on trees.

Rival and the other contributors show that an abundant world is associated both with life in the present and with autonomy. The independence daily displayed by Huaorani in gathering food is elaborated into extremely egalitarian relations of consumption, based on a mutual surrender of identical products within the longhouse. Autonomy seems to be based on individual self-sufficiency.

Among the Górale, in contrast, domestic relationships involve mutual dependencies. Households are prized precisely insofar as they are constituted through differences of gender and generation. Yet, even among these peasants, freedom from the moral order of kinship is found in dealings with other people *outside* the village, where Górale become independent individuals. As tricksters and traders they dupe powerful and endlessly gullible outsiders who are associated with the immoral order of authority in the state.

Hungarian Rom appear to be more like the Huaorani than the Górale, stressing individual autonomy in many aspects of their lives. In dealings with their own kind as well as with the outside world, Rom value their independence. Their autonomy is intimately connected with their orientation to the present. Just as a denial of labor is associated with a lack of concern with planning and saving, so do Rom domestic arrangements downplay the transmission of identity and authority through time. Rom, in some situations, obliterate the differences between elder and younger and undo kinship hierarchies based on seniority.

The title of Rival's chapter introduces another important theme: these people are victims as well as autonomous and free spirits. The Huaorani are not exceptional when they live life constantly on the run, as the prey of more powerful neighbors. On the other side of the world in the Philippines, the Buid—who share a similar ideology—imagine themselves the prey of powerful spirits, who seem to be bigger and more aggressive versions of themselves (Gibson 1986:154). These cases offer vivid images of the precarious nature of this way of life. Such people know that they are threatened not only with exclusion but also with extermination.

1

"Brothers" and "Orphans": Images of Equality Among Hungarian Rom

Michael Stewart

It is considered desirable that:

1. *The Gypsies should be forbidden from begging . . .*
2. *They must dress like other poor people . . .*
3. *The violins must be removed from those who live from music, and broken up, and the value of these refunded . . .*
4. *This nation should really forget its old customs: to this end the council orders the building of houses in a suitable way in rows with the other [that is, peasant] houses . . .*
5. *The speaking of their language shall be forbidden them . . .*
6. *All children under the age of fourteen are to be removed and stabled in Catholic peasant families*

—late eighteenth century[1]

If the category of "endangered child" is interpreted strictly, almost all of the young children living on Gypsy settlements should be taken into care. . . . Taking their children into care is also a way of assimilating Gypsies.[2]

—late twentieth century

For at least two hundred years, the Hungarian state has hoped to assimilate its Gypsy population. This aspiration has at times been forcefully pursued as public policy—less so at other times, when it has been assumed that the modernization of society will itself bring about the desired "end of the Gypsies." Insofar as the state has tried to influence and shape Gypsies' lives, one important tool of policy has been an effort to determine the kind of households (both the physical buildings and the moral environment) in which Gypsies live. In the socialist period the living conditions of Gypsy families was one of the litmus tests for sorting out those Gypsies "worthy of," or "ready for," assimilation and those whose time had yet to come. To encourage the recalcitrant, propaganda pieces were published— with titles like "The End of the Settlement," or "The Last of the Gypsy Camps"— in which the horrors of the past were contrasted with a brave new world: no more tents, caves, or mud-brick houses; from now on the Gypsies would live in row upon row of identical, concrete, barrack-type houses. Although the state encouraged and coerced all Gypsies to live in conditions it defined as suitable, this was not the only goal of communist housing policy. Making use of the inevitable social and economic differentiation within Gypsy communities, communist bureaucrats "privileged" certain Gypsy households, those that seemed to be making efforts to improve their domestic surroundings, with further encouragement towards assimilation.

In earlier work, I have discussed how Gypsies represented their communities as "brotherhoods" of equal men and so defended their communities against the state's divisive demands that upwardly mobile households split off and join the majority society. From the perspective of a community imagined as a "brotherhood," in which everyone is supposed to share their meager resources, households already threatened to breach the solidarity of the men. Accumulation or private consumption within households represented a potentially threatening ethic. As my earlier writings have tried to reflect, this male centered perspective has great rhetorical importance in the lives of both the men and women with whom I lived. Women, for instance, helped their men sustain "brotherly" activities by scrimping and saving on the domestic budget. But, with hindsight, it also seems to me that I have been, in part, overly influenced by my own gender and the limitations that this imposed in terms of the experiences and discourse to which I had access—given that adult Rom society is rather strictly sex-segregated most of the time. I was further constrained by uncritically adopting an unarticulated model of the public and private, which led me to *expect* to find an opposition between a male, public space and a female, private one. In this chapter, I look at a different way in which Rom constructed their communities (as groups of equal and parentless "boys" and "girls," as children, and more particularly, as "orphans").[3] This, I believe, was another way the Rom slipped out of the grasp of the state that wished to reform them out of existence.

Dependence

To make any sense of the way Rom of Hungary deal with their disadvantaged social position, three general points need to be borne in mind. The first is that for the Rom there exists a categorical, dualistic division of the world into Rom and non-Rom, that is, the non-Gypsies or *gažos*, as they are known in Romany. Day by day this boundary is reasserted and reinforced, so that almost any positively valued activity can be interpreted as characteristic of the Rom, and not the *gažo*, way of doing things. The *gažos*, the proverbially "foolish" non-Gypsies, are in some ways seen as a lower form of humanity, as people who simply have not understood the proper way to live. The Rom, by contrast, know that it is possible to live "easily" and "luckily," thanks to their "Gypsy work," which I gloss metaphorically as the ability to find ways of harvesting without sowing (see Stewart 1997:17–26).

The second crucial point is that the reality of Gypsy lives on a settlement in the 1980s was anything but "easy" and "lucky." They faced grinding poverty, multiple disadvantages, and repeated misfortune. Indeed, from a strictly economic point of view, it would be hard to imagine a group of people less blessed with good fortune than the Rom. In all likelihood, these Rom are descendants of people who were enslaved in the Romanian principalities of Moldova and Wallachia for several centuries up to the middle of the nineteenth century. In Hungary, Gypsies have provided cheap labor for generations of peasants and, under communism, they filled the dirtiest and lowest paid jobs in the nationalized economy. To take just one marker of their relative material position, in 1983, when 32 percent of all Hungarian citizens had cars, only 4 percent of Gypsies in the area of research did (*Hungarian Statistical Handbook* 1984; *Dongó Beszámoló* 1984).

It is important to stress here how their structural disadvantages in Hungarian society led to daily humiliations for even wealthy and prestigious Rom when it came to dealings with the authorities and powerful *gažos*. Most Magyars (I use the term "Magyar" to refer to members of the Hungarian ethnic group and the term "Hungarians" for citizens of Hungary) in a town like Harangos, a prosperous north-Hungarian town where I lived in 1984–1985, assumed that the Gypsies were dirty, feckless, lazy, deceitful, promiscuous, culture-less beings. What was even more disturbing was that it seemed acceptable behavior to accuse Gypsies openly of these failings. Rom, of course, were well aware of disparaging *gažo* attitudes and would spend a lot of effort trying to avoid situations in which they could be humiliated.

Within a Rom settlement, a rich and successful horse dealer could plausibly claim to me that he was a "king" *(kraj)*, a man above the others, both his fellow Rom and the *gažos*. One such man used to boast to me of his dealings with "big peasants . . . big gentlemen . . . big comrades." As I traveled with him among the peasants—who also saw themselves as a marginalized population in communist Hungary—time and again I saw him manage situations to his own advantage. In these encounters, in which my friend worked his networks of connections with apparent ease, it was easy to forget how limited were the contexts in which he could sustain an elevated status. The structural weakness of the position of this great Rom dealer was mercilessly exposed one day, while visiting a collective farm to bargain for some fodder. When we arrived the boss's secretary peremptorily commanded my friend to wait outside, and when the "boss" himself came out, the Rom had to put up with a patronizing lecture on the failure of Gypsies to plan their fodder needs. All of a sudden, the man who so impressed me normally with his grace and charm seemed shaken and appeared to lose his poise: for at the

As part of the communist campaign to raise Rom living standards, "old style" Gypsy settlements were bulldozed. Here one resident rises above the occasion (Michael Stewart).

end of the day, he remained a *cigány,* meaning a "Gypsy" who could, with impunity, be humiliated in public.

The third point is that from 1961 to 1989 the Gypsies were subjected to an official assimilation campaign that aimed to bring them into the "ruling" working class and end their "usurious" activities as traders. Trade was seen by the ruling communists as an activity that exploited the "productive labor" of the "honest" workers and was deemed "anti-social" and "retrogressive," even in the petty form that most Rom practiced. More than any earlier effort to "solve the Gypsy problem" in Hungary, the communist policy involved a systematic assault by the authorities on Gypsy communities, their particular economic adaptation, their language, and their culture.[4] Though it is fair to say that all around the world Rom, and other Gypsy communities, live within a state of siege vis à vis the outside, non-Gypsy world, nowhere was this more true than in Eastern Europe under communism.[5]

Gypsies as Children in Official Discourse

In 1984–1985, apart from heavily armed police (mostly looking for defaulting fine payers), the only official to visit with any regularity the site where I lived was a woman whose role combined that of midwife and social worker for families with small children. Though teachers, local counselors, and other officials were supposed to visit the Gypsy families, none came because the Rom, who lived be-

The bulldozers get to work (Michael Stewart).

yond the edge of the town in a separate settlement, had a (wholly misplaced) reputation for blood-curdling violence. In part because the midwife was dealing with "innocent children" (this was her term), she felt a rare sympathy for the Rom. But she was also, I discovered, paid a supplement for these visits. The Hungarian socialist state was worried about the Gypsy population "explosion," first because they thought it was rendering Gypsies poor in the short term, and second because they feared that, in the long term, the Gypsies threatened to overwhelm the majority Magyar population.[6] The bonuses paid to the midwives were to ensure that someone handed out free contraception to Gypsy mothers.[7] Though Rom husbands sometimes objected to the midwife's visits for this reason, for the most part such women provided one of the few nonhostile links between the Hungarian state and the Gypsy population.

I was fortunate, therefore, to be lent the text of a report by Mrs. Tokaji, a midwife who worked in Harangos while I lived there. Her study dealt in general with "the role of the midwife in raising the health-culture of backward social layers."[8] She defined her goal, in the official jargon of the time, as the "final rooting out of the disorderly life" of the Gypsies. The midwife had a special role to play in this since "the fact is that the Gypsies characteristically have a strong emotional bond with their children," and, therefore, the midwife could approach the Gypsies more directly than other state functionaries. She could, especially, hope to have some influence in the all-important area of child-rearing, since, "if we want the Gypsies to become equal members of our society of workers . . . we will have to reduce to a minimum the regressive influence of the family circumstances which encourage the preservation of their traditions."

In particular, Mrs. Tokaji singled out the "psychic and mental characteristics" of the Gypsies. Using the publications of an influential amateur linguist, Jozsef Vekerdi, she talked of Gypsies as children who have failed to "grow up" into adult behavior and commented that "amongst them instincts rather than consciousness determines their actions . . . .The preconditions of rational argument are still largely waiting to be created. . . . Their actions are carried out on the first impulse that takes them. In a given situation they act without weighing up and considering the consequences." Because of this, Mrs. Tokaji explained, knifings were common among the Gypsies. "They only live for today . . . in hunting for happiness they seek to satisfy immediately their bodily and physical needs. . . . their thought is hindered by the poverty of their language."[9] Instead "in their adjustment to the world the decisive role is played by their sensory organs. The Gypsies even call themselves nature's children." Given their low cultural and intellectual level, it had to be recognized that they were incapable of grasping a problem in its entirety.

In her fundamental assumption that the Gypsies were "nature's children" and thus incapable of looking after their own affairs, Mrs. Tokaji captured the essence of the paternalist, socialist state's perspective on the Gypsies.[10] A colleague of Mrs. Tokaji, a local doctor, told me you could see Gypsies' childlike mentality in the way they decorated their houses with what he called a "jumble of colors," in the passion of arguments that would be forgotten the next day, and in their inability to save their resources from one day to another. More brutal perhaps were the words of one local communist leader who wrote:

> How many times have we declared that they in themselves don't have the strength to resolve their astoundingly severe problems? How many people realize, too, that they don't have their own social institutions, thinkers, intellectuals. Their advocates, their representative forum, can be nothing other than the socialist society, the socialist state which feels it is its responsibility to help them.[11]

In texts like this it is possible to see that the rhetoric that portrayed Gypsies as people who have not "grown" into responsible, adult behavior shaped high-level policy as much as the interactions with lowly officials like Mrs. Tokaji. Though occasionally some officials recognized that in reality low wages were the source of Gypsy poverty, for the most part the emphasis was put on their "child-like" lack of planning and spendthrift behavior. And it was this "blame the victim" schema that shaped the disciplinarian understanding of the socialist state's main effort to "help" the Gypsies, to "raise them" (as one does children) from their condition: the decision to ensure all Gypsies were engaged in socialist waged labor. From the early 1960s all Gypsies were to be compelled to take on employment in factories and farms. The provision of socialist waged labor was meant to provide the main social force for breaking them from their lifestyle. In part this was seen as a way of ensuring all Gypsies had access to regular incomes. But there was an even more important moral aspect to this policy. By participating in *collectives* of cooperating workers, by engaging in *productive* activities (as opposed to using their wits in trading), and by applying *sober methods of calculation* to their work, it was thought Rom could be persuaded to abandon their individualist, short-term, spendthrift, and potentially exploitative mentality.[12] As part of the campaign to wean Rom from their attachment to the thrills of trade, the police were encouraged to carry out spot checks on horse markets in certain areas of the country to ensure that all traders also had full-time, socialist employment. In theory, those without jobs could be charged with "socially dangerous work-avoidance." On numerous other occasions the Gypsies found themselves at the rough end of council and state efforts to help them "adapt and assimilate." In 1976, for instance, the local council in Harangos confiscated many of the Rom's horses—in order to further encourage them to live from waged labor alone. And every year until 1984 there had been a collective bathing of the entire Gypsy population of one settlement—but not of the few Magyar families who still lived there—organized by the Public Health Department and policed by an armed detachment sent down from the local military base.

As important as battles over the sources of wealth and livelihood were struggles over the meaning of household. It was the belief of state officials that by recasting the Rom household in what they saw as a proletarian (but we might characterize as a petty-bourgeois) framework, the Gypsies could be prized out of their separate communities and into the supposedly welcoming arms of the Magyar community. From the point of view of the local state, on whom responsibility devolved to demonstrate efforts in "assimilating" the Gypsies, it was above all home life that became the target of their opprobrium and intervention. Though Rom have their own sense of order and personal cleanliness, council officials would typically comment on how well particular houses fitted, or did not fit, their own sense of an "orderly" *(rendes)* home. The presence of particular items of furniture could also be diagnostic. Thus the absence of a kitchen table might indicate "a low cultural level" to an official, even though many Rom did not eat from a kitchen table, since people tend to eat together out of a bowl on the floor. And the "ability" of parents to control their children, notably by ensuring that they attended school, was also an important sign that all was "in order" in a Gypsy family. In all these and other ways, local officials from the council were, in effect, trying to establish the bases within the Gypsy family on which the state policy of assimilation could build patterns of reliable and respectable behavior and authority that could be called on.[13] There were, of course, incentives and threats. Those Rom who seemed to be regular wage-workers and "upwardly mobile" were to be offered the chance to leave the Gypsy settlement (with all its practical difficulties, such as lack of running water in the home, unpaved roads, distance from shopping and other facilities) and be re-housed in modern accommodation. For others, however, and of course these were the majority, there remained the tactic of taking Gypsy children out of their homes into state care. Thus in a 1977 report concerning the town where I lived, Gypsy family life was seen as the "breeding ground" of antisocial behavior. It was for this reason that council officials often raised the idea in conversations with me of taking more Gypsy children into state care. And unlike so many policies proposed in this town for "raising" the position of Gypsies, this one was implemented. While in 1976 there were only twelve Gypsy children in care, by 1980 that number had risen to thirty-three and by 1985 to forty. Of all the children in care, 28.5 percent were of Gypsy origin, this in a town where Gypsies made up less than 5 percent of all children in school.[14]

Gypsies as "Children" in Their Own Discourse

In the context of attitudes like those expressed by Mrs. Tokaji and many others, it may seem odd that the Rom would represent themselves as "boys," "girls," and "orphans." It might almost seem as if they were adopting one of the symbolic forms by which they were denigrated. Indeed at the height of the celebrations that punctuate the life of a settlement, when Rom are supposed to display greatest "respect" *(patjiv)* to one another, they address each other as boys, begging permission to sing to the others. Elsewhere I have discussed how, when the men begins to sing, they create an intense sense of equality and brotherhood (Stewart 1997: 181–203). What I wish to consider in this chapter is the significance of addressing one another as boys: Why is it that the term *rom* (married male) tends not to be used and is instead substituted by a word that literally means unmarried male or boy? The puzzle concerns women as well as men, for it is polite to address a woman of any age as girl *(šej)* rather than married female, *romni*.[15] To preempt my argument somewhat, I will suggest that in addressing each other thus the Rom create a view of their own society in which equality is constructed around the downplaying of all forms of seniority, those imposed by the state as well as by parents.

In order to understand this usage, I look first at the construction of the other egalitarian model of community, that of "brotherhood." This second, and rhetorically dominant model, plays on a highly gendered distinction of social action. In this model, especially pronounced in the celebrations of Rom men, drinking and singing together express the central values of *romanes*, the Gypsy way of doing things, and are associated with "brotherly" values. Manliness is associated with the expression and creation of equality among Rom in horse markets where men joust with *gažos*, Hungarian peasants. In such contexts the world of brothers is opposed to that of the Rom households to which these men also belong.

Horses, Men, and the Construction of a Community of Brothers

With their horses and the horse trade, Rom men created a zone of freedom. In the horse fairs and countless deals that went on between the big markets, they sustained an image of the economy in which abundant wealth was out there to be garnered or gleaned by those with "the luck" to know how. With horses, the Rom took a symbolically treasured object from the dominant social system and managed to invert the meanings attached to it by the *gažos* to such an extent that the Rom's activities with horses sustain an entirely alternative vision of social relations in which the Rom and not the *gažos* were on top. In particular, through trading in horses, through the commodification of these animals, the Rom could play on their ability to make the *gažos* sustain the Rom.

Whenever I visited Rom, I was soon taken by the men to inspect and photograph their horses, with the young boys set up on their backs and the men of the household standing around them. But the aim of keeping horses was not so much to display their beauty as to sell them back to the *gažos* or to swap them with other Rom. These trades were exemplary cases of "Gypsy work" *(romani butji)* and, as such, it was legitimate to interrupt almost any other activity in order to pursue the chance of a deal.[16]

The meaning and importance of horse deals for the Rom derived in part from the contrast between their role as *traders* and that of the *gažo* peasant *producers*. The peasant came to market to buy or sell an animal he needed in his agricultural work. But the Rom were not so constrained. Whereas a peasant had to buy a horse with an eye to the long term, Gypsy dealers *(kupec)* could pick up any piece of living flesh if they could turn it around fast enough to make a small profit.

Rom did not conceive of their relationship to horse markets as passive price-takers, rationally calculating their best course of action in a market over which they had no control. For them, everything happened as if prices were the result of the game of bargaining. Thus, for the Rom, the market was as much a political as an economic forum. The horse fair was an arena where the relations between the Rom and the non-Gypsies could be redefined. By making a profit on trade in the animals that above all stood for gentlemanly feeling, Rom put themselves in a position of symbolic power over the *gažos*. By taking hold of prices and manipulating them they could act out a control of the *gažos*. In the market arena, the role of the trader was to organize, persuade, or cajole others into participating in exchanges. Rom acted on the market in order to alter the terms of trade, to back their hunches, and grasp imaginatively possibilities unforeseen by others. They could then persuade and coerce their exchange partners to see the world as they themselves saw it. This achievement was all the harder and all the more pleasurable because for the peasants horse deals were always risky exposures of the self, since the value of a man on the market was no more than the value of the horse he brought with him.[17]

To sustain their position as the "bosses" of the market, Rom attempted to establish their potency over the *gažos* in a number of media, including dressing up in the style of richer landowners or members of the gentry who did not "labor" to live. But it was above all in their speech *(vorba)* that the Gypsy dealers realized their power, since it was by acting "like interpreters" between unfamiliar speakers, as one man put it to me, that they brought off their deals. Through their speech, Rom said, "we make money turn around, turn around and come to us," and they emphasized the ease with which this might be done, as a dealer "rotated" goods between customers. Explaining their trade, men would customarily use a gesture in which the fingers of one hand were lightly touched into the palm of the other at right angles and then their position rapidly reversed, suggesting an exchange of items between one hand and another. The lightness of touch and rapidity with which the hands swapped places seemed to embody the mesmerizing speed, ease, and efficiency of the dealer "rotating" goods between customers.

In the market, the power of the Rom to alter the terms of exchange with the *Gazos* and make money from them depended on their speech. This, however, was only one way they celebrated this activity. Another way in which the Rom asserted their agency in this matter was by saying that Gypsy men's success on the market depended on their "luck" *(baxt)*. Luck was something found in all dealing. Luck for the Rom was something that inhered in the game of dealing and more particularly adhered to them when they played with a *gazo*, confronting him and persuading him to part with his wealth or to give a horse for less than its value. As luck, efficacy, prosperity, and happiness, *baxt* was one of the constitutive qualities of the Gypsies, just as diligence was of the peasants. The notion of "luck" had at least two different aspects for the Rom. First, it opposed them to the dominant work-ethic. The ideal was a deal in which they had not "worked" on the horse in the narrow "peasant" sense of the word "work"—punishing, physically exhausting, sweat-expelling, earth-shifting effort. In dealing, the Gypsies let money grow without the steady preparation of the "soil." A second aspect was to introduce the element of volition into the Gypsies' market rhetoric. For the Rom, "luck" as efficacy, as the successful manipulation of the *gazo* trader, implied a background of conscious action. This was so because it was only through maintaining proper relations with their wives, and thereby keeping themselves pure, that Rom became lucky. In other words, when facing outwards towards the *gazos* their success might be represented as labor-denying "chance-luck," and, when facing inwards to their own community, "success-luck" could be seen as the effect of the Rom men's wills exercised in an area of social life that they had some control over: their relations with women.

This symbolism of luck recapitulated the dual way Rom treated their horses: by turn as commodities and as sexually available women. By playing on two ways of representing objects, as alienated things and as personalized products, Rom masked the fact that horses came from the *gazos*. On the one hand, as pure commodities, mere prices, horses were set apart from their loving peasant producers. But equally, by representing horses as available "women," the Rom alienated the hostile *gazos* from their own horses.[18] The social importance of this symbolic masking also derived from another equally important alienation taking place in all the brouhaha of the dealing. For most Rom, horse-dealing was not a financially profitable activity. In order to enter the horse trade each year, men needed to input wealth from outside the sphere of horse trading, and this came by and large from the efforts of their wives in raising pigs for sale. Despite the fact that a Rom's wife was normally responsible for most of the effort in raising pigs—by scavenging for discarded food in the rubbish bins of the town—when it came to selling pigs, women were kept out of the exchange; their labor did not give them control over the income. Their removal from the horse business was even more formalized. The Rom (men and women) gave two express reasons for this. First, women were said (and believed themselves) to be incapable of controlling a horse, though everyone assumed that any seven-year-old boy could control a tame horse. The second reason was that any female involvement, any comment a wife might make during the dealing, could spoil a man's luck. For the Rom, it seemed that they could be successful with their horses only if they kept them in an arena apart from that associated with the non-Gypsies and Gypsy women. So, just as the *gaźo* producer was separated from his product, likewise the role of Gypsy women in producing the money that enabled the purchase of horses was also symbolically devalued.

Horse dealing provided one way that these Gypsies appeared to live without the weight of labor; but in order to be "lucky," the Rom had to distinguish the activities in this sphere from all other forms of production. This sphere had also to be separated from the sphere of biological reproduction. Thus it was precisely the mark of women's biological fertility, their menstrual blood, that made them dangerous to the horse dealer because this blood symbolized the *gaźo* way of doing things: labor, growth, biological reproduction, durational time. Gypsy business belonged to a different order of reality. And this order of reality was celebrated in drinking sessions that went on informally after markets and more formally at moments of arrival and departure of Rom from the settlement. These celebrations, known locally as *mulatśagos*, from the Hungarian term for intense partying, were the high point of social life in the settlement. In them men shared food (eating from one bowl), drinks (often dovetailing their drinking so as to all consume one type of alcohol), and, above all, speech. It was especially through this shared speech—"*vorba*," which was categorically always "true"—that men became brothers to one another and asserted their unity against the outside *gaźo* world.[19]

Orphans

So far I have presented a number of symbolic constructions relating to Rom identity: Labor has been opposed to trade, brothers to households, masculinity to femininity. But what of the original suggestion that Rom are "children"? I want here to consider what it meant to the Rom to be a "boy" or a "girl," and I will begin by looking at the way Rom treat their own children. One of the most striking aspects of Rom life to an outsider is the difference between Rom behavior toward their children and that meted out in the surrounding *gaźo* environment. In most Magyar families, one finds a common European pattern, by which parents expect their children to display morally exemplary behavior—to be the "little angels" of folk talk. Children are commonly subject to a monotonous barrage of commands, protective injunctions, and disciplinary complaints. To sit with Magyar families is to have to hear over and again the phrase "don't do that" or "that's not allowed" *(nem szabad)*. By contrast, in the eighteen months I spent with Hungarian Rom families, I can hardly recall a single occasion when I heard an equivalent phrase addressed to Rom children.

Though this may at first appear a trivial contrast, in fact the compulsive fashion in which *gaźo* parents across the European and North American continents discipline their children for eating the wrong sort of food, watching too much television, and a host of other "bad" behaviors indicates just how very differently the Rom conceive the world. Expressing a rare insight into this very general middle-class form of behavior, a British journalist recently asked, "If bringing up children is a way of saying yes to life, then why is it that one spends virtually every waking hour saying no to them?"[20] He went on to list some of the orders he had given out during the previous weekend:

> Don't stick your head in the washing machine
> Stop blowing your nose on my trousers
> Don't shout
> No, we can't go to Africa for lunch
> Don't bite the toothbrush
> Stop rubbing lemonade on your hair
> Don't wipe your hands on your mother
> Don't shout
> Don't drink your juice with a fork
> Stop sitting on my head
> No you can't put your pyjamas on inside out
> Don't poke your finger in your brother's ear
> Don't post the house keys through the letter box
> Don't shout
> Mummy's hair dryer isn't a good way of warming the bath
> No you can't watch the late news tonight
> No you can't sleep in the bath tonight
> Please don't shout
> Stop sitting on the dishwasher door
> No you can't wipe your brother's bottom
> Don't look at the pictures, look at the words
> STOP BLOODY SHOUTING![21]

With the exception of those items that concern personal hygiene (for which Rom children early on learn a strict code of "shame") and the prevention of life-threatening dangers (and with Rom children even this is normally achieved by quietly and unostentatiously removing the danger, not by remonstrance), there is not a single command in this list that one might expect to hear in a Rom settlement.[22] Socialization for the Rom is not a matter of bringing "wild" or "pre-cultural" beings into the sphere of the civilized but is instead a gradual absorption into the relations that constitute *romanes*, "the Gypsy way." Children are presumed to be born with their character, with their "will" *(voja)* established. Living with them is a matter of learning about their personality, not shaping them into a mold. They are not dressed in clothes that emphasize their difference in status from adults (for instance in the unisexual jumpsuits that are fashionable among other Europeans). Rom children wear smaller versions of their elders' clothes. Nor is maturation a matter of imposing an authority structure on children.[23] If a child has a tool that others need, s/he may be persuaded (not ordered) to relinquish it or, failing that, the others will wait. *Force majeure* has no role here. In particular, this means that Rom have not been brought up to accept a voice of authority. A great value is put by the Hungarian Rom on the autonomy of will of each individual. Just as people did not intervene when a grown man in a fit of self-destructiveness knocked down part of his house, so, when the children in a neighbor's home broke several windows one morning, the mother bewailed her plight, cursed, and even shouted about them to her friends, but there was no question whatsoever of stopping the children, let alone punishing them.

In fact, parents who tried to order their children about were roundly told off by other relatives for their bossiness. I was at first rather shocked by the casual way children treated their elders, often simply ignoring their requests. Again, the contrast with local peasants was striking. In the Magyar village, relations between brothers were inflected by the authority of relative age, but, among the Rom, the child-parent relation was strongly tinted by the egalitarianism characteristic of relations between brothers described above. It was not at all the case that elders were never respected but rather that any attempt to use the formal respect due to age as ascribed authority, so as to coerce others, was bound to fail. All respect was personal, contextual, and achieved, not in any sense ascribed. There was, if you wish, no context in which personal charisma could be turned into traditional authority. The value of personal autonomy was simply too great.

In contrast to the gendered model of brotherhood, an image of social relations as taking place between boys and girls who are also orphans dissolves, or at least recasts, the opposition of "brothers" (men) and "households" (women) into a more inclusive image of community. Here all Rom are implicitly "parentless children." As such, the orphans are expected to help one another. Although adults rarely had a right to interfere in one another's business, concern for children's autonomy meant that if a Rom hit a child, others did intervene. By treating the children in ways that implied their lives were the concern of all, Rom seemed to be trying to construct an image of the community as a unity. Adults sought petty forms of assistance from other people's children on the settlement. The neighbor's child, even if one was not on particularly good terms with her parents, might be sent to the shop or asked to guard the sleeping baby. Equally well, children could expect to share the attention of adults. They were, for instance, allowed to choose where and with whom they spent their time and with whom they lived. In one case the children of a woman's first marriage lived with her mother, who carried out the daily round of a caretaker. The mother was insistent that this was not her or her second husband's wish; rather, her mother wanted some grandchildren with her. And if the children, too, had not wished it this way they would have returned.[24] It was acknowledged, of course, that most children were emotionally attached to their parents, but for that very reason, I believe, adults sometimes teasingly "kidnapped" children, persuading them to come off secretly on a trip for a few hours without letting anyone know of their whereabouts, as if to remind them that their commitment to their parents and their home was balanced by ties to other Rom and the whole community.[25]

Lest the general argument I wish to make be misunderstood, I should emphasize that I am not saying that Rom thought of themselves as children in the way we think of children. As caretakers of one another, living in households that were quite unlike those of the *gaźos*, which have senior and junior generations, Rom "boys" and "girls" were inevitably autonomous persons, like our "adults." To press this point home, I would just note that the behavior of Rom children in Hungarian schools is a source of constant friction, since they refuse the subordinate position non-Gypsy children are raised to accept. And even where teachers are sympathetic, a gulf of misunderstanding can frustrate communication. One researcher, for instance, tells the story of a boy who gave flowers to his teacher after having received a good mark in class from her. She presumed this was a gift from his parents in an effort to secure her "protection." In reality it was the gesture of a boy used to establishing his own relations with adults (Forray and Hegedűs 1985).

In a radical rethinking of the received wisdom about hierarchy, Chris Fuller, with reference to the Indian caste system, has suggested that the image of the autonomous actor is often the preserve of higher status persons keen to disassociate themselves from their dependency on lower status groups (1988). In the face of upper-class pretensions to have no need for the poor, lower caste Hindus stress on the contrary their dependence on their superiors. In Hungary (and more generally in Europe), however, the Rom have found themselves increasingly excluded from any place in the wider social order; they are treated as though they could be discarded from the social division of labor and are unable to assert any claim on the *gaźo* authorities—they are "orphans" of the capitalist and socialist systems, if you wish. As such, as people with no social superiors to protect them (but also none to discipline them), with only each other to depend upon, the Rom have come to represent themselves as autonomous people without protectors—as orphans.

If all are orphans, then all remain beholden to help each other in the never-ending trials of life, where none are protected by seniors of any sort. This throws a fresh light on inter-household relations in Rom communities and in particular on the value of sharing goods, activities, and personnel between houses. In earlier work I have talked of the opposition of "brotherly" and "household" values, saying that if the Rom lived in a state of siege in relation to the *gaźos*, the Rom household stood in a similar relation to "the brothers". In this light, many aspects of daily life on a settlement seemed to express a desire to render permeable the walls of the household and to suggest that Gypsies should be open to one another independently of their household ties.[26] Thus, for instance, food is passed between houses, and no fixed mealtime is kept in Rom families, as if to deny the idea of an exclusive, private home. The same intention seemed to underlie the custom by which Gypsy yards were left open, or did not have gates at all, whereas every Magyar house on the settlement was kept secure behind a locked iron gate. Nor did a Rom ever lock her front door when there were members of the family on the settlement. At almost any time of night or day, unless a towel hung over the door indicating that someone was washing, a guest might enter a house without any preparatory greeting or warning. Rarely did I see a Gypsy make another feel that an unexpected visit fell at an inconvenient time. Even when we arrived with a party of men after midnight on one occasion, our host was out of bed, offering drinks and coffee in a matter of minutes and making us feel that he would be happy to talk with us through the rest of the night.

Rom ideas of social reproduction were not so much rooted in an ideology of sustaining a house and handing on the capital associated with it (land, for instance) as in an alternative ideology of mutual nurture and shared social activity. Sharing activity, food, dress, language, and persons was thus a form of the continuous nurture of one another, a constant reinvention of being (see also the chapters by Astuti and Harris in this volume). For this reason, it seems to me, the Rom were fiercely insistent that Rom stepparents should love their acquired children exactly as their own.[27] The masking of a person's past behind their present, achieved identity was also reflected in the names individual Gypsies acquired. A Rom's name was not a fixed marker of an identity that existed outside a network of relations, as our names are, but was more like a nickname that had been acquired as a marker, and often a comic one, of a place in a network of relations.[28] A person could have several names, either over time or at once, each relevant to a particular set of social relations.

In all these ways, we can see that Rom notions of time differ somewhat from those in the world around them. Rom did not construct childhood as a period of life distinct from adulthood, nor adulthood as a status into which one enters after a temporal period of development and a more or less ritual moment of transition. If all are children and remain so forever, there is no place for generational difference, no need for growth, no need for change. It is possible to live in a continuous unfolding present in which life is a process of becoming.

The Anti-Authoritarian Community

The two models of social relations among autonomous Rom shaped interactions with the Hungarian state in rather different ways. Especially after 1961, the socialist state was intent on assimilating the Gypsy population of Hungary into "the working class." This was a campaign fought on a number of fronts, some involving repression of Gypsy activities and others involving encouragement of rapprochement to Magyar behavior and norms. Elsewhere I have described how the attempt to divide and rule the Rom was defeated by the practices of brotherhood

(1997:50–72). The idioms of equality discussed in this chapter indicate another way the Rom eluded the attempt by the state to find bases within their communities which they could use as bridging posts for establishing the kinds of hierarchies and authorities they needed to turn the Gypsies into obedient members of the Magyar working class.

This anti-authoritarian view of the family should not be seen simply as a strategic reaction to state control. It was also a creative and productive framework within which Rom grew up free to move from one house to another, to eat where they pleased, and to ignore demands made on them by kin and non-Gypsies alike. This cultural form was, I would argue, surprisingly politically effective.

Just as parental authority was drastically restricted among the Rom, so there was no other relation between men outside the family in which a person had the right either to lead or in other ways to stand over people.[29] Indeed, given the nature of relations with the *gaźos*, the question of leadership became particularly acute in relation to the state authorities who traditionally assumed that Gypsy communities had leaders. In fact there is a special term in Hungarian for these: *vajda*. In some communities where there was a *gaźo* resource that could be monopolized by one man (such as permits for dealing in scrap materials, or a cooperative farm that had a need for occasional Gypsy labor in large numbers), such figures emerged. In the late 1980s these leaders came to assume national political importance when the Popular Front—a formally apolitical organization that in reality carried out aspects of communist policy that the party wished to distance itself from—sought out these men to provide a "respectable" Gypsy leadership with whom they could do business. In Harangos there were no scarce non-Gypsy resources and no *vajdas*. Even so, officials' preference for dealing with such designated leaders meant that policemen, council officers, and even representatives of national governments sought out such figures when trying to deal with the Gypsies collectively.[30]

One day, a local council representative came to visit the settlement on which I lived, and he was greeted by a large group of frustrated Gypsies complaining about the lack of running water, the lack of proper roads, and the consequent refusal of ambulances to enter the settlement.[31] Immediately, he stated that he was unwilling to deal with so many people at once and asked to speak to the *vajda*. One old man pushed himself forward claiming to be the leader—maybe in the past he had once acted as a spokesperson in some negotiation with *gaźo* authorities—but before so much as a word had been exchanged, his own son stood up and ridiculed him to the official as a drunken illiterate. No one came to the old man's defense. For what all the Rom there knew, was that in Romany the word for *vajda* was *mujalo*. And the other meaning of *mujalo* is "informer."

Notes

1. Points one to five are from an order dated July 14, 1772 and signed by the Bishop Eszterházy, who officiated in the area where I worked two centuries later. (Cited in Breznay

1932:283). Point six is from a more complete version of the same decree promulgated in Vienna, the full text of which can be read in Guy (1975:207, 209); and Gilliat-Smith (1963:50–53).

2. These two statements are taken from unpublished annual reports made to the Hungarian government in 1977 and 1985 on measures taken in dealing with the Gypsy question in Harangos.

3. I want in particular to thank Sophie Day, whose comments during the workshop at the London School of Economics that prepared this book suggested the current form and content of this paper. Maria Phylactou has also provided some much appreciated editorial help.

4. With the exception, of course, of the Nazi attempt, mostly confined to western Hungary, to deport the Gypsies in 1944 to the death camps.

5. See Luc de Heusch for the original use of the siege metaphor (1966:89)

6. This was a common theme in conversations with Magyars about "the Gypsy question."

7. At the same time the Hungarian state made extra payments to any citizen who had more than two children, as part of its natalist policy of halting the overall population decline that developed under socialism. Gypsies benefited from these centrally allocated funds like all other Hungarian citizens.

8. Quotes are from verbatim notes in possession of the author. Mrs. Tokaji is a pseudonym.

9. Needless to say, none of the local midwives spoke Romany, which was spoken by a little less than half the Gypsies in the area of Harangos.

10. It would be quite wrong to imagine that Mrs. Tokaji's opinions reflected an extreme anti-Gypsy attitude. To the contrary, the tone of her text is considerably warmer and more sympathetic (though more intensely patronizing) than many official publications. This report was prepared for examination as part of career advancement within the public health service and therefore we can assume Mrs. Tokaji had, if anything, bent over backwards to present an "acceptable," "socialist" attitude.

11. Károly Bebesi, "Where from, where to?" *Dunántúli Napló* (local paper) 18 October 1981. Even as he wrote, Comrade Bebesi was mistaken or deliberately misleading: there were Gypsy and Rom intellectuals, but the state did not wish to let them play a role in articulating their people's political wishes.

12. Trade was seen as exploitative of the labor of "producers," since it did not create any new object of value (see Stewart (1997:97–111).

13. I see this process in terms similar to those described by Althusser in his discussion of the way the "individual" comes to feel addressed or "called out" by ideology (1971:160–170).

14. There had, however, been a reversal of this policy at the national level with encouragement given instead to weekly boarding schemes. The situation since 1989 has changed in some respects.

15. The collective term of address *"šejale"* (girls) is rare outside of songs. Katalin Kovalcsik suggested to me that its use in songs may reflect the fact that it was used more as a term of address in the past, since songs often act as unconscious repositories of historical practice (personal communication).

16. Though there were a few animals known as Romany horses, through which Rom attempted an especially radical rejection of dependence on the non-Gypsies, their more important efforts concerned the normal *Gažo* horses, those that came from the *Gažos*. These were trained and raised by them and therefore responded to commands in Hungarian. See Stewart (1997:23–25) for a discussion of Romany horses.

17. For the Rom dealer, too, esteem was linked to the value of his horses, but his success or failure in trade was more fundamentally an expression of his "luck."

18. By symbolically assimilating horses and women, the Rom men established a fantasy image of non-Gypsy, female availability which was hardly lived out with real non-Gypsy women.

19. At such moments, when all the Gypsy men acted in concert, they achieved an ideal of brotherly behavior that was expressed in a "light, fine mood" (voja) and that inspired them to accept, outside the context of mulatśago when relations among men were often more fractious, the egalitarian demands of the ethic of sharing among brothers.

20. T. Sutcliffe, "Mummy's hair dryer isn't a good way of warming the bath," The Independent, 2 February 1998, p.15.

21. T. Sutcliffe, "Mummy's hair dryer."

22. The Rom expressed considerable surprise, indeed some disgust, that gaźo children of two or three years of age should require adult assistance in using the toilet. Rom, I was proudly told, are self-sufficient in this way shortly after they walk.

23. Most non-Gypsies seem to take it utterly for granted that we should give our children commands. I recently watched a man in a restaurant prevent his son liquidizing his ice cream in the bowl before eating it. I suppose he was embarrassed in some way. But would the same adult have criticized an adult friend for this behavior, I wondered. What was the father trying to establish?

24. I say "shared" here, rather than "given," because there was no question of reciprocity. But perhaps the suggestion that the mother was the actor here is wrong, since I suspect it was the children, too, who decided to share their lives with their grandparents.

25. See also Rena Gropper's penetrating discussion of Rom attitudes towards childcare, from which I drew inspiration in looking through my field notes (1975:123–138). Gropper notes many ways in which children are expected to choose their most important relationships.

26. The rhetorical stress on openness to others' needs derives its significance from the fact that ties within households were, most of the time, as strong if not stronger than those between "the brothers."

27. See also Gropper's account of being encouraged to swap her own child at birth with one born to one of her Rom brother's (1975:128).

28. See Williams for a discussion that informed and inspired these observations (1984). Nicknames, too, protected Rom from identification by gaźo outsiders; see also Okely (1983:174–175) and Day (Chapter 7 in this volume).

29. In theory, young people were supposed to treat their in-laws with great respect (patjiv) but the difficulties of doing so in a community so taken by an egalitarian ethos meant that few couples lived near either set of parents.

30. This is also, incidentally, the explanation for the appearance of the various "kings" and "emperors" of the Gypsies in parts of Eastern Europe since 1990, especially in Romania. They are exploiting niches created by gaźo credulity.

31. This man's visit was formally prompted by the first elections to the local council since the late 1940s that offered a choice of candidates. I suspect, however, that if I, an exotic foreigner at whom he was keen to take a closer look, had not being living there he would never have "spoilt" his Saturday by coming out there.

2

Incorporation and Exclusion in the Podhale

Frances Pine

Góral w gory spoziera	*The Góral looks at the mountains*
I łzy rękawem ociera	*And wipes away his tears with his sleeve*
Bo góry porzucić trzeba	*Because he must leave the mountains*
Dla chleba panie dla chleba	*For bread, lord, for bread*
Góralu, czy ci nie żal?	*Góral, are you not grieving?*
Góralu, wracaj do hal!	*Góral, come back to the high pastures.*

Popular Górale Song by Michał Bałucki

Stories of Tricksters and Migrants

"Góral are you not grieving? Góral, come back to the mountain pastures"—this refrain speaks to the migrant worker far from home. In Polish songs about the Górale, and in the songs that the Górale sing and the stories that they tell about themselves, these are recurrent themes. The Podhale, a land dominated by the peaks and high pastures of the Tatra Mountains, places and anchors these people in their stories, memories, and personal narratives. But the same stories tell of loss and grief, of endless struggles against the rugged landscape and harsh weather, against the intrusive state, and against relentless poverty.

Like some of the other people discussed in this volume, the Górale occupy and move between several different social and economic worlds. In daily village life, they appear similar to other east European peasants: Reciprocal bonds between kin and houses are strong, and a collective morality underpins village social and economic organization. Hard work and industry are highly valued, and economic security is seen as the just reward of labor. When the Górale enter the outside world, however, as traders, entrepreneurs, and migrant laborers, they em-

phasize individualism above collectivity. Here it is not hard work that brings reward but individual skill in dealing, in making connections. Above all the "real"
Góral relies on his or her wits to transform, reverse, and even transcend the existing social order, for just a minute. So, Górale heroes are tricksters and entrepreneurs; Janosik, the greatest Góral hero, was an eighteenth-century mountain bandit who stole from the rich to help the poor. On one level, such narratives
celebrate Górale individualism, resourcefulness, wit, and creativity. On another
level, one hears a more haunting undertone of loss, exclusion, and powerlessness.
In the end Janosik is betrayed, caught, and hanged by agents of the state.

These trickster and bandit-hero stories are indicative of an important difference between the Górale and the "proper peasants" of eastern and central Europe
(see, e.g., Fél and Hofer 1969). The self-sufficient, Calvinist farmers, whom Fél
and Hofer took as their model, managed through endurance, patience, and toil to
make their lands prosper. The Górale clearly recognize that in their own circumstances this is not possible. Trickster behavior, which "proper peasants" would
only tolerate among youthful bachelors, may be performed by all Górale, men
and women, the married as well as the ("irresponsible") unmarried. But it is acceptable only in the context of dealings with outsiders. It is almost as if the
Górale behave like "proper peasants" within the village and like "Gypsies" in the
outside world. The Górale are famed in Poland for their autonomy and cunning.
Fél and Hofer's friends, by contrast, were known outside their village, in Budapest for instance, for their sheer hard work (1969:348). It is this combination
of an orientation towards continuity—the preservation of the past in the present
within the village—and a willingness to operate as if living in a permanent present (when *outside* the village) that I explore in this chapter.

The stories that most please the Górale are those that tell of a one-off, successful sting. In the early 1990s, Western tourists were pouring into the Podhale, buying out the shops and markets and continually searching for "authentic" Górale
experiences—a torch-lit sleigh ride through the snow, a campfire in the forest
with wild boar sausage and vodka. At that time, a Góral friend told me "the circus
bear story," which she swore was true:

> A German tourist accosted an old Góral man, saying that he wanted to go bear-hunt-
> ing, and he would pay him exceptionally well to be his guide. The old Góral agreed
> and they arranged to meet the next day. The old man sat and thought: he knew that
> there were no longer any bears in this part of the mountains, but it seemed a shame
> to disappoint the German, and to let that wonderful fee slip away. Then he remem-
> bered that there was a circus in Nowy Targ that week. Off he went to Nowy Targ, and
> arranged with the circus people to borrow their bear for a day. They loaded the
> mangy old animal into a cart, went to a particular spot in the mountains, and let the
> bear loose in the forest. The old man then went and met the German hunter, who
> was driving a range rover, equipped with binoculars and rifles and all the parapher-
> nalia of a great hunter. They drove up into the mountains, and the Góral said that

they were in luck: there had been a sighting of a bear and he knew just where it might be. They reached the place where the bear had been deposited and, sure enough, almost immediately glimpsed the animal in the forest. Greatly excited, the German jumped from his vehicle, grabbed his rifle and, mounting his extremely expensive state of the art mountain bike, set off through the forest after the bear. The bear loped on for a bit, and the German, finding the terrain too rugged even for his bike, dismounted and took up the chase on foot. The bear looked back and saw what was happening. Delighted, he turned in a circle, got on the bike and rode away. The astonished German took off in hot pursuit, shouting and waving his rifle. The bear glanced around, and seeing the running figure behind him, dismounted and walked on his hind legs up to his pursuer, took him in his arms, and began to dance, waltzing away with him into the sunset.

The activities of the Górale who successfully engage with the world outside their village, like the antics of this trickster with his bear, involve juggling, balancing, and often producing something out of nothing or, at least, out of very little. Their success rests on the ability to read accurately dominant stereotypes and to use these to their own advantage. In the late 1970s I witnessed the preparations for sending the grandfather of a certain house to his daughter in Chicago. The grandfather was very old, of fragile appearance, and possessed an enormous sweetness and innocence of nature that shone out from his face. At a time when it was extremely difficult for Poles to get visas from the Americans or passports from their own government, he managed to obtain both, saying that he merely wanted to see his grandchildren and would not stay long. On the eve of his departure his wife and daughters washed and groomed him until he shone and then packed the things he was to take. First they packed a suitcase full of brand new shirts and sweaters ("They will think they're for you to wear—you mustn't say they're to sell"), painted eggs, silver, amber, and other trinkets ("They'll think they're presents for Hela and the children—you mustn't say they're to sell"), and vodka, smoked cheese, and sausage ("Well, you tell them you have to eat while you're there"), and cartons of Marlboro ("Well, who are they to know that you don't smoke?"). Next they moved on to the grandfather himself, first wrapping him in several beautifully tanned and dyed sheepskins and then covering these with layers of new shirts, sweaters, and several pairs of new trousers. Finally, when the old man was rigid like a stuffed doll and could barely bend his arms and legs, they buttoned him into a new sheepskin coat, tied around his neck a sign—on which was written in English, "Hello. My name is John and I am going to Chicago" (in case he got lost changing planes in New York)—and took him on a sled to the train station, where he and his wife caught a train to Warsaw. It was the first time he had left the Podhale. At the Warsaw airport, his wife handed discreet envelopes of American dollars to the customs controllers, wished them merry Christmas, and asked them to look after her fragile old man. He passed through customs without having his cases opened. His first letter home announced his safe arrival, expressed his amazement at all things American, and commented that he had been very hot and uncomfortable on the plane but had not drunk anything because (not surprisingly, considering the number of layers he was encased in) he did not want to have to go to the toilet. While he was in Chicago, he helped his son-in-law with some carpentry and looked after his grandchildren while his daughter was at work. Everything he had brought with him was disposed of for a tidy profit. After some months, he announced he was homesick, and he was packed up again in a similar fashion, this time by his daughter, and sent home. His wife met him at the airport and explained to the customs controllers that the many, ornate plastic flowers at the top of each suitcase were gifts from American Poles, to place on monuments to the war dead. The grandfather watched, looking old and fragile; the customs people closed the cases without further ado; and he and his wife traveled back to the village. From the sale of the contents of his cases and from his many layers of coverings, they made a tidy profit again. Villagers generally were extremely pleased with this story, and retold it often, always lingering over descriptions of trickery and stressing both how easy it was to bribe officials on both sides of the Atlantic and, with even more glee, how gullible they were in assuming that such a sweet old man was as pure and innocent as he appeared.

Landscape and History

The Górale are peasant-pastoralists who live in the Carpathian Mountains on what is now the Polish-Slovak border. Originally Vlach shepherds, they migrated along the Carpathian ridge, eventually settling in the Tatra Mountains. There they gained usufruct rights to lands owned by the Polish king and held by local nobility, becoming sedentary farmers, although often, of necessity, continuing to do other things as well.

In the past five hundred years the Podhale (literally, beneath the high pastures), where the Polish Górale live, has been consecutively part of the Polish Kingdom, the Austro-Hungarian Empire, the Polish Republic, German occupied Poland, socialist Poland, and now post-socialist Poland. Like many mountainous regions onto which states inscribe political borders, the sociogeographical position of this area has been ambiguous. On the one hand, the remoteness of the mountains and their inaccessibility, particularly during the cruel and long winter months, reinforced the exclusion of the local peasant population from the political and economic centers. On the other hand, trade and other traffic had to cross these mountains, and market towns grew up on the main routes, providing local villagers with venues for selling surplus produce and crafts. Equally, the fact that the mountains formed the border between empires and nations provided the Górale with opportunities for trading, dealing, and smuggling in the terrain with which they were familiar but which seemed hostile and inaccessible to outsiders. Nowy Targ, the home of a famous periodic market, was by the fifteenth century already well placed on a trade route (initially) between Poland and Hungary.

From quite early on, therefore, the Górale were simultaneously excluded from, or marginal to, the states in which they were politically situated, and they were actively involved in a transnational trading circuit. From the mid-nineteenth century until the early 1990s, the inhabitants of the village where I do research had extensive dealings with both the market itself and the trade and transport routes that spread out from it. While there can be no doubt that until at least the 1950s most villagers lived in poverty, the existence of the market afforded them some opportunity not only to buy and sell, but also to forge links with people from outside the region that could lead to temporary work or to further deals, and to gain access to knowledge and information networks extending far beyond the Podhale itself. This paradoxical exclusion from the center and incorporation into the wider outside stage is a major feature of Górale culture.

The village was founded at the beginning of the seventeenth century, comprising initially about twelve families with usufruct rights to arable land, pasture, and forest. Until 1848, when they gained the right to own their lands, the peasants worked their farms and rendered dues in the form of produce and labor to the manor. Early parish records from the village indicate little specialization: Occasionally a man is identified as a blacksmith or a servant, a woman as a midwife, but on the whole villagers are registered as peasant farmers.

The hundred years after emancipation were marked by a series of ongoing hardships and intermittent crises, as the practice of partible inheritance among both sons and daughters created ever smaller and more dispersed holdings, as high birth rates stretched local resources beyond endurance, and as outbreaks of cholera and plague, crop failure and famine weakened the population. Even without such trials, the poor soil, high altitude, and long and bitter winters would have militated against successful farming. Very few families at any given time were able to maintain a self-sufficient household on the basis of their landholding; even fewer were able to sustain this self-sufficiency over generations. Records from the late nineteenth and early twentieth century show lands being mortgaged and then forfeited to non-Górale money lenders in the nearby town. Some families sent their young daughters into domestic service in the manors and town houses; both males and females of all ages also worked as day laborers for the local manor. Others went farther afield. Old villagers I spoke to in the late 1970s had memories of their parents and kin walking to Budapest to seek work; many highlanders set out for America as part of the massive wave of economic migration to the New World that swept across Galicia in the late nineteenth century. Some who left returned in later years; those who remained abroad frequently maintained contact, sending kin money and parcels and often helping other family members to migrate in their turn. This period was one of relentless, harrowing poverty; it was, at least partly, this poverty that forced Górale villagers to turn to trading and marketing, smuggling and banditry, and above all to temporary migrant labor, and that molded the form of their relationship to the outside economy for years to come.

In many respects, the Górale epitomize both socioeconomic marginality and cultural resistance to incorporation. Renowned throughout Poland as colorful renegades, an image that they themselves deliberately cultivate, they also maintain an ordered and highly moral internal social structure, in marked contrast to their often ostentatious rejection of external power regimes. Górale difference is continually accentuated in sets of images that juxtapose the inside and the outside. The inside (the Górale house and community) is portrayed in contradictory ways, both as subjugated by, and as subversively superior to, the state and external economy (outside). Each of these images is at least partly accurate; there is no single picture that could encapsulate Górale history and culture, nor all of the complexities of their relationship with external power structures.

In their dealings with the outside, the Górale attempt to circumvent or subvert the laws and regulations that are imposed on them and to maintain symbolic boundaries that allow them to keep outsiders out. They themselves, however, through choice and necessity, move constantly between their village economy and the wider local, national, and global spheres; hence the boundaries they erect are, by definition, flexible and porous ones—allowing movement out of the village, while ideally letting outsiders in only under certain circumstances and only to a certain degree. In fact, Górale control of this boundary is largely illusory; villagers are often compelled to conform to the rules of the state and to bow to the greater power of external economic orders. Their communities are regularly penetrated by outsiders in the form of state and church officials, tourists, and, increasingly in the post-socialist period, individual entrepreneurs and speculators. However, through their emphasis on the centrality of the house, the development and maintenance of their own practices, particularly around work and gender, and their very public performance and elaboration of Górale identity in ritual and ceremonial, they reinforce—at least symbolically—the resilience and cohesion of their own "culture" and social order (Pine 1997).

In the Górale social world (Pine 1996), the house represents the correct and moral social order. To use Schneider's (1980) term, it is a "core metaphor" for kinship, identity, and belonging; it contains, defines, and generates both productive and reproductive labor; and it is based on legitimate hierarchies of generation and gender. The state, and in earlier times the landed gentry, represents an encompassing but inherently repressive external order that at various points in history has threatened the integrity of the house: draining its resources through taxes and payments in kind; appropriating its members through armed service, prison, and exile; diverting its labor through service to the manor and regulated waged work under socialism.

In their daily lives, Górale villagers reinforce their positive identity associated with the house, wider kinship, and community rather than their more ambivalent identity as peasant workers within the Polish nation and state. By this I do not mean to suggest that there are no internal conflicts within Górale households or communities. There are many such conflicts: young men argue with their fathers and brothers about the use of land and other resources; young women argue with their parents about the work they should do and the person they should marry; spouses fight about money and alcohol; and fights and more entrenched feuds between different kin groups are common. Further, even during the socialist period there was marked stratification between rich and poor houses within villages (Pine 1988, 1996). However, the ideal of a moral community in which members are bound together by shared place, kin ties, and labor is very strongly upheld, and it is easy for villagers to gloss over internal differences by referring to this ideal, at least in the construction of their identity against the outside.

Górale Identity in Relation to the House

The mountain landscape, the closed village community, and the house-based farming family are seen by the Górale as the core of economic and social life, an ideological representation that both disguises the extent of their interaction with and dependence on the outside world, and keeps that world at a distance. Villagers know each other by their *przydomki*, the name of the house, which extends to all its members whether by birth (through either mother or father), by adoption or fostering, by marriage, or by service. Only local people know each other's house names, and this local knowledge allows them to place and situate each other within a shared world and to effectively exclude outsiders. The state and the church, on the other hand, impose a bureaucratic system of surnames that villagers use in their dealings with official bodies.[1] Thus, even in the naming of persons, an inside and an outside system exist.

Although it is probable that the ideology of the house was elaborated partly in emulation of the great houses and patriarchal families of the local gentry, there was also a long established Górale tradition of agnatic clans, whose members exercised economic and political control in the more remote mountain regions beyond the reach of the state. Until as late as the 1920s, parts of the high mountains were dominated by *rody* (clans), groups of agnates and their families who lived in large extended houses, owned and worked the land on a corporate basis, and exercised predatory control over lowland villages (Dobrowolski 1966). These *rody* villages represent the house in its most developed and self-contained form, providing the prototype for the smaller, more interdependent houses of the lower highlands where I work. The bandit-like behavior of *rody* members, their virtual autonomy, and the closed nature of their communities are echoed in stories of Górale heroes, most notably in the Janosik cycle, in which this flamboyant and fearless Góral preyed on the rich and was the benefactor of the poor, until he was betrayed by a woman (no doubt an outsider), captured, and hanged. The bandit who disregards the laws of the state but obeys the laws of the highland community, who outwits the more powerful outsiders but who is always at risk from them as well, serves as both a model and a cautionary tale to young villagers still. The stories symbolically challenge the power of the dominant political and economic order, which is seen as endangering local values and autonomy, and at the same time validate local village leadership and house authority.[2]

Górále social memory of pre-war class relations reveals the bleaker side of patterns of power and subversion. When I first began fieldwork in the late 1970s, the older villagers' memories of their own experiences, and of family stories that had been passed down to them, portrayed the gentry as mean, harsh, and uncaring towards the peasants. In one story, which ends with a reversal of power, a landowner was so loathed that a group of villagers confronted and overpowered him, tied ropes around each of his legs, fastened each rope to a strong horse, and sent the two horses racing in opposite directions, tearing the hapless man limb from limb. Other stories, less dramatic but more poignant, recount tawdry tales of neglect and greed, of refusal to help in times of famine, and of seduction and abandonment of village girls.

Anti-clerical tales also revolve around the greed, worldliness, and dishonesty of priests. Several priests were said to have fathered the children of young village women; one was reputed to be a pedophile who abused his altar boys, and was also said to have attempted to steal the miraculous icon that adorns the altar of the village church.[3] Others were said to live "as if married" with their housekeepers, one of whom was believed to be a witch. Priests were accused of overcharging at funerals and weddings, refusing to perform marriages for people who were too poor to pay, and even refusing to give children proper funerals unless their parents paid exorbitant sums. It was said that they demanded produce when they knew children were going hungry, appropriated village land by underhand deals, and generally behaved in less than pious ways. Similarly, lawyers and innkeepers were portrayed as encouraging village men to drink and then, when they were unable to pay their debts, taking their lands as forfeit.

Many of these stories probably contain substantial truths; for instance, land records from the nineteenth until the mid-twentieth century show frequent mortgaging of lands and transfers of land title to pay off debt to non-villagers, who are listed as innkeepers and advocates. Regardless of their veracity, however, the stories testify to the villagers' view of outsiders in positions of power and authority. On the whole, they paid and obeyed when they had to but denied any indications of docility by private expressions of disrespect, ridicule, and "small acts of everyday resistance" (Scott 1985), such as stealing fire wood from the manor lands and pilfering crops from their fields. Villagers also appropriated rituals and paraphernalia from the church and incorporated them into their own house ceremonial. These ceremonials celebrated and underscored both the moral authority of the senior generation—particularly the male household head—and the continuity, fertility, and reproduction of the house, its land, and its people (Pine 1997). Thus in the domestic ritual before the church wedding the bride and groom are blessed by their parents with consecrated water from the church. At the year's first ploughing, the senior couple take grain and a straw wreath or cross, blessed in the church, and bury them in the newly plowed earth (Pine 1988).

Domestic rituals carry far more weight than those of the state, which are ignored if possible and minimized if not. Church rituals and religious practice are given more respect. With a few exceptions, however, priests—like state officials, urban middle classes and intelligentsia, and gentry in pre-war days—are shown a public face of humility but in private spoken of with derision. Here we can see two competing claims to power and authority, one that is seen as an imposition from the outside, but that has at least to be formally obeyed, and the other that is generated from within the community. This latter commands actual obedience and regulates social relations in practice.

Górale memories of the war also reflect this identification with the mountain community rather than the nation. A fortune teller was shot by the Nazis in the early 1940s. Villagers say this was because she read in the cards of the German commander that Germany would lose the war. Furious, he ordered her execution. In fact, it seems more likely that she was shot because she and her family were helping the Polish partisans and possibly members of a partisan brigade. While this would have been highly valued as heroism in wider Polish society, for the villagers such activity was almost irrelevant; what they stressed was that she confronted outsiders in authority with the transient nature of their power.[4]

This anti-outsider focus was clear in all villagers' talk about the war. For example, an old woman recounted her memories of the war, when the mountains were both a rest and recreation area for the Germans, and a center of partisan resistance. She found these years a time of total confusion. During the day, the villagers would be warned that the Germans were coming and would hurry to take their cows to the forest to hide them. They would return after dark, only to be warned that the Polish partisans were coming, and then they would round up their cows and go back to the forest to hide again. As she said, "They came in the day and they came at night, and we didn't know what was happening and we were always afraid." In other memories, the trickster element of Górale cunning was stressed: the village leader was so clever that he managed to entertain simultaneously a group of Germans in one room and a group of partisans in the other, and neither knew the other was there, and both believed he was their man. In fact he was, of course, a man of the village.[5]

The Socialist Period of Economic Expansion

With the establishment of socialism in the late 1940s, the local gentry lost their power, and the Górale found themselves in a new relationship with the outside world. The new bureaucracy, however, expanded and extended the state's influence enormously. Although agriculture was never successfully collectivized in Poland, production, distribution, and marketing were strictly regulated from the center. Most industry was state owned, and education and health care were also centrally controlled. In the 1950s, attempting to rebuild after the devastation of the German occupation, the socialist government followed the Soviet model and implemented a massive industrialization program supported by extensive infra-structural development.

The impact of this development drive on the Podhale was profound. Small factories were opened in the region, and the service sector was greatly expanded. For the first time in the history of the region, villagers were guaranteed regular waged work, which carried with it substantial benefits. Improvements and innovations in transport and communications created unprecedented opportunity. Villagers could travel away to work with relative ease, and outsiders from other parts of Poland and the rest of the socialist bloc had easy access to the Podhale. The tourist industry flourished, as skiers came in the winter and hikers in the summer, all of whom were provided with accommodation, meals, entertainment, local crafts, and numerous other services, all for a price. The local economy, after centuries of underdevelopment, began to expand (Pine 1993).

However, the integration of the Górale into the Polish state remained complex. While the Podhale economy expanded, hostility to the state and the privileging of the local social order became if anything stronger than before. Rather than seeing these developments as emancipating, villagers interpreted them as yet another, even more extreme, attempt by the state to curtail their local autonomy and undermine the authority properly vested in the house.[6] Concerning integration into the informal or second economy, however, they were more positive.

By the 1970s, the Polish national economy was in dire straits, suffering the consequences of a badly managed centralized distribution system and unrealistic quota system, and the "second economy" grew directly in proportion to these troubles. In the Podhale, informal activities ranged from letting rooms to tourists privately (i.e., unregistered and untaxed) and private sales of wool, sheepskins, and crafts in the market to the private production and sale of vodka, to smuggling and dealing in gold, horses, and other goods, and to temporary migration to the United States to work illegally. These activities provided a major source of income and allowed people to continue to farm their lands, to invest in farming equipment, and to build ever bigger and better houses.

Waged work in the socialized state sector was consistently undervalued (Pine 1994; for comparison, see also Stewart 1993). People maintained that they worked only to secure benefits and a pension, that pay was so low it was worthless, and that they worked in order to have access to scarce goods and perks. The house economy consistently took priority over state-regulated domains; children were kept home from school; and adults took sick leave or holiday leave during planting and harvesting. Pilfering from the workplace was commonplace, as it had been from the estates of the gentry in the pre-war years, and was regarded as just compensation for poor wages and bad treatment.

In the informal economy during the socialist period yet a third set of rules and moralities applied, which contrasted strongly to those regulating both involvement with the state and work for the house. For instance, farmers deeply resented the state's compulsory quotas for meat deliveries to the cooperative but thoroughly enjoyed exercising their trading skills selling meat privately in the market.

Women downplayed their waged work in the weaving cooperative but embarked with enthusiasm and vigor on weaving done at home, for private sale, with high quality wool smuggled from their state workplace. Whenever possible, people bought and sold through the second economy; they also used informal connections to obtain building supplies, vodka, machinery, and fertilizer. Many village men worked informally as builders, drivers, carpenters, and plumbers; the most respected village women were those who knew how to "*targować*" (deal in the market, bargain and trade).

If the house economy represented the legitimate authority, hierarchy, and sociality of the kin group, and the state economy stood for oppression and interference by an illegitimate authority of the dominant class or group, the informal economy took on the mantle of the realm of the individual, acting for the house (and to some degree, by definition, against the state) but also transcending the demands of the house in pursuit of immediate self-interest. Because ideally this self-interest eventually fed back into the house, it was morally acceptable. And because it involved ingenuity of a kind that subverted or disregarded the dominant authority of the state, it was applauded.

This notion of self-interest deserves closer examination. The advent of widespread wage labor and universal education and literacy during the socialist period generated certain changes in the Górale social order. Most significantly, the younger generation gained access to a new range of alternatives to farming and to a set of skills that enabled them to deal with outside bureaucracy in ways their parents could not. Despite these changes, most young villagers wished to remain in the Podhale, and most continued to view the land and the house as the most important source of security and identity. In the Podhale, as in the rest of Poland, family and personal networks were the basis for economic survival, social relationships, and moral values, not only to a far greater degree than state institutions and ideology but also in opposition to them (Wedel 1992). However, so much Górale economic activity was outside the state sector and only semi-legal (if legal at all) that villagers masked and downplayed these dealings. Women and girls spent hours knitting in the evening; this was performed as kin or family labor, while the sale of the finished garments to market women, or in the marketplace itself, was clandestine. Similarly, teams of highly skilled builders, or sheepskin craftsmen, tended to portray their deals in terms of kin and neighborly reciprocity, rather than as work generating substantial income. Thus the house and farming economy came to be over-emphasized as a stage on which the hidden economy could be performed and its profits presented, particularly through elaborate and expensive ritual and ceremonial, in disguised form.

Gender and Generation

In the post-socialist period, the need for such subterfuge has been largely, if not completely, eliminated. The ubiquitous sphere of alternative economic practice that was both shielded behind the house and upheld it, is now revealed, made explicit, and acknowledged. Indeed, this is the stuff that the new Polish capitalism is made of. The Górale division of labor is in practice fluid and negotiable, which makes it particularly well suited to the kind of flexible entrepreneurship and kin-based survival strategies that flourish in the new economic order (Pine 1996). This is nowhere more apparent than in issues of gender.

The proper order of the house revolves around the authority of the senior couple, the male *gazda* and the female *gospodyni*. Men and women have clearly defined tasks within the domestic domain and within farming and house-based production, but the division of labor is not rigid; if necessary, women may drive tractors and lead horse-drawn plows, men may cook, milk cows, and plant potatoes, and nobody considers this inappropriate.[7] Both women and men are judged according to certain criteria connected to the well-being and prosperity or fertility of the house. Hard work, knowledge, and experience are highly valued. Young unmarried men are expected to be somewhat wild, to drink with their cohort, and from time to time to be involved in the ultimate demonstration of youthful masculinity: fights with outsiders and occasionally with other villagers. Young unmarried women are expected to be somewhat flirtatious, and even overt sexuality is not frowned upon. This is the one period when individualism is encouraged in the inside, within the village community, without being seen as opposed to the interests of the house.

However, both men and women, when they marry, are expected to settle down to activities that increase the fertility and productivity of the house and its land. It is here that the emphasis on conformity and mutuality becomes explicit. Behavior that is accepted, and even applauded, as the performance of masculinity and femininity before marriage, must be transformed after marriage into behavior channeled toward the interests of the house. Transgressions such as adultery or drunkenness are viewed with ambivalence: things that constitute essential parts of the public display of gendered behavior but that also should be controlled because of their potential to disrupt the proper processes of production and reproduction. What is not tolerated is excessive behavior. Men who are chronic alcoholics are eventually excluded from farming exchanges, which seriously undermines their house economy. Women who have too many children, or who fail to care for their children, put at risk the successful reproduction of the house and farm. And men who are excessively violent in the house disrupt its very core: the relationship, with its proper balance of authority, between husband and wife.

When Górale villagers operate in the outside world, however, an entirely different set of acts and judgments is set into motion, and it is here that they can be seen to be not so much "proper peasants" as talented entrepreneurs. The gender and generation rules that operate within the village are suspended or even reversed; what is applauded is individualism, entrepreneurial skill, and innovation. During the socialist period, for instance, mothers of young children were granted American visas and Polish passports because the officials, certain that no woman would abandon her baby, believed their promises to return in a few weeks. In fact they would work in Chicago for two or three years, making the equivalent of a life's earnings by Polish standards, and then return, bringing with them highly valued dollars as well as cases of goods to sell at the market. Their children, in their absence, had been cared for by their own mothers or sisters and although they certainly missed them, they had no worries about their safety or well-being, nor doubts about their own performance as mothers. Their ability to play on gender stereotypes and their sense of the market enabled them to do what all good Górale mothers should do: provide for their children.

Some of the most common metaphors for the loss of national autonomy in the immediate post-socialist period were those associated with the seduction, corruption, and betrayal of Polish women by foreign men. But for the Górale, such stories simply have no evocative meaning. The opening of the borders with the West has brought numerous opportunities and Górale women have been quick to pursue work as housekeepers and *au pairs* in Italy and Germany, as cleaners and factory hands in Greece, and as farm laborers in France and Germany. Indeed, they have an established cultural precedent for such migration. Rather than threatening the integrity of the house and the social order, such action consolidates it.

There are many stories and legends of successful migrants; the reality, as everyone knows, is often much harsher and bleaker. Illegal immigrants are badly treated, exploited, and humiliated. Some migrants are cheated and lose their earnings, or spend them unwisely, and return with little or nothing to show for their time away. But in the broader picture, the stories of loss and failure are forgotten; everyone who goes away and comes back rich is proof of the legendary trickster skills of the Górale and of their ability to play and to win in the informal economy. The reality in between fades to a shadow, to be summoned up again only in the stories that contrast the hostile and antisocial outside world with the moral and good community of the mountain villages.

The Joy of the Market

For the market women, traders and migrant laborers themselves, the time after leaving the house and before re-incorporation is one when individualistic skills, desires, and tricks can be legitimately pursued. On Thursday morning, the day of the big local market, market women get up at four A.M. to milk the cows and prepare breakfast for the house before setting off with their goods. As soon as they leave the village behind, the mood of the women lightens. Traveling in twos or threes on the bus, or in the cart or car of a neighbor or friend, they chat and gossip and exchange jokes and information. They discuss the sweaters and cheeses they are carrying to sell, the price of wool at the moment, the worry that Russian traders are taking their business. Once they reach the market, they stand together, holding up sweaters, often with leather bags full of smoked cheeses at their feet and sacks of homespun and carded wool behind them. They laugh and call out to passers by, tourists and professional intermediaries alike, "Come on my darling, look at this sweater—it's the last one like it—buy two and I'll give it to you cheap. Yes, my darling, it's the best quality." They haggle and gesticulate and perform the deal with their bodies, clearly excited by the contest of wills and intoxicated with their own words, rhythms, and rhetoric. Some men perform in the market in similar ways, notably those who are very successful livestock traders or horse dealers. But the real, flamboyant skills lie with the market women. Once they have sold all their wares, they walk about the market, still charged with the adrenaline of dealing, buying treats to take home to the children, haggling over prices of imported clothes, food, and household commodities. When they have managed to get an exceptionally good price, or to unload a bad batch of cheese or an underweight sweater onto an unsuspecting tourist, their delight is palpable.

It is in the performance of the deal, in the active agency of the dealer, that the liberating individualism of this trickster behavior is most clearly seen. Such moments are confined to the transactions in which the trader, and most particularly the market woman, is acting as a sole agent in a space that is neither defined by the rules of the house nor oppressed by those of the state.[8] By contrast, within the house economy and the village community there is little place for the pursuit of individual desires or skills and, looked at purely from that perspective, the Górale do indeed appear to be "proper peasants." Likewise, in the context of waged labor, trickster behavior (like pilfering, cheating, and rearranging reality) has to be disguised. The women who left the socialist weaving cooperative with wool hidden under their coats hurried past the reception desk, eyes averted and head bowed to the ground. These individualistic acts were subversive, and were celebrated after the fact, when the wool had been brought safely home, when the ambulance that had been used for carting illicit coal had been returned to the hospital, when the money had been slipped to the official, accepted, and hidden away. In contrast to the market, in these contexts there is no moment in which the performance of "the deal" takes over the body, words, and space of the dealer. It is only at the market in the moment of dealing that the individual is able to transcend the enduring structures of both house and state and perform, unattached and unencumbered, completely in the present.

This brings into focus a difference between the Górale and other peoples represented in this volume. For the Rom, for instance, Stewart shows how the individual continually attempts to transcend the drudgery of everyday life, the painful weight of the past, and the uncertainty of the future. This "presentism" is perhaps most clearly seen in the ambivalence with which men view the household and the demands of the domestic economy. The world of domestic consumption and reproduction is associated with the house and is located in the labor, time, and energies of women. Social value is created outside the household, in relations between men. There are similarities between this and Strathern's account of Mount Hagen, despite the very different ethnographic context. There "rubbish" women, standing for the self-interest of subsistence production and consumption in the household, are contrasted to "big" men, who create social value and status through exchange outside the household (1988:132–167). Closer to home, discussing poor peasants in Greece, Papataxiarchis (1991) describes male "friends of the heart," whose shared *raki* drinking and gambling in public spaces is opposed to their kinship practices, which are located in domestic space. Bloch, in yet another context, shows that Merina associate men with social value and kinship and women with individual households, which are potentially divisive to the deme (1975:210). For the Górale the parallel contrast seems to be not male/female, but inside/outside and married/unmarried.[9] Górale men do "live in the present," drinking and gambling and fighting, during their adolescence and early adulthood. So, too, do women, although to a lesser degree, through their sexual flirtations. However, once a person has become adult and married, this period should be left behind, and the interests and reproduction of the house should be placed first. The house and the community provide the boundaries that protect the individual from an intrusive state; and for the Górale it is this outside space that is the proper place for the performance of individualism, self interest, and "presentism." But, of course, this outside, the locus of their "present," is not really within their control.

The history of the Górale is one of ever-increasing incorporation into the state (and the church) and the market. In between the house economy and the traditional marketplace lies the limbo where the Górale go and work for state industry, or for local enterprise, for poor wages and some benefits. Since the advent of the socialist period, this has perhaps been the most solid and consistent source of money and livelihood; however, it is consistently the most denigrated—precisely, I think, because it is here that the real impotence of the Górale is most clearly experienced and their real dependence upon, and encapsulation by, the outside political economy most blatant. In the post-socialist economy, the state continues to be represented in negative terms and blamed for the factory closures, cuts in benefits, high prices, and, most of all, the ongoing crisis in private farming.

As this penetration by the state and outside economy grows, the Górale themselves both emphasize their autonomy and individualism more and more in some aspects of the external economic order, and focus within their community on ever more elaborate rituals of local identity and belonging. The Polish state and tourist board advertise tourist trips to the mountains with colorful posters of "authentic" Górale, dancing, playing music, or herding sheep. Villagers invest in expensive traditional costume, to be worn at weddings and to local Marion festivals that honor, not surprisingly, Mary in her aspect as protector of those who travel far away; in other words, they reclaim their image by constantly reinventing it within the local community. When they move into the external world, the most successful become flamboyantly modern, driving western cars and buying up-to-the-minute consumer goods. As the potential for both incorporation and penetration is realized more than ever before, villagers respond with more elaborate, and more exclusive, performances of local identity and more audacious acts of entrepreneurial individualism in the external world.

Notes

The research on which this paper is based was funded by the (then) SSRC (Social Science Research Council) in 1978–1980 and the ESRC (Economic and Social Research Council) in 1988–1990 (R0002314) and 1991–1995 (R000233019). Additional funding was received from the British Council in 1977–1979 and in 1981.

1. Górale refer to house names as "how you speak to a person" (*jak sie mówić do nei/go*) or "whom they are from" (*od kogo oni są*). For surnames, they speak of "the way you write yourself" (*jak się pisać*).

2. I am grateful to Sophie Day for a comment that helped to clarify this relationship for me. I would argue that the legitimacy of authority that the state claims is in practice vested in the house.

3. This icon appears to have reached the village in an equally dubious way: it was brought from Russia by the same priest during the war—the fact that it was probably stolen by him originally did not give him any special rights over it in villagers' eyes, nor negate what they felt was their right to have and keep it!

4. Other stories, told by historians rather than villagers, paint a less honorable picture. The Nazi plan to exterminate the Poles excluded certain Górale, whom they called *Goralenvolk* and saw as the true Aryan race. Individual Górale were issued *Goralenvolk* cards, which testified to their Aryan nature. Looking through the old archives, I came across one of these cards made out to a woman other villagers believed to be a witch.

5. In the late 1970s, I was frequently told by villagers, "I am a Catholic, not a communist." In fact some of those who stated this were simultaneously members of the party and practicing Catholics, and most village farmers were members of the Peasants' Party—an offshoot of the Workers' Party (Communist Party)—and of the Agricultural Cooperative. However, all distinguished clearly between such political memberships, which they viewed as entirely pragmatic, and Catholicism, which they viewed as a matter of faith and belief, regardless of their disdain for the clergy.

6. When I first went to the village, it was winter, and I was struck by the sight of groups of boys and young men swaggering along the icy street, brandishing long poles that looked like hockey sticks. Later on I learned that these were homespun versions of the *ciupaga*, the Górale walking stick with an evil pointed metal tip and a small axe-like head, that men use for support walking up mountains, in Górale dancing, and as a weapon of defense and offense, and that is now sold, in mass-produced and modified form, as a tourist trinket throughout Poland. When I asked the young men why they carried these sticks, they answered, as if stating the obvious, "to beat up tourists."

7. Women retain ownership of their own land and property after marriage and control their own money and often the household budget as well.

8. Górale market women can be distinguished from other Polish peasant women who market produce both by the range of goods and products they sell, and by their selling performance. For instance, in central Poland, where I have also done research, villagers tend to sell either agricultural surplus or items like socks or tights, products of cottage industries that have sprung up following factory closures in the restructuring process. In this area, "dealing" has negative connotations, associated with Gypsies and, indeed, the Górale, while "honest hard labor" is seen as the only positive route to economic reward. Some villagers seem almost ashamed to have to sell their produce and, overall, their demeanor when selling is quiet and watchful.

9. See, for comparison, Harris (1980) and Pina Cabral (1986).

3

Prey at the Center: Resistance and Marginality in Amazonia

Laura Rival

When compared with Andean state formations or Caribbean and Central American chiefdoms, most postcolonial Amazonian societies appear to be marginal. They are committed to living in the present and deny the long term and transcendence; that is, they share the same 'cultural syndrome' as the other social groups discussed in this book. Amazonian societies are remarkably egalitarian; their political institutions and ideologies are not generally conducive to domination, coercion, or oppression. Sometimes historical change is denied, ignored, or rearticulated in mythic terms that refer to an unchanging primordial era, a time when animals and humans were not differentiated; sometimes it is wholeheartedly embraced, not as a nostalgic reference to ancestral traditions but as the process through which kinship is created anew in each generation (Gow 1991). Personal autonomy is highly valued and central to the organization and continuity of social groups. Endogamous kindred-based residential groups represent the social ideal of identity, sameness, and undifferentiation in many Amazonian societies. As a result, the incorporation of "others," considered necessary for social reproduction and cultural continuity, becomes a source of both danger and creativity. Moreover, exchange is looked upon with ambivalence and often altogether avoided.

However, this apparent lack of concern for continuity and reproduction is, to a large extent, deceptive. In most cases, social life is structured by institutions that, although wrongly characterized by earlier anthropologists as "clans," "phratries," or "lineages," nevertheless exist; they are generally reproduced through key rituals.[1] And we now know that pre-conquest Amazonia, far from being "the exclusive habitat of egalitarian hunter-horticulturists living in small villages" (Viveiros de Castro 1996a:182), was the land of agricultural chiefdoms (see, in particular, Roosevelt 1993). Furthermore, as Harris stresses in his contribution to this volume, the production of kinship, however located in the present from the emic point of view, requires great inputs of work, a pervasive ideology oriented towards production, and the strong commitment of individuals to the "morals of consanguinity" (Viveiros de Castro 1996a:189). Finally, when the anthropologist starts looking beyond the longhouse or the village, she finds that warfare and predation are essential components of social reproduction (Menget et al. 1985; Descola 1993; Viveiros de Castro 1992). As soon as she analyzes the interrelations between indigenous sociologies and cosmologies, she discovers processes of symbolic exchange involving life-taking, cannibalism, and violent death that "cross socio-political, cosmological and ontological boundaries, thereby playing a constitutive role in the definition of collective identities" (Viveiros de Castro 1996a:190). Amazonianists disagree on how to best interpret lowland South American warfare. Menget and his co-authors (1985) speak of symbolic exchange and symbolic production, Descola (1993) of structural contradictions, and Viveiros de Castro (1992) of the irresistible longing to be killed and devoured by a cannibal god as a means of achieving immortality.

The Huaorani do not imagine themselves as achieving their true humanity by becoming immortal, divine predators. On the contrary, they see themselves as the victims of predators, as prey constantly on the run, fleeing persecution, death, and being eaten. Huaorani people do not seek transcendental immortality; rather, they consider earthly life really worth living, even if it means living in constant danger of being killed and eaten up. The good life they aspire to requires that they secure complete cultural and political autonomy and that they reproduce without the intervention of external creators. Huaorani people are, in this sense, even more committed to the here and now than other Amazonian groups. This is what I attempt to establish in the rest of this paper. I start by presenting basic ethnographic facts, and I then move on to discuss the way in which Huaorani social categories are structured around two central principles drawn from natural phenomena. One is the prey-predator relationship, the source of extermination. The other is the large, emergent fruiting tree, symbol of reproductive power and androgynous fertility. In the conclusion, I contend that Huaorani social principles and social life are ill-understood as devolutionary outcomes. Rather, they point to the distinctive absence of belief in immortality and to the traditional political choice of autarky and endogamy against all forms of superior others, be they powerful neighbors, ghosts, or spirits.

At the Margins of Predation: the Huaorani's Timeless Present

Huaorani people are more mobile, autarkic, and endogamous than most other Amazonian hinterland groups. We will probably never know whether they are the descendants of sedentarized and sophisticated cultivators. But there is little doubt that their way of life has, for centuries, depended more on foraging activities than on agriculture. Their rejection of elaborate gardening corresponds to a specific historical experience and a particular form of social organization. Like all other people discussed in this book, they are fiercely egalitarian and present-oriented. Highly mobile (more by preference and more as a means to conflict resolution than as a way of adapting to dispersed resources), living in small groups, and owning minimal property, Huaorani people are disengaged from future concerns and long-term planning. They "procure" rather than "produce" food (Bird-David 1990, 1992; Ingold 1996), give away rather than exchange and reciprocate, and share belongings upon demand (Peterson 1993). They also, in some sense, come to share a common substance through living together. Until recently, they viewed their way of life and cultural and political autonomy as depending on their complete avoidance of inter-ethnic contact and exchange. And although only one small group still clings to autarky today, "contacted" and "pacified" Huaorani continue to rely on forest abundance as a means of coping with the peripheral situation created by petroleum development.

The longhouse residential group *(nanicabo,* plural form *nanicaboiri)* constitutes the basic social unit of Huaorani society. A typical longhouse comprises between ten to forty-five members: usually an older couple (often a man married to one, two, or three sisters), their daughters (with, when married, their husbands and children), and their unmarried sons. It shows no age or sex segregation. House groups regularly move between their longhouses built on hilltops and a series of secondary residences and hunting shelters. Most *nanicabo* members hunt small arboreal species and gather everyday—generally alone, except children, who tend to hunt and gather in bands. Considerable time is invested, and great interest is shown, in hunting and gathering activities, which are often subsumed under the term *omëre äante gobopa* (literally, "forest visiting in order to bring something back"). There is no reason not to recognize the productive nature[2] of these extractive activities, even if Huaorani people do not see them as "work." Finally, it should be stressed that to gather and hunt in the forest is not experienced as a hazardous occupation, for the location of resources—even game—is well known and predictable.[3] Hunters rarely come back without game. In fact, returns are high, and everyone eats at least 200 grams of meat each day. The meat is immediately shared, boiled, and often eaten with nothing else. There is no particular rule as to who should get which part. Before the introduction of shotguns in the mid-1970s, birds and monkeys were exclusively hunted with blowpipes, and white-lipped peccaries *(Tajassu peccari)* with spears. The white-lipped peccary (the only ground animal considered edible) was hunted only occasionally. There were no other weapons—no traps, bows and arrows, or clubs—and most other animal species were tabooed (Rival 1996/b). Fishing, an activity popular with women and children, was marginal. Fruit was, and still is, as relished as the fruit eating animal species that make up the bulk of the hunt. This is particularly true of *daguenca* (the *Bactris gasipaes* palm fruit) that, when in season, becomes the main staple. Hunting is discontinued during the *daguenca* fruiting season.

The longhouse economy is structured by the sharing of forest food individually obtained by each producer. The goal for each producer is to obtain enough food to feed her/himself and share with co-residents. The individual's ability to extract from the forest, and carry back to the longhouse, large quantities of food to share and consume with co-residents expresses the central value of personal autonomy. Even young children make sure they always possess enough foodstuff, not only for their own consumption but to give away—especially to their grandmothers, mothers, and older sisters. There is, inside the longhouse, a constant mutual giving away of food. Men, women, or children cook the food they bring back on the existing hearths (each identified with a married woman and equally used by her husband and children) before sharing it with whoever happens to be around. The sharing of cooked food may be preceded by the sharing of unprocessed food, especially meat. In this case, the person who brings raw food to the longhouse may give part of it to specific co-residents, who are free to use it as they please—they can cook it for themselves and others or redistribute it further. If someone feels entitled to a share but has been ignored, she or he may assert her or his claim by asking directly the bringer for some gathered fruit or hunted game. In this way, givers may be free to redistribute their catch according to their own priorities, but they also have to respond to the claims made by co-residents. Gibson's comment that "in pre-capitalist systems exchange relations serve not to mask political relations, but to express them" (1991:171) entirely applies to the Huaorani situation, where demand-sharing corresponds to the assertion of egalitarian principles.

Nanicabo food sharing is not based on reciprocity, for the act of giving and receiving are totally dissociated. Social partners equally disengaged from property relate to one another by sharing food in a way that creates neither competition nor dependency. Nonreciprocal relations produce a collectivity (the *nanicabo*) in which givers never become creditors, nor receivers debtors. Huaorani syntax illustrates the independent co-occurrence of these two social actions. Two expressions, *pono* and *goro*, are used to mean "to give." When *pono* is used, the grammatical subject (the verb nominative) receives something. The morpheme *po*, which also exists as a verb form meaning "to come," can be used to mark a movement "toward." *Goro*, which means that the speaker is giving something away, is derived from the verb *go*, which means "to go."[4] The morpheme *go* marks a movement "away from." To give is therefore either "to give" or "to be given," an action expressed in the active not the passive mode. Giving and receiving are conceptualized grammatically as acts of displacement. The focus is on the movement of objects, not on who owns them.

Ongoing residence forms the sociological basis on which the economy of sharing develops. The repeated and undifferentiated *action* of sharing turns co-residents into a single, indistinct substance. Sharing practices express and continuously reassert togetherness. The principle by which people come to share a common substance (i.e., become related) through acts of feeding is general: fathers feed semen to fetuses, mothers breast feed infants, and *nanicabo* co-residents continuously feed each other.[5] People living in the same longhouse gradually become of the same substance, *aroboqui baön anobain* (literally, "of one same flesh"). In other words, the physical reality of eating the same food and sleeping together builds up into a common physical essence, regardless of blood ties. This is the clearest indication that living together is more valued than being related genealogically (Rival in press/a, forthcoming).

Persons and communities are processes that unfold in time through the cumulative experience of living and sleeping side by side, day after day. Food sharing corresponds to the undifferentiated feeding process, itself part of a wider organic process. When a *nanicabo* member is sick, all residents must respect the same food prohibitions. It is this shared collective curing effort that helps the patient to recover his or her good health. As relatedness results from the fact of collectively consuming or avoiding food, collective fasting can also express sharing. It is not so much the kind of food eaten that matters but the relation of consumption that it creates. *Nanicabo* members share the same substance not only because they feed each other, but also because they sleep, work, live, and defecate together. They share illnesses, parasites, a common dwelling, and a common territory. Each *nanicabo* is known to others under a collective identity derived from its corporal and communal existence. Members of a residential unit are described as having a certain smell, a certain way of dividing up the work amongst themselves, a funny way of cutting their hair. They are said to be taller—or shorter—than the norm; their skin is darker or lighter, and so forth. Of course, such merging of individual selves within a singular collectivity is stereotypical. However, it is significant that residential solidarity, which social actors see as based on the moral principles and social practices attached to the experience of togetherness, be represented in organic terms. Finally, if living together turns people into the same substance, the process is not irreversible. Certain members may become estranged from the *nanicabo*; they may spend more time away visiting distant relatives. By disengaging from the intense economy of sharing, and by residing less constantly within the *nanicabo*, they lose some of the common substance, and differences surface. The sharing of a common substance lasts only as long as it is sustained through continuous sharing practices. It is not permanent and can be discontinued. However, reversing the process is an extremely serious matter. Individuals who leave one group for another cease to be kin; they may become *huarani* ("enemy other") and undergo a change of identity marked by the adoption of a different personal name and the acquisition of a new spouse.

As in many Amazonian societies, residence is uxorilocal, so men must progressively integrate the sharing economy of their wives' house groups. Married couples, although embedded within the *nanicabo* sharing economy, are distinguishable by the more ritualized way in which they give to, and receive from, each other. Transactions between husbands and wives, unlike those practiced with other co-residents, are strictly reciprocal; one gives in response to what one receives and vice versa. Whereas co-residents tend to obtain food independently, and then share it out, married couples seem to engage in complementary activities, each reciprocating to the other goods and services of a different kind. However, each spouse controls the food each one carries back to the longhouse, regardless of who has hunted or collected it, and each is entitled to give it away. This indicates that although the conjugal pair forms a productive unit, each spouse remains an independent food sharer within the *nanicabo*. Marriage organizes the production of goods, not their circulation.

Conjugal reciprocal exchange is closely related to complementary production. Men and women know how to do, and can do, almost every item of their society's cultural repertoire. However, when married, they tend to specialize in certain activities. Many activities become the regular task of one member of the conjugal pair, although this implicit division of labor may vary from one couple to another or from one longhouse to the next. Moreover, spouses spend at least as much time sharing tasks and engaging in complementary ones. Therefore, if conjugal complementarity introduces a certain division of labor, it is not normative in the sense that different domestic and productive tasks are equally valued. Difference is not translated into hierarchy, and general practice is not converted into a rigid code of conduct. As I have argued elsewhere (Rival in press/a), the reciprocal nature of marital life is due to its reproductive function. The marital relationship demands the rigorous respect of mutual obligations because conjugality is before all joint parenting.[6] Marriage is about producing children, that is, increasing the number of *nanicabo* residents. Whereas the association of autonomous and self-sufficient producers sharing their products forms a suitable base for *nanicabo* sociality, it is not sufficient to bring into the world new members. For this, married couples must turn into productive units and *work harder* (a fact continuously stressed throughout the wedding ceremony). Balanced reciprocity between husbands and wives ensures a real increase in work output. Moreover, it ensures that fathers and mothers share equally in the procreation process and the growth of children (Rival 1998a).

Surrounded by Predators

The history of this isolated group, whose language is not attached to any known phylum, and whose cultural borrowing was literally nil at the time of contact in the early 1960s, is still poorly known. To the best of our knowledge, Huaorani people have lived for centuries in the interstices between the great Zaparo, Shuar, and Tukanoan nations, constituting nomadic and autarkic enclaves fiercely refusing contact, trade, or exchange with their powerful neighbors. The core of their ancestral territory seems to have been the Tiputini River, from where they appear to have expanded east, west, and southward until they occupied most of the hinterlands between the Napo and the Curaray Rivers in the aftermath of the rubber boom, which caused the disappearance of most Zaparo communities (Rival forthcoming). It is quite clear from ethno-historical records, oral tradition, and present practice that Huaorani people have not participated in, nor depended upon, the great inter-ethnic trade networks of the Upper Marañon described by missionaries and travelers. In contrast to the situation found among Amerindian groups surrounding them, their material culture and means of production have been indigenously manufactured from locally found raw materials within each independent, self-sufficient longhouse. Their insistence on not depending on anything external also explains why the objective of warfare is to kill off and exterminate, not to incorporate, outside powers (Rival 1996/a).

This extreme closure corresponds to the perception that "true human beings" *(huaorani)* are under constant threat of being captured and eaten by non-Huaorani *(cohuori)*, who are all, as the old Aca once told me, "cannibal predators *(quènhuë)*[7] living on the other side and stealing people (especially children) to butcher, smoke, and cure their flesh and eat it as if it was monkey or peccary meat." The dual opposition *huaorani-cohuori* is absolute and ontological. The Huaorani, as a people, are radically different from all non-Huaorani, defined as cannibal others. The difference is categorical, or essential, in the sense that *huaorani* are victims of *cohuori*. *Huaorani* and *cohuori* are like two different species, two different kinds of beings. The only possible relationship between *cohuori* and *huaorani* is unilateral predation. Literally, *cohuori* are predators and *huaorani* prey. This is continuously repeated in everyday conversation about the past, especially when trekking along rivers where violent fighting with Zaparos, Quichuas, rubber tappers, and explorers occurred.

Ontological predation is also at the center of three popular myths that relate the origin of hardwood and deadly spears, the predatory activities of demonic vampire bats, and the nature of life in the world tree at the beginning of time:

How the Huaorani Acquired Hardwood Spears

At the beginning of their history, Huaorani people had only spears made of balsa wood, which were too blunt and soft to kill. They were at the mercy of numerous cannibals and under the constant threat of being killed off. Their only protection against these powerful enemies was to live in hiding. One day, the son of the sun visited them and taught them the existence of peach palms. Having learned to make hard palm wood spears, they were able to defend themselves. Until this day, the Huaorani have survived as a separate group. Peach palm wood spears, therefore, are essential for the survival of a separate ethnic identity. Without them, Huaorani people would have succumbed to the genocidal actions of over-numerous "others".

When Vampire Bats Exterminated Huaorani Children

Tonquitay (demonic vampire bats) caused a lot of hardship in former times. People's lives were miserable, for despite all their care, the bats would come at night to steal their young children in order to kill them and eat them. The bats lived on a giant rock as hard as cement in the sky. The sky, attached to tree tops by climbers, was close to earth. What people took to be wild turkey bones thrown on the ground by birds of prey were in fact the bones of Huaorani children. The children had to work hard for the bats. The bats were the bosses, the children the slaves. Those who refused to work were killed and eaten up.

The World Tree, at the Beginning of Time
In the beginnings of time, the earth was flat; there were no forests, no hills. The earth was like a dried, barren, and endless beach, stranded at the foot of a giant *ceibo* tree. This tree, attached to heaven by a strong vine, was the only source of shade against the strong sun. Only seedlings growing under its protective shade could escape the merciless heat of the sun; this is why there were no hills and no forests. There was no moon, and no night either. All that was alive dwelled in the giant tree. It was like a house. The living slept in the tree and fed on its fruits. There were no gardens; there was no need to visit; and food was shared by all. In those times of beginning, people formed one big group. Humans and animals were not yet separated. Only birds were different and lived apart: the doves, the only game obtainable, and the dangerous Harpy Eagle, who swooped down on people and doves alike. Life in those times would have been good to live, if it had not been for the giant preying bird.

Each of these myths highlights an important aspect of the relation of predation. The first myth stresses that since the military capacity of resistance is limited, Huaorani autonomous existence as a separate, viable collectivity is constantly under attack. Flight and self-segregation are, therefore, essential to survival. The very same social anxiety is expressed in the second myth, although anxiety about biological reproduction is, this time, focused on the survival of the young. The most revealing element in the third myth, the myth of origin, is that the prey-predator relation is so primeval that it even preceded speciation.

While Huaorani people view the *cohuori* as an undifferentiated class of cannibals that stands in absolute opposition to them, they see themselves as relatively differentiated in "us"*(huaomoni)* and "others"*(huarani)*. A known (and genealogically related) person is classified as either *boto guiri* (my relative), or as *huaca* (unrelated). All co-residents and, more generally, members of allied longhouses define themselves as "us" *(huaomoni, guiri)*, that is, as having at least one forebear in common. But not all *guiri* live together in the same longhouse or even close by. Some necessarily live with *huarani*, potential affinal allies, who may as well turn into enemies. The dual opposition *huaomoni-huarani* (us-others)is never categorical but results from what I would call a statistical effect. When someone, for example the old Aca, says that a person is "other" *(huaca)*, she means that there is no common name between this person's name set and hers. Since grandparents give their names to their grandchildren, this in turn indicates a lack of genealogical connection between her and this person. By the same token, Aca also implies that her parents and grandparents, and this person's parents and grandparents, lived in distinct parts of Huaorani land, and that, therefore, they probably never met. Aca, on occasion, calls the group she identifies with *huaomoni*. It is most likely that within her *huaomoni* group, the majority will, like her, call the person in question *huaca*. But there is almost certainly someone in the *huaomoni* group who will depart from the majority and recognize this person as a relative, referring to him or her as *boto guiri*, "my relative." These exceptions are crucial for linking up local groups that would otherwise remain completely closed in upon themselves.

The dual opposition between *huaomoni* and *huarani* structures marriage alliances. The autarkic closure generated by the *huaorani-cohuori* absolute predatory difference correlates to a high degree of endogamy (Rival 1996/a). When demographically stable, the overall population is divided into dispersed networks of inter-marrying longhouses separated by vast stretches of unoccupied forest. For greater security and autonomy, longhouse residential groups tend to isolate themselves from most other groups. Marriage alliances create solidarity and unity between longhouses that exchange marriage partners. These loose aggregates maintain relations of latent hostility with all other groups, actually called "others." Although longhouses unrelated by marriage avoid meeting (and often ignore each other's exact location), isolation is relative, as—in theory—potential kin ties can always be revived, especially when spouses are scarce or social disruptions caused by warfare too acute. "After all," as I have heard informants say, "all Huaorani are alike, they speak the same language"; and they are, I would add, equally the preys of *cohuori*.

One—possibly two—groups, known as the Tagaeri, are still defending a strict autarky, refusing all contact, including contact with their "civilized" kin. Recent attempts by some of their relatives to "pacify" them and exchange marriage partners have failed, causing one death on each side. This conflict occurred despite the close ties (i.e., classificatory brothers) existing between members of the two *huarani* groups. No simple explanation of this failed attempt to renew contact can be offered. However, it can be related to the fact that even a close kin can turn into a *huarani*, simply by joining a longhouse that is part of a different *huaomoni* group. In fact, Huaorani oral tradition is replete with stories of cannibalistic spirits *(huene)* who kill their victims by pretending to be close kin (siblings, parents, or offspring) visiting the native longhouse after a long absence. Physically distant kin who have not interacted with each other for a long time are socially distant, to the point of being "others." So, for the Huaorani, it is not affines but kin who live with "others" who may turn into dangerous "cannibal others."

Such dangers are avoided when "we-people" *(huaomoni)* stay together, feast together, marry endogamously, and avoid meeting "others" or "enemies" *(huarani)*; that is, when pairs of brothers and sisters exchange their children in marriage (bilateral cross-cousin marriage is both an ideal norm and a common practice), or sets of inter-marrying brothers and sisters continue to live close to each other, forming the core of feast groups. In other words, the principles of balanced reciprocity, equivalence, and symmetry equally infuse marriage alliances and conju-

Huaorani take pleasure in the abundance of the forest (John Wright).

gal intercourse. People today no longer live on hilltops away from rivers in highly dispersed, semi-autarkic, and transient collective dwellings; but many marriages still unite in sequence pairs of brothers and sisters. Moreover, it is still the case that pairs of brothers and sisters remain in the same *huaomoni* group by marrying some of their children together. This explains why a significant proportion of contemporary marriages are double cross-cousin marriages.

Permanent Guests in the Giving Environment

Personal autonomy and autonomy from powerful, predatory neighbors would not be possible if the forest was not a "giving environment." The "natural abundance" of the forest is manifest in the fact that people gone on treks do not cultivate but *find* useful plants and cultigens in old camps and abandoned housesites, or along rivers or trails. Huaorani people, like other Amazonian trekkers and foragers, largely depend on anthropophytes or semi-domesticates (Balée 1994). They also use a whole range of more or less intentional management practices to encourage the continuous growth of certain fruit trees and palms in old sites and to facilitate the propagation of certain plant species (Rival 1993, 1998a, forthcoming). Although a thorough botanical survey of Huaorani land is yet to be conducted, there is little doubt that forest inventories should reveal large

Missionaries mistakenly translated huentey as "laziness" (John Wright).

patches of anthropomorphic forest, that is, of forest modified by past horticultural activities—either non-Huaorani or Huaorani. Even more interesting anthropologically, and more directly relevant to the present discussion, are the following facets of Huaorani life: (1) the way in which they understand the relationship between past generations and the living people who make forest resources bountiful, (2) their shamanic practices to increase game availability, and (3) their creation and celebration of abundance in ritual.

There is no word in Huaorani to translate literally what I call "natural abundance," but this does not mean that the term does not capture the indigenous representation of the relationship between living people, the forest, and past generations. A number of superlatives, emphatic suffix markers, adverbial forms, and, above all, speech diacritics (tone of voice, wordless exclamations, gestures) are used to convey the ravished pleasure and enthusiastic excitation caused by the sight—or the recall—of an abundance of useful resources and food stuff. Hand made objects or processed products do not cause such admiration and enthusiasm. For example, none of the aforementioned superlatives would apply to a large manioc garden under production, or to a hip of hunted game, or to collected nuts. A peccary herd passing by may cause much excitement ("there were so many, many, many of them!"), but no one would exclaim "they are so many of them!" at the sight of twenty hunted, dead peccaries waiting to be butchered and cooked. Similarly, a palm grove with ripening fruit will cause people to exclaim: "there is so much fruit, it is ripe!"; but no one will marvel at the five or six big jars of fruit drink lining the longhouse wall. To convey analytically that human activities in the environment may be anti-productivist, yet social—i.e., not mere foraging—is not an easy task. The meanings inherited from Greek philosophy, Christianity, Hegel (with his principle of domination and objectification), and Marx (with his theory of increasing socialization through the intentional transformation of nature) all converge to form the deeply rooted Western conception of productive labor as the quintessential expression of human nature and as the most social and most powerful means for self-realization (see note 2).

What makes Huaorani thinking so different from our own is that they conceive the natural environment as comprising elements that are the direct manifestations and concrete objectifications of *past* human labor. The presence in the forest of abundant resources is thought to result from the subsistence activities of long dead people (Rival 1993, 1998b). A hilltop is covered with producing palms because "the grandparents used to live there, they built their longhouse on it, they lived together without splitting up, and made gardens to feast with the enemies. Do you see this fish poison vine? My grandmother must have made it grow here, look, there used to be a creek down there, she fished in it." Those are remarks I heard over and over again while walking through the forest with informants. In the course of living, a residential group hunts, gathers, and manages a whole range of useful plants along hunting trails and streams. People cook and eat, discard fruit seeds, throw roots, and cut down trees, which gives light for other tree species to grow. People are totally aware of these processes and of the intimate, symbiotic connections between their being alive (i.e., producing and consuming) and the state of the forest.

People are also conscious that their present activities are making similar activities in the future possible. However, such awareness is devoid of moral implication and has nothing to do with the modern notion of planning for the benefit of future generations, since the future and the past are envisaged from the point of view of a continuous, timeless present. The dead do not ask for anything, so no exchange takes place between the living and the dead. What they "give" to the living is not really a gift, anyway; it is more like a by-product, a consequence of the fact that they spent their lives giving to, and receiving from, each other; today's useful resources are the legacy of their sharing economy. So the living owe nothing to the dead. As a matter of fact, although the living can recognize the activities of past people in the forest, they can never be sure whose they were. Informants would say somewhat hesitantly, as if aware of the conjectural character of the statement being made, that such plant had been put in such place by those of the "X" *nanicabo* ("X" standing for the name of a remembered [great-] grandfather or [great-] grandmother). When residential groups are so mobile, and when so many different historical groups (not all Huaorani) lived in the region, how can we know with certainty whose activities have generated abundance? What matters, anyhow, is that human work can be recognized in the landscape and identified as *the* source of abundance for the living.

But what human work, what labor, is being recognized? To answer this important question requires the exploration, however brief, of Huaorani ethno-semantics. There is no general word for "work" in this language but a whole range of terms for the specific making of particular objects or the doing of specific tasks.[8] All these forms of "doing" and "making" are considered creative activities.

The term *baromipa*—literally, "child making," that is, to procreate—is sometimes used for the making of artifacts and weapons. This is the term the Summer Institute of Linguistics has selected to talk about the creation of the world by God. Hunting and gathering activities, by contrast, are often subsumed under the term "forest visiting to bring something back" *(omëre äante gobopa)*. Clearing the forest to plant a manioc field is "doing in the bush" *(omëre quëqui)*. This term is sometimes used today by men opening seismic trails for the oil companies operating on Huaorani land. The preferred expression for this activity, however, is "work journeys" *(omëre gomonipa)* (Rival in press/b).

In a sense, moral connotations attached to "work" are even more revealing than semantic categories. Huaorani people feel strongly that individuals should choose freely when and how to work and that work should be undertaken with pleasure. It is believed that to oblige someone—or to force oneself—to do something leads automatically to disastrous effects. From what I could observe, people would neither give orders nor accept them outside of preparations for a drinking ceremony. As for the ethos of happy working, I noted one exception: carrying heavy loads across the forest. Everyone complains bitterly about this one activity, considered dreadful and toilsome, but necessary.

This rapid exploration of ethno-semantics would remain incomplete without the mention of one key indigenous concept: *huentey*. This term, wrongly translated as "lazy" by school teachers and missionaries, refers to the state of perfect stillness and tranquillity felt by, and flowing from, someone lying chanting gently in a hammock. To be in a *huentey* state is to be in a state of perfect inaction and contentment. *Huentey*, the opposite of activity and movement, is a form of "social work" that helps restore harmony in the longhouse. As such, *huentey* is considered essential for preventing tensions, bad feelings, and the risks of scission.

It is against this semantic and ethical backdrop that past human activities are said to "have made the forest grow" or that past people "did" *(què)* and "lived" *(huè)* in such and such part of the forest, by which it is meant that subsistence and ceremonial activities have encouraged the *natural* growth of useful forest plants.

Is this representation of the forest a straightforward observation, denoting sound ecological knowledge? Only in part, for some connections between resources in the forest and people are ritualized, whereas others are used metaphorically or symbolically. For example, as I have shown elsewhere, house groups converging on chonta palm (*Bactris gasipaes*) groves during the fruiting season see in the fruit the end-product of the activities of particular dead people, that is, their direct ascendants (Rival 1992, 1993); and the couple responsible for the organization of a manioc[9] drinking ceremony is symbolically assimilated to a fruiting tree (Rival in press/b). More to the point for the present discussion is the fact that feast goers, through the performance of dances and songs, transform themselves into birds gorging on a fruiting tree.

Drinking ceremonies are organized whenever there is an abundance of fruit. Moreover, they are invariably treated as potential occasions for marriage celebrations. Over a hundred songs are sung during the night of an ordinary fruit festival, many of which end with verses that mean approximately: "When a tree is heavy with ripening fruit, birds of all species gather on it. They sing out of joy, and they sing to call more birds to partake in the feast. We true humans are like birds: we drink fruit and enjoy abundance. And when no fruit is left, we people, like birds, leave separately, each one going his or her own way."[10]

The message is clear and straightforward. The feasting group is represented as a momentary collectivity made up of free and independent individuals who share no more than the transient pleasure of consuming abundant food together. People chant for hours on about the vivid colors of feathers and fruit, the sounds emitted by, and the movements of, the flying creatures, as well as the sweetness and abundance of the juices that have brought them to congregate. The message of these endless sensuous descriptions is that no obligations or rights bind feast goers together. They are independent or, even more, *unrelated*—as many different bird species. Feast sharing stands in contrast with longhouse sharing, and each relates to a different construction of autonomy. Feast sharing is not really sharing at all but rather the partaking of naturally abundant food from a tree-like source. Human-birds are unilaterally consuming from a naturalized source (a tree-couple), in total freedom and independence. Nothing binds them to the source or to each other, except the gregarious pleasure of congregating and celebrating. By contrast, within the longhouse, each one is in turn receiver and giver; and the daily practices of this particular form of food sharing—characterized by repeated, but not reciprocated, acts of giving away—create lasting bonds of shared substance, crystallized in enduring social units.

Insight into the relationship between autonomy and the unilateral feeding that takes place between feast goers (birds) and the couple (fruiting tree) who has taken responsibility for organizing the drinking ceremony is gained by examining the term for "guest" (*ne eñaca*, "the one who is born") and the term for "host" (*ne ocöinga*, "the one who is at home"). Hosts are in the house, or of the house, and as such they are required to give to their guests, unilaterally and upon request. A host, by giving away to the guest without expecting anything in return, is like a reproductive couple, a nurturing parent, a tree. A guest, on the other hand, is a pure consumer, just like a newborn. Guests are exogenous to the *nanicabo* they visit but would slowly become part of it if they were to prolong their visit. A visitor is entitled to anything she or he sees and would like to have. But if she or he stays on for more than a day, she or he must start giving away as much as she or he receives, thus entering the ambiguous category of half-visitor, half-refugee resident. This is why visiting patterns are highly restrictive, especially for women.

The host-guest relationship, predicated on the facile transformation of providers of "natural abundance" and unilateral givers (parents, hosts, forebears) into natural objects (trees), partly explains the ways in which Huaorani people have reacted and adapted to outsiders, particularly corporate ones. Missions and companies are impersonal donors with the unlimited capacity to create "natural abundance," that is, to provide enormous quantities of food and manufactured goods upon demand. Most manufactured goods used in Huaorani households today are neither purchased nor traded but *given away* by missions, oil companies, and other governmental or private institutions. Besides, these manufactured objects are treated exactly in the same way as naturally abundant resources. Their sight generates the same exhilaration as a troop of monkeys, a tree covered with ripe fruit, or a pack of peccaries.

The host-guest relationship also clarifies manioc cultivation practices in present day sedentarized villages (which roughly correspond to former feast groups). Manioc, *the* easily accessible source of starch food, must now be grown on a larger scale and used almost daily. This is due to the fact that, on one hand, village life intensifies visiting (and the regular consumption of food drinks) and, on the other hand, children, who are more numerous and less involved in subsistence activities than traditionally, spend most hours of the day, most days of the week, at school. Families nevertheless evade these new obligations and constraints by trekking away from the village and its school as often as possible and by maintaining a system of sharing by which one household produces manioc for, on average, five households. Thus the majority of the people still behave as "guests" in relation to a minority of "hosts" and thereby sustain the anti-productivist vision of an abundant, giving world.

Conclusion: Prey That Do Not Turn into Hunters

Huaorani society has expanded both demographically and spatially since the 1950s. It also has, despite the present situation of intense contact, achieved a remarkable degree of isolation. The present state can be described as one in which units of sharing are reproduced with their egalitarian and anti-productivist structures, and this is done as the units remain fairly independent from each other. Each maintains its own autonomy and self-sufficiency by securing direct access to the new sources of natural abundance. The political and economic context in which Huaorani society is enclosed has favored both this strategy of reproduction and a dualist vision of the social world. Surrounding colonists and indigenous groups are still perceived as predators—albeit no longer cannibals.

And the motive of recent killing raids has been to avenge deaths thought to be caused by Shuar and Quichua predators. Other types of outsiders, by contrast, are treated as sources of natural abundance and harassed with continuous and vastly inflated requests for manufactured goods. There has been no attempt to domesticate exchange; people simply shy away from it.

All over the world, the cultures of indigenous and tribal peoples have been gradually marginalized. As these people continue to face an unequal conflict with powerful external political and economic forces, most populations studied by anthropologists are de facto marginal to central powers. So what is so distinctive about the Huaorani? I would argue that it is the fact that these marginal people constitute themselves in collectivities whose essential, embodied qualities are not derived from productive labor but from shared experiences of consumption. Like the Greek peasants discussed by Papataxiarchis (see Chapter 8) and the Hungarian Gypsies described by Stewart (see Chapter 1), the Huaorani create and reproduce their separate and autonomous identity by devaluing their participation in social relations of production and by giving priority to nonproductive forms of sociality. They, concomitantly, treat powerful outsiders and dominant forces as sources of endlessly renewable wealth. Both the practice of valuing sharing in consumption over cooperating in production and the treatment of oppressive political and economic agents as free sources of wealth and creativity are two sides of the same coin. By which mechanism, therefore, is this peripheral collectivity tapping external, dominant powers, turned into an expansive productive force that reproduces the collectivity? This reproduction, I wish to argue, is accomplished by eliminating reciprocal exchange through a process of naturalization.

As I have shown in this paper, the Huaorani sharing economy is not based on the devaluation of productive labor, but rather on the radical attempt to eliminate exchange. Society is structured by demand-sharing and by reciprocal exchange confined to marriage alliances between two longhouses united by cross-sex sibling ties and to daily transactions between husbands and wives. Within the longhouse, co-residents are both producers and consumers. Their creative power, which derives from both production and consumption, is neither denied nor devalued. On the contrary, it is seen as prolonging its effects beyond death, for the forest, far from being a pristine environment external to society, exists as the product of the productive and consumptive activities of past peoples. Both the forest and society are regenerated through the business of ordinary life, without need for accumulation, surplus, stealing, or the transfer of life energy from one sphere to another. The Huaorani vision of life is not limited fertility but natural abundance.

Identity is not naturalized, or essentialized with reference to a narrative of origin as a means to hiding power differentials (Yanagisako and Collier 1995). Rather, we find the naturalization of social relations. Starting with the most inclusive level of social interaction, that between *nanicabo* co-residents, we find a system of representations focusing on common living (from food sharing to substance sharing) as an organic process. The notion of shared substance does not constitute the naturalization but the biologization of social bonds; *nanicabo* sociality is in part biotic. At the most exclusive level, the absolute lack of sociality between *cohuori* and *huaorani* is naturalized as the animal-like relation between predator and prey. The naturalization of the diachronic relation between past and present people consists in making the dead the source of plant food freely tapped by the living, as in the ritual association of *huaomoni* groups with the *Bactris gasipaes* palm groves created by their forebears, or as in the ritual transformation of the couple hosting a drinking ceremony into a fruiting tree and of their guests into gorging birds.

Social relations are, therefore, modeled after two distinct natural processes. The aggressive relation between prey and predators, as found in the animal kingdom, is marked by extreme hostility and separation. It is in the nature of the more powerful *cohuori* to reproduce themselves by continuously snatching the creativity, vitality, and life force of *huaorani* people. The latter can do no more than elude contact with cannibal attackers, move about as much as possible, and count on with their own forces, hence the political choice of radical isolationism. By contrast, the life-sustaining relation between people and forest plants, particularly fruiting trees (and the impersonal agencies perceived as fulfilling a similar function), is characterized by great generosity. It is in the nature of trees and other food plants of the forest to give continuously to humans without asking anything in return. For the Huaorani—as for the Buid of Mindoro, a group of egalitarian, marginal forest dwellers in the Philippines—"the autonomous growth of plants [and] their apparently inexhaustible capacity for spontaneous regeneration . . . provides an example of a life form in which struggle and aggression are unnecessary" (Gibson 1986:186). Both populations associate the power to generate vitality with spontaneous growth of vegetation, reproduction, and continuity and do not, therefore, depend on the acquisition of, nor can they be appropriated by, external political or religious powers. This leads me to contend that Huaorani culture represents society from the viewpoint neither of prey turned into hunters (Bloch 1992a) nor of cannibal enemies (Viveiros de Castro 1992); rather the Huaorani represent prey that evade being eaten and surrender, that circumscribe exchange to reciprocity between husbands and wives and between brothers and sisters, and that reproduce in autarky. To my mind, such clearly deep-seated processes of naturalization constitute an additional proof, *contra* Claude Lévi-Strauss (1968) and Donald Lathrap (1968), that not all marginal nomadic bands found in Amazonia are devolved agriculturalists who adopted a hunting-and-gathering mode of existence only recently (Rival 1998b). Huaorani people form an autonomous society of consumers whose marginal condition results from the social, political, and economic choice of privileging political autonomy through autarky over the desire to access manufactured goods and other foreign commodities. How much longer they will access commodities as if they were fruit on a tree, and how much longer they will be able to play the card of accommodation without incurring the risk of distortion, remains to be seen.

Notes

1. Lévi-Strauss's concept of the "house" has proved very useful to explain the social organization, as well as the ideologies, of kinship and gender of some Amazonian societies (Hugh-Jones 1993, 1995; Lea 1992, 1995).
2. I use the term "productive activity" in the sense intended by Marx. However, what Marx actually intended with the primordial character of labor and the primacy of production in all societies is far from clear or consistent. As Balbus (1982:16) points out, Marx sometimes conceives of production as a transhistorical, universally applicable theoretical category, and he equates the human condition with production; at other times, he is careful to stress that the category of production is more relevant to characterize some historical periods only, particularly the rise of capitalism. This leads Balbus to argue (1982:30) "that the ambiguity of Marx's formulation comes from the fact that he tends to equate the process of production as a whole with productive activities and the social relations of production. This is highly problematic for non-capitalist societies, where the determination exercised by the mode of production may, in practice and for each, mean something radically different." This is why Ingold (1996), following Bird-David (1992), now prefers to talk about hunting and gathering as "procurement."
3. Contrary to the Piaroa situation reported by Overing (1992), shopping is not assimilated to gathering and hunting activities. Shopping is an extremely stressful activity. The Huaorani have very little practice or understanding of town retailing, which involves a great deal of personalized dealing, bartering, and good knowledge of price fluctuations. Moreover, they never have enough money to get what they see and want, which leaves them in a state of anxiety generated by scarcity and limited access.
4. That the English "to go" is "go" in Huaorani is completely fortuitous, but it has not gone unnoticed. Summer Institute of Linguistics missionaries translating the Bible into Huaorani, amused by the word correspondence, brought it to the attention of their native helpers. Many Huaorani mentioned this fact in the course of language work or informal conversations. Although it could be seen as mere pleasure in telling an amusing anecdote, I believe there is more to it. The single word that Summer Institute of Linguistics missionaries and Huaorani had in common was in fact the root used for "to give." And this is what really caught my informants' attention. The powerful outsiders who made peace with those who had killed their close relatives were before all those who endlessly gave away food and manufactured goods. (Five Wycliffe Bible translator missionaries were speared to death by the Huaorani in 1956. The wife of one and the sister of another made peaceful contact with "the killers" in 1958.)
5. Bird-David (1992:39) has shown that the sharing economy of hunters and gatherers, i.e. the fact that they give without expecting an equivalent return derives from their particular view of the environment as a sharing parent who gives unilaterally and provides for the needs of its human children.
6. Conjugal division of labor and balanced reciprocity are relaxed when the couple's children are all married. Then they may sleep in separate hammocks and cook on their own hearths (this is the only time when a man has his own hearth). The old spouses are now equal and independent *nanicabo* residents. They no longer form an economic partnership differentiated from the *nanicabo* sharing economy.
7. "Animal killers" (i.e., predators, in vernacular, *tenohuenga*) comprise first and foremost the harpy eagle *(quenihuè)*, the jaguar *(miñe)*, the nutria *(ompure)*, and a number of

fish and birds that eat fish. Snakes are sometimes included. The animals on which these animals prey are simply "food" *(quenguinani)*. Noteworthily, this term stands in contrast with the term for pet, "that who is fed' or "that who has received food from humans" *(queninga)*.

8. There are a few additional and highly specific terms to cover collective enterprises such as house building or canoe making. The term *tabado*, from the Spanish word for work *(trabajo)*, is used for the long-term salaried occupations of young, schooled men, for instance, the public relations jobs offered by Maxus to ONHAE (The Organization of the Huaorani Nation of the Ecuadorian Amazon) leaders.

9. Although gardening was a part of precontact Huaorani life style, it was exceptional and was practiced mainly for ritual purposes. Even if fast-growing food plants have been cultivated before contact, people have subsisted mainly on forest food. Huaorani manioc gardening requires little time and energy input. It hardly transforms the forest cover and, compared with the elaborate practices and rich symbology found elsewhere in northwest Amazonia (Descola 1994; Whitten 1985; C. Hugh-Jones 1979; Bellier 1991; Guss 1989; Journet 1995), appears rudimentary. A few of the most striking differences can be cited for illustration. Huaorani manioc gardens, which are usually abandoned after only one harvest, are small in size and poor in varieties. The soil, hardly weeded, is not cleared of all its vegetation cover, nor is it burned. There is no strict gender division of labor (gardening does not represent the secret domain of female knowledge) and no belief in the need to combine garden technology with magic. Given a general lack of planning and concern for securing regular and continuous supplies of garden crops, households can spend months without any. Finally, manioc roots are never brewed into beer. Quichua Indians—for whom manioc beer is the sacred mark of social and cultural identity and not a mere staple—profoundly despise the Huaorani way of growing and preparing manioc.

10. *Tomëmo behuenqui ponga abi tomëmo behuenque bamenenga abi eëmo amina bamenguina amina.*

Two Marginal Individuals

Part Two turns from "cultures" to individuals. In some ways, these individuals are exemplars of their social groups, but they also step beyond surrounding norms. Neny, for example, (a Vezo "mother" in Madagascar) is an avid trader. She can be seen as a woman who embraces Vezo values wholeheartedly: the love of the present moment, the lack of wisdom, and the refusal to think of tomorrow. Yet, Neny loves trading so much that "she can't be bothered to be married," and she runs her household so badly that her guest, Astuti, is no longer encouraged to live there. In this way, she is seen to be extreme and to be oriented even more extensively to the short term than her Vezo peers. As an exceptional person and also an older mother, Neny just manages to juggle her passion for trading with the long-term saving and planning associated with care of the dead and with kinship obligations. It is interesting that her neighbors contrasted Neny to her daughter, who was judged far more harshly for her "addiction" to the market and her failure to make a home. The younger woman had not balanced obligation and pleasure.

Uchiyamada's heroines, Lilli and the goddess Kali, can also be seen as cultural exemplars. Lilli is an untouchable widow living with her two sons in Kerala. As an untouchable, she is unable to remove the pollution that stains her and the rest of her kind both inside and outside. And, again like her fellow untouchables, she is unable to prize herself out of chronic debt to the rich. Yet, like Neny, Lilli seems to be uncommonly skilled and persuasive, an exception as much as a type, who makes her own place in the world. These powerful individuals can be seen as threats to the stable, long-term order.

Both contributions dwell upon the pleasures these women find in the present moment as they leave aside various kinship obligations and household chores. Astuti argues that both marketplace and sea are turned into resources for Vezo foraging and shows that Neny comes to lose herself in the pleasure of striking a deal and making a profit. She is alert, excited, and absorbed in what she does. Lilli, too, loses herself in the stories she tells about her beauty and her transgressions across various boundaries between the inside and the outside, between one caste and another, between the worlds of erotic love and the family.

Uchiyamada explores the extent to which Lilli exhibits a strategy common to low status women in the area. He shows how untouchable women remain divided, and he argues that this sense of division is characteristic of those who live at the margins, in contrast to those occupying the center. Accordingly, the discussion of gender by Pine in Part One is elaborated: a sense of division is common to many of the women represented in the volume, and many seem to achieve a gratifying individuality as they leave home and family behind. But, most return. They do not resolve a sense of division but at best capitalize on their status in between and on the move.

4

At the Center of the Market: A Vezo Woman

Rita Astuti

The Vezo of Madagascar are people who are committed to life in the here and now. In the way they define their identity, in their economic attitudes, in their political inclinations, they emphatically deny the determination of the past over the present. There is, however, a significant limit to their presentism, for unlike the Hadza (Woodburn 1982; Bloch 1982), the Vezo do not go as far as to ignore their dead. By tending to them, they become committed to long-term reproduction.

In this chapter, I illustrate the unresolved tension between short and long term among the Vezo by looking at a single individual, one of my Vezo adoptive mothers, whom I shall call Neny (literally, "mother"). Her particular story recapitulates the wider one I have constructed out of my fieldwork; but it also presents a new twist, which has important ethnographic and theoretical implications. Neny's story opens an analytical space for the recognition (and enjoyment) of those fleeting but highly salient moments in which the present entirely disengages itself from the past and from the future.

The Vezo in the Present

The Vezo are fishing people who live on the western coast of Madagascar. As I have discussed in more detail elsewhere (Astuti 1995a, 1995b), to describe the Vezo as fishing and coastal people entails much more than a description of their livelihood and their place of residence. To assert, as my informants did, that "the Vezo are people who struggle with the sea and live on the coast" *(olo mitolo rano, olo mipetsasky an-driaky)* is to assert that it is what people do and where they live that makes them what they are *(maha-Vezo ny Vezo)*. What is asserted, however, is as significant as what gets denied, namely that "the Vezo are not a kind of people" *(Vezo tsy karazan'olo)*. To be un-kinded means that one's identity is not determined by descent, that one is not born Vezo, that Vezo-ness is not an inherent, intrinsic feature of the person.

The performative nature of Vezo-ness frees the Vezo from the burden of the past. In the construction of their Vezo selves, the past has no role to play, since what makes one Vezo is not one's Vezo heritage or one's Vezo ancestry. Children of Vezo parents are not said to be Vezo until they have learned to swim, fish, and sail—in other words, until they have learned to perform Vezo-ness in the present. Similarly, any stranger can be transformed into a Vezo, whereas Vezo people themselves can be transformed into something else (typically into their in-land neighbors, the Masikoro, who are cultivators and cattle-keepers). In all cases, what one is depends on what one does in the here and now, rather than being predicated on essential qualities of the person inherited from the past.

Because Vezo-ness is not grounded in descent or securely attached to the past, the way in which people talk about Vezo identity is pervaded by a considerable sense of contingency. Repeatedly in the course of my fieldwork I heard that such and such a person was no longer Vezo but had turned Masikoro (miha-Masikoro) because he had made a silly mistake while sailing back to land. I also heard that a Masikoro person I had just met was very Vezo (Vezo mare) because he knew how to build canoes. Although these exchanges should not be taken too literally, as they are often meant as teasing jokes or flattering compliments, it is nonetheless significant that such jokes and compliments actually work—they work because, for the people concerned, being Vezo and Masikoro are contingent ways of doing to be realized in the present, rather than fixed states of being derived from the past.

The denial that the past determines the present extends beyond people's understanding of what it means to be Vezo. Short-termism is the most dramatic feature of Vezo economic ideology and, to a great extent, economic behavior. Fishing is described as a form of foraging (mitindroke), which consists in finding a little something everyday to be consumed immediately; it is contrasted with agriculture, which requires long-term investment in the land, long-term planning, and the careful management of crops through time. Vezo foraging, on the contrary, does not involve the past and does not project into the future. It is as if Vezo people started from scratch every day, relying on the fact that the sea is an abundant and generous container of fish, which people extract and use to "buy money" (mivily vola) for their needs.

The problem, however, is that the sea, as everyone knows all too well, is also entirely unpredictable and unreliable, and does not allow small-scale foragers like the Vezo to search for food on their flimsy, un-motorized canoes everyday. The uncertainty of fishing calls for the same kind of "wisdom" that the Masikoro are said to have: the ability to save in the present in order to ensure one's future. But the Vezo take pride in the fact that they are not wise (tsy mahihitsy), that they are unable and unwilling to plan ahead. And so, after a good catch at sea that, in just one day, earns them a considerable amount of cash (often equivalent to the paltry monthly wages of an average civil servant), they rush to the market to buy fat and tasty food, snacks for the children, nice clothes, perhaps a warm blanket. The lack of wisdom is evident the next day when the catch is poor and the money short, and people are forced to eat tasteless soupy rice with no side dishes. When this happens, people typically express "surprise" *(fa tseriky)* at the fact that they have so little to eat (note that people are never surprised when things turn out well).

Both Vezo surprise and lack of wisdom have a significant temporal dimension. Surprised and unwise people are those who act in the present with no knowledge of the past and no expectations of, or plans for, the future. Vezo rhetoric of "unwisdom" and their oratory of surprise thereby define a world in which there is no past and no future, only acts in the present.

If, in the realm of economics, the Vezo boast about their short-termism, in the realm of politics, they find ample scope for denying—even mocking—the power of the past over the present. If any statement sums up Vezo attitudes towards political authority, it is that the Vezo are people who dislike ties and bonds *(tsy tiam-Bezo fifeheza)*. The ties and bonds disliked by them are as varied as the constraining power of custom and tradition; the ambiguous inequality that exists among affines; the coercive authority of powerful foreigners, whether the Sakalava kings of the distant past, the French administrators who replaced them, or the present-day—much less powerful, but nonetheless obnoxious—government representatives. For the purpose of the present discussion, Vezo perceptions of their customs and the memories of their relationships with Sakalava kings best illustrate their refusal to let the present be determined by the past.

Customs *(fomba*: ways of doing things) are things of the past: things that are done in the present because they were done in the past.[1] And because they are things of the past, customs are "difficult" and "serious" *(raha sarotsy)*; they constrain people who must obey them to avoid falling "dead on the spot" *(maty sur place)*. It follows that the more customs people have, the more their actions in the present (what they must, as well as what they cannot do) are determined by the past. But what if people are, as the Vezo perceive themselves to be, too "soft" *(malemy fo)* and "easy" *(mora fanahy)* to withstand the constraints and the "difficulty" imposed on them? The answer is: They will have fewer and easier customs.

Whether Vezo customs are in actual fact any less numerous or "difficult" than those of other people is clearly a matter of judgment. What is significant here is that my informants considered themselves able to decide which customs their soft nature and easygoing character could cope with and thus able to manipulate the things of the past in order to accommodate their desires in the present (for an example, see Astuti 1995a:64).

Although the Vezo are able to manipulate ties and bonds imposed by their own past, they cherish memories of how their forefathers responded to political constraints that were inflexible and intractable. These are tales of how the Vezo dealt with Sakalava rulers *(mpanjaka)* who, up to the colonial period, controlled the western regions of Madagascar, demanding tributes and allegiance from the local populations. Sakalava rulers, like any other holders of power and authority, are described by the Vezo as *masiake*: wild, aggressive, unpredictable; their demands were inescapable, for a refusal to comply was punished by death. So what did the Vezo do? Were they able or willing to endure subjection? In their present-day recollections—a sort of heroic and defiant assertion of their character—the Vezo present themselves in the act of fleeing: "If the king came to the coast, the Vezo would just take to sea, because they couldn't be bothered to wait at the village to meet him".[2] I am not concerned here with the historical accuracy of this claim;[3] rather, I am interested in understanding what the Vezo claim to have fled. Sakalava rulers were interested in collecting tributes from the coastal regions (see Astuti 1995a:73), but they also came to "survey people's ancestors" *(mitety raza)*, asking people who their ancestors were and where they had come from. This was a deeply significant political act through which Sakalava rulers attempted to transform previously autonomous people into subjects of the monarchy by subsuming their local, descent-based histories into the history of the Sakalava monarchy (see Feeley-Harnik 1978). By taking to the sea with their canoes, by refusing to pay tribute and to be questioned about their past, the Vezo avoided this incorporation.

But their flight, as it is remembered today, can also be read as a refusal of the notion, shared by Sakalava rulers and their other subjects, that people's identity can only be constructed by reference to the past, whether one's own or that of powerful others.[4] By fleeing, the Vezo seem to have opted for an alternative mode of defining identity, a mode in which people are determined by what they do in the present rather than by their own or someone else's past.

The Vezo and Their Dead

The Vezo deny the determination of the past over the present, but they are not without a past that impinges upon them. Their past is their ancestors: *raza*, people of the past who are now dead *(olo taloha fa nimaty)*. By remembering and working for them, the living create and sustain the (otherwise denied) connection between the present, the past, and the future, which transcends the impermanence of their (of all) human lives (see Bloch 1992b). As can be expected, Vezo people's interactions with their ancestors are fraught with contradictions, for it is through their ritual work for the ancestors that the Vezo confront the limit to the short-termism and presentism that shape their lives.

Vezo people stress the difference between the living and the dead[5] and go as far as to assert that the dead become so different from what they were in life that they cease to be human.[6] For example, whereas the living are un-kinded, Vezo ancestors are divided into kinds; whereas the living shape their identity contingently and contextually in the present, the identity of the ancestors, who can no longer perform Vezo-ness, is determined and fixed by descent (Astuti 1995a).

To preserve and enjoy their lives, the living devote time and efforts to keep the dead away, raising a barrier *(hefitsy)* between life and death, between the coolness of their villages and the heat of the cemeteries, between the fluidity of life and the fixity of death. Raising this barrier, however, is a paradoxical enterprise, for in order to keep the dead away, the living are forced to engage with them. The deal is straightforward: The dead will refrain from interfering with their descendants (by making them ill, appearing in their dreams, preventing them from having children, etc.), if their descendants will remember and care for them by staging complex and expensive rituals aimed at building solid and lasting tombs.

What interests me here is the fact that in the process of staging complex funerary rituals to remember and care for the dead, the living become inevitably, if only momentarily, overshadowed by death. In these ritual moments—which are considered extremely dangerous and difficult *(sarotsy mare)*—when the barrier between life and death is down (only to be raised again), the living become kinded like the dead already are and like they themselves will become in their future existence. They become wise and have to plan ahead in order to save the vast sums of money needed to keep the dead happy for some time; and they subject themselves to the ties and bonds imposed on them by the ancestors—who are *masiake* (wild, aggressive, and unpredictable), just like any other powerful ruler. In those moments, the Vezo are unable to sustain the claim that the past does not determine them, for in those moments they create the past and anchor their existence to it—only to disengage themselves from it once the ritual is over.

Neny and the Long-Term Transactional Order

At the time of my first period of fieldwork among the Vezo of Betania, Neny was the person who made all the crucial decisions that affected my stay and my work in the village: She decided that I could stay in the empty house of her brother-in-law; she decided when to allow me to share meals with the family; she instructed her husband that it was time to call on the ancestors to introduce me to them; she overlooked my attendance at my first funerary wake; and so on and so forth. She was in her early fifties, the eldest of a group of five siblings, mother of five children, married to an older man who was obviously unable to assert his authority over and above that of his wife. Following an incident towards the end of my stay, when Neny's husband finally decided that he had had enough of being bossed around and, in a sudden fit, threw Neny out of the house with all the furniture (only to be repeatedly humiliated in the process of asking her to come back), I was told by various people (including Neny's husband) that Neny was just like a man *(manahaky johary ampela io)*.

Throughout my stay, I never failed to be impressed by Neny's strong character, by her strength and determination in whatever enterprise she undertook or in whatever opinion she held. Both in her household and among her siblings, she always put on the role of the wise, responsible, judicious mother/wife/sister, whose job was to bring people to their senses by reminding them of their duties and responsibilities, making sure that they did not drink too much, that they did not dance too wildly, that they did not get into fights, and so on.

Neny, of course, often preached what she herself did not practice. For example, she was the person whom I most often heard expressing surprise *(fa tseriky zaho)* at the fact that we did not have any substantial food to eat for supper—for she had spent all the money the previous day on vast quantities of expensive but fat and succulent pork! She told me more than once, almost mocking herself, that "the Vezo make a lot of money, but they don't know how to manage it" *(zahay Vezo mahazo vola maro fa tsy mahay mampiasa vola zahay)*; she would explain that, like the *kalanoro* (invisible creatures who live in the forest), the Vezo eat up all the food they have prepared for lunch without giving any thought to the evening meal: "In the evening there is no food and one just sits around" *(lafa hariva, laoke tsy misy, de mipetsaky avao teña)*. Like all my other Vezo informants, Neny took great pride in her lack of wisdom, in the short-termism of her economic decisions, in her alleged inability to save and plan for the future. It was therefore somewhat surprising to hear Neny preaching to her siblings and other relations that they had to be wise and stop squandering their money on good food, rum, and fancy clothes.

The sudden discovery by Neny of the wisdom that she normally so proudly lacked has to be understood in its context: a number of long and laborious family meetings held in her eldest brother's house to organize the construction of the ancestral tomb. As mentioned earlier, this is a very expensive undertaking, which requires the gathering of a huge sum of money necessary to buy the building materials and food and drink for the crowds invited to attend. At the meetings, Neny spent her time exhorting her siblings to be wise, while accusing them of not being so. Her injunction was that each one of them must put aside a small sum every day from their earnings and remove it immediately from their own houses, handing it over to their eldest brother for safekeeping. In her authoritative view, this was the only way to avoid having the money spent on food, rum, or snacks.

Through her wisdom, Neny was voicing what her family knew only too well, namely, that in order to meet their responsibilities towards the dead, they would have to plan and save. Thus, while it was taken for granted that the small sums of money to be set aside daily for work on the tombs would otherwise have been spent in immediate gratification, people also recognized that to spend money in such a way was incompatible with their duty towards the dead. Grudgingly and with great efforts, they all finally gave in and followed Neny's advice.

Because of her character, her age and status, Neny obviously felt that it was her duty to remind every one that in order to succeed in building a permanent and lasting tomb for the dead, the living had to abandon their customary Vezo behavior. Incidentally, by doing so, she drew my attention to the existence of two clearly separate, if related, "transactional orders" among the Vezo: on the one hand, transactions concerned with the reproduction of the long-term, everlasting ancestral order; on the other, short-term transactions concerned with individual self-interest and immediate but fleeting gratification (see Parry and Bloch 1989). The difference between the two transactional orders can be understood in no better way than by looking at the outcome of each: lasting tombs for lifeless people on the one hand; transitory, sensual enjoyment on the other.

Neny's display of wisdom in those family meetings supports Parry and Bloch's analysis of the articulation between long- and short-term transactional orders. They argue that the transient world of self-interested, short-term individual action, although not "immoral" in itself, must at some point be converted into long-term reproduction of the social order. Neny's often pedantic and slightly infuriating sermons seem to confirm that the strongest censure (voiced in this case by Neny, who feared that it might otherwise be voiced directly by the ancestors, with disastrous consequences) is evoked when individual involvement in the short-term cycle becomes an end in itself, no longer subordinated and converted into reproducing the transcendental order (see Parry and Bloch 1989:26–27). On hearing Neny preaching and scolding her siblings, one would have come to the conclusion that the transcendental order always wins out by controlling, if not entirely motivating, people's behavior. A closer look at Neny outside those family meetings, however, reveals other possibilities.

Neny at the Center of the Market

The day I left Betania after my second visit to the field, a crowd of relatives and close friends, dressed in their best clothes, escorted me to the airport. The most senior person accompanying me was Neny. As we crossed the inlet of water that cuts Betania off from Morondava, Neny was distinctly restless, for she was going to miss the market. As we sat on the canoe that shuttles people back and forth across the inlet, she stretched her neck to peep inside the baskets of fish balanced on her friends' head; as we got off, she ran to the front of our procession and squatted down with other women who were inspecting some smoked fish that was being offered for too high a price. As we walked past, Neny's fellow traders began to tease her: Couldn't she stop trading even for one day? Was it really too much to stay away from the market? Even when she had to see her adoptive daughter off with a proper blessing and good wishes? Neny laughed, stood up, and rejoined us.

Neny is one of a large number of Vezo women who, in different capacities and to different degrees, trade fish at the Morondava market. At the time of my last visit, having no fish of her own to sell, she devoted herself entirely to complex arbitrage activities, which involved buying fish on the beach to resell at a higher price in the market. By doing this, she did not aim to accumulate capital and expand her commercial activities, but simply hoped to make enough of a profit to buy her family's daily provisions.

Neny operates at the end of a long chain of transactions that originate far away from the marketplace. Early in the morning, women from the south of Morondava set off from their villages carrying baskets of smoked and fresh fish. As they move northwards, they encounter other traders waiting along the beach to buy their fish. If a deal is made, the new owner will most probably resell the fish far-

Women haggle over the price of fish on the coast of Madagascar (Rita Astuti).

ther north, increasing the price slightly and securing a small profit. This may happen more than once, until the fish finally reaches the market. Although most traders will walk the whole distance to the market to collect part of their payment and to buy some provisions, only women like Neny, who live a few kilometers away from Morondava, can afford to spend the entire day trading at the market.

Time is a critical factor in the organization of the fish trade. Lack of time and flexibility means that the women who live farther away from Morondava are willing to sell at a price lower than their fish can ultimately fetch. Neny, on the other hand, perceives her profit to be a direct consequence of her hard work at the market: sitting long hours in the heat, often hungry and thirsty, returning home in the evening tired, and with her hands and clothes stinking of fish.

The fish trade, however, is not just a matter of time and hard work; it also involves taking risks. The trade is risky because fish is highly perishable and because supply and demand are extremely volatile. While both sources of risk are beyond a trader's control, what marks off a skillful trader is her ability to identify and avoid transactions that will "kill off" her money.

First of all, a trader must be able to evaluate the quality and quantity of the fish she buys, and she must do so without damaging the fish through excessive handling. Despite the chattering and loud jokes, the four or five women squatting around the fish baskets can fool no one as to what they are actually doing: calculating how much fish they have in front of them, its quality, what it will fetch when sold at the market, and how long it will take to be sold off.

Success depends equally on a trader's ability to predict conditions of supply and demand in the marketplace. The first thing Neny does in the morning is to inspect the footprints of people heading towards the market. She recognizes the prints of most of her fellow traders (even when they wear flip-flops!), and this gives her an idea of how much fish has already gone by that morning. She also knows what the weather has been like, and she can thus make a rough estimate of the size of the previous day's catch. To this, she adds snippets of information drifting down the beach—be it about the crew of a Japanese trawling ship that has bartered a live goat for ten baskets of fish down in Antsatsabo, or a funeral in Begamela that may keep some of the regular traders away from the market for the day.

In sum, Neny's task is to predict the future as best as she can. Observing her in action on the beach, I felt that, with a few contextual adjustments, she would fit Simmel's rendering of market competition rather well: "Innumerable times competition achieves what usually only love can do: the divination of the innermost wishes of the other. . . . Antagonistic tension with his competitor sharpens the businessman's sensitivity to the tendencies of the public, even to the point of clairvoyance" (Simmel 1955, quoted in Hirschman 1982:1472).

Neny may not be clairvoyant; but she is sharp, sensitive, and tense. She is, in fact, just like the "pure entrepreneur" described by Kirzner (1973), whose main characteristic is alertness: the ability to see and a heightened sensitivity to detect new opportunities for profit making. It is Neny's alertness—detectable in her brisk movements, her tense posture, her searching eyes, her unfailing concentration even when she pretends she is not paying attention—that makes her such a successful trader.

"She Can't Be Bothered to Be Married"

At the start of my second visit, Neny told me, rather apologetically, that I was to live at her brother's house rather than with her. The explanation she offered was repeated, this time with reprobation, many more times by other women as well. Almost every day, they told me, Neny came back from the market after dark *(mimpoly mantoñaly)*. When everyone else had finished eating and was relaxing outdoors, the fire was just being lit in Neny's kitchen *(ketsiky mantoñaly)*; all in all, her handling of matters in the house, and especially in the kitchen, was quite unacceptable *(tsy mety)*. And while there was no doubt, even in Neny's mind, that it would be inappropriate for me to live in her house, these women thought that it was no longer appropriate even for Neny's husband, for her two daughters and son, and for her grandson.

Why did Neny behave like this? Her own explanation was simple: She stayed late at the market so as to make more money. Thus, after selling the fish bought in the morning, she looked for more, most probably buying it from those traders who, unlike her, wished to return home before dark. These last minute transactions are both extremely risky and potentially very profitable. Although Neny told me how important it is for a trader to resist the temptation of buying when the risk is excessive, I suspect that she often forgot her own wisdom. Most of the time, she seemed to be able to pull it off, but sometimes she did not and, as a result, lost some of the profits made during the course of the day.

Neny's relatives did not resent her desire to increase profits; what they did object to was her apparent inability to stop and to achieve what was deemed a correct balance between making money and looking after her family. A similar lack of balance was evident when she escorted me to the airport and was teased for her failure to put her adoptive daughter before the market. The market had become an "addiction," and Neny had lost all sense of proportion. On one occasion, someone suggested that Neny behaved as she did because "she can't be bothered to be married" *(tsy mahefa manambaly)*. Knowing Neny and knowing her rather lethargic and resentful husband, this seemed a plausible explanation.

The criticisms waged against Neny's near obsession with the market need to be put into perspective, for, although Neny's behavior was reprimanded, in some ways it was also tolerated, if not admired. The same women who criticized her also recognized her formidable skills in trading and praised her for being a very Vezo woman *(Vezo mare ampela io)*. This is because trading fish is one of the things that makes people Vezo *(mahavezo)*—and Neny, thanks to her multifaceted skills and addiction, happens to be particularly good at it. But this is not all. At least in the eyes of her women friends (but also in the eyes of some men), Neny is "very Vezo" because she has effectively taken control of her household, thanks to the skills and intensity of her trading. She is therefore a living example of the prototypical Vezo woman, one who makes all the decisions *(ampela Vezo manao decision)*.

In any case, Neny was in a very strong position to withstand (perhaps ignore) criticism. After all, she is a middle-aged woman with grown-up children and a docile if resentful husband; she can afford to break family rules and disregard marital values. The importance of her specific structural position in allowing her to do this becomes obvious when compared with Mena's case. Mena is one of Neny's daughters; she married a few years ago, moved out to live with her in-laws, has conceived a couple of times, but has failed so far to bear a child. Mena often trades in Neny's company, and she is often as late as Neny in coming back from the market. But, both her age and, no doubt, her perceived infertility make her behavior far more objectionable than Neny's. In her case the conflict between market and marriage was judged much more harshly—most vocally, perhaps not surprisingly, by Neny herself.

Yet, the fact that Neny more than Mena can get away with what she does, does not explain her motivation for doing it. A crucial if easily neglected element in understanding her commitment to the market is the enormous pleasure she takes in it.

The Pleasure of the Market

Neny, it is true, would probably never admit that she enjoys trading. When she returns from the market, she complains about tiredness, poor health, the sun and the heat, and she reminds her audience—her husband, her two daughters, her son and grandson—that it is for their benefit that she works so hard. But when I got her to talk about what she does in the market, and when she discussed her achievements and intricate trading plans with friends and relatives, it was hard to miss the excitement in her voice and the glitter in her eyes.

Much has been written about the social aspects of markets in Africa and elsewhere. Most famously, Bohannan and Dalton have provided a list of the most significant noneconomic functions of marketplaces in the African continent (1962:15–19): They are points for dissemination of information, places to meet friends and kinsmen and exchange news and gossip, as well as occasions for finding sexual partners. Although Neny undoubtedly enjoys the noneconomic aspects associated with the Morondava market—if nothing else, the company of her fellow traders is more enjoyable than that of her husband—what she really enjoys most is pure, "neo-classical" profit maximizing, as regards both ends and means.

Neny needs to make money; this is why she trades in the first place. But she also seems to like making money, finding in trading the same deep source of pleasure and excitement that Gell (1982) has attributed to bazaar traders in India. As Gell puts it, "There is a sense in which trading, as an activity, must, almost by definition, be a source of subjective gratification, since to trade is to accept a more-valued commodity in exchange for a less-valued one. That is happiness" (1982:149). Neny never expresses her happiness in so many words but her satisfaction is evident when, after a day spent at the market, she returns with a basket full of rice, meat, coffee, and sugar cane balanced on her head and proceeds to instruct her eldest daughter on what to cook for dinner. She makes money; she eats well; she is in control; and she loves it.

There is, however, another element at play, which pertains to the specific means deployed by Neny to achieve her ends. I referred earlier to the skills she masters, to the unfailing concentration and alertness with which she meets the intellectual challenge of predicting and controlling a complex range of variables (the weather, the funerals, the footprints, the Japanese fishing trawlers) and of estimating potential profits and losses. Every day, on the beach and at the market, she applies her mind to this guessing game, imagining new scenarios, exploring new possibilities, and finding new solutions. It is this guessing, imagining, and exploring that Neny finds so enjoyable and absorbing. In those rare moments when I could find her relaxing outside her home, she could think of no better way to entertain us than to recount how she predicted a price increase the previous day, bought fresh fish cheaply, smoked it, and resold it the following morning at a large profit. She was obviously pleased with her practical achievement, but it was also clear that she derived a rather more rarefied aesthetic pleasure from the calculations, the suspense, and the power of her imagination.

The challenge that confronts Neny in the market, of course, is not merely intellectual. She spends her days taking risks that, although carefully assessed and if necessary circumscribed, are nonetheless unavoidable. This is what gives fish trading its buzz, why it seems to absorb its participants to a much higher degree than, for example, the often sleepy and rather laid-back rice sellers. Taking risks not only keeps people alert, it also creates an anticipation of success that can never be taken for granted and that, for this reason, is all the more enjoyable if it can be achieved. Although Neny followed a similar routine every day, she nonetheless had something new to say about it each day; instead of emphasizing routine, she chose to stress variability, chance, and change in strategy and in results. The thrill of figuring out, working in, and exploiting a new environment every day is thus central to Neny's aesthetic enjoyment of the market.

The pleasure that Neny derives from the market, from the beauty of pure competition and abstract calculation, tells us something of crucial importance about motivation and ultimately explains Neny's behavior. For the intensity with which she devotes herself to trading, including the additional hours she spends at the market every evening, is surely the expression of a sought-after pleasure: not, primarily, the pleasure of making an extra bit of money, but rather the pleasure of imagining, predicting, and testing new ways of doing so.

In those moments of acute concentration when her mind ticks hard, Neny is a different woman from the eldest, wisest, and at times most infuriatingly conscientious family member, who worries that her relatives will be unwilling to rein in their self-interest to pay their respects to the ancestors. When she is at the center of the market—a skillful, alert, and successful trader—she gets so absorbed in what she does (and does so well) that she forgets all about her husband, her children, her adoptive daughter, and even, I suspect, her ancestors. She may be criticized for doing so, but when she is at the marketplace, she forgets about the criticisms too. In those moments, Neny seems to be able to transcend the transcendental order and to win over it by creating a world as fantastic as that of the ancestors—a world in which she is no one's wife, no one's sister, no one's mother but only a skillful, alert, and calculating fish trader. In those moments, Neny succeeds in entirely, if only momentarily, disengaging herself from her past and her future and in being fully absorbed in the pleasure of the present.

Notes

The two periods of fieldwork among the Vezo of western Madagascar on which this essay is based (1987–1989; July–August 1994) were supported by Wenner-Gren grant-in-aid and by grants from the Central Research Fund, University of London; the Centro Nazionale delle Ricerche (CNR), Rome; the Istituto Italo-Africano, Rome; the University of Siena; the British Academy. I thank all these institutions for their support. I would also like to thank the participants to the workshop on marginality held at the LSE in 1996 for their comments on an earlier version of this paper, Maurice Bloch for his enthusiasm for Neny's pleasure in the market, and Lorenzo Epstein for his invaluable assistance in making sense of it. I am grateful to Sophie Day, Akis Papataxiarchis and Michael Stewart who, through the efforts of producing this book, have shared their friendship with me.

1. *Fa fomban' olo taloha,* they are customs of the people of the past; *fa fomba bakañy bakañy,* they are customs that come from the past.

2. *De lafa niavy andriaky ny mpanjaka, de roso an-driva ny Vezo, ka tsy nahefa mipetsaky an-tana mandramby azy.*

3. See Koechlin 1975:46–8, 64, 95 for comments on the mobility of the Vezo as a means of avoiding political control. Similarly, Grandidier and Grandidier 1908–1928, 1:376, n. 4 noted that, prior to French colonization, the Vezo were frequently pillaged by the Sakalava kings (see also A. Grandidier 1971:14) and that they did not hesitate to migrate when they had reason to fear a raid. For the first significant contribution to the study of Vezo-Sakalava relations, see Marikandia 1991.

4. So that "severed from his past, a person has no identity in the present" (Feeley-Harnik 1978:411).

5. *Ny maty ny velo tsy miaraky, tsy mitovy;* the dead and the living are not together, they are not the same.

6. *Lolo reo tsy olo fa biby;* they aren't people, they are "animals."

5

Two Beautiful Untouchable Women: Processes of Becoming in Southern India

Yasushi Uchiyamada

I would like to tell you two love stories of untouchable women. One is alive; the other has been dead for many years. My first heroine, Lilli (pseudonym), is a widow and prostitute *(veeshr)* in her mid-fifties; she was a neighbor of mine when I lived in a village I call Nagarajanadu, in Kerala, South India, for eighteen months in 1992–1993. The second is goddess Kali (Pavumba-Kali), enshrined in what used to be a forest in a neighboring village, Pavumba. I collected fragments of stories about these two untouchable women when I returned to Nagarajanadu for six weeks in May–June 1996 and three weeks in August 1997.

The two heroines have many things in common: They are untouchables; both are concubines of high caste men; both are beautiful and dangerous. What I shall *not* do in this paper is to link the *life* of an untouchable woman with a *myth* of a goddess so as to reveal the homology between the two: to place structure above desire; to look for the origin of manifestations. I attempt to follow the flow rather than to analyze—to follow the itinerant "becoming-women" (Deleuze and Guattari 1986, 1988) who cross several boundaries, realms, and hierarchies. These women will not be confined within the grids of a cultural logic concerning purity and pollution, a static Dumontian social structure. In conclusion, I present a performance by, rather than a cogent analysis of, an old untouchable female beggar who I encountered at the Pavumba-Kali temple. Her cryptic bodily movement seemed to be pointing at a qualitatively different way to understand this process of "becoming at the margins."

What It Is to Be an Untouchable

He was afraid to take the child in his arms. He was a scavenger. How could he take that child with hands that had cleaned out latrines? . . . Even though a scavenger bathed he still stank. Would something bad happen to the child just because he touched it? He must grow up without coming close to a scavenger. (Pillai 1993:71)

This is a passage from *Scavenger's Son* by Thakazhi Sivasankara Pillai, a well-known local novelist who lived not far from Nagarajanadu. Chudalamattu is a young scavenger whose late father was a scavenger. He loves his little innocent son who is yet to know what it is to be an untouchable. Chudalamattu's concern is how to make his son touchable. He therefore does not touch his son. Yet, it is inevitable that the scavenger's son will become a scavenger.

One evening I was sitting in a crowded tea shop at Pallimood junction. Across the table sat a young Pulaya man with a dark complexion (*pula* means pollution in Malayalam). I knew his face. He was a scavenger whose job was to clean the latrines of shops and offices at the junction. After taking a cup of tea and a snack, I left the tea shop. It was very dark and there was nobody on the road. The scavenger was following me. He suddenly ran up and asked me if I thought he stank. Because there were no clean caste people looking and preventing him from approaching me, and probably because I told him that he did not have a foul smell, he suddenly hugged me and rubbed his palms and arms against my head, face, and body, smearing and passing onto my body the imaginary pollutant that made him an untouchable. When he finished smearing me, I asked him what he was going to do the following day, for I wondered what he would do after transferring pollution to a foreigner. He replied that he was going to clean latrines.

In the past, untouchables in Kerala were allowed neither to approach public space nor to enter the houses of people from a higher caste, for untouchables were believed to pollute the latter merely by drawing near. Social differences were materialized spatially, although it was made to appear as if moral/substantial differences resulted in social/spatial distances. In Kerala, this led to "pollution at a distance." In mid-nineteenth century Cochin, for instance, it is known that Pulayas polluted Brahmans at a distance of sixty-four feet and Izhavas from a distance of thirty feet. Parayas polluted Brahmans at a distance of seventy-two feet (Alexander 1968:51, 58). The Brahman priest of a local Nagaraja (Snake-King) temple told me that Brahmans were allowed to worship Nagaraja in front of the chamber of the deity in the inner courtyard of the temple, whereas Nayars worshipped the deity from the outer courtyard. Izhavas worshipped Nagaraja from an outer wall of the temple. Pulayas, Parayas, and Kuravas worshipped a separate image of Nagaraja erected in the low-lying wet land known as *punja*. Moreover, high status Nayars and Syrian Christians had the right to kill untouchables if the former encountered the latter on a public road. In the princely state of Travancore (Nagarajanadu was under its suzerainty from the mid-eighteenth century), untouchables were not officially allowed to enter public temples until the Temple Entry Proclamation of 1936. Yet, "pollution at a distance" continued to be observed in open and subtler forms. Kathleen Gough, who revisited a village she called Pālakkara in Central Kerala in 1964, reports an incident where Nayar temple committee members prevented untouchables from entering the village goddess temple (Gough 1970). In 1992–1993, 1996, and 1997, I witnessed daily the negotiation of "pollution at a distance" in subtler forms at thresholds such as verandas and entrances of private homes. Untouchable men were not normally allowed to step across these threshold spaces. Yet, I have seen many untouchable young men with tenth standard education venture to place one foot on the veranda, while balancing on the other foot, which remained outside the threshold. The potential forward movement suggests a willingness to step into the domestic space of high caste people. Yet, its simultaneously frozen aspect suggests the effects of forces that prevent crossing the boundary. I have never seen untouchable women challenge the threshold from the front. They would rather approach from the back, and they often slip through the back gate quietly.

To make this chapter easier to follow, a simplified caste hierarchy in Nagarajanadu and its vicinity can be provisionally *represented* as follows:

Nambudiri	Brahman priest, landlord
Nayar	warrior, farmer, landlord
Syrian Christian	trader, farmer, landlord
Artisans	goldsmith, blacksmith, carpenter, mason
Izhava	ex-untouchable palm wine maker, tenant farmer
Pulaya	untouchable former soil slave
Paraya	untouchable former slave, basket weaver, gravedigger
Kurava	like a member of a hill tribe, owner-cultivator

Pulayas were the soil slaves who produced paddy for their Brahman, Nayar, and Syrian Christian landlords. As soil slaves, Pulayas were attached to the land rather than to people. When the ownership of land was transferred from one landlord to another, the ownership of the soil slaves was also transferred to the latter. From the viewpoint of soil slaves, landlords would come and go, but soil slaves remained with land/soil. Without soil slaves the production of wealth (i.e., paddy) was impossible (Uchiyamada 1997a).

Parayas played the important role of absorbing the malevolence and sins of their high caste masters as sin eaters and gravediggers, without whom the maintenance of the *dharma* (righteousness) of the kingdom was impossible. As I have discussed elsewhere, the release of high caste people was dependent on the constant removal by Parayas of malevolence from their bodies and domestic space (Uchiyamada 1997a).

Kuravas were regarded as the least cultured group: "tribal" people who had their own territories, shrines, and sacred ancestral houses. They have been losing their ancestral land to encroaching Syrian Christians, and to a lesser extent to Nayars and Izhavas, since the mid-nineteenth century. In Nagarajanadu, Kuravas officially owned 61,067 square meters of dry land in 1907, which had decreased to 48,538 square meters by 1989. These figures, which are based on official land records, are deceptive, for many Kuravas do not have title deeds for their lands (Uchiyamada 1995:38–45, 231–239, 243–245). As "tribal" owner-cultivators, Ku ravas were less integrated into the dominant social order than Pulayas and Parayas. Syrian Christians and, to a lesser extent, Nayars are still encroaching on to the territory of Kuravas (Uchiyamada 1997b). Further, Nayars and Izhavas have extended their control over the shrines of Kurava ancestors so as to complete their domination of the Kurava territories (Uchiyamada forthcoming).

Potiyamma (Dust-Mother) was a Pulaya single mother of three children. She squatted behind the house where I lived after her late father, Karamban, was evicted from his ancestral land during the land reforms. Potiyamma called his land the "soggy place." She once told me about two views of the *punja* (the wet lands) that she had dreamed repeatedly. In one dream, Potiyamma's mother, who was Karamban's second wife, goes to the *punja* where her husband is working in the "mud" *(cheli)*. She brings him lunch. He is angry because she is late. The violent husband beats up his wife, who falls down in the *punja*. Her body is stained with mud all over. Her sympathetic neighbors working in the *punja* rush to carry her out of the *punja* and wash the mud off her body. In another dream, Potiyamma herself has a clean body. But she falls into the *punja* because she is careless. Her body is stained with mud. Karamban beats up Potiyamma because she soils her body with mud. The first dream is about a violent force that polluted the body of Potiyamma's mother. The second is about Potiyamma's own carelessness that resulted in polluting herself (see Prakash 1990). Both these dreams are about Potiyamma's anxiety over pollution.

The Malayali term *cheli* signifies both "mud" and "semen." Similarly, the waterlogged and chaotic *punja* is simultaneously a dangerous and potent place from which rice is produced by soil slaves attached to the soil. Karamban was the heir of the soil slave lineage. Potiyamma hated this man, her father, who beat up his second wife, as well as herself; thus, she dreams about her violent father. During the 1930s, a violent incident occurred in the "soggy place." When Karamban temporarily moved to his first wife's natal house in Ochira, the Nayar landlord and his mother's brothers demolished the Pulaya family's ancestral house, filled the well, and sold the land to a Syrian Christian landlord. So, when he returned from Ochira, Karamban found that his ancestral land was in the hands of a Syrian Christian and he had to move to an adjacent plot, from which he was evicted in 1967.

These facts, however, are not central to the present analysis of Potiyamma's dream. What interests me here is the polysemy of *cheli*. In her dream, Potiyamma's mother was beaten by her angry husband. She fell down into the *punja*, and her body was polluted with *cheli*. Her neighbors washed her and removed the *cheli* from the surface of the body. Potiyamma's mother was also impregnated by *cheli* ejaculated into her womb by Karamban. Potiyamma's body is clean on the surface; yet, she is the product of the *cheli* (semen) of the "soil slave," who worked in the *cheli* (mud). Careless Potiyamma fell into the *punja* and stained her outer body with *cheli*, which caused Karamban to beat her.[1] I shall leave the possible interpretations of Potiyamma's dreams to psychoanalysts, for what I hope to suggest is simpler and more modest: Potiyamma is troubled by the unwashable *cheli* that stuck to her body from within as well as without. The mud that stuck to Potiyamma and her mother is a visible marker that reveals the invisible inner substance of their bodies.

Lakshmi, a Paraya woman who squatted at the back side of my former house, was possibly the poorest person in Nagarajanadu. She was about fifty years old, a widow with three daughters and two grandchildren. She was small and thin with a dark complexion and earned her living weaving baskets. She was indebted to a Syrian Christian merchant with whom she had to sleep occasionally. Her second daughter was the concubine of a Syrian Christian farmer. My neighbors called her Echimi (a corrupt form of Lakshimi) because they thought that the poor untouchable widow did not deserve to be called by the name of the goddess of prosperity. During the monsoon season (June–August), many untouchables were without sufficient work and food. It was raining as usual one morning, and as I prepared my coffee and looked at the wet roofs of my neighbors from the veranda, I noticed that smoke was not coming up through the thatched roof of Lakshmi's mud hut. Lakshmi had not bothered to light her hearth because she had no rice to boil. On the following morning, too, I saw no smoke. The local shopkeepers would not sell her rice on credit; she had no means to repay her debt. After exhausting all means to borrow either money or rice in the neighborhood (she had already borrowed money from me and rice from Potiyamma), she decided to apply for the Kerala widow's pension scheme. She had previously applied to the *panchayat* (village council) office for the pension, but her application was turned down. Unfortunately, she did not have the death certificate of her husband, and to obtain it she required a substantial contribution for the doctor issuing the certificate. This time, in a desperate attempt to seek help, she visited a Pulaya social worker who was known for his ability to extract political favors, but she came back later empty-handed.

I do not have enough space here to introduce all my former untouchable neighbors, but in addition to those I just mentioned, there are a few more important characters surrounding Lilli, who is introduced below. Joseph is a converted Pulaya. He is a fat and garrulous jack-fruit leaf seller whose hut was located between those of Potiyamma and Lakshmi. Joseph is a distant relative of Potiyamma. Joseph's elder brother, the late Uncle Thankappan, was a respected communist activist. Uncle Thankappan's wife, Greesi, was a poor widow. She often visited higher caste neighbors during lunch and eyed their food jealously. Reputed to have evil eyes with the power to damage food if not given a share, my neighbors gave her food. She once told me that she hoped to live without begging. Greesi died before I returned to Nagarajanadu in 1996. Joseph has two sisters, Rachel and Anna, both of whom are married and do not live in Nagarajanadu.

Lilli: An Ethnographer's Representation

I do not remember when and how I met Lilli, a converted Roman Catholic Pulaya woman. But, upon my return to Nagarajanadu in 1996, Lilli confidently told me, as well as her neighbors, that she was the first person in the village to meet the Japanese anthropologist. Although she was not the first person I met in Nagarajanadu, I do clearly remember that I recorded her genealogy as I sat on the veranda of Lilli's house, early during my stay in the village. Lilli served me a glass of tea with goat's milk (poor people's milk) and a plate of jack-fruit (poor people's food during the monsoon). I noticed that she had a swollen goiter in her neck. She was cheerful, friendly, and a bit malicious. In retrospect, I suspect that she was trying to turn me into a potential patron. When I was about to leave, she asked me to give her several thousand rupees, which, she said, she needed for removing her goiter. She was extremely insistent. Her theatrical expression, bodily movement, and the tone and pitch of her voice—a collage of submissiveness, arrogance, manipulation, and genuine despair—made me feel embarrassed and uncomfortable as I prepared to retreat to a bungalow that my landlord called the fortress. Ever since, she has been cheerful, inquisitive, insistent, and sarcastic, but she has never failed to cover her upper body with a discolored cotton towel, occasionally with a pink nylon shawl. If she was without towel or shawl, she would cover her blouse with the edge of her blue dhoti,[2] a sign of feminine modesty, whenever we met. It was a strange sign. She was covering and asserting herself at the same time. This ambiguity and oscillation is the main theme of my tale. Many people told me that she was a bad woman. As a bad woman, Lilli was extremely skilled in abusing people. Whenever Lilli and her untouchable neighbors abused each other, hurling derogatory sexual remarks at each other in public, my non-untouchable neighbors would shut the windows and tell their children to stay home.

Lilli was about fifty years old when I first met her. She had two married daughters, four grandchildren, and two unmarried sons in their early twenties. She lived with her two sons in my neighborhood. I soon became close to her sons and dropped into her house often to chat with them. I was told that Lilli's husband had been run over by a bus in 1985 while riding a bicycle on his way to the local market. Yet, the state bus company and the driver were not prosecuted. Lilli filed a case against the company and the driver for dangerous driving and killing her husband. She demanded 65,000 rupees (about 1,500 pounds sterling) for the loss of her husband. While I was in Nagarajanadu in 1992–1993, the court ordered the accused to pay Lilli 15,000 rupees (about 350 pounds sterling). When I returned to Nagarajanadu in 1996, Lilli did not know why she had not been given the compensation from the bus company and the bus driver.

During the busy farming seasons, I sometimes saw Lilli working in the fields as an agricultural worker. When a new house was built in front of hers, Lilli was given a job at the construction site as a casual laborer. I suspected that the landlord, who was Lilli's long-term client, had recruited her so that he could visit her on the pretext of visiting the new house. I saw them talking at the site during the day. My neighbors told me that they were having sex in the bush behind. I gradually learned that the image of sexually innocent and chaste Indian women was a fiction. Many people I knew, both married and unmarried, seemed to be having sex in bushes and in tapioca gardens. Many unmarried girls became pregnant. An

Izhava tailor who impregnated a Pulaya girl was beaten up by her brother and fled from the village. A Syrian Christian girl who had an affair with her relative became pregnant and was sent away, but she returned home after a while and continued to live as if nothing had happened. In the paddy field, agricultural workers flirted with each other, and they seemed to enjoy it greatly. According to Lilli, many unmarried girls in the neighborhood went to the government hospital in Mavelikkara for abortions. People in Nagarajanadu, high and low caste alike, men and women, seemed to be as promiscuous as people in Tokyo and London. Yet, according to the dominant discourse, it was only untouchable women who were particularly loose and promiscuous.

More than a month had passed since the beginning of the monsoon in 1993. There were no agricultural activities in the paddy fields, which were flooded and had turned into a large lake. Many poorer untouchables were suffering from lack of income and food, and many of them could not find enough to eat. When I passed in front of Lilli's house with my research assistant, Raghu—who lived, and still lives, next door—Lilli came out of her house and talked to me. In fact she shouted loudly so that people in the neighborhood could hear her oratory: "Don't tell anybody. Somebody has stolen my son's ninety rupees. He was hiding one hundred and fifty rupees in his diary. He kept his diary in a box. He suspects that Kochchumoon stole the money. Anyway I have made a vow there."

It was rumored that Lilli went to Malayalappuzha and made a vow to goddess Kali, feared by the locals for her power *(shakti)* to cause misfortunes. Lilli called the thief a "bastard mother-fucker" *(tantayilla taayooli)*, a "short and curly" *(milannum kuyilannum*, literally "peacock and cuckoo"), and "buffalo" *(kannaali)*. This was the kind of language that people without shame used. I saw my neighbors listening to Lilli from their houses. Varghese, an old Syrian Christian man, was one of them. Lilli continued:

> When my aluminum vessel was stolen, that vessel cost me twenty rupees, I made a vow [at Malayalappuzha]. I prayed, "Let me see the vessel with my own eyes again." One year later, when I visited George, I found my vessel at his house. It was Varghese who had stolen my vessel from my house and given it to George, because he was furious with me. But they had to give me fifty rupees.

Lilli made it known that she had a relationship with George, Varghese's second son, and that the angry old man had stolen the aluminum vessel from the prostitute's house and given it to George to vent his anger. But he had to pay fifty rupees later, when the Pulaya prostitute spotted the vessel at her client's house with the help of goddess Kali at Malayalappuzha. Potiyamma, whose son Kochchumoon was accused of having stolen ninety rupees from Lilli's house, was listening too. But she was not worried, because she seemed to think that her son's name was used as a decoy. Greesi, the converted Pulaya widow of late Uncle Thankappan, listened quietly to Lilli's oratory with other members of her family. Thinking back, Greesi did look worried. Nearly three years later, when I returned to Nagarajanadu in 1996 and asked Lilli about the money, she smiled and said to me, "Greesi died," and she winked by closing both her eyes. Lilli suspected that Greesi's son had taken the money.

During my visit in 1996, I stayed with my former research assistant, Raghu. Lilli seemed happy to see me again. Before inquiring about my family and job in Japan, she covered her blouse with a filthy cotton towel, performing an act of feminine modesty that honored me. This time, I wanted to ask about her life, which I had failed to do in 1992–1993. As before, I did not know how to ask Lilli to tell me about her life. So I put it euphemistically and said, "Do you know stories about women exploited by men?" Lilli smiled and said, "Yes, I know a lot. But I charge a lot. Come back tomorrow. I have no time now." From the next day, Lilli told me her stories.

The following is a life history of Lilli that was reconstructed by Raghu and myself from fragments of stories that Lilli told during May and June 1996. As I listened to Lilli, I realized two important things: one about myself and the other about her, or about the relationship between us. As she narrated the erotic and romantic stories, Lilli seemed to be observing my responses and reactions and constantly changing the course of her (re)actions in such a way that I thought she was trying to seduce me. She talked about her beautiful body and lovemaking. She talked also about a beautiful girl she had met a few days previously and told me that the girl was suitable to be my wife. It seemed to me as though she were trying to be either my lover or mother, perhaps both. For Lilli, the fact that I was married did not stop her from attempting to make me marry the beautiful Pulaya girl. Marriage *(vivaaham)* meant something different for Lilli than the modern notion of monogamous marriage, possibly something similar to older Malayali "marital" *(sambandham)* relationships. Perhaps she was mixing up the two and moving freely between them.

In these conversations, Lilli used her skill as an orator and "prostitute" to seduce me. For my part, I had to make an effort to appear "cool" and undisturbed by her seductive talk. Raghu commented on Lilli's speech and said to me, "She starts talking from a higher level, gradually lowers the level of her talk, and finally falls on the ground with a man to copulate with him." In the section that follows, I shall tell her life history in the spirit of her own self-representation, rather than subordinating her voice to my own.[3]

Lilli: A Self-Representation

I have experienced many happy and unhappy things in my life. I lived with my husband for twenty-five years and there was no trouble between us. Actually, there were troubles, but they passed unnoticed. After his death, life is worse. I want to be with a new husband.

I was fourteen when I married Daniel. I thought George was going to be my husband, because both George and Daniel visited me often, and I liked George. When the marriage was fixed, I learned that it was Daniel. What can I say after the marriage is fixed?

I was very beautiful to look at. Charles's elder brother, Podiyan, wanted to marry me. Podiyan was a teacher at Sunday School. I answered more questions than any other students could. Podiyan told me that he wanted to marry me. He did not know that my marriage was already fixed.

After I got married, Podiyan followed me to the junction when my husband was not around and said, "I have a desire to come with you."

My neighbors were Izhavas. Izhava boys were enchanted with my beauty. If I were not married, Izhava youths would have eloped with me.

I was very beautiful. Have you seen my photographs? [She proudly showed me an old photograph, and I asked her if I could borrow it.] Many young men like you were attracted to my beauty.

Lilli feels miserable after the death of her husband Daniel, who was an agricultural worker, and now wishes to remarry. She tells of her beauty and her marriage with Daniel. Lilli likes George (this person is different from the second son of Varghese), who is one of the most prosperous Pulayas in Nagarajanadu today. Podiyan, a retired Pulaya government official who married a high caste Syrian Catholic nurse in Kottayam and who now passes as a Syrian Christian, is in love with Lilli, who is beautiful and bright. Lilli's beauty is such that Hindu Izhava youths desire to elope with her.

Do you know Rajan? Do you know how much we loved each other? My family worked at his house. I met him at his house and "worked" (had sex). I was the only one who was allowed to enter the house to prepare curries. There was no bathroom in that house, just a shed in the garden. Rajan and I brought water from the well to the shed together. We chatted, looked at each other, and fell in love. He used to come here at night. There were bushes in front of the house. So it was very convenient. At that time he was studying typewriting in Mavelikkara. He went to the typing school by bicycle. I took a bus from Pallimood junction and went to Mavelikkara. We met there after school was over. We chatted. I took a bus from Mavelikkara. He rode his bicycle. He went in front of the bus. We met again at Pallimood junction. From there we would come back together, chatting. It was such a great love.

Once he sent me a love letter that was not clear, because he wrote it in the garden. I told him to write clearly. So he wrote a letter in his house. His mother asked, "What are you doing?" He said, "I am writing a story" and went out. His elder sister came in and read the letter. This caused trouble. My husband did not tell anybody because he was a proud man. After that we stopped "working" there.

After that, he used to come here, and we "worked" in the bush. One evening, as we were "working," Bhaskaran Pillai and Uncle Thankappan were sitting near the bush. We did not notice them, but they saw us. Bhaskaran Pillai went to Rajan's house and told them what we were doing. Soon after that, Rajan was sent to Pune. From Pune

he sent me letters: "Love is long. Love is short." "Kiss. Kiss. Kiss. All over your body."
[Lilli gestured how Rajan's kisses covered her entire body.] I wrote back. Where did I
keep this letter? I kept it in the back of a photo frame. My husband found it. But, by
the grace of God, Rajan's name and address were not on the letter. My uncle's daughter was mistaken and scolded for hiding such a letter.

Lilli talks about her relationship with her lover Rajan, a son of her Syrian
Christian landlord. Lilli is the only untouchable woman who is allowed to enter
the house and prepare food for her masters: These acts have sexual connotations.
She is seventeen, and Rajan sixteen, when they fall in love. At first they talk, and
then they make love. Lilli's eldest daughter is already born. Lilli's husband does
not say anything because he is a proud man. Lilli and Rajan "work" (have sex) at
Rajan's house. After Rajan's family discovers the affair, Rajan and Lilli "work" in a
nearby bush. One evening, Bhaskaran Pillai (a Nayar neighbor of Lilli) and Uncle
Thankappan (a Pulaya next door neighbor who was a respected communist activist) see Lilli and Rajan having sex in the bush. Rajan is sent off to Pune.

One evening I was peeling tapioca at Rajan's house. After everyone went to bed, Rajan came up to me. As we were having sex, Louis fell from his bed and everyone woke
up. They saw what we were doing. Louis was in love with Rachel from next door. She
was eighteen years old then. That was when I gave birth to Shibu [Lilli's fourth child]
at my natal house. Everybody from this house was attending Samuel's brother's wedding. So there was no one in this house. My husband came back from the wedding
and lay down in the middle of the room. He heard a noise and found Rachel and
Louis having sex in the next room. He caught both of them. But Louis was strong.
He kicked my husband and ran away. My husband dragged Rachel to a coconut tree
and tied her with her half sari. Rachel said, "Let me go free in the name of your children, or Uncle Thankappan will kill me." He freed Rachel when he heard this. Louis
gave Rachel money to buy clothes.

There are similar affairs between many Pulaya girls and high caste young men
in the neighborhood. Lilli talks about a love affair between Rajan's younger
brother, Louis, and Uncle Thankappan's sister, Rachel. Louis gives Rachel money
to buy clothes, an act that is informed by the older Malayali "marriage" (sambandham) relations or sexual unions.[4] When Lilli's husband finds the couple
making love in his house, he ties Rachel to a coconut tree. The important theme,
which recurs in Lilli's tale, is that man ties woman, and woman resists being tied
down. In Kerala the groom ties a golden *tali,* which has the shape of a leaf,
around the bride's neck at marriage. The bride is thus tied to her husband and to
his house upon marriage. Rachel resists being tied to a coconut tree.

Anna was having an affair with Johnny. When Uncle Thankappan found this, he tied
Anna to a plantain stem and went away to bring a sickle. Anna plucked out the plan-

tain tree and ran away. She came to our room, and I looked after her there. When Uncle Thankappan asked me about her, I said, "I did not see her." At night I boiled hot water for her to take a hot bath. I gave her food three times a day. At night I slept with her. So the room was not searched. After a while, Anna went into the next room and Johnny came in. It went on like this for three days. My husband did not notice what was going on. After their affair became public knowledge, Johnny was married off and sent away to Pala. One day before Johnny's marriage, Anna and I went to the east side of Bruce's house to see Johnny at night. Anna and Johnny embraced each other and cried. What a cry it was! One night Johnny came to my house with a ribbon and asked me to give it to Anna. I hid the ribbon under my pillow. So it was damaged a little bit. But Anna was happy. When wife-takers came here to see Anna and Rachel and asked me about their behavior, I said nothing about their affairs.

Rachel's elder sister, Anna, and Johnny, the eldest son of Varghese, are having an affair. One day Uncle Thankappan finds out about the relationship. He ties Anna to a plantain stem, but Anna plucks out the plantain tree and runs away. Here again, a woman is resisting being tied down by a man and continues to have an affair with her lover. Lilli hides Anna and her Syrian Christian lover, Johnny, in her house. When wife-takers come to the neighborhood and inquire about Rachel and Anna, Lilli does not tell them about the affairs of her neighbors.

One day Joseph came here and asked Kunjumol to lend him an agricultural tool. Kunjumol said, "You better buy one yourself at Kayankulam when you exchange a bank draft." [Kunjumol is ridiculing Joseph.] Joseph said, "I can earn what your mother earns by other means." Kunjumol replied, "Money is money. My mother does not earn money as your sister, Rachel, does—at the cremation ground at the south side of your house!

Joseph, Uncle Thankappan's younger brother, and Kunjumol, Lilli's eldest daughter, abuse each other. Joseph tells Kunjumol that her mother earns money through prostitution. Kunjumol tells Joseph that his sister receives money from her lover for aborting fetuses. Receiving clothing from a sexual partner conforms to the older *sambandham* relationships. In contrast, the act of receiving cash for sex marks the recipient as a prostitute. Kunjumol admits that her mother receives money for prostitution, but she tells Joseph that what his sister, Rachel, does at the cremation ground, viz. receiving money for abortion, is more debasing than prostitution.

Pavumba-Kali: A Detour to a Local Kali Temple

I shall now make a short detour to a local Kali temple at Pavumba. The purpose of this excursion is to tell a story of a goddess believed to have been a Kurati (Kurava woman), who was a concubine of a Brahman priest in her former life. Goddess Kali at Pavumba (Pavumba-Kali) is known for her beauty and malicious "power" *(shakti)*. The goddess is especially popular among women, particularly those who wish to join their lovers.

> Long ago, this area was a deep forest. It was the time when people observed untouch-ability. In the forest was a Shiva temple, which was served by a Brahman priest. (The Brahman family that serves the Shiva temple today is unrelated to this priest of the past.) This Brahman fell in love with a beautiful Kurati, whose skin was the color of gold. The Kurati became pregnant. The prohibited liaison was discovered. Learning that the angry people would soon kill them, the Kurati and her Brahman lover com-mitted suicide. The Kurati cut her throat and died in the forest. The Shiva temple was polluted. After that no one entered the place again. The temple fell into ruins and the place was covered with woods. Dire malevolence afflicted the region. Some people believed that the forest of Pavumba had healing power. They came to the for-est with offerings. One day, two women from a neighboring village came to Pavumba. In the forest, one of them was possessed and said, "I wish to sit here." Peo-ple laid a stone and performed puja in the forest.

This is a summary of various fragmented stories about the origin of the Pavumba-Kali Temple. I was told that the goddess did not allow the myth of Pavumba-Kali to be *represented* either in a written form or as a formal perfor-mance.[5] My strategy, then, is not to generalize but to follow the ways in which the original event *repeats* itself in a creative way (Deleuze 1994).

When I visited the Pavumba-Kali Temple for the first time during the mon-soon in 1996, I saw a man in his thirties, whose wife had left him recently, offer a fowl to the goddess. I learned that the man made a vow to offer 501 rupees, should his wife return home within a week. I also met Karambi, an eighty-six year old Kurati, who was begging beside the shrine of Pavumba-Kali. (A later meeting with Karambi is described at the end of the chapter.)

The Kali temple at Pavumba is a peculiar place. The temple yard is divided into two. The western half is the realm of a Shiva temple, and the eastern half of a Kali temple (see Figure 5.1). The symbolic space of the western half is organized in ac-cordance with the dominant social and religious order: the *dharma*.[6] In this realm, all the shrines face east. Parvati, the auspicious wife of Shiva, is seated on the left side (north side) of her husband. This symbolic order confirms the dom-inant relational hierarchy. For the time being, I shall *represent* rather than *repeat* it in a simple form as:

husband : wife :: right : left

A Brahman priest attends Shiva, Parvati, Ganesh, and other minor guardian deities in this realm. Nothing is extraordinary here; the symbolic order of the temple "reflects" the dominant social order (Dumont 1959).

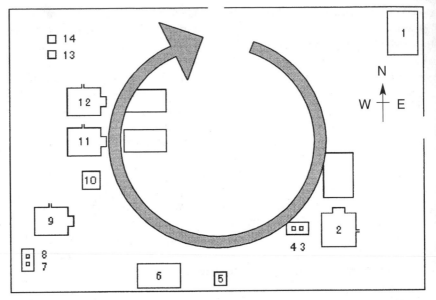

1 Temple Office   2 Pavumba-Kali   3 Kurava Ancestor   4 Brahaman Ghost
5 Well   6 Brahman Priest's shed   7 Nagaraja (Snake-King)   8 Nagayakshi
(Snake-Queen)   9 Shastavu   10 Ganapati (Ganesh)   11 Shiva   12 Parvati
13 Yakshi   14 Matan

FIGURE 5.1   The Two Realms of Pavumba-Kali Temple

In stark contrast, Pavumba-Kali is seated facing north. On her left side (west side) is Kurava Ancestor seated on a small pedestal. Farther on its left side is the ghost of the Brahman lover of the goddess. Thus, in the realm of Pavumba-Kali, the status of the Brahman lover is lower than that of Kurava Ancestor:

concubine : patron :: right : left

Kurava : Brahman :: right : left

The dominant social and religious order, which is organized according to the principle of a purity-pollution hierarchy, is disturbed and reversed in this realm. Moreover, Kali demands blood rather than vegetarian offerings. She wears a glittering red sari. She loves jewelry. Four fearful faces of Kali, with wide-open eyes and a protruding red tongue, gaze in four directions from the roof. Eerie, red, deformed human figures hang from the eaves. The priest is a low caste Izhava man.

Devotees, the majority of whom are sexually active women in their twenties, thirties, and forties, are usually seen sitting on a platform, which is located in front of Pavumba-Kali's chamber. After getting off the bus, a woman may enter the temple from the north entrance. Then she may proceed to the temple office to purchase a ticket for an offering, such as a fowl, or she may walk straight to Pavumba-Kali's shrine with a small offering, such as a bottle of coconut oil. Having worshipped Pavumba-Kali, the devotee may sit quietly on the platform, thinking about the goddess for a while, often for hours. She then crosses the invisible boundary that separates the two realms towards the west and quickly worships Shiva, his wife, Parvati, and their guardian deities, before leaving the temple from the main northern entrance.

Sexuality and Fertility

Two contrasting female images are found in this temple yard. One is Pavumba-Kali, the deified former untouchable mistress who killed herself in the forest by cutting her own throat. The other is Parvati, auspicious wife of Shiva. Both Pavumba-Kali and Parvati embody *shakti*, female sexual power. The former represents *shakti* in the form of a dangerous and destructive sexual power, and the latter in the form of controlled and productive fertility. Pavumba-Kali was pregnant when she committed suicide in the forest; thus she terminated her own and another's life. In other words, she refused to have her life and fertility controlled by the dominant men of Pavumba, and by killing herself and her fetus, and being reborn as the beautiful and fearful goddess, Kali, she also transformed her sexuality into something antithetical to marriage and kinship. Parvati, on the other hand, gave birth to Brahmanical deities such as Ganesh. She is an idealized wife and mother. Her *shakti* is controlled by her husband, Shiva, and by the institution of the family. There is a sharp contrast between the image of Kali, a single goddess who is beautiful, fertile, and angry, on the one hand, and the image of Parvati, the auspicious wife of Shiva and the mother of Ganesh, on the other.

Ann Gold has written, "Students of South Asian society, mythology, and psychology frequently portray the cultural image of Hindu women as ambivalently construed and inherently split" (1994:30). Gold notes that these "split" images of Hindu women derive from observing them rather than listening to what women say about each other (1994:33). She also notes that the authors of these images are men rather than women themselves (1994:37). The point is valid. Gold listened to obscene songs and stories narrated by respectable high caste women and extrapolated, "positive attitudes toward reproduction and pleasure . . . coexist with more austere Hindu precepts" (1994:44). Thus, Gold attempts to *synthesize* female sexuality (whore) and procreation (mother), as they are expressed in the songs of women, *within the institution of the family*. In her own words: "We have the new mother, with baby by her side, as a teasingly seductive, and potentially once again fertile, wife—the total collapse of the erotic whore/fertile mother kind of split image"

(1994:55). She listened to women rather than men. Yet, the limitation of her *synthesis* is that she listened to respectable high caste, rather than untouchable, women.

Let us return to the temple yard at Pavumba. As I noted above, there are two contrasting images of goddesses in the same temple yard. What Gold did was analogous to *synthesizing* the "split" that exists *within* Parvati and not *between* Parvati and Pavumba-Kali. As a result, sexuality and fertility as experienced at the margins are totally left out of her account. To recap, Parvati is maternal and erotic; her sexuality and erotic beauty are channeled to her husband, Shiva. In contrast, Pavumba-Kali, whose prospect of becoming the wife of the Brahman priest was denied in her former life, is autoerotic. Although she seems to take pleasure in this, her desire is never satisfied. She is therefore jealous and angry.

Now let us proceed from the "split" space of the Pavumba-Kali temple to the "split" selves experienced at the margins by considering Dr. Razina Viswambharan's column in a Malayalam women's weekly, *Mangalam* (1996:25).

The Four Laws of How Women Should Behave

Dear Elder Sister,
I am writing this letter with worry. I am a twenty-year-old housewife. My husband is my mother's brother's son. We have been married for five years, but we do not have a child. But this is not what annoys me. I weep every day. He hates me and does not even look at me. He is in love with our relative Cheriyamma. He went out with her and bought her whatever she asked him. Both of them promised that they would never do it again. But within a few days, they started seeing each other again. Because of the pain, I can hardly talk. I live like a servant. . . . I don't know what to do. I do not have the courage to commit suicide either. I am waiting for your advice.

                                                                    Mrs. S.R. Alapuzha

Dear Younger Sister,
. . . Do you know the four laws of how women should behave? Be like a minister in the administration; Be like a maid at work; Be like Lakshmi [the wife of the ideal king Vishnu] in appearance; Be like a prostitute in bed. Try to win your husband's love through good behaviour. The house and its surroundings should be kept tidy [a Minister]. Go and finish your housework, including cooking, at the right time [a maid]. . . . If the wife fails in these matters, the husband is not satisfied with her, and gradually leaves her. . . . Put a red mark on your forehead, and make up your face after taking a bath [suggesting a metamorphosis from Lakshmi to a prostitute]. Men do not like women who cry and complain all the time. . . .

                                                                    With Love,
                                                                    Elder Sister

The columnist tells Mrs. Alapuzha to behave in ways strikingly similar to the image of the "new mother" proposed by Gold: the new mother, with baby by her side, as a teasingly seductive, and potentially once again fertile, wife—the total collapse of the erotic whore/fertile mother kind of split image. The "four laws" referred to by the columnist of the popular women's magazine, the symbolic order of the Shiva/Parvati temple, and the explication of the whore-mother synthesis by Gold seem to share a common cultural logic. The reason is simple. They are the artifacts of the regulatory dharma. Now let me juxtapose the high caste whore-mother synthesis with Lilli's, as well as Pavumba-Kali's, whore/mother "split" images.

One afternoon, I asked Lilli to explicate the four laws. On this occasion, her explanation of the first three laws was similar to the columnist's exegesis. But the last one was different. Lilli said:

> Women who sleep with their husbands are not prostitutes. Prostitutes sleep with men who are not their husbands. People go to prostitutes because they are not sexually satisfied. I did not have that [i.e., I did not get sexual satisfaction from my husband], so I . . . Men and women in Kerala are highly intelligent in these matters.

On another occasion, I asked Lilli why Johnny, Rajan, and other men slept with untouchable women. Lilli explained:

> That is love. If the wife cannot satisfy her husband, he loves a woman without thinking about her caste. . . . A clever wife has more than one husband without being noticed. This is the meaning of "be like a minister in the administration."

Lilli's reading of the four laws is radically different from that of the dominant and high caste view. Lilli is proud of her seductive beauty. She says that she was so beautiful to look at. Lilli enjoyed being gazed at and fancied by higher caste men. She took pleasure from having sex with Rajan and did not seem to feel guilty, in stark contrast to the middle-class urban women in Delhi, described by Thapan, who suffered from the oppressive gazes of others, and who experienced their own body as "bodies for others" (Thapan 1995). Lilli's justification for taking pleasure from sex with her higher caste lover was that she did not get sexual satisfaction from her husband. Her understanding of female sexuality is a female-centered and self-centered one. In contrast, Dr. Viswambharan, the columnist of *Mangalam,* advises Mrs. Alapuzha to be an erotic whore and a good wife at the same time, if she is to win back her husband's love. Gold similarly argues that the image of Hindu wives, as they are *represented* (not *repeated*) in songs they sing, are seductive and reproductive at the same time. Dr. Viswambharan's prescription is a husband-centered one. Gold's "new mother" is narrowly confined and family-centered. In either schema, an Indian women enjoying erotic love outside the institution of family does not have a place. The family is the holiest institution in India. Reproducing the family reproduces caste.

For Lilli and other untouchable women, falling in love with high caste men involves crossing the boundaries of family and caste that separate untouchable selves from higher caste people. Lilli's erotic beauty, which provoked high caste men's sexual desires, moved Lilli from the confinement of an untouchable family to a different terrain. It gave her a sense of self-worth. Moreover, Lilli has established *bandham* relationships with Rajan. The notion of *bandham* connotes sexual, conjugal, and kinship relationships. Lilli still sees Rajan, whose wife now works in the Gulf. Lilli's romance with Rajan was a sexual one. This *bandham* relationship seems to have spilled over into the realms of conjugal and kinship *bandham* relationships. I began to think about this possibility when I learned that Lilli received rice, money, and saris not only from Rajan himself, but also from his mother when she married off her two daughters.

A Commentary

The Kali/Parvati "split" enabled Lilli to traverse the bounded terrains of family and caste. This "split" seemed to have given Lilli a freedom, sexual satisfaction, and a sense of self-worth. This transgression across bounded terrains gave her material gains, too. Yet, this is secondary according to Lilli's self-representation. Lilli told me that she loved Rajan, and not for money. She said, "I gave him money when he was young and without work." She seemed to be saying that she was not a prostitute, as she did not receive money from Rajan for sleeping with him. After all, Lilli told a long love story for several days without talking about prostitution.

My point of departure begins where Gold ended. Gold listened to women's songs. But she was not critical enough about the possibility of reproducing an image of the "new mother" that would only constitute yet another set of "boundary processes" (Sibley 1995), separating gendered subjects once more by divisions of family, class, and caste. Let's listen to what untouchable women say about themselves. Yet, this still is not enough. We need to follow the trajectories of these "becoming-women," who are inherently "split," who cross the boundaries of family, caste, and social structure in a passing moment, in a liminal space that is created by the spilling over and heterogeneous *bandham* relationships. As will become clearer towards the end of the chapter, there is a moment when the "split" becomes ontologically meaningless.

It was early July. The monsoon had just set in, and paddy fields began to flood again. It was time for me to return to Tokyo. I had to give Lilli a cash gift before I left Nagarajanadu. Yet, I did not know how to do it without damaging our relationship. Lilli seemed to have sensed my concern. She told me that she wanted to replace the door flaps, which were badly damaged by termite tunnels, and that a marriage negotiation for her eldest son was about to take place at her house. I gave Lilli a cash gift of 1,500 rupees as my contribution towards the cost of replacing the front door, so as to help the outcome of her son's marriage negotiations. This transaction made me appear as though I were one of the philanthropic landlords in the neighborhood who was sympathetic to the untouchable widow and her family's well-being. The ambiguous relationship between Lilli and myself; the relationship between a "bad woman" telling erotic tales and her potential "son" listening to her stories, was temporarily eclipsed when I handed over the cash gift and Lilli responded by folding her palms.

Pavumba-Kali Revisited

I returned to Nagarajanadu during the monsoon in early August 1997. The front door and window flaps of Lilli's house were all replaced with new ones. At her house, I was introduced to her daughter-in-law, who was apparently pregnant. Lilli's eldest son's marriage negotiations had been successful. I returned to Lilli the old photograph that I had borrowed. Lilli asked if my wife was jealous because I had brought back a picture of a beautiful woman. She then complained that her beauty in the photograph had decreased because I had gazed at it. I protested and told her that the picture was as beautiful as before.

While in Nagarajanadu, I inquired as to the whereabouts of the Izhava tailor who had made Shobha, a daughter of a Pulaya *mantravaadi* (magician), pregnant and was beaten up by her brother before he fled the village in 1996. I found him in the nearby town of Mavelikkara. He was working as a tailor in the town and was married to the Pulaya girl. Shobha had been a beautiful young woman when I visited her father, Kocchucherukan, a well-known *mantravaadi*, in 1992. But what struck me about Shobha then was not her beauty but her open smile and her friendliness. It also seemed that she freely smiled and conversed with my Izhava friends. I began to think the following: "This is not Hawaii. Why does Shobha smile so openly? Is she a prostitute?" When I was told that the Izhava tailor had made Shobha pregnant, I was not at all surprised. Unlike the Kurava lover of the Brahman priest, Shobha has successfully crossed the boundary that separates untouchables and non-untouchables by using her charm and pregnancy. She now lives in the town of Mavelikkara with her Izhava husband and her Izhava son.

*   *   *

One Friday morning, Raghu and I went to Pavumba in the rain. I saw two women sitting on the platform in front of the chamber of Pavumba-Kali. One was in her twenties and wore a green sari, and the other, who seemed to be accompanying the young woman, was in her forties and wore a red sari. After worshipping Kali, and then proceeding to the divine couple, Shiva and Parvati, in accordance with what other people did at the temple, I sat down at the north entrance next to an old Kurava beggar who did not have his left leg. As I saw people circumambulate the temple yard clockwise, Karambi (the eighty-six year old beggar mentioned previously, from my 1996 visit) came back from the shrine of Pavumba-Kali and sat down next to me. A middle-aged couple who had completed the circumambulation walked towards the north entrance. They were about to pass the gate when the Kurava beggar said, "Hey! Give me something before you leave. I am Mother's person." The couple stopped short. The husband, who was walking a few steps ahead of his wife, searched for money, came back to where the beggars sat, and handed it to them. When the devotees heard the Kurava beggar say, "Hey! Give me something before you leave," they hastened their steps. But, when they heard the voice say, "I am Mother's person," they stopped as if spellbound. Without fail, they offered the Kurava beggars a fifty paisa coin, a one rupee coin, or a few one rupee bank notes. This, I thought, was extraordinary, for people do not usually give money to beggars once they manage to pass them in places such as bus depots and railway stations. If they do give something, they would normally give only small coins, such as five or twenty paisa.

It was around midday, or the time of the day when human activities become most vulnerable to the attack of spirits. Karambi quietly stood up and moved slowly and shakily towards the realm of Shiva and Parvati. It seemed to me that her movement was a sign of some sort. Karambi seemed to be causing metamorphoses in the temple yard. I saw the Brahman priest close the chamber of Shiva. He put on a white long-sleeved shirt, lowered his *mundu* (white waist cloth), and left the temple yard from the north gate. Karambi staggered to Parvati's chamber, offered a coin, folded her palms, and worshipped the goddess, before proceeding to the chamber of Shiva. At the shrine of Shiva, Karambi worshipped the god quickly without making an offering. She then proceeded to the shed of the Brahman priest, who had returned. He opened the door and offered her rice gruel in a small stainless steel vessel. Karambi consumed the rice gruel beside the well, washed the vessel, and placed it at the threshold of the Brahman's shed, before moving on to the pedestal where Kurava Ancestor and Brahman Ghost were seated. At the ancestral altar, Karambi grabbed tobacco, which was placed there as an offering, and moved to the chamber of Pavumba-Kali where the two women, one in a green and the other in a red sari, were worshipping the goddess. Karambi stood near the devotees while they received small bananas from the Izhava priest as *prasaadam* or sanctified food. Karambi, who stood between the image of Pavumba-Kali and the devotees, demanded her share. Each of them gave Karambi a half portion of the sanctified banana. The old Kurati immediately ate *prasaadam* in front of the shrine of the deified Kurati concubine, without showing any respect for the goddess, as if she herself were a form of the deity. After consuming the *prasaadam*, Karambi slowly came back towards the north entrance with a bunch of tobacco in her hand. As she closed the reversed circle, the temple space seemed to have returned to normal.

Karambi's counterclockwise circumambulation, which took about twenty to thirty minutes, is methodologically important for a qualitatively different understanding of becoming at the margins. All too familiar binary oppositions—such as structure/anti-structure, pure/impure, order/chaos, Parvati/Kali—that constitute the dominant conceptual grid were made redundant through Karambi's extraordinary movement. When Karambi moved at first to the shrine of Parvati and worshipped the goddess, Parvati was made into Pavumba-Kali. As she moved on to the shrine of Shiva, Shiva was transformed into the Brahman Ghost, or the prohibited lover of the Kurati. The old Kurati appeared to my eyes as though she were a form of Pavumba-Kali, who was also a Kurati in her former life. At the ancestral pedestal, Karambi, who was facing north, stood at the south side of the pedestal as she grabbed a bunch of tobacco, as if she were Kurava Ancestor herself. At the chamber of Pavumba-Kali, she did not face the goddess, but turned north and demanded her share from the two devotees. Karambi's cryptic performance erased the "boundaries" and the "split" that separated order from chaos, pure from impure, Parvati from Pavumba-Kali, and the goddess from the beggar. Parvati was Pavumba-Kali and Pavumba-Kali was Parvati. Shiva was the Brahman Ghost and the Brahman Ghost was Shiva.

The presence of the dharmic order in the western half of the temple yard forces devotees of Pavumba-Kali to move to the chambers of Shiva and Parvati before they leave. Although they spend hours at the chamber of Pavumba-Kali and worship Shiva and Parvati quickly, they not only inevitably *synthesize* chaos with order, anti-structure with structure, but also subordinate the former to the latter as they circumambulate the temple yard. What Karambi did was not a mere reversal of the dominant *synthesis* as in theses of "ritual reversal" (Gluckman 1963; Gough 1959). The Kurati's counterclockwise circumambulation at midday engulfed and erased the dharmic order. At this point, all forms of "division" such as whore/mother and Kali/Parvati become redundant. Karambi's bodily movement brings about the becoming that cannot be *represented* within the given symbolic order. Thus, her processional and lived *repetitions* of the Pavumba-Kali myth are highly particular. Karambi's performance seemed to be impregnated with a body of knowledge that was neither logical nor language-like (Bloch 1992b). What kind of knowledge is this? Is it analogous to what Deleuze termed "unknown knowledge" (Deleuze 1994), which impregnates the actions of participants, becoming visible in a certain moment and space?

I am convinced that the static "ritual reversals" theory of Max Gluckman and its variants—such as the Dumontian "replications at the bottom" theories (e.g., Moffat 1979) or the "model and copy" theory of Clifford Geertz (1984)—cannot effectively explain the creative flows of becoming at the margins. I am equally unsatisfied by the early *Subaltern Studies* that presumed an *a priori* "autonomous domain" at the bottom (Guha 1982), for, as I have discussed elsewhere, the power of marginal people is feared by the politically dominant precisely because it is generated and exercised *relationally* (Uchiyamada 1995). Nor is the recent overemphasis on performance satisfactory. I have made an attempt to link the *lived desires* of untouchables and a *becoming myth* of a deified untouchable concubine in a roundabout way. What is yet to be explained is the genesis of these desires at the margins among "becoming-women."

Notes

I would like to thank Tadashi Yanai for taking me to "La Pedera" in Barcelona, which inspired the way I think about becoming. To Dorinne Kondo, Caroline Osella, Filippo Osella, Veronique Benei, Helen Lambert, and Masakazu Tanaka for their comments, I am also indebted. I thank Michael Stewart for his encouragement. The text has benefited greatly from Sophie Day's detailed suggestions. I am deeply grateful to my former neighbors in Nagarajanadu. Earlier versions entitled "Two Beautiful Untouchable Women: Sexuality, Desire and Becoming at the Margins" were presented at a workshop on marginality held at the London School of Economics on 27–29 September 1996 and at the South Asian Anthropologists Group Annual Conference held at the School of Oriental and African Studies on 11–12 September 1997.

1. This dream could be read as a commentary on Potiyamma's sexual relations with her elder sister's husband, who fathered all of her three children. It is possible to describe this relationship with her elder sister's husband as "sororal polygyny," which was not uncommon among Pulayas. Nevertheless, Potiyamma was unhappy about the arrangement. She never told me about her relationships with her "husband," even though we chatted almost daily. In fact, once Potiyamma described herself to me as a beautiful bride riding a horse on the day of marriage. Yet, the groom was conspicuously absent from the image. This fragmented evidence suggests that Potiyamma had suffered from the institution of "polygyny," from violence and above all from the image of her polluted body.

2. A colored cloth wrapped around the lower body.

3. Readers who wish to follow the flow of Lilli's narrative might be advised to skip my commentary.

4. See Gough 1959 and Fuller 1976:99–122.

5. An Izhava temple priest told me that a few years ago a Malayali professor visited the temple to collect the myth of Pavumba-Kali. But he was not successful. A Malayali dramaturgist, I was told, attempted to present the myth of the goddess on the stage, too. But he had to give up his plan because during the rehearsal Pavumba-Kali always possessed the actress who was playing the role of the heroine. I take the myth of Pavumba-Kali as one that is unrepresentable. I have therefore made an attempt to follow the flow of the becoming myth rather than representing it.

6. Fuller argues: "The king plays a central role in Hinduism by guaranteeing the overarching moral order of society and the cosmos—the dharma in a holistic sense. Without a king, there is anarchy and the "law of the fishes" (when the big just swallow the small) prevails." (1992:19). This view is in line with the worldview of the dominant caste Nayars. Yet, this worldview, *which is constitutive of the dominant social order rather than its reflection*, is not necessarily shared by untouchables (see Uchiyamada 1998).

PART THREE

Single-Sex Worlds

These chapters advance the arguments in Part Two concerning the different strategies that can be observed within a "culture." The prostitutes, bachelors, or poor peasants and day laborers are, "culturally" speaking, British, Greek, and Japanese, respectively. And yet they have found a distinctive way to live within these cultures. Some of the common threads derive from their confrontation with state definitions of their role and place in the social order. More than most of those discussed in this volume, but like the Gypsies, these people are heavily constrained by official policies and laws. Gill shows how Japanese day laborers, in a defensive reaction, refuse to have anything to do with the state at all. Prostitutes in London and poor Aegean peasants likewise achieve a radical separation from the mainstream in at least some aspects of their lives. One way of gaining independence involves a reevaluation of money. These people tend to associate some forms of money with hierarchy and dependency, and they renegotiate its meaning through spending it rapidly or gambling without thought for the future.

Like many other people who orient themselves to the here and now, these three groups face a dilemma when it comes to reproduction. The title of this part, "single-sex worlds," suggests that these are people who do not reproduce at all. This is true of the Japanese day laborers and some Greek bachelors. Some of the London prostitutes manage to reproduce "alone," having children through assisted reproduction (such as in vitro fertilization), or setting up female-headed households in which the figure of the father is displaced.

Like the Rom and like Lilli, these examples provide radical reworkings of conventional households. This point again brings to mind a hunter-gatherer literature. Several earlier authors have talked of the hunter-gatherer ethos under the descriptive label of "individualism," implying a distrust of knowledge beyond personal memories and experiences and a dislike of all binding ties and commitments (Woodburn 1968; Morris 1982:459). These chapters also show how individuality may be opposed to other important values invested in the household, in the same way that the short term is opposed to the long term. The fact that these people continue to live "in the present" despite the heavy costs that they acknowledge—having neither their own children nor their own conventional households—has to be understood in terms of the positive pleasure they experience, as well as in terms of social and economic exclusion. One of the sharpest critiques made of the "culture of poverty" literature was that it blamed the poor for their situation. In response to this criticism, ethnographers might be tempted to invert conventional rhetoric and attribute "marginality" exclusively to global processes. But this perspective would suffer the same problems as the one it attacks, since it makes it difficult to acknowledge that the way of life of Aegean Greeks, day laborers, or prostitutes may exacerbate a structurally imposed marginality. In some situations, marginal people may celebrate their "feckless," "irresponsible," or "spendthrift" behavior for the very real freedoms it confers. For much of the time, a present orientation works, in the sense that it is more enjoyable, pleasurable, and sociable (productive of happiness) than life in the long term. Many of the people here see themselves representing a way of life that is far superior to the "mean, tight-arsed bastards" who have forgotten why they are earning money in the first place and who have forgotten all the arts of sociality (see Miller 1994:82–134).

6

Wage Hunting at the Margins of Urban Japan

Tom Gill

Japanese industrial relations have long been associated with close, long-term relationships between employer and worker, and metaphors describing the stereotypical company in paternalistic and familial terms have been commonplace.[1] The model was never true for more than a minority of Japanese workers, and in recent years discourses centered on the "core and periphery" model (Chalmers 1989) have been steadily gaining acceptance. A core of elite workers enjoys the security of long-term contracts, whereas a periphery of increasingly easy-to-dismiss workers gives the employer the flexibility needed to vary the workforce in tune with changing economic conditions.

Day laborers *(hiyatoi rōdōsha)* are on the outermost rim of the peripheral workforce. As the name suggests, they are typically hired by the day and can be laid off the next day if not required. Their chief employer is the construction industry, which is especially vulnerable to changes in economic conditions, tendering outcomes, and the weather. It is a highly hierarchical industry, with a few giant general contractors at the top manipulating a long string of subcontractors, sub-subcontractors, and sub-sub-subcontractors, to whom work is passed on at increasingly unfavorable terms. The small companies toward the bottom of the chain may have no more than half a dozen regular employees. When big contracts come along, they will supplement that workforce by taking on day laborers.

Day laborers operate in various ways, and depending on which definition one employs, they may be numbered at well over a million in the Japanese economy.[2] However, my own research has focused on those— perhaps 100,000 in total— who maintain the traditional day-laboring lifestyle and who are currently suffering from severe unemployment. This traditional orientation entails finding work at a *yoseba*, an urban casual labor market. Work is transacted very early in the morning, either informally by street-corner recruiters called *tehaishi* or formally

at the casual labor exchanges that are run by the government in a rather unsuccessful attempt to legalize, organize, and control casual labor.[3]

Yoseba day laborers usually stay on their own, in cheap lodging houses called
doya (a slang inversion of yado, standard Japanese for an inn). A doya room is
typically only just big enough to lie down in, and the cheaper ones tend to be very
dirty. Toilets are shared, and there are usually no baths. The rent is very cheap
compared with any other hotel but remarkably high compared with a small
apartment, especially when the cost of using public baths is factored in. Often
these lodging houses are concentrated in places called doya-gai. This term—
which can be derogatory, depending on usage—carries associations similar to
those of the American "skid row." In three famous cases, the yoseba and doya-gai
are in the same place: Kamagasaki in Osaka (ca. 20,000 men), San'ya in Tokyo
(ca. 12,000 men), and Kotobuki in Yokohama (ca. 8,000 men).[4] Other smaller
yoseba, such as Sasashima in Nagoya and Chikko in Fukuoka, do not have doya-
gai and the men must commute from lodgings elsewhere.

Marginal Geography

Yoseba are very clearly defined zones with perceptible borders setting them apart
from the surrounding cityscapes. They tend to be located in fairly central city districts with good rail and road access, reflecting their original raison d'être as a
convenient supply of instant disposable labor to city industries.[5] Entering the
yoseba is almost like arriving in a foreign country. One crosses a road and immediately becomes aware of the change in atmosphere and in behavior. People sleep
in the gutter, piss in the street, wander around rather than walking in a straight
line, have plenty of time, and talk to strangers—modes of behavior seldom seen
in the rest of the city, except late at night. There are wrecked cars abandoned in
the street and shacks built by homeless people in the hedgerows. Kotobuki is the
one part of Yokohama where you can park illegally with little risk of having your
vehicle towed away by the police.

The marginal status of the yoseba is encoded in its proximity to other places
inhabited by marginalized groups. Thus there is a marked tendency for yoseba to
be located adjacent to baishungai—red light districts. San'ya, for example, is next
door to the Yoshiwara, Tokyo's most famous pleasure district; and Kamagasaki is
next door to Tobita, which like Yoshiwara has a history of licensed prostitution
dating back several hundred years.[6] Nowadays at least, day laborers cannot afford
to patronize prostitutes on anything like the scale that would justify this proximity. Rather the patrons of Yoshiwara and Tobita are mostly mainstream males. My
impression is that the proximity of yoseba and baishungai has more to do with
shared outcast status than with a patron-client relationship between the two.

Yoseba also tend to be next to, or to overlap with, Burakumin districts. The Burakumin are a despised outcast group within Japanese society with a long and
contentious history (see DeVos and Wagatsuma 1967; Yoshino and Murakoshi

1977). They are another marginal group in Japanese society, but one with markedly different characteristics than day laborers. Their identity is hereditary, whereas that of day laborers is acquired; they maintain family life, whereas day laborers generally do not; they tend to be sedentary, whereas day laborers are mobile. In my thesis (Gill 1996:35–40) I discuss the possibility that Burakumin and day laborers may be the cultural descendants of the Eta and Hinin, two contrasting outcast groups of the Edo period. For now, suffice it to point out that these two groups are often to be found in roughly the same part of town.

In some *yoseba* one also finds various facilities for people with mental or physical disabilities. This is especially so in Kotobuki, where there are workshops for blind people, people confined to wheelchairs, and people with learning difficulties. This stems from the difficulties faced by local authorities in locating such facilities in more "respectable" districts, where the residents invariably complain. The *yoseba* is a more tolerant area and hence tends to become a dumping ground for people who, for virtually any reason, do not fit into mainstream society.

It is generally possible to trace the formation of the *yoseba*, and its proximity to other despised districts, to deliberate state policy. For hundreds of years, central and local governments have dictated where casual workers will gather through zoning regulations. These dictate where cheap houses and lodging places may be built, just as licensing systems have been used to restrict prostitution to particular districts and discriminatory legislation has been used to confine Burakumin to specified places, typically near rivers, where the land is not well suited to human habitation.[7]

Thus the *yoseba* may be despised by the mainstream, but it also has its value, both economic (supply of cheap, flexible labor) and social (dumping ground for misfits). A senior Yokohama police officer told me that, despite Kotobuki's high rate of crime, he and his colleagues had no intention of trying to clean the place up or shut it down: "Given that human nature, and therefore cities, are not perfect, it's not a bad idea to concentrate the problems in one place. The relatively high rate of crime in Kotobuki must be seen in the light of the lower rates in other parts of Yokohama. The two are surely connected."[8]

A leading activist in the Kotobuki day laborer union once compared Kotobuki to an *ubasute-yama*—in Japanese history, a mountain where old women would be left to die when they had outlived their economic usefulness. The police officer quoted above compared the same place to a *kakekomi-dera*, or temple of sanctuary. Actually the *kakekomi-dera* were Buddhist nunneries to which married women would escape if they wanted a divorce. Three years of religious observances would automatically dissolve the tie of marriage.

It is interesting that both these similes refer to institutions designed for women. Perhaps this is another instance of different categories of social discrimination being lumped together, like the concentration of polluted zones around the *yoseba*. Anyway, the distinction between mountain of abandonment and temple of sanctuary is that between involuntary victimhood (stressing the *yoseba*'s usefulness to the mainstream) and deliberate escape (stressing the *yoseba*'s use-fulness to the people at the margin). I found a similar ambivalence among day la-borers themselves. Some would curse the day they entered the *yoseba*; others, per-haps a majority, were glad it was there. It was, after all, a community.

Solitary Men

Some day laborers are skilled. The *tobi*, or spiderman, who does dangerous high-level construction work, is a traditional day laborer category. So is the *daiku*, or carpenter. However, most day laborers do work requiring physical strength rather than acquired skills. Even for unskilled workers, wage levels are quite good com-pared with, say, British casual wages, or indeed with Japanese wages for manual work done on a more regular basis. On the other hand, demand for labor fluctu-ates violently in response to economic trends, seasonal cycles, the weather, and so on. Also a man's employment prospects decline steadily as he gets older. Since so-cial security is rather inadequate in Japan, many day laboring careers end in homelessness, illness, and early death. Life expectancy for day laborers is reck-oned to be some twenty years shorter than for the general male population of Japan.[9] These factors make it almost impossible for day laborers to sustain family life: Nearly all are bachelors or divorced/separated, and many, perhaps a majority, are also estranged from their natal family.

Apart from a few working in shops, restaurants, and so on, there are very few women in the *yoseba*. It is an almost exclusively male society. It has not always been so. As late as the 1960s whole families sometimes lived in tiny *doya* rooms, and there were quite a few female day laborers, sometimes called *yoi-tomake*. But during the 1970s and 1980s, Japan's economic growth gradually made marriage to a day laborer ever less attractive to women, besides furnishing easier work in service industries that made hard manual labor a steadily more avoidable occu-pation.

As a result of these two factors, it is fair to say that in contemporary Japan nearly all *yoseba* day laborers are single men. They do not reproduce, and it fol-lows that people are very seldom born into the *yoseba* as they may be born into a ghetto. Rather, they come to the *yoseba* in the course of their working career. I found that the great majority of *yoseba* day laborers had rural backgrounds. Some had come to the *yoseba* temporarily in the first instance, as migrant labor-ers making use of its function as a convenient temporary labor market. Others had been fired from previous employment, acquired criminal records, got di-vorced, become addicted to alcohol, or in some other way been disqualified from mainstream society. For them, the anonymity of the *yoseba*, where false names pass unquestioned by recruiters and landlords, is a great attraction in a society that usually insists on identification for everything.

Out of all the men who drift into the *yoseba*, a certain percentage end up stay-ing. They may find that the longer they stay, the harder it is to get more regular employment, as the blank on their CVs gets longer. They may be unable to return to the mainstream life of family and company because of an addiction, typically to alcohol or gambling. A few of the skilled workers may judge that they are better off selling their skills to the highest bidder every day, rather than working permanently for a single employer, and some of these people may actually live away from the *yoseba* and simply use it for work contacts. Then again, some people stay in the *yoseba* because they cannot think of anywhere else to go, or just because they like it.

Present Orientation

During the two years I spent doing fieldwork in Kotobuki and other *yoseba* (1993–1995), the most striking attitude I encountered among day laborers was a powerful orientation to the present moment. This is captured in day laborers' conceptualizations of space and money. *Genba*—literally, "present place"—signifies the workplace, typically a building site, which may be different every day. The word has proletarian machismo: It suggests that actual work, in the here and now, is being done—as opposed to meaningless, unreal pen-pushing work. *Genkin*, "present money," means "cash in hand," as in *genkin shigoto*, a cash-in-hand job, usually meaning a single day job for which you are paid on the day. This is not the only kind of job transacted at the *yoseba*: Period contracts of seven days to a month or so are also available. Period contracts offer greater security of income, though usually at a somewhat lower rate of pay. I observed that during the recession of the early 1990s, when jobs were very scarce, the take-up rate for one day contracts at the labor exchanges was virtually 100 percent, whereas a substantial proportion of period contracts failed to find takers.[10]

My impression was that the length of delay was a direct function of the balance of power between capital and labor: When unemployment was high, as it was during the recession, one day cash-in-hand contracts declined more rapidly than period contracts, and the net result was that day laborers were made to wait longer for their money. This delay was resented; like the London sex workers described by Day in this volume, day laborers insist on freely spending their earnings and object when the small rewards from everyday drudgery are denied . . . , channeled into welfare funds, rents, insurance and so forth that give a false promise of future security.

When day laborers work by the day and are paid by the day, they come about as close as one can in an industrialized society to practicing "immediate return," as defined by Woodburn in his analysis of African hunter-gatherers (see, for example, 1981). Perhaps, like the Gujarati laborers described by Bremen (1994:133–287), Japanese day laborers may be characterized as "wage hunters and gatherers." Although, of course, cash is itself a store of value and hence introduces an element of delayed return absent from traditional hunter-gatherer societies, the delay is rarely very long for a day laborer. Money is soon spent, and

A day laborer in a lodging house. He averts his face to avoid identification. Note the very sparsely furnished room with minimal possessions. This man can leave tomorrow (Nakajima Satoshi). (Originally published in *Tanshin Seikatsusha* by Nakajima Satoshi. Osaka: Kaifu-sha, 1990.)

A different lodging house. Some day laborers live in the same room for decades (Nakajima Satoshi). (Originally published in *Tanshin Seikatsusha* by Nakajima Satoshi. Osaka: Kaifu-sha, 1990.)

many day laborers have the principle of not working again until they are broke—a practice long ago observed among casual workers in other industrialized countries.[11] Several day laborers quoted to me a proverbial saying dating from the Edo period: *Yoigoshi no kane wa motanai*—"Money is not something you keep overnight."

Gambling is a major *yoseba* institution—illegal bookmakers take bets on horse, bicycle, and power boat races, and there are other games as well: dice games, one-armed bandits, mah-jongg for cash stakes, and *pachinko* (a Japanese version of pinball, played for cash prizes and hugely popular). This is a particularly effective way of preventing the accumulation of money and inequalities of wealth within the *yoseba*, since the nature of the odds means that ultimately excess wealth owned by gambling day laborers is transferred to the coffers of the gambling establishments.[12]

Day laborers very seldom gamble against each other, preferring forms of gambling that pit the punter against a professional house. Solidarity is expressed by *not* creating debts among friends (see Chapter 8 of this volume). At the same time, the *yakuza* (members of the so-called "Japanese mafia") who run most of the gambling establishments, may perform a similar role to that of the out-of-town professional gamblers in the Greek case who ensure that the community remains a net loser.[13]

A lot of money is also spent on alcohol in the *yoseba*, though there are sturdy minorities who neither drink nor gamble. Drinking practices also express solidarity and present orientation. The copious American sociological literature on skid row includes numerous references to "bottle gangs," semiformal groups of drinkers who contribute to the costs of buying a bottle and among whom some kind of record is kept to ensure that participants get a fair deal.[14] I found no such institution in the *yoseba*; rather, people would share alcohol with more or less anyone who rolled up. Some people were always giving, whereas others always took. There appeared to be no sense that drinks given were to be repaid at some time in the future.

Most day laborers have very few possessions other than some basic clothes and occasionally a few tools. Indeed, possessions are widely viewed as an annoying encumbrance, since they hamper mobility. The few men I knew who *had* acquired a roomful of possessions complained that they had to pay the rent on their *doya* room even when they were away working on period contracts or at other *yoseba*.

The disadvantage of a lifestyle oriented to the present is that it renders people extremely vulnerable to bad weather, bad luck, and aging. This vulnerability is characteristic of day laborers, as has been all too obvious during the Heisei Recession.[15] Without savings, they are very soon in trouble when jobs dry up. They may be forced to leave the *doya* for want of money to pay the rent and be reduced to sleeping rough. Even this is romanticized in the slang word *aokan*, a contraction of *aozora* (blue sky) and *kantan* (simple). It is a simple life, under a blue sky. But day laborers also describe their position more bluntly with another proverbial expression: *Hiyatoi o korosu ni wa naifu ga iranai, mikka ame fureba ii-yo* ("You don't need a knife to kill a day laborer. Three rainy days in a row is all it takes").

This powerful orientation to the present—getting the reward for one's labor immediately and spending it immediately—recalls Orwell's observation in *Down and Out in Paris and London* that "when you are approaching poverty, you . . . discover the great redeeming feature of poverty: the fact that it annihilates the future. Within certain limits, it is actually true that the less money you have, the less you worry . . . You think vaguely, 'I shall be starving in a day or two—shocking, isn't it?' And then the mind wanders to other topics" (Orwell 1986:16).

A number of American sociologists have also discussed "present orientation" in association with lower social class, juvenile delinquency, and mental illness. As Murray puts it: "Deviant behavior is related to deviant time orientation" (Murray 1984:155). He also quotes Wiseman (1970), who suggests that skid row alcoholism programs often fail because the counselors are oriented to the future and the alcoholics to the present. Liebow argues that the present orientation of his street-corner informants is in fact a realistic orientation towards a future that is "loaded with trouble" (1967:68–69).[16]

Yoseba naturally attract the attention of the social services and of well-intentioned volunteers. As in Wiseman's case, the relations between helpers and day laborers may be characterized as a dialogue between future and present orientation. For example, in an attempt to inculcate the saving habit among day laborers, the Yokohama social services have set up a special bank in Kotobuki. It has no computers or cash machines, just old-fashioned ledgers. However, it stays open until 8:00 P.M. in recognition of the fact that day laborers are often away at work during usual banking hours. It is lightly patronized. The people running it told me that one of their principles was to allow any number of transactions on an account in a day. Some savers would deposit a day's wage on getting back from work and then withdraw it at intervals of hours or even minutes in the course of the evening—so uneven was the struggle between long-term security and present gratification.

The majority of volunteers are Christians, for whom future-orientation takes on an existential dimension.[17] They give out food and blankets to homeless men, and some of the groups attempt to make converts. The idea is that the men should look after their physical health in the present life and look to their spiritual well-being in the hereafter.

As with the special bank, the battle with this orientation to the present is a tough one for the Christian volunteers. The number of converts appears to be rather small, and when it does happen, the meaning of conversion may differ for the missionary and the convert. Consider the following field note, recording an encounter in front of a liquor store around 5:30 A.M. on a mid-winter morning:

> There was a thin little old man drinking *shōchū* (strong barley-based liquor), face
> lined with grey dirt. Said he was diabetic and had a dicky heart. "You need to be care-

ful," I said. "I'm already sixty so it doesn't matter if I die," he replied. "I've been a Catholic for ages so I'll go to heaven. I go to church properly, every Sunday. They give you wine and bread, you know, just like this"—and he stuck out a twitching little tongue. (Field notes: Wednesday, 5 January 1994)

Ironically, this man's avowed acceptance of the Christian concept of an afterlife has become a justification for self-destructive behavior in the here and now.

Death in the *Yoseba*

The other marginal groups discussed in this volume also show strong elements of an orientation to the present, but there is always some modification: The Greek gamblers must not lose so much as to ruin their families or spend their wives' dowries (Chapter 8); the London sex workers veer uneasily between the pleasure of immediate consumption and the delayed gratification of long-term plans for businesses and families (Chapter 7); for Vezo fishing people, death and the need to erect expensive funeral monuments puts a brake on the prevalent short-termism (Chapter 4). Yet, none of these factors is present in the *yoseba*. The men are mostly bachelors or divorcees; for the former the shame of failing to sustain a nuclear family is not an issue; for the latter the shame has come already, usually long in the past. It is widely recognized that very few people emerge from the *yoseba* to make exciting new careers, and most men are resigned to permanent residence. As for death, the absence of kinship ties means that there is no obligation to maintain graves or other monuments.

Nevertheless, death is a subject of consuming significance to Japanese writers who study the *yoseba*. The short life expectancy mentioned above, and the fact that dead bodies are sometimes found in the street in the *yoseba*, are unavoidable facts of life: hence such books as Aoki Hideo's *Yoseba Rōdōsha no Sei to Shi (The Life and Death of the* Yoseba *Worker)*, an academic work that sees the early death of day laborers as the ultimate form of capitalist exploitation, and Funamoto Shuji's collection of militant tracts, *Damatte Notarejinu-na (Do Not Be Silent and Die in the Gutter)*, a call for day laborers to abandon quietism and take action against their capitalist exploiters. Furthermore, Ifunke (1991) and Higa (1993) focus on the untimely deaths of particular day laborers.

The day laborers I knew showed a variety of attitudes toward death. A substantial proportion was frightened of dying without known kin. People who die in this way are called *muen-botoke* or "unconnected Bodhisattvas." It is the post-mortuary equivalent of the detachment from family characteristic of many day laborers, and it seems to bother them more than their this-worldly predicament. Some men may permanently break off all contact with their natal family but still keep a scrap of paper on them with an address or telephone number, so that next of kin can be contacted in the case of their own death. Notification of their death may be the first their relatives hear of them for decades.

Scene outside the Welfare Center in Sanya, Tokyo, February 1991 (Morita Ichiro). (Originally published in *Tokyo Streets* by Ichiroh Morita. Tokyo: Sanichi Shoboh, 1993.)

One man told me that he fully expected his family to put his ashes in the family grave after his death, although he was equally certain that they would not welcome him home alive. Because of the collapse of his marriage and his subsequent spendthrift ways, it would bring shame to his family if he returned to their small rural village alive. Once dead, however, the situation would be reversed: It would bring shame to the family if they did *not* inter him in the family grave. I suspect that as well as shame such behavior would also carry a risk of supernatural pollution *(kegare)*, which Namihira (1977:47–52) associates with the failure by the kin of the deceased to conduct elaborate post-mortuary rituals.

How prevalent such attitudes may be I do not know. But it may be significant that although Buddhist priests take little or no interest in day laborers while they are alive—leaving volunteer activities to Christians and various left-wing groups—when men do die as *muen-botoke*, Buddhist temples will provide the equivalent of a pauper's burial. When this happens in Kotobuki, it is customary for the monks of Tokuon-ji, a nearby Buddhist temple, to cremate the corpse and perform the appropriate ceremonies. The monks also hold *kuyō* memorial services at a small Buddhist altar behind the employment exchange in Kotobuki during the sacred periods of mid-summer and new year, commemorating the souls of those who died with no one else to say sutras for them.

Some men said they viewed death with equanimity. Nishikawa, a self-confessed alcoholic, put it this way:

My old man died at the age of sixty, and I expect to do the same. The liver won't hold out forever. But I've no regrets. So long as you live a life that's rich and interesting, it doesn't matter whether you live to sixty or eighty. Besides, salarymen don't live much past sixty either. They tire themselves out and die soon after retirement. There would be no rational point whatever in trying to stop drinking, or to drink less.(Field notes: 3 February 1995)

Sakashita, who did dangerous high-level construction work, had a slightly different view. He claimed that his lifestyle was designed to accommodate the possibility of sudden death:

I'm not afraid of death. I'm aware of the possibility. If you fall, that's it. It's all over in a flash. But I'm ready for death. I can go any time. I've designed my life that way: I've no wife, no kids, and no regrets that I have no wife or kids. If I'd started a family, I'd have to take more care of my own life, I would have to think of the others. I'm better off on my own. I can die any time and it won't bother anyone. That is real freedom. I'm that sort of guy and I can't change. (Field notes: 26 March 1994)

Oppositional Identity

Thus different men find different ways of dealing with the prospect of death. It may well be that at one level present orientation is a particularly prevalent mechanism for coping with death. But it is also the cornerstone of a group identity predicated on opposition to the mainstream.

The category to which day laborers most often contrast themselves is the "*salaryman*," the stereotypical white-collar worker at a big company. He must commute vast distances from his cramped family apartment to the same boring workplace every day, bow and scrape to a dictatorial boss all day long, work many hours of overtime (often unpaid) to display loyalty to the company, flatter the boss at drinking sessions and golf outings he would rather avoid; and when he finally goes home he has an equally dictatorial wife and demanding children waiting for him.

Against this caricature, some day laborers like to picture themselves as free, autonomous, transacting individuals. Their social relationships are based on choice (friendship) rather than obligation (kinship, workplace relationships), and they are in control of their working lives. The simple freedom to decide for yourself whether or not to get out of bed and go to work is often mentioned, and some men prefer to describe themselves as "free workers" (*jiyu rōdōsha*) rather than as day laborers. This mind-set has developed in opposition to an industrial culture in which companies have tended to intrude into their employees' lives far more than in most capitalist systems. In fact, many day laborers have lived a more conventional lifestyle in the past; their departure from it is variously represented as their rejection of it or its expulsion of them, according to circumstances and the man.

Certainly day laborers have to make larger choices and decisions about their work than salarymen do: when to work, where to work, whether to work, and what sort of work to do. These issues, which rarely present themselves to the regular employee, are an ever present concern to day laborers, who view themselves, again rather like the London sex workers, as freelance entrepreneurs. The terms on which they work demand strategy—for example, some day laborers will try to work for as many different *tehaishi* as possible, playing them off against each other to maximize the wage when casual labor is in demand and presenting each day's work as a personal favor, so that when the balance of supply and demand swings against them, they can call in favors from as many *tehaishi* as possible.

This strategy of limited engagement with numerous employers has a long history. Yokoyama Gennosuke, a social critic writing in 1899, says that day laborers of the time responded to exploitation by cultivating a relationship with their *oyakata* (boss), which he describes as "extremely weak." The majority of them worked on different jobs in different places every day, and they would not hesitate to work for a different *oyakata*, if he was offering one or two sen a day extra. They had "no sincerity or compassion towards the boss," Yokoyama rather quaintly observes ([1899] 1985:34). He further mentions that although bad diet has broken the spirit of the poorer day laborers, they are still apt to remark that they "wouldn't do something so stupid as to get a steady job" ([1899] 1985:40)— a comment that may still be heard in the *yoseba* today.[18]

Despite the sometimes highly competitive labor market, many day laborers did stress egalitarian relationships among themselves. There were of course unmistakable distinctions about the mastery of skills, the degree of workplace success, the standard of accommodation, and so on, but these were relatively small compared with the elaborate pyramidal hierarchy associated with the larger type of Japanese corporation. I mostly found that day laborers would share food and drink, even with strangers, on terms that resembled "sharing" more than "exchange" (Woodburn 1998). Street conversation, often accompanied by the free sharing of alcohol described above, helped to create something like the "imagined egalitarian community of shared moods and shared character" described in this volume by Papataxiarchis (see Chapter 8).

I have said that an orientation to the present is the cornerstone of the day laborer's oppositional identity. The *"salaryman,"* as conceived by day laborers, must be oriented to the future because he has his children to think of. They must have a stable home, so he must have a long-term loan. To pay the long-term loan he must have a long-term job, and to keep the long-term job he must avoid behaving in ways that might upset his employers or fellow workers. In addition, Japanese corporations have a range of systems for delaying the return to labor. About a third of annual remuneration is held back in the form of summer and winter "bonuses." Likewise, retirement payments will build up over the years and will not necessarily be paid at their full value if the employee leaves the firm before retirement.

These factors, more than any culturally given sense of loyalty, bind workers to their employers and effectively oblige them to obey the company at the cost of sacrificing personal freedom. Samuel Butler once said that it was ridiculous to speak of a man having free will if he was in the jaws of a lion; the popular view among day laborers, and among some salarymen themselves, is that a man in the jaws of the company has just as little ability to exercise free will.[19]

Oppositional identity in the *yoseba* was not based only on occupation. Day laborers had to deal with the fact that they were outside that other dominant institution, the family, as well as being outside mainstream employment relations. Some would present this as a positive decision on their part, as in the case of Sakashita, quoted above. More often it would be presented in passive terms. For example, I noticed that men who admitted having been married in the past nearly always portrayed the breakup of their marriages in terms of being kicked out by their wives rather than in terms of having walked out.

Another recurrent theme in my conversations with day laborers was about the *yoseba* as a place where the conventions and distinctions of mainstream society did not apply. Thus, one could make friends instantly, because all were in the same boat. The *uchi/soto* (insider/outsider) distinction, portrayed as central to Japanese social relations by virtually all observers (e.g., Doi [1973] 1981:40–44; Nakane [1970]1984:125–127; Hendry 1989:39–42), was thought to have little significance within the *yoseba* because everyone there was an outsider anyway. Likewise people would talk straight all the time, rather than using *tatemae* (saying things for form) for outsiders and *honne* (saying one's true feelings) for insiders. Sometimes, however, overly direct speech led to outright fistfighting.

Yoseba friendships were very variable. I met men who claimed to have known each other for several decades, and chance encounters between people who greeted each other as old friends happened frequently. Sometimes one partner in a friendship would drift off, destination unknown, and the other partner would do no more than shrug his shoulders. Among the more alcoholic men it was virtually impossible to judge the age and depth of friendships. For example, people would insist they had known complete strangers (such as myself) for many years. Sometimes a friend would take on a role usually associated with kin, such as escorting a sick man to the doctor or helping in negotiations with social services. However, I never felt I was in the presence of a friendship that carried the sheer weight of obligation associated with kinship.

Autonomy and Dependence

Death on the street is no longer necessarily the final act of the present-oriented lifestyle. Most day laborers remain excluded from the state pension system because they do not keep up their contributions and there is no universal minimum pension. However, in recent years, central and local government have finally begun to extend welfare benefits to elderly day laborers. It is one of the ironies of *yoseba* life that men who set great store by independence and autonomy some-times become completely dependent on the state for their livelihood in old age. In theory, any Japanese citizen who cannot support himself or herself is eligible for welfare (*seikatsu hogo,* sometimes translated as "livelihood protection"). In practice, social welfare is not easily granted by the Japanese authorities, and simply being unemployed is not usually admitted as sufficient grounds for eligibility. Most city governments will put people on welfare only if they can prove that they are physically incapable of working, even though this is nowhere stated in the official criteria. However, the city of Yokohama is more liberal than most in its interpretation of the criteria, and in recent years has tended to attract would-be claimants from other cities with harsher regimes. This tendency, at a time of a prolonged recession in the construction industry, where most day laboring jobs are found, has resulted in a steady increase in welfare recipients in Kotobuki: the number of recipients finally passed half the population (about 4,000 men) by the end of 1994. As Stevens puts it: "This *yoseba* has changed from the macho day laborers' settlement to the 'welfare town'" (Stevens 1997:244).

Attitudes to welfare vary widely. To some, going on welfare is the ultimate admission of failure: a de facto admission that all the talk of freedom and the rejection of conventional lifestyles was just so much drunken bragging. These men would sooner die on the street than take money from the state—and it is convenient for local administrators to exaggerate their numbers. To others, welfare is just another form of income, part of the "natural abundance" (see the Introduction to this volume) of Yokohama's relatively liberal postindustrial environment; there is no contradiction in going on welfare, since, unlike the despised salarymen, they do not predicate their identity on work. Yet others take the pragmatic view that they will work while they still can but will apply for welfare when necessary. Whether they will be *granted* welfare is of course another matter.

By encouraging day laborers to demand welfare as a right guaranteed by the Japanese constitution and earned by long years of debilitating and under-rewarded labor, the day laborer union in Kotobuki is attempting to change the perception that claiming welfare is an un-masculine, helpless form of behavior.[20] They lead day laborers in negotiations with local authorities, sometimes staging protest marches and sit-ins. Hence "receiving welfare" (passive) is rewritten as "getting welfare" (active).

The fact is that changes in the Japanese economy have sharply reduced job openings for day laborers in recent years. Technical developments, such as the increasing use of container transportation at the docks and of prefabricated units on construction sites, have been accompanied in the 1990s by a severe slump in the construction industry, which is the major employer of day laborers. At the same time, the day laborer population has been aging rapidly, to the point where the average man is now in his fifties. It has become steadily harder to maintain the old day laboring lifestyle, and its more positive aspects have been whittled away. It may be that Kotobuki's change in character from "worker's town" to "welfare town" is part of a broader trend that makes the day laboring lifestyle increasingly hard to sustain. That is not to say that casual labor is going to disappear. On the contrary, unemployment is rising in Japan, and casual labor is rising with it. But it has been culturally repackaged: It is done in different industries, by different people, and with different descriptions. Nowadays, casual labor is increasingly done in the service sector by younger people, many of them female, and the grimy industrial associations of "day laborer" have been replaced by the feel-good connotations of *frītā* (a contraction of "free arbiter") or by other more neutral terms. Recruitment is handled by large, legal companies that nevertheless take just as large a cut of the casual wage as the *tehaishi* standing on the street corner. Casual labor is alive and well; solidarity and community are dying on their feet.

Notes

1. Abegglen (1973) and Vogel (1979) were influential in establishing the familial image of the Japanese company. The concept is interestingly problematized by Kondo (1990).

2. According to the Ministry of Labor (MoL), there are fewer than 50,000 day laborers in Japan, whereas the Labor Statistics Bureau of the Management and Coordination Agency (MCA) says there are about 1.2 million. The MoL only counts people carrying the official handbook issued to day laborers to enable them to use the special unemployment insurance system for day laborers; the MCA uses a much broader definition, including everybody working on contracts of less than thirty days' duration. A majority of day laborers as defined by the MCA are women, many of them home-workers. My own figure of 100,000 *yoseba* day laborers covers the MoL definition plus those (a roughly similar number, in my semi-informed opinion) who do not carry the handbook for various reasons.

3. A few of the *tehaishi* are themselves day laborers or former day laborers. Others are representatives of particular shipping or construction companies; others are small time entrepreneurs; and yet others are *yakuza* (gangsters) or the employees of *yakuza*. Where the *yakuza* are not directly involved in labor recruitment, they usually take a daily or monthly payoff from the non-*yakuza tehaishi*.

4. For recently published monographs on Japanese day laborers, see Fowler 1996 on San'ya, and Stevens 1997 on volunteer activities in Kotobuki.

5. Note that the American skid row, too, was originally associated with casual labor rather than with social failure. It is a corruption of "Skid Road," deriving "from the skidways on which lumberjacks in the Northwest transported logs." (Bahr 1973:32) Bahr says that the original Skid Road was a line of "lodging houses, saloons and establishments . . . contiguous to the "skid road" running from the top of the ridge down to Henry Yesler's mill" in Seattle. He does not put a date on the emergence of the name. In any case, the term "on the skids," meaning "down on one's luck" is a later back-formation.

6. Sometimes the same language is used to describe day laborers and prostitutes: the word *tachinbo*—"one who stands" (on the street corner)—is applied to both professions, for instance, and *nikutai rōdō* (physical labor) describes both kinds of work. In both cases the worker has nothing to sell except his/her own body. The strategy of the divided self described by Day (Chapter 7) is common among day laborers. They will characterize their

custom of working and resting on alternate days as being necessary to preserve the strength of their body as a tool for doing work; and they will see no contradiction between this and their habit of getting very drunk on their days off, which is something they do to their "selves" rather than their "bodies." One day laborer even compared his body to a car—it ran on alcohol just as a car ran on petrol (Field notes: 7 March 1994).

7. Kotobuki, the Yokohama *yoseba* where I did most of my fieldwork, is the most modern instance of this zoning policy. After Japan's defeat in World War II, large numbers of day laborers gathered at Sakuragi-cho, close to the Yokohama docks, where there was much casual work to be had unloading supplies brought in by vessels servicing the allied occupation. The workers lived in *doya* and in old ships moored near the docks, known as "floating hotels." In 1956, the city government, influenced by complaints from shopkeepers at Sakuragi-cho, made a conscious decision to shift the *yoseba* a mile or so east and inland to Kotobuki. The *doya* at Sakuragi-cho were torn down; the floating hotels sunk; and their owners were compensated and given permission to build *doya* in Kotobuki, which at the time was an empty piece of land, having just been released from requisition as a transport depot by the departing allied forces. The first *doya*, appropriately named the Kotobuki-so, opened there in October 1956; the casual labor exchange was shut down at Sakuragi-cho and reopened at Kotobuki in April 1959; and in 1961, despite local protests, the blood bank was also moved to Kotobuki (selling blood used to be an important source of emergency income for day laborers).

Thus in just a year or two, the whole scene was shifted east and inland to its present location. Within five years (1956–1961), sixty-three *doya* had been built (Saito 1994:131). They were filled immediately: The high growth economy had spawned a large population of day laborers. Here, then, is a modern example of how the state can locate and control a *yoseba* without needing to force individual people to go there.

8. Field notes: 1 February 1994.

9. Officials of Junichiro, the Kotobuki Day Laborer Union, estimated the average age at death of day laborers in Kotobuki at 56 (Field notes: 24 February 1995). Life expectancy for Japanese males was recorded as 76.36 years in 1995 (Ministry of Health and Welfare).

10. For example in 1995, the Kotobuki Labor Center advertised 26,012 person days of work on one day contracts, and 25,662 contracts were taken, for a take-up rate of 98.7 percent. It also advertised 35,564 person days of work on period contracts, of which 27,076 days were filled, for a considerably lower take-up rate of 76.1 per cent. For the ten years from 1986 to 1995, the average take-up rate was 95 percent for one day contracts and 77 percent for period contracts (Kotobuki Labor Center statistics).

Partly this difference is due to the bad reputation of some employers, who are said to keep workers in barrack-like dormitories and to feed and pay them badly. On the other hand, period contracts at dormitories save one the cost of renting a *doya* room and are generally recognized as being the only way to save money: being away from *yoseba* society, and often with one's wages withheld, prevents one from spending them.

11. In his classic prewar study of American casual laborers, Carleton H. Parker notes that most of those he knew would stop working as soon as they had enough to live on (1920:78–79). R. Williams makes exactly the same observation about British casual dock workers (1912:31–32).

12. The Kotobuki bookmakers use the same odds as those used at the courses and at legal off-course gambling centers. These odds are calculated by a computerized totalizer to

factor in a 25 percent margin to the house. This substantial margin goes to the government as a betting tax at legal establishments and into the pockets of *yakuza* at illegal ones. Note that gambling is just as much a part of Japanese popular culture as saving is. Although the average Japanese household saves 15 percent of its disposable income—a high figure by Euro-American standards, but lower than it used to be and far behind South Korea and Taiwan—Japan as a whole spends some 5.7 percent of its GNP on gambling. This latter figure is probably the highest in the world, at least for industrialized countries. Per capita sales of betting slips are 2.3 times higher than in the U.S. and four times higher than in Britain. Japan also has *pachinko*, a multi-trillion yen gambling enterprise that dwarfs race-betting and lotteries and is not shared by any other country to any significant degree. (Sources: On savings, Bank of Japan statistics for 1993; on gambling, AERA magazine, vol. 7 no. 30, 25 July 1994:32–39.)

13. Day laborers certainly feel an affinity for romantic losers, as evidenced in the widespread support within the *yoseba* for the Hanshin Tigers—a very popular but notoriously unsuccessful baseball team, comparable to the Chicago Cubs in the United States, or perhaps to Manchester City in English football.

14. The bottle-gang debate of the 1950s and 1960s is summarized in Bahr (1973:157). Some observers stress flexibility, others formality. The most formalized account is by Rooney, who compares the bottle gang to a business corporation: "The management of the capital is handled by a leader who acts as general chairman. Each member is a stockholder and maintains rights to consumption of the communally purchased bottle of wine " (Rooney 1961:449). Giamo (1989:182–183), visiting the Bowery at the end of the 1970s, finds the same institution with the same name, twenty years and the width of America away from Rooney's study.

15. Official government records state that Japan was in recession for thirty months from 1991 to 1994. In the *yoseba* the recession is generally though to have started in 1990 and still to be in progress at the time of writing (1997).

16. Murray himself trumps everybody by arguing that time in skid row is cyclical, rather than linear. He gives two reasons: (1) "One's primary goal is survival, a goal which must be re-achieved every day"; and (2) "the cyclic schedules of the institutions which affect the homeless" (Murray 1984:157). In the *yoseba*, the first point applies to some of the older, weaker inhabitants; the second point does not apply in terms of the one-day cycle, since the vast majority of residents are not in the kind of regimented shelters common in U.S. skid rows, which chuck the men out every morning and let them back in the evening. (Homeless shelters are still rare in Japan, and they tend to limit residence by specifying a maximum number of weeks rather than by limiting hours of residence in the day.)

In my own view, all sorts of conflicting conceptualizations of time coexist in the *yoseba*, as they do anywhere. The cycle of the seasons is very important to day laborers, some of whom abandon their spendthrift ways as winter approaches and attempt to save money to tide them over this most difficult time of the year, when jobs are scarce and conditions harsh. I met one who practiced a form of hibernation, taking on tough period contracts through November and early December and using the money to live in a sauna/cinema complex for a month or so over New Year (Field notes: 19 October 1993). A few others were saving money towards their retirement. They were, however, a very small minority.

17. According to the Annual Survey of Religions published by the Agency for Cultural Affairs, Christians made up only 0.7 percent of the Japanese population at the end of 1994.

However, the strength of the charitable imperative in Christianity makes them a major presence in the *yoseba*.

18. One could go back still further. In the late sixteenth century the warlord, Hideyoshi, banned day laboring because he saw it as a threat to the feudal relationship between master and man (Leupp 1992:16). The term became almost synonymous with escaped peasants, who illegally fled the rural rice fields to work for cash in the cities of Tokugawa Japan (Leupp 1992:160). After various other attempts to control and regularize casual labor, the shogunate started to build labor camps called *ninsoku yoseba* (literally, "navvy gathering places") in the late eighteenth century, which were essentially forced labor camps for people who hadn't actually committed any crime (Leupp 1992:165–175). The term *[i]ninsoku yoseba[i]* appears to be the origin of the modern word *[i]yoseba[i]*.

19. In recent years, the terms *karō shi* (death by overwork) and *tanshin funin* (forced relocation by the company, leading to separation from one's family) have made frequent appearances in the media, and there have been several highly publicized legal actions attacking companies for inflicting these evils on their permanent employees. These factors must be set against the early deaths, mostly from rough living, of so many day laborers.

20. The mainstream unions in Japan have no interest in day laborers, whom they tend to view as nothing more than possible threats to their members' livelihoods. However, there is a history of left-wing activists trying to organize *yoseba* unions, and today there is a National Federation of Day Laborers (*Hiyatoi Zenkyo*, in its Japanese acronym), grouping unions from the *yoseba* in Tokyo, Osaka, Yokohama, Nagoya, Fukuoka, and Naha (Okinawa). Annual conferences have been held since 1984.

The Kotobuki union, Junichiro, seemed to operate more like a pressure group campaigning for day laborers' rights than a union in the conventional sense. Its leaders were a mix of present and former day laborers and middle-class activists; rather than collecting dues they defined all day laborers in Kotobuki as de facto members. The union negotiated with employers over unpaid wages, industrial injuries, and so on; and with the local authorities over policy on public works employment, social security, homelessness, and such. It also attempted to raise political consciousness among the workers and provided a certain amount of food, shelter, and so on to those who needed it during the colder months. My impression was that day laborers respected the efforts of individual unionists on their behalf but seldom felt more than a fleeting sense of solidarity with the union itself.

The official English translation of Article 25 of the Japanese constitution states: "All people shall have the right to maintain the minimum standards of wholesome and cultured living. In all spheres of life, the State shall use its endeavors for the promotion and extension of social welfare and security, and of public health."

7

Hustling: Individualism Among London Prostitutes

Sophie Day

When London prostitutes work, they say that they are *on the game*. This metaphor can be read in several ways. It is not simply the obverse of being *on the job*, a common English way of describing (noncommercial) sex, nor simply a reference to the tyranny (especially for women) of marriage. When prostitutes get paid for services that other women apparently give away for free, they consider that sex is very like other forms of female work.[1] To be *on the game* is, above all, a reference to the market that prostitutes represent as though it were a business of the intellect, involving calculation, a sense of timing, risk, and luck—in contrast to the mindless drudgery of "straight" jobs. The imagery suggests that prostitutes create and control a market in which they are autonomous and individual players. In this chapter, I explore the conditions that shape this rhetoric, as well as some of the difficulties that cause women to become stuck on the game.

Unlike many of the people discussed in this volume, London prostitutes constitute neither a culture nor a society, nor do they reproduce themselves as a subculture. At times, it is possible to talk of a community, or to note that groups of friends and colleagues spend a great deal of time together. From conversations with women over a period of five years, as well as from interviews and observation in a variety of settings where prostitutes worked and spent their time, I derived a sense of occupational identities and common ways of behaving.[2] These women worked in all the major sectors of the industry identified in London, including on streets, through agencies and madams, in flats (apartments), through private referral, and in saunas or clubs. By and large, the orientation of prostitutes to their present business was framed by dramatic discontinuities with what went before and what they hoped they would achieve. Even women who have worked for many years present sex work as a strategy for the short term, and they continue to insist that it is legitimate work, in explicit opposition to claims that it is morally wrong. They self-consciously present what they do as "sex work," which involves a public and alienable aspect of their persons comparable to all sorts of other uses of the body in the workplace.

This chapter focuses on white English women and presents two contrasting strategies. I describe a divided self, associated with the majority of women I knew, and an undivided self, which I consider to be a minority position. It is hard to be precise about the sociological correlates. First, prostitutes come from all sorts of backgrounds, and the contrast I describe may exaggerate the extent to which these are associated with the work itself, an issue that might be resolved through further research with women after they have left prostitution. Second, various associations will suggest themselves. It will seem as though the minority attitude should be found among higher status prostitutes who work for themselves, perhaps "on call" by telephone. It will seem as though the minority attitude describes the successes rather than the failures. I associate the correlates particularly with a contrast between the younger and older that overlaps with these other differences. Prostitutes in their twenties or younger tended to maintain strong distinctions between different aspects of life, whereas women in their thirties or older tended in the opposite direction, towards an undivided self. This contrast is idealized: These year bands relate to the time spent in prostitution and, indeed, to differences among individuals, as well as to chronological age; moreover, prostitutes switch between these practices. Nonetheless, the majority strategy seems to implicate a transitory lifestyle, even a stage in the life cycle like adolescence, whereas the minority strategy is more common among lifelong career prostitutes.

In the next and the longest section, I provide a context for aspects of work, or "hustling," in which these strategies are elaborated. Hustling is highly valued by prostitutes, largely because it constitutes a positive and personal achievement against all the odds—such as policing, legal discrimination, out and out exploitation, and violence. For the majority of prostitutes, this form of business activity is associated with an individualism that is nevertheless bounded by the market. At home, women do not act as discrete, isolated individuals but situate themselves inside valued relationships based on commitments to home and family. The self is stretched, as it were, in several directions and internalized or even dissolved inside other people through roles such as "partner" or "mother." However, as shown subsequently, this divided self often proves difficult to sustain, and the problems may help explain the emergence of what I call a more "radical" individualism akin to the *kefi* described by Papataxiarchis (Chapter 8). In some situations, the image of the hustler appears to spill over into other realms of life outside work, and the person comes to live more or less exclusively in the present. At the end of the chapter, this figure of the hustler is reconsidered from the perspective of dominant concepts of the person in England.

On the Game: Playing the Market Against the State

Most prostitutes distinguish sharply two aspects of the wider society: the market and the criminal justice system (or, more broadly, the state bureaucracy as a whole, including tax, local government inspectors, and so forth).[3] They represent the market and commerce in highly positive terms and consider the state to be purely repressive.

Most of the women I have known suggested that they began to work as prostitutes for the money, to "get rich quick," and they talked of their own "greed." It was the profits envisaged through work in an informal and often illegal sector of the economy that attracted them and, critically, the fact that these profits were to be made in a short period of between one and five years. Experiences vary. In practice, most sex workers in London make a precarious living, and many women do not earn much. They experience difficulties in meeting rents and everyday bills and work for longer than they had intended. I last saw one woman when her telephone line had been cut off, her mobile had gone, and she owed money on the rent. She had worked as a prostitute in London in a wide variety of ways (working from streets, in saunas, flats, and through agencies) and in related areas of the informal economy. She had always wanted to earn enough to open her own agency, once her mortgage had been secured, but she had failed.

Nonetheless, most women make a great deal more money than they have previously in low paid service jobs, in part-time work while at school, or when they were unemployed. Women also secure unexpected riches through short trips to other countries and through particular clients. Thus at the successful end of the spectrum were women who sustained affluent lifestyles and talked of school fees, furnishings, holidays, and the other requirements of everyday life, so as to calculate exactly what they had to earn from their lucrative business. They also talked about processes for laundering pots of money; the sums were not very large in absolute terms but constituted windfalls that were otherwise unaccounted for and so could be used to fund businesses, property, or training schemes at home. Even though popular images suggest that money is more readily available in some types of prostitution than others, the women I knew found no recipe for tapping into these possible sources of wealth. For example, there was little variation in earnings by workplace within the study group as a whole, suggesting that individuals could not readily increase their earnings by moving to a particular sector within the business.

Fluctuations in the money supply, rather than an absolute shortage, led women to calculate their future moves, to take risks, and to share their local knowledge in conversations about clients and about state interference—all in an attempt to increase their control over the supply of money. Women talked about the most profitable work, where to work, which clients to pursue, and what services to offer. Practices sometimes changed on a daily basis. Earnings were generally measured against some abstract idea about the money available out there: "I made or didn't make my money"; "you will or can make your money"; less often, "the money is or is not there." By and large, it is assumed that the money is out there, if only you know how to find it—through luck as much as judgment (Day 1994).

Some women, particularly those who worked as "employees"[4] in saunas or clubs, considered prostitution a job that would yield a predictable minimum wage, and they restricted their work to certain times and places. But the majority, from diverse backgrounds and working in all sectors of prostitution, considered sex work a freelance business (Day 1996). They continually tried to maximize their earnings by following the market (where the money is supposed to be) and adopting a highly flexible approach to their work. Women constantly moved to different sectors of prostitution: they worked abroad, and they invested in alternative and often innovative activities involving telephone lines, "virtual" sex on the Internet, and so forth.

The women I have described considered themselves to be, first and foremost, businesswomen. Prostitution is *not* thought to be like other forms of work, since the women involved do not subject themselves to the indignities of wage labor where they would have to answer to a boss. When prostitutes talk of "making their money," they often indicate further how they glean an income through business acumen and not through wage labor. They make it seem as though the market can be taken for granted: Money can be made if individual prostitutes are sufficiently enterprising and creative. By implication, the uses to which they put their bodies become inconsequential when compared to the calculations of where the money is and how to get it with the minimum of effort. Money grows on trees; clients are easy to find; the drudgery of work can be avoided; and the prostitute is in control of her very own market. All that a woman has to do is to gather money from gullible men out there. This is a very positive notion of the market, which is echoed by several other authors in this volume (for example, Astuti, Pine, and Stewart).

Business was not just a source of wealth. It was a zone where women were their own bosses. Most prostitutes I knew operated independently in market dealings and played the active role in negotiations. They selected their clients, fixed the prices, and organized the services for sale, the time allotted, hygiene, and other factors, as one of many examples illustrates.

Anna[5] explained how she had learned to spend very little time with "punters" (clients or customers of prostitutes), to insist upon "durex" (a brand name that is often used to refer simply to condoms), to avoid kissing, and to keep her clients on top of, rather than inside, her bed. She went on to explain how she ensured her own safety: "I've got tight security because I can see who's actually at the door, and if I don't like the look of someone, you can't tell from down the stairs looking through a camera, I call them up." It mattered hugely how you presented yourself:

> I know if you're frightened yourself that other person is going to take advantage, so never show you're scared of them. All right, I've probably got two minutes to make up my mind, either do they stop or go, do I like them, do they like me, what are we

going to do, is it going to stay on board. I've got probably a minute and a half to find out, is he going to stay, and usually I know in that minute what we're going to do, do I like him, what his attitude's going to be like in bed, do I like him.

Anna screened her clients once they had come up the stairs, interrogating them and following various house rules—rules, for example, about washing. As she had said earlier, "you need front and amateur theatricals to be a good hooker." Independence at work, earnings, safety, and even the creation of a client in the first place are all seen to derive, in part, from prostitutes' skill and a sense of mastery of their own business environment.[6] In these ways, it seems that the market does indeed belong to the prostitute. If the ability to act the boss and remain in charge is important, so, too, is the continual invention of new and different looks, the creation of appropriate personae, along with biographies and roles to sell. Business was fueled by a constant diversification in the types of sex and the "pretense" or illusion (Oldenburg 1990) offered for sale. Artifice is crucial to prostitution; it keeps women alive and solvent.

However, illusion, "front" or amateur theatricals, can equally be seen as *mere* rhetoric with little content. Prostitutes depend upon a market demand that is not fixed but highly volatile. Clients who purchase services are as likely as prostitutes to consider themselves in charge and, often, to have got the better bargain.[7] Equally, there are wide fluctuations in the prices that women are able to charge. Accordingly, it is important to recognize the partial nature of this very positive representation of the market and of free enterprise, which acknowledges no role for the clients who buy services and who are often difficult to find. Even more striking, however, are the constraints associated with the criminal justice system and the administrative state machinery that deals with commercial sex. These make it well nigh impossible to walk the streets or, it seems sometimes, to do business at all. When prostitutes say that the market is theirs, they do not talk of the exploitation, robbery, assault, imprisonment, and murders that are inflicted on them every day by a variety of men, including clients, managers, and agents of law enforcement.

It is virtually illegal to work as a prostitute in the United Kingdom; prostitutes can operate legally if they work invisibly and alone, without advertising and without associating with any colleagues. Likewise, prostitutes can spend time with other adults outside work only if they share none of their earnings. In practice, this means that it can become illegal to associate with other people even when you are not working. The laws invoked here relate to "pimping": male associates are charged with living off immoral earnings, whereas female friends are generally prosecuted for controlling or managing prostitutes. In addition, a criminal record can make it difficult to travel abroad, and known prostitutes may find it difficult to keep custody of their children. Sex workers generally react more strongly to the criminalization of their private lives than their work, and they consider the state to be at its worst in penalizing them for having a private life at all.

In the UK today, personal autonomy is widely associated with a free market and success in business (Dilley 1992; Heelas and Morris 1992; Carrier 1997). In associating liberty with their position as free agents in a market, prostitutes are making use of a view of moral behavior that is widespread in the UK. In particular, when they see themselves as entrepreneurs, who simply avail themselves of rich pickings and take advantage of market opportunities, they invoke categories that the government of Margaret Thatcher successfully propagated as *the* model for good citizenship. By associating themselves with such highly valued moral categories, prostitutes counter their social stigma. Ironically, however, it seems to be the very regulatory role of the state in their lives that makes this rhetoric so convincing.

Prostitutes are not fully conscious of this irony, that is, the positive role of the state in forging this view of the market, because they focus almost exclusively upon its repressive role and talk of their negative personal experiences with state officials. Thus when prostitutes talk about the iniquities of the law, they discuss arbitrary policing and the extreme isolation in which they are forced to work, which makes their work very dangerous. Prostitutes experience little protection and complain that society at large has joined hands with a punitive state machinery in labeling prostitution and prostitutes deviant. What they do not talk about is the way in which broader state policies render only specific types of market activity possible, namely freelance business conducted by individuals. In other words, the hustling that is so highly valued by prostitutes—in opposition to dominant models of respectable behavior—can also be seen as an inevitable, structural consequence of state regulation.

The state is seen as a zone of oppression, whereas the market, which enables prostitutes to become rich, enshrines a realm of freedom. Thus for prostitutes different aspects of the state are divorced from each other, and one set of economic state functions—maintaining an overarching free market, along with the circulation of currency and so forth—appears to be totally disconnected from another political set—enforcing laws that control sexual behavior. In this way, it seems that a positive view of the market depends, at least in part, on a negative view of what prostitutes call the "state" or the "law" and that the way in which women present the market as their own creation is, in fact, intimately connected to specific processes of state criminalization. What might be seen as another form of "wage hunting and gathering" among London prostitutes is fostered, if not largely created, by punitive laws and policing that make women operate as solitary individuals almost all the time. These laws make the problems of state policy very much more obvious to prostitutes than possible shortcomings in the market.

More general processes of social exclusion reinforce the effect of state systems of control. For example, a general disapproval of commercial sex means that prostitutes create distinct personae, along with appropriate biographies, for their families as well as for clients. They frequently possess at least two legal identities, using one as a private citizen and another for work. Most aspects of the present are distanced from a previous life (and, by implication, the future) through severing or attenuating ties with family, friends, or colleagues, moving to a new home, and sometimes, for all intents and purposes, disappearing from earlier social networks.

These few comments about the occupation suggest an individualism that is forged through state repression *and* through generally admired moral and economic values. It is an individualism embodied in the figure of the entrepreneur or the hustler and highly valued by prostitutes; it is also an individualism that is limited by everyday social practices among these women, who, in fact, depend upon each other to get by. To conclude this section, and before elaborating the two strategies mentioned in the introduction to this chapter, let me summarize these different, even competing, strands of hustling.

Despite, or rather because of, criminalization, prostitutes in London enjoy many of the advantages of working in that archetypal free market, the informal sector. By definition prostitutes are invisible to the state bureaucracy that regulates the formal economy, and thus they have the opportunity to do business without the restrictions of fixed work hours, managerial interference, and state inspections under which legal businesses operate. Prostitutes see themselves making their own lives through entrepreneurial activities in the space between the informal and the illegal. Here prostitutes see themselves as hustlers operating as free, solitary, and independent individuals.[8] They remain poised to take advantage of every opportunity and to judge rapidly the potential costs and benefits of alternative courses of action. They approximate perfect market atoms or monads.

This is the rhetoric. At the same time, women share a great deal of information, as noted above, and they depend upon each other to hide from the state and confer some mutual advantage in a very competitive market. In practice, prostitutes do not operate as solitary individuals all or even much of the time but work, gossip, and party with other prostitutes and associates, depending upon where they work (flats, streets, agencies, and so forth), as well as upon their own backgrounds and preferences. These clandestine, informal, and personal networks appear to make the life bearable.

Hustling in London is described as a game. When prostitutes call themselves freelance businesswomen, they are asserting a precarious personal achievement, against the odds. The odds—in the form of repressive laws, policing, and social disapproval, as well as more widespread problems that face small businesses the world over—are stacked high. But the game itself confers a freedom that can be characterized in both positive and negative terms. It can be played with creative human activity that is not managed or controlled by any boss, and it thus contrasts with the routine drudgery of wage labor. However, many prostitutes find that their social life is restricted. This does not mean that they have less of a social life than other people but that, for the majority, it is hopelessly divided. For a great many women, work remains distinct from the homes that they have built at the same time. A domestic social world connotes greater permanence and stability than the working environment. It is built around a spouse figure, secured

more safely by the production of children, and associated with a respectable domesticity. Even though many prostitutes I knew were friends with other sex
workers (visitors, godparents, child-minders, neighbors, and so forth), there were
several points when these two worlds—which exist as much inside the person of
a prostitute as outside—cannot be integrated, as shown in the next section. It is
mostly younger women who are likely to try to inhabit two distinct social realms,
within the terms of what I have glossed as a majority strategy.

The Divided Self

Like many other people in the UK, prostitutes often present themselves in two
parts, public and private, which/who are invested in different activities and visible in different places. Unlike others, however, prostitutes experience a particular
legal and social stigma, according to which, in their working capacity, they appear
to be "merely public women" who have either no private life or no right to a private life. I have suggested in earlier work that this is because they appear to con-
found the "normal" distinctions between the two: selling what cannot be properly sold and making public what should rightfully remain private (Day 1990).
Prostitutes, however, claim to be clear about the distinctions between public and
private, especially when it comes to sex. They claim that their work is legitimate
and thereby constitutes part of the public realm, and they negotiate constantly
shifting boundaries between those aspects of the sexual that can be alienated
from the person and those that remain integral to a sense of self. As they demonstrate the existence of a public realm, so they lay claim equally to a private realm,
for the two are constituted mutually. Accordingly, many prostitutes present
themselves in the same way as other people—in two parts.[9]

   It is, however, much more difficult to construct and maintain this private
realm than it is to demonstrate the legitimacy of the commerce. Initially, I did not
know how to react to what prostitutes told me about their private lives. Many
women said that all they wanted was a husband, all they dreamed of was children,
all they were saving for was a home of their own. They tested their fertility and
looked after their man. These women wanted to become housewives and mothers, sometimes with jobs, yet their aspirations often appeared to be exaggerated
and lifeless. At the very least, their dreams seemed old-fashioned. I was taken
aback and wondered whether I was being teased.

   In these conversations, hustling was decisively relegated to the public domain
of the market, which provided a means to build a home. The unsavory business
of sex work, disagreeable to many prostitutes themselves, was seen as a short-
term interlude in life, a present bracketed from past and future, and it was also
distanced from the "real" or "inner" self by means of these values attached to domesticity and to motherhood especially. Many prostitutes wanted a respectable
life, at home if not at work and in the future if not now. Many were saving for a
fundamentally bourgeois future, to which they made substantial sacrifices. These

dreams also informed everyday activities and plans for the immediate future. Women entered training and saved for jobs[10] that could be integrated into their home life, even if the earnings were trivial. Some said that they would return to hairdressing, others trained as nursery nurses and secretaries. Some made down payments on cars and on houses.

Commonly, bits of the lifestyle were tried out for size, and they were also altered radically as circumstances changed. Women who had appeared to be totally committed to motherhood, for example, changed their minds rapidly when they fell pregnant or when they left the game. Often, the homes that were imagined appeared to be remote from anything prostitutes had experienced themselves.[11] I give two brief and poignant examples. Rachel was earning a great deal of money at the end of the 1980s, and, like many other English people at this time, she dreamed of a home of her own. Although she managed her finances poorly, she earned so much that she could not help but acquire a flat in the end. Her home was in the center of town, so that she could work more easily on call and in a smart district. Some months later, a close friend of Rachel visited the Project (Praed Street Project), telling how they had quarreled. I asked about the flat, and the friend explained that Rachel did not know how to make a home: It looked just like the interior of one of the hotels where they worked. Fabrics matched, luxurious carpets were fitted, but the flat contained nothing of Rachel herself. When I next saw Rachel, she had lost her flat but confirmed that it had never been a home, nor come to life. She could not explain why.

Jane moved in a different circle and earned what she said was just enough from working mostly in rented flats. Over a period of several years, Jane saved for her own home. This process took much longer than it should have, but eventually, five years after I met Jane and many more since she had started saving towards her various targets, Jane bought a house in the suburbs. She put a brave face on the difficulties she had furnishing the house and, especially, living there alone. After some months, Jane began to complain about her neighbors, who watched her every move and seemed highly suspicious of all the men coming and going. I realized that her predicament was similar to Rachel's: Jane had turned her house into a workplace. At one level I was not surprised, as she had often worked at home before. But I was taken aback that she should have saved up for so long only to buy such an inappropriate place for work. I had thought that she chose a house on an estate in the distant suburbs precisely so that it could not be turned into a workplace and would therefore remain remote from prostitution. In fact, I suspect that this was Jane's intention but that it had been thwarted by the fact that she could not make her money. It seemed to me that both these women assumed that a home would follow automatically from the purchase of property, and both were disappointed. Certainly, other women found it difficult to sustain a refuge beyond work that gave meaning to their lives. Rachel lost her home rapidly. Jane made hers into a workplace. These brief examples suggest that women may invest in domestic lives that remain difficult to realize and insubstantial, despite the very real strength of prostitutes' commitment and attachment to these ideals.

In the majority ideal, public and private realms remain separate and ranked, with the home a beacon sustaining an unpalatable business now and promising a different future. Yet, if or when a home takes a more tangible shape, it may be difficult to separate from the realm of work.

Money, and Why It Is Easier to Spend Than to Save

Unlike many of the people described in this volume, prostitutes explicitly claim that they want to rejoin the mainstream. But they want to do so in a better position, with some money or capital. They consider their work short-term, and they want to accumulate money, setting various targets and goals through which to make a different future. Buying homes, paying for training, and starting a business are all options. Prostitutes face two rather different obstacles in achieving these goals. First of all, the informal and illegal nature of the work causes particular problems. Unlike those who work in a formal sector, these women do not automatically save as they earn, and it is difficult to launder untaxed money so as to invest in a business or buy a house. They therefore depend on shady practices among lawyers and accountants. In addition, overheads from working are rarely predictable, except insofar as they exceed expectation—whether in the form of fines, equipment, or the costs of employing sticker boys to advertise and maids to screen clients.

Secondly, prostitutes find themselves complicit in destroying the very fabric of their future as they attempt to build their homes. The two women I mentioned earlier, Rachel and Jane, made their homes alone. Most women, however, consider homes to involve also significant relationships, and any prostitute with a personal or intimate sexual partner is faced with difficulties in constructing a solid distinction between the private and public aspects of her person. Some women do not let partners know about their work; others refuse to share any income. Most, however, spend at least some money in their personal sexual relationships. Few prostitutes have no money. Usually, they have so much more cash than other people that they find themselves supporting, and thus creating, pimps out of boyfriends, girlfriends, sisters or mothers.[12] They then worry about the possible financial dependency of their partner and, inevitably, about potential pimping or "poncing."[13] Similarly, women worry about relatives and friends living off their earnings and merely feigning a personal interest. It can be difficult to spend money in any significant personal relationship, since women wonder whether their friends are more interested in their money than in their love.

In this situation, women may refuse to spend on or in key relationships with other adults and thus find that they can only, indeed must, spend on themselves. According to standard accounts of English kinship practices, a person appears alienable and discrete only in her commercial dealings. This public individual contrasts with a private person, who is involved in relationships of sentiment, love, and kinship constructed around an inner core, which is inalienable and constituted relationally.[14] It is as though the competitive and atomized individualism of the marketplace was contrasted to a more satisfying individuality outside work. If prostitutes find it hard to use money in their private and personal relationships, one option is to expand the public uses of money and a market morality. In a sense, they then confirm the stereotype to which they object so strongly, namely, that prostitutes are purely "public women."

At work, women consider themselves to be exploited against their will, but at home they consider that they may turn friends and families into dependents in a more active fashion, albeit unwittingly. Through exchanges, such as gifts and, more to the point, theft, such relationships of dependence and domination are more serious in the long term than in the short term. Rachel had initially saved through a shady lawyer and lost her money. Another woman bought property through her boyfriend, who likewise stole it. Jane had planned to set up a small haulage company in Jamaica with a boyfriend, who then disappeared. In the face of these and similar experiences, a future based on a secure and trusted partnership becomes impossible to realize, so it may be easier simply to spend now and to spend on yourself.

Sometimes, this can be phrased in positive terms as a freedom to spend money on nothing. Earnings are often described as cash, which contrasts with other kinds of money because it is so easy to spend at once. For example, a woman currently in social work said: "I earned a great deal of money then. I didn't save anything. It went on clothes, stuff for the house, things for [her son]. I used to walk down Bond Street. . . . I was very materialistic. The more you had, it didn't seem to mean much. Stupid things. £200 on frozen food one day, I had to take it home in a taxi from Fortnum's [an expensive shop]." But, as this quote suggests, London prostitutes frequently told me that their money simply disappeared; they were puzzled by their failure to hold on to it. Although many were committed both to immediate consumption and to longer-term productivity from their earnings, they often found it easier to spend now than to save and invest in a different future. Women found that they could not make money productive in significant personal relationships. If the phrase *on the game* can be used to gloss a valued image of the entrepreneur in the marketplace, another phrase can be introduced to indicate the difficulties that women face in using their earnings. This consists of just one word: *addiction.* I understand this to refer to the perceived need to spend immediately rather than invest in the future and make long-term plans. Money, as the English say, "burns a hole in your pocket."

One woman, Julia, wrote to us at the Project, "it's been a dreadful decompression, but I think I've just about detached from my addiction now." Julia had worked for the money, and she missed it now that she worked as a secretary in a straight job and lived with a boyfriend from an earlier holiday romance.

The use of the term *addiction* suggests that women like Julia experienced little choice in what they did with their money. Accordingly, spending and sharing money in the present can be seen as an unfortunate necessity, as well as a positive freedom. At the very least, it may provide a brake on the process of drawing other people into prostitution and uniting ideally separate domains of life. The more quickly prostitutes get rid of their money in trivial contexts and meaningless shopping, the less likely it is to contaminate key relationships and compromise key ideals. At the same time, of course, the immediate use of earnings makes it hard to set up a family and a more respectable future.

It seems that the sense of division I have associated with prostitution is fundamental. Not only does it involve marked separations between different aspects of the person and the world at large, but it also encompasses a striking contradiction in women's attitudes to their present activities, which I have tried to describe in these few comments about money. Women work as prostitutes in order to make enough money to carry on with their lives. They find that they cannot make their homes or move into more respectable jobs because they are unwilling, as much as they are unable. The process involves either setting up on your own, which can be very lonely, or contaminating relationships with key friends and relatives who would belong to the domestic idyll. In the process of moving on, this future loses its attraction. Past and future therefore can remain bracketed at a distance from the present, as women find themselves addicted instead to the game they have joined.

Becoming a Mother

Often in our conversations, prostitutes talked of how they wanted to make money *and* children for the future. Only an external body is invested in the market, carefully circumscribed and bounded. An inner body, marked especially by the cervix, is kept out of the work process. This is commonly associated with current or future sexual partnerships, which characteristically anticipate procreation (Day 1990). If a home connotes some kind of permanence and a colonization of the future, then children both complete and extend this picture in a way that other adults can never do. Children stand for the future.

In the study group as a whole, there was a marked commitment to motherhood and significant worry about infertility. Many women were frightened that their work would make them sterile because of genital infections and "too much sex." These concerns seemed to lead women into repeated pregnancies, for they wanted to prove that they could conceive. As Karen said, "I want to know if I can get pregnant."

Just as women experience difficulties in rendering their earnings productive, so, too, they find it hard to turn pregnancies into children. It sometimes seemed that women did not so much want children as the possibility of having them. On falling pregnant, some women found that they could not negotiate their pregnancies while working. Should you stop work or take your pregnant inner body into the marketplace? Who was the father? Women would work one month on and one off, or six months on and six off, so as to be better able to determine paternity. Some became concerned about paternity, along with the potential ill effects of continued work, after, not before, they had fallen pregnant.

Most pregnancies were terminated: Of 267 participants in a study we conducted from 1989 to 1991, 134 women reported a total of 225 terminations. Ultimately, however, pregnancies often bring sex work to an end. They provided a common excuse for moving into an uncertain future, at least for the time being. Younger women, who remained pregnant, generally returned to their families, often in other cities. Anne and Karen, for example, relied primarily upon their parents for support during this time. They were pleased to have become mothers but frustrated at being poor, and the putative fathers had disappeared. Anne had expected more, for she had been very much in love. Karen, to the contrary, claimed: "I don't want no man around me. . . . I don't care who the father is. I know who the mother is. . . . Don't worry, I'll never hold it against my child. It doesn't bother me—as far as I'm concerned, he hasn't got a father, he'll never have one. . . . I'll say, 'I'm sorry that you haven't got one; you have me and that's it.'"

I had the sense that pregnancies turned prostitution into a particular stage of the life cycle among these women, akin to student life in other circles. I remained unclear about the relative importance of sex work subsequently; when they initially left their work, we lost touch with many research participants in the Praed Street Project. But it seems that many do return to sex work or combine prostitution with other jobs some years later.

Prostitutes, like other people, lose their children; they also set up extended or nuclear families and, especially, single parent families. Those we knew who had and kept their children tended to build households in which the father figure floated in and out of the home or disappeared altogether. I have suggested that income differentials cause difficulties between partners. But, in contrast to their concern regarding adults, prostitutes are not at all concerned about turning their children unintentionally into pimps or ponces. To spend on children is positively valued and might even define a good mother.[15] Accordingly, mothers may turn from their sexual partners to their children for intimacy and authentic relationships uncontaminated by the market. In these circumstances, the role of father and husband tends to become more attenuated.[16]

It should be recalled, once more, that social and legal processes of exclusion apply to the whole person and not just the domain of work: "Prostitutes are deviants." If it were true that you really gave yourself away through selling sex, then you would have no "inner body" and no personal life. The ability to conceive shows that prostitution has not robbed a woman of her personal self; she can, after all, make money at work and children at home. Terminations, then, successfully reconstruct the desire for future rather than actual motherhood. For most women, it is enough for now to demonstrate the ability to earn and to conceive; it is then possible to imagine that these abilities can be made productive in the future in the form of jobs or businesses and children. But motherhood and the market alike become largely personal achievements among a smaller group of women who have their children and their businesses or jobs simultaneously.

The Undivided Self

Many of the prostitutes I knew became stuck in the business and worked for longer than they had intended. They made less money than they had imagined, saved little, failed to complete a training or to launch themselves in some concrete way into a different life. They became entangled in cross-cutting ties that were largely contained within a subculture. Some women I knew left the work regardless, and the majority of prostitutes in London probably work for less than five years (although it is unknown how many return to the work over their careers).

However, I also knew women who had clearly adjusted incrementally to a different kind of prostitution. These were older women in their thirties and forties; and the group certainly included some who had once left the game, supposedly for ever, with their children-to-be. But not all these women were mothers returning to work; many simply continued to do business in prostitution and elsewhere—in the beauty industry or sales of some kind, including insurance, tax advice, rentals, and, traditionally, property dealings.

So far, I have shown how many women confine their hustling—on the game—to a market domain. In the face of the difficulties outlined above, it is not surprising to find that some women abandon this attempt to sustain two different lives. These others embrace unity in the form of a valorized "individual." This is what I call the minority strategy of a radical individualism.

Here, the hustler is embraced as an icon across a wide range of activities, and the public woman happily goes home. The boundaries between the market and domestic life are much more permeable than those described previously. Some women appear to be mistresses or friends at work (when they are earning) and not prostitutes at all. Equally, some become "kept women" at home. The minority strategy can be traced in such varied relationships with clients and other men.

Many prostitutes cultivate multiple ties with their clients. Men commonly provide these women with a regular income, as well as with income for meeting unusual expenses. Many men are well connected and constitute a valuable clientele, as women diversify within and outside the industry. These men are a source of additional clients through referrals and sometimes provide capital and customers for new businesses. More often, they provide advice and indispensable professional services as accountants, lawyers, doctors, brokers, and the like.

These men are equally important to the process of moving on, providing a stepping stone out of the industry altogether. Kay had the odd regular, about whom she spoke little, as she retrained and worked for a small salary. Laura had two regulars who paid her college fees and her mortgage as she qualified for a new job over a period of three years. She made up her money by working now and again and referring old clients to her colleagues, who paid her a commission.

A third woman trained as a legal secretary, sustained by a single client who wanted to marry her, whereas a fourth broke a drug habit and brought up her son through the support of just one man, who wanted exclusive (sexual) access to her. Such women tended to consider themselves ex-prostitutes, as they earned only a supplementary income from the odd regular client or traded one service for another on the side. Only a few seemed to break totally with the industry.

Some prostitutes refuse to see regular clients because they act as though they are friends with special rights. The prostitutes dislike the constant pretense and artifice required to make it look as though such men had privileged access, and they refuse to act the part of girlfriend. Some have been abused by regulars, who are recognized in retrospect to have got the better bargain by not having to measure out the minutes in precise quantities of money. Generally, however, it is only regulars who can tide women over the bad times and only regulars who can provide a platform to a different way of life. With good management and luck, regulars can even constitute a gold mine.

The majority of women I knew in all sectors of the industry cultivated regular clients, but only some managed to keep these men and create a business out of them. As they did so, difficult issues about the use of money and motherhood (discussed in the previous section) were more or less automatically resolved in the movements of these men from domestic settings to the market and back again. The men had made holes in the fabric separating the two domains and thus connected them. In this situation, some women embraced the lack of division in their lives and turned it to good use. In order to contrast the two strategies on the game at the heart of this chapter, I shall briefly indicate key differences in the use of money and motherhood.

For the majority of women, there is a tension between spending now and saving for a different future. But for the minority, money spent now on ephemera and luxuries enables a constant refashioning of the person for sale (that is, an investment for the future). Perhaps the most obvious examples are to be found in physical transformations, which range from expensive fitness and health regimes to plastic surgery and a wide range of medical treatments, such as hormone replacement and even "non-sexual" procreation. When Karen—mentioned above—was particularly fed up with her work, she said with some vehemence that she would have a laparoscopy: in other words, a virgin birth through *in vitro* fertilization, where the egg would be implanted through a laparoscope. In fact Karen did become pregnant, but through a client, and she returned to her home outside London, saying that she would explain to the child that it had no father.

Physical changes such as these expand the notion of personal achievement so that even aging ceases to be a fact of life that is taken for granted and becomes instead a personal choice. While prostitutes justify these forms of consumption in terms of the boost they give to their earning power, they also lay claim to a personal status that is entirely achieved. From this perspective, the future is merely an aspect of the present; there is little contrast between spending and saving, and no great tension between frittering money away and productive investment.

Generally, motherhood is not taken for granted as a natural stage of life among prostitutes. To the contrary, it is a personal achievement of an unusually arduous nature that involves layers of pretense, illusion, and artifice amidst families carefully negotiated into existence. These families rarely approximated to prostitutes' original aspirations, and some women, like Susan, found it easier to accommodate the continuities between different kinds of work at home and in the market than to shore up the boundaries between them.

Susan had worked on and off for more than twenty years. Her status as a mother, she told me, did not come easily or naturally when she fell pregnant twenty-two years ago. She had undergone a back-street abortion, which caused an infection. Later, she had an emergency operation for fear of pregnancy in her fallopian tube. As Susan explained it, "the tube had curled up over my right ovary. They cleared it." After investigations for infertility while she was married, Susan eventually got pregnant:

> I had my only son through having eggs removed. I had a cyst in one ovary and had a wedge resection. This takes about nine months to grow back. The doctor scratched the surface, which was very hard. There was pus and things. This seems to have released an egg on 13 January 1978.
>
> Prior to that, I had had fertility drugs which had over-activated, and the tube curled round and was removed. This was my other tube. The tube [that had originally been operated on] was blocked. I did meditation exercises for a year. I think this is what opened it up. It was self-healing. I had a book to visualize and imagine what was down there and the fallopian tubes and so on. I did this religiously morning and night for months and months. The doctor announced that it had all opened up, what was previously blocked. I did lots of yoga too, which helped to get pregnant.
>
> At the time, I wasn't working [in prostitution]. I was married and did a bit of modeling.
>
> I tried to get pregnant for three or four years, with drugs and so on. After the ovary was scratched and the egg released, I was told I had forty-eight hours to conceive. There were problems with my husband, aggravation. He went out gambling the first night. The second night, we both went to a party and got drunk. Eventually, we had sex the following morning when he obviously thought there was no chance I'd conceive, and then he insisted on sex three times over the next three days, ostensibly to conceive but, really, thinking there was no chance and just to have sex. So, I got home on the Friday, and I must have conceived 5.00 A.M. on the Sunday morning.

Motherhood was just as important to Susie as to other women, but it was not of a qualitatively different order from any other enterprise on her part. What she said about getting pregnant and having a child was similar to other accounts she gave about her dealings with schools, clients, businesses, and medicine. For example, Susie's husband required handling in the same way as a client, and men mentioned subsequently also spanned the usual divide between market and personal relationships. Thus, Susie made a trip to the United States to renew a liaison that had finished some eighteen years previously. Before she left, she explained that the trip cost more than an airfare: She had to diet, have unwanted hair removed, and so forth. While the trip failed to cement a relationship, Susie was quite prepared to think of marriage and resettlement in California. She preferred to work with "regular" clients or even "sugar daddies," who were like boyfriends as well as customers. In fact, when I last saw her, she had set up home with an ex-client, much to the dismay of her colleagues. Sex work created openings and supplied Susie with capital as well as customers in a major high profile and legal health club during the late 1980s. Susie's son, however, was not involved in any of these businesses, and he was sent to boarding school on a music scholarship for a number of years, so that his mother could maintain the one separation that remained very important to her; she worked only when school was in term.[17]

These few comments about Susie introduce major points of contrast between two strategies on the game in London—strategies that alternately adopt and dissolve a sense of division between different aspects of life. The most successful women I have known in the London sex industry have at least partially dissolved the boundaries between public and private and, in so doing, have embodied a thoroughgoing commitment to the present. These women fashion—or at least act as though they were—a single, unitary, discrete, and autonomous individual who makes money and who makes herself. Money, children, and relationships are all personal achievements of the same kind, aspects of a juggling act that combines in various ways motherhood, sex work, and a range of continually new and generally short-lived businesses. These more "radical" individuals have created an entire world of artifice that constitutes a relatively seamless whole, spanning what remains divided for other people into the private and the public. The minority strategy draws no particular contrast between the individual hustler in the marketplace and the relational person cocooned in a family or, more accurately, a domestic haven where there is no need to pretend or to wear a mask. For the minority, the whole of life constitutes a personal achievement, whether at work or at home, as the hustler moves from the marketplace to the hearth and back again.

This minority strategy appears to enable prostitutes to avoid becoming "stuck," since pregnancies can be turned into children while women are still involved in sex work and, indeed, busy building upon their relationships with clients so as to diversify their economic base. Yet, this minority strategy may simultaneously rob women of a refuge or haven, presented in terms of a utopian future—a "natural" kinship and truly creative or unalienated activity. Perhaps these dangers account for the minority status of the radical strategy.

Conclusion: Hustlers

In this chapter, two contrasting occupational strategies have been outlined alongside two different "individuals," or concepts of the self. Both are associated with hustling. Prostitutes present themselves as though they had achieved the freedom of the market through their own wits and as though they were self-made businesswomen who had internalized everything of value from the wider society and rejected the rest. However, I have argued that prostitutes are also forced to make their own way at the margins of mainstream society. They are led to pass over many relationships, intentionally or unwittingly, including those with bosses, colleagues, and state functionaries in general. Prostitutes practice a marked individualism at work *both* because they achieve their own desires *and* because of the place ascribed to them through criminal and other sanctions.

Prostitutes do not constitute a culture, nor do they create homogeneous occupational identities. If, at one level, this chapter has made two aspects of working ideologies apparent, it may be in danger of simultaneously reifying them. To conclude, I should make it clear that women shift from one orientation to the other and often occupy a position only transiently. In addition, the two strategies that I have outlined reflect a broader discourse in the UK, where both constitute valued ideals or norms of behavior.[18]

Numerous television soaps and thrillers, as well as art exhibitions, press coverage, and popular commentaries have featured prostitutes in recent years and explored processes of exclusion, style, and the freedom to live outside relationships that are normally taken for granted.[19] These suggest that images of prostitutes have a broad appeal, and one reason for their popularity may relate to this contrast between different concepts of the individual—concepts that are closely associated with class and gender hierarchies in the UK.

Both in rhetoric and in significant everyday practices, prostitutes become the subject or owners of a market. Such "possessive individualism" (Macpherson 1962) implies that "ownership" of oneself (body and soul) can become the foundation for control of an entire market in sexual services. This image seems to fit with the populist platform associated with Margaret Thatcher in the later 1980s (when this fieldwork was conducted), where success in business was epitomized in the figure of the self-made entrepreneur who had no need of politics or state regulation.

Such individualism is restricted to the marketplace in the majority strategy and extended to a range of other activities by the minority. Most prostitutes I knew embraced a divided self and attempted to insulate some relationships from the ravages or, at least, competition of the marketplace. The majority concept of hustling may be associated with "bourgeois" or middle class notions of respectability that have a curiously old-fashioned ring in certain situations. However, some of the women I knew undid this distinction between public and private in favor of a less divided and a more fluid, situational notion of the self. For example, in the minority strategy, women came to create a family as well as a market out of their own unitary bodies and persons. This concept of the self can evoke modern ways of behaving by appealing, for example, to notions of flexibility, technological innovation, and diversity.

Through a process of contrast, this "modern" person might also evoke elite notions of individuality, where people—and men in particular—are not divided between work and home but are simply themselves, in accordance with their own inner nature. The entrepreneur/prostitute, then, seems able to achieve what others have been given—others who are born with privileges of male gender, genealogy, and property, and who therefore can remain intact (or undivided). Prostitutes might magically appropriate the attributes of other (socially superior) English individuals simply by acting as though they owned themselves.

In the process of recuperating dominant images to legitimate their own practices, prostitutes make other "English individuals" intelligible. They reveal the considerable advantages attached to personal choices that are sustained by a host of relationships associated with pedigree, property, and gender, and that often remain invisible (Bouquet 1993; Macpherson 1962; Pateman 1988). Prostitutes also make the values associated with this individualism appear faintly ridiculous when they attempt to embody society within their own persons or divide themselves into two, a literal act that may appeal only to those who have few other choices. In this way, they show that it is not, in fact, automatically enabling to be an individual, whether in the market or in other realms of life. Practices described in this chapter reveal the emptiness of a "freedom" to live altogether outside relationships that are normally taken for granted and in accordance with the radical, modern, and also elite version of individuals; these practices also reveal the difficulties of sustaining a more fulfilling personal life in accordance with the restricted, old-fashioned, and also bourgeois version of individuals. It is only in reaction to negative stereotypes that the hustler, through enterprise, makes a market, a family, and herself; and it is only in the context of extreme discrimination that the personal autonomy achieved by prostitutes makes sense.

Notes

1. As in: "Marriage . . . often turns into the crassest prostitution—sometimes on both sides, but much more generally on the part of the wife, who differs from the ordinary courtesan only in that she does not hire out her body, like a wage earner on piece work, but sells it into slavery once and for all" (Engels 1973:79).

I should like to thank the many participants in this research and particularly Helen Ward, my long time colleague, for their help. And, accordingly, I refer to some of our collaborative research with the term "we" rather than "I" in what follows. Thanks also for comments from participants in the workshop that led to this book and from seminars in the anthropology departments of Goldsmiths College and University College London and the University of Edinburgh, and for editorial help from my coeditors, Brian Morris, Maria Phylactou, and Jonathan Weber.

2. This research was part of a collaborative project in London with women working in the sex industry from 1986–1991 (in what follows, the terms *prostitute* and *sex worker*, and *prostitution, commercial sex,* and *sex industry* are used interchangeably). Participants came from different countries and backgrounds and worked for varying lengths of time. In our survey,

280 women said that they had been working for between a month and thirty-four years, with a median of four years (Ward et al. 1993); many, however, stop and start repeatedly. The research involved clinical and epidemiological studies as well as anthropology. From the end of 1991, the National Health Service has supported our project, the Praed Street Project, which now includes a range of medical and nonmedical services (Ward and Day 1997).

3. In shorthand, the "state."

4. In fact, such employees are usually self-employed in legal terms, thus the qualification.

5. Names are pseudonyms, and some biographical details have been changed slightly so as to preserve confidentiality.

6. Similar skills and attitudes were also described and observed in dealing with other people involved in the business, such as agents.

7. During interviews, some clients explained how they shopped around to get the best deal. These men considered that consumer choice determined the shape of the market and the relatively strong position of the buyer (Day et al. 1993).

8. In fact, only some women used the term hustler (or whore). Various terms are used but the most common are "business" or "working girls."

9. This brief comment is very general, but the division between different spheres of prostitutes' lives, as well as their extensive interconnections, are such general features in UK society as a whole that I pass over a more detailed discussion in favor of issues that I consider more particular. The conventional division between work and home is not only fantastical, but it is evaluated in many different ways. Space precludes a discussion of the extensive literature on gender, but it might be noted that work—rather than home—has been seen as a haven for women in the present day when they become single mothers and their second marriages break down (see, for example, Hochschild 1997).

10. I am unclear about how far earnings from sex work subsidized later work in the formal sector, but the amounts seemed substantial.

11. I do not mean to imply that prostitutes come from bad or broken homes, for I suspect that these ideals are remote from everyone's experience.

12. See the next section for comments on the use of money and children.

13. See Day (1994) for various meanings of these terms. For the present purposes, they can be treated as synonyms and glossed by reference to what are perceived as legal definitions: making a living from prostitution indirectly, through your girlfriend or wife.

14. See, for example, Schneider (1980) and Carrier (1992) on general images of kinship in North America and northwest Europe.

15. Those with adolescent or older children never voiced concerns about pimping, but I am focusing on young children for I do not have a picture of the developmental cycle overall.

16. Not all women lived alone with their children or tolerated a father at home grudgingly, but the father/husband figure became an optional rather than a fixed presence. In conversations about relationships that lasted between parents, prostitutes took on a lighter tone that seemed to reflect more flexible relationships that could be negotiated more easily. Of course, men also take on a range of roles. Some fathers, husbands, and boyfriends were reported to do most of the childcare, whereas others did become involved in the business and would manage a woman's affairs or provide protection.

17. The contrast that I have drawn between the two strategies should not be exaggerated, and this example shows it to be a matter of degree: Susie maintained distinctions between her activities and scarcely ever worked during school holidays.

18. Whilst it is possible that these strategies resonate with other individuals in other countries, I restrict myself to white women in the host country, the UK. Furthermore, I restrict myself to the "ethnographic present" of the late 1980s, when Thatcherism was influential, although I suspect that these notions of individual achievement have a long history.

19. Television in the UK, for example, has included three series of a soap about prostitution in the Midlands; the "stickers" that advertise prostitution in telephone boxes have also been the subject of an art exhibition; there has been wide press coverage of issues surrounding prostitution, such as the creation of toleration zones for work, the taxation of earnings, prosecution for raping women at work, and related issues. At the time of editing, there is a six part documentary series of interviews with prostitutes fronted by one of the BBC's leading female presenters.

8

A Contest with Money:
Gambling and the Politics of
Disinterested Sociality
in Aegean Greece

Evthymios Papataxiarchis

Gambling in Greece is an illegal activity unless it occurs in a licensed place. Yet, despite its well publicized suppression by the authorities, it enjoys a great popularity, especially in the countryside. As it is linked to rapid economic transformations, a thriving underground economy, and a black market in money, gambling highlights cultural idioms that have been particularly salient in the course of the 1980s.[1] It epitomizes a spendthrift attitude at the grassroots level, a privileging of consumption over production, and a commitment to the "present" that is combined with a disregard for the future. In political terms, as gambling usually develops at the interstices of legality and illegality, it reflects the problematic relation of the Greeks with the state and the law. Therefore, in many respects, the analysis of gambling provides a key for understanding Greek "normlessness," that is, both the way individual Greeks fail to conform to institutional rules and the way the Greek government fails at times to meet the expectations of its partners in the European Union.

In this paper I will offer a local, historically minded and ethnographically based insight into spendthrift behavior and the more general emphasis on the "present" that underlies this behavior. I do this through the analysis of illegal forms of card playing and dice throwing as I observed them in Mouria, a village community of north Lesbos.[2] More particularly, I will discuss gambling in the context of the coffee house as an aspect of a counter-hegemonic space that was historically established in conditions of the prolonged political and economic marginalization of the island. In this context, gambling becomes an act of resistance to market and state domination, an act of defiance against money. Through multiple inversions, a position of heavy monetary dependence is symbolically transformed into one of autonomy. Here, I will specifically focus on the recon-ceptualization of money (and of the economic more generally) that is achieved in gambling and try to show how these new meanings are invested in oppositional as well as transformative ways of relating to the state.

Let me start with a preliminary note on reciprocity and politics. Gambling has often been defined as a form of "negative reciprocity," since it engages actors who are in the business of taking from one another (Sahlins 1965; Mitchell 1988). Yet in contrast to other forms of negative reciprocity, gambling seems to be highly politicized.[3] This is primarily due to a widely observed link between gambling and processes of commodification, monetization, and hierarchical encompass-ment within dominant orders—a link that is facilitated by the role of money as a morally ambiguous symbol that indiscriminately crosses boundaries. So there are some cases where gambling is seen as "gifting" and as antithetical to capital accu-mulation (MacLean 1984) and others where gambling is an innovative response to capitalist strains (Mitchell 1988), leading to a radical reconceptualization of some basic social givens of the economy (Verdery 1995). In these examples gam-bling is depicted not just as a competition between players but also as the site of antagonism between the local society and encompassing orders (see Wasserfall 1990; also Zimmer 1987; Geertz 1973). Here, I will try to pursue this line of analysis and show how gambling practices contest the external boundary of the local community by rearranging the semantic properties of money, which is fun-damentally a "symbol of limitlessness" (Wasserfall 1990:335), and by turning against hierarchical encompassment. This is not a static opposition but a process of "mutual appropriation" between hierarchical levels (Thomas 1991:3).

More particularly, I will treat gambling as a form of "constructive resistance." Most of the politics of gambling involves a rich symbolic "work" of inversions be-tween taking and giving, dependence and autonomy, hierarchy and equality. In employing the concept of "constructive resistance," I want to focus on resistance as creative action and not as passive reaction to the conditions of domination. I am talking about agency that emerges in engagement with overarching power re-lations, and about culture as the bottom line of all politics and the foundation of the creative act of contestation. This implies a broad notion of resistance as a contest over hegemonic meanings that may be implicit or explicit (see Kaplan and Kelly 1994). Further, I want to suggest that a considerable "portion" of the work of resistance amounts to a conceptual redefinition of dependence and that this cultural work may be politically effective in renegotiating the content of par-ticular power arrangements.

Context: Political Marginalization and Economic Dependence

Some notes on the historical aspects of marginalization are necessary for under-standing the politics of gambling in Aegean Greece. Since its formation in the early nineteenth century, the Greek state has been internally perceived as a colonizing force, the institutional agent of a "western" hegemonic project (see Herzfeld 1987). This attitude was enhanced by the application of a highly centralized model of communal organization that contradicted earlier experiences of communal self-administration under the Ottoman *millet* system. The historical first comers to Greek unification gradually resolved this problem through clientelist forms of political integration. The latecomers, however, were firmly established at the political margins (see Mavrogordatos 1983). Politically excluded and denied equal access to state controlled political and economic resources, some of these new Greek territories, to which Lesbos and the big islands of the eastern Aegean belong, eventually turned to radical, antistate politics (as did the refugees that came to Greece in the 1920s).

North Lesbos represents an extreme example of the radical politics that emerged as a response to long-term marginalization. During the Nazi occupation, and the civil war that followed—when the state lost control of many rural areas in Greece—the procommunist National Liberation Front (EAM) enjoyed massive support in this region. The sense of local autonomy, which was sustained through late Ottoman rule, was institutionalized in forms of popular government, and unionization was strengthened. Consequently, the outlawed Communist Party of Greece became the dominant party in the region during the postwar decades. The internal migration that linked these rural communities to the big urban centers, and the rural/urban ties that resulted, strengthened organizational links with the primarily urban, communist left and contributed to the reproduction of a radical, left-wing politics of protest and resistance against the repressive, authoritarian state of the post–Civil War era.[4]

These historic conditions of political marginalization have been closely interwoven with a whole set of economic hierarchies and dependencies. Mouria's agricultural economy is largely an olive monocultivation. Since the Tanzimat, the Ottoman reform in the middle of the nineteenth century, the local economy has been linked to the regional and international market in olive oil. Monetization has been one consequence of this link. Another effect was the stratification of the land tenure system and the social differentiation between a small group of big commercial landlords (*afentika*, bosses) and the bulk of dependent laborers. Mouriani have vivid memories of the *ekmetalevsi*, exploitation, that lasted until the interwar period. To illustrate their sufferings, Mouriani refer to their dependence for work on the commercial bosses, who dominated the local society as well as the process of indebtedness. During this late Ottoman period, money came to be invested with semantic properties that made it the core symbol of domination and hierarchical exploitation.

After unification, the local political scene altered dramatically as a result of the economic decline of the commercial landlords and their replacement by agents of the Greek state. The state gradually assumed a number of key economic roles and provided a new form of economic organization and dependence through cooperatives. Despite the integrative intentions of the state, during the interwar and postwar period, economic dependence came to be part and parcel of a process of political marginalization from the state. The experience of economic decline, which was shared by the elite and by poor peasants alike, fed a strong resentment of political marginalization. Resentment gradually turned into a politics of protest against the state. These developments shaped an idiosyncratic "peasant communism," one that is often distinguished by an inter-class alliance of the economically declining and politically alienated elite with the mass of peasant laborers

All this resulted in a paradoxical situation after 1974, when democracy was restored shortly before my fieldwork. No doubt the debt situation probably intensified, but the political conditions, in the context of which economic dependence was being resisted, improved. The broadening of the political arena in the course of democratization reached its climax with the coming to power of the Socialists in 1981. This improved the organizational conditions under which the politics of antistate protest were conducted. However, at the same time state controlled cooperatives and banks assumed a greater control of the local agricultural economy through loans and price controls. Now the debt situation became more overtly political, as it encapsulated and could be made to stand for the problematic relationship between the localities and the state. The potential for conflict was increased by the fact that even though economic dependence increased in many respects, money was becoming cheaper: The price of labor was increasing at a greater rate than the price of land, and alternative occupations emerged. Accordingly, debt could be addressed more readily. In all these respects, then, this was a transitional period.

The Coffee House and the Capitalist Order: Reciprocities, Money, and the Self

In Mouria, gambling takes place exclusively in the coffee house where the main activity is drinking. And this physical setting offers an immediate clue as to its nature and significance. Despite the fact that, as we shall see, gambling is technically disassociated from drinking, it is informed by the same set of values. In the Greek coffee house, drinks are often treated as gifts, the exchange of which is governed by a quasi-ritual code called *kerasma*, "treating to a drink." *Kerasma* has a tripartite structure of giving, receiving, and reciprocating; these acts are accompanied by a set of more or less formalized greetings. The exchange of primarily coffee or *raki*, a strong alcoholic drink, underlies all major forms of sociality in the coffee house: casual commensality, the more stable dyadic ties of emotional friendship, or the circle of associates who drink together. In one way or another, *kerasma* bases all forms of coffee house sociality on reciprocity (Papataxiarchis 1992) and in so doing suggests alternative cultural understandings of the self, compared to those associated with the world outside the coffee house.

Coffee house reciprocities can be divided into two categories. On the one hand is the interested give-and-take, often based on kinship or other economic or political ties, and on the other hand is the disinterested sharing based on a notion of natural sameness among men. Interested reciprocity focuses on the mutual exchange of drinks, usually coffee or other nonalcoholic beverages, and here the generous offering of drinks is unashamedly combined with acts of remuneration. This interested reciprocity, which I call "exchange proper," corresponds to relations that have a temporal content, that is, relations that are extended through clearly registered acts of give-and-take in time. In such exchanges, I see a self emerge that is governed by *symferon* (self-interest), an interested self, defined in relation to "external" factors of identity, such as one's domestic/marital situation, occupation, or economic and political status. Since these external factors always vary in some degree, "exchange proper" goes together with an identity premised on socioeconomic, political, or other kinds of difference: The alliance of different qualities allows for "productive" investment.

Disinterested reciprocity, on the other hand, corresponds to relations of emotional friendship that are independent of kinship, economic, or political allegiances (Papataxiarchis 1991). As an alternative to the household domain, such friendships capture the festive spirit of the coffee house, in which freedom and performative autonomy can be achieved. As reciprocity comes to be governed by disinterestedness, it fades away and turns into a form of sharing reminiscent of Huaorani sharing practices described in this volume by Laura Rival (and see Woodburn 1998).[5] This transcendence of interest is ideally achieved in a *parea*, a circle of emotional friends who stop applying the code of *kerasma* and share drinks as "free gifts." In this context sharing brings forward a self governed by *kefi*, a disinterested self.

Kefi refers to an emotional state of joy and relaxation, depicted in images of lightness. It is achieved when the heart, the assumed center of emotion, is freed from the worries and concerns of this world. It further connotes a rationality that does not rest on reason but on sentiment. Actions that appear unreasonable from the viewpoint of economic or political calculation and self-interest may be fully comprehensible in terms of the actors' emotional preferences, "making *kefi*" (Papataxiarchis 1994). *Kefi* is thought to be an exclusively male property and suggests an identity premised on a natural affinity between men. Further, in the rhetoric of the coffee house *kefi* and *symferon* are juxtaposed, as two opposed forces that split the self and constitute alternative and mutually exclusive principles of action.[6] In actual practice, however, they are combined to make alternative strategies through which the achievement of autonomy is pursued.

One of these strategies involves a "fundamentalist" interpretation of *kefi*. It is an oppositional model that dynamically juxtaposes "joy" to "interest," thus insisting on the resistant qualities of *kefi*. This romantic model idealizes "true" agency as a theory of a self "made" in performance. Performance is conceived as a form of "self making" *(ftiachnomai)*, the self being both subject and object of "making," yet always in close reference to another self. This strategy seems to be linked to the process of symbolic inversion of margin into center and of dependence into autonomy, as it describes a self governed entirely from "within." Association and identification with others in this strategy is based on a sameness between self and other that is achieved through the performative transcendence of all external (i.e., class, marital, party, political, etc.) difference. This strategy is particularly popular among the many bachelors and the poor of Mouria.

The other strategy, I call *kefi* "realism." Instead of juxtaposing "joy" to "interest" in a fundamentalist fashion, here "joy" is turned into "interest," thus subordinating *symferon* to *kefi* and mixing the two. Agency in this model has two aspects, "internal" and "external," "performative" and "instrumental." In this respect it can be associated both with resistance and accommodation. *Kefi* "realism" deals with the hierarchical and exploitative environment in which some people try to change the balance of forces in favor of the cosmological camp of *kefi*. Because space is allowed for *symferon*, this "realistic" strategy has a dialogic quality. The juxtaposition of "emotion" and "interest" is in time resolved in favor of a compromise between the opposed forces.

The "fundamentalist" ideology of the disinterested self refers to a paradise lost, a world without money, dependent labor, or social hierarchy, a world built on allegedly "natural" similarity among men—the only safe basis of social equality. And it promises, as a minimum, a temporary yet instant salvation from the evils of living in this world of antagonism and material gain, a solution that can become more permanent if it is repeated regularly and consistently in the coffee house.[7] In actual practice, however, this soteriology works not as effective liberation but as an interpretive framework: It provides the cultural materials to construct alternatives to the evils of capitalism. And money is one of the core symbols of capitalist domination that is subjected to conceptual re-elaboration.

Mouriani distinguish various categories and subcategories of money. They distinguish, for example, between "traditional" and "modern" money. "Traditional" money, usually in the form of old, silver coins—out of circulation—is morally neutral and used for traditional, ritual purposes and not as means of payment and exchange. "Modern" money, on the other hand—the main means of exchange, payment, and calculation in the present-day world of commercial exchange, borrowing, and wage labor—appears to be a negative moral and symbolic force. Men in the coffee house share the general view that money—especially in its paper form, as *metrita*, cash—is *vromiko*, filthy, stinking, and has no "value." This image is captured in the widely held idea that one needs to wash one's hands after money has been touched.

This strong antipathy towards money seems to be more marked among men who rely on wage labor or depend on loans from the bank and who are more exposed to money. In their perspective money is personified; it takes the form of *mamonas*, a spirit that appears to upset the correct order of things. According to one of the big gamblers of Mouria, in this modern era "*mammon* has mastered them all." Under "his" influence, men allegedly surrender to the dictates of self-interest and adopt attitudes of saving, accumulation, and profit. They prefer money-yielding-work rather than money-consuming-leisure, and they pay less respect to the values of education and pleasure with friends. Moreover, in pursuing self-interest men are enslaved to the forces that promote selfishness, competitiveness, and divisiveness in the male world. From this point of view, money burdens the heart; all it does is foster worry, anxiety, and misery, while suppressing the joy and lightness of *kefi*.

In Mouria, households rely on money for their daily reproduction. Yet men's strong antipathy toward "evil" and "dirty" money results in a generalized but fruitless effort to avoid it. One solution is avoidance-through-substitution: Where possible, peasant producers substitute money with a traditional means of payment and exchange. Family farmers, for example, sometimes use olive oil in major transactions (e.g., buying land) or in dowries. Further, when in need, they do not buy labor in the wage market but arrange reciprocal exchanges between households (called *synalama*).[8]

Another solution is avoidance-through-handing on. This strategy highlights the gendered character of resistance to money. Women are assumed to be closer to money than men. Men, therefore, pass their small daily or weekly earnings to their wives who store it and spend it in small everyday transactions, as well as in larger household oriented "investments," for ritual and other purposes. In other words, by running the household women seem to resolve male ambiguities towards money. Women further extend to money their ability to transform natural, unprocessed products into "culturally" processed ones (see also Dubisch 1986). Women somehow "domesticate" the monetary earnings of the household just as they cook and clean. Thus they make money part of the order of the household and an essential ingredient of its present welfare and future reproduction.[9]

A third strategy is avoidance-through-separation. One feature of this strategy is the insulation of disinterested reciprocity from money, thus reaffirming the opposition of *kefi* to *symferon* and suggesting that *kefi* has no "material" basis in "interest." So, for example, whereas in a treating to a coffee that is related to "business" money is fully acknowledged—the treat is initiated by putting its monetary equivalent on the table—in the sharing of *raki* in a *parea,* money remains invisible. The money that buys *raki* appears at the conclusion, behind the scenes and with a certain diffidence, thus contributing to the image of *raki* as a "free" gift. This suggests that separate spheres of monetary circulation, for "domesticated" and "raw" money, exist.

Avoidance of money is, however, a strategy with limited effects since it cannot deal with its growing and overarching presence in everyday life. Many accounts are left open with the exploitative and alienating aspects of short-term acquisitive exchange. When money is so visibly present, and in big quantities, the disinterested self cannot successfully go on hiding from it. On the other hand, the overabundance of money, especially in its "raw," "wild" form, also creates an environment that favors a more offensive strategy, a strategy of open confrontation with money and what money stands for. It is in this context that gambling assumes its relevance.

Gambling: A Contest with Money

The gambling practices I deal with here are governed by simple and strict rules. Competitive card playing for high stakes is called *tzogos*, from the Italian *giuocco*, card playing. The term metaphorically means lots of noise and suggests a big event. The throwing of die is called *koumari*—from the Arabic *qimar*, the origins of which remain unclear—and means gambling. The most famous of the village gamblers are known as *koumartzides*.

Gambling "proper," that is, competitive card and dice games for huge amounts of money, forms one pole spatially, temporally, and morally within the field of reciprocities. Gambling takes place at the coffee house, and it starts soon after the *raki* drinking session is concluded. Yet in many respects, as we shall see, it is clearly demarcated from the commensal activities that precede it. And, in the first instance, the image of aggressive, antagonistic taking from a fellow man associated with winning at cards seems to be fundamentally opposed to the disinterested sharing that has earlier been celebrated in the course of drinking together in the same place by the same men. This apparent clash between positive and negative reciprocity provides the paradox that gambling represents.

Mouriani are very proud of the reputation of their village as the "casino" of Lesbos. They say that Mouria is preferred by outsiders because there is "freedom" in the village. In principle, gambling can take place all the year round, but the gambling season starts around November and reaches its climax at Christmas and the New Year. The gambling sessions are judged by the sort of people who participate, the amount of money played, and their duration. The longest gambling sessions that I observed during my fieldwork lasted almost thirty-six hours, whereas "ordinary" sessions start at night and may last for a few hours and sometimes until the following noon. The amounts spent are not easy to record accurately but sometimes reach tens of thousands of drachmas. In principle, any man can participate in a gambling round, if he claims to know the rules and does not have the reputation of a bad loser, that is, of a man who does not or cannot honor his debts. Yet, ideally, the men involved are unrelated. They often come from different localities or different drinking circles, *pareas*, in the same locality. In fact, gambling depends on the availability of outsiders, who usually, directly or indirectly, know each other. The more distant the men involved, the grander the occasion. When two "professional" gamblers from Mytilene visited Mouria and joined a few players from nearby villages, they gave rise to the most exciting and celebrated session of that particular year. In sociological terms, the gambling circle seems to be outwards oriented and non-bounded.

Tzogos takes place at night. The players occupy the big table at the corner of the coffee house, which is specially covered with green felt for the occasion. They start with light poker. This is a kind of warming-up exercise that goes on until the last clients leave the drinking place and some latecomers join the circle. Then the manager closes the doors and draws the curtains, which remain closed until the end of the session, thus marking the total seclusion of the gamblers and their immediate environment from the rest of the local society. This is the only instance of the coffee house becoming totally secluded. The village, which in ordinary circumstances has the coffee house at its very center, is suddenly excluded. Everybody in the village knows what the closed curtains mean, and everybody respects the players' desire for seclusion.

For the players themselves the coffee house supplants the community at this moment. The closed curtains place the players in an artificial state of darkness and night in which they remain until the session is concluded. This reflects the general mood of the occasion. Faces are tense and sober, guarding against the mistake that can be interpreted as an attempt to cheat. Argument hangs in the air; the slightest wrong movement and everyone is ready to take offense. In fact, this happens rarely. My impression is that the rules are strictly observed. Players are mainly silent. Words may be exchanged only if a dispute arises. The tone of discussion then quickly rises to a climax, an interlude of expressed tension, followed by another prolonged phase of silent participation. Soon, the contestants manifest symptoms of tiredness. Brandy or coffee are often employed to sustain them, yet *raki* is avoided. The atmosphere of *tzogos* is something of an anticlimax to the festivity that it succeeds. It is dark, heavy, and silent against the light and noisy mood of the *raki* drinking session.

The total seclusion of the coffee house is often attributed to the apparently illegal status of gambling. It is true that policemen stationed in the nearby head village are expected to arrest gamblers when a formal complaint is made. Yet, the most fierce opposition to gambling seems to stem primarily not from the state but from the realm of the household and women. Mouriani tell stories of wives who have informed the gendarmerie on their husbands, thus hoping to put a brake on an activity that threatens household finances. In fact, they were often successful, thus increasing the workload of magistrates in the district capital, Mytilene. However, the fines imposed do not put a stop to the gambling. Instead, they appear to inflate the reputation of gamblers. The big gamblers of the village do not hesitate to recollect with pride the number of times they have been charged with illegal gambling. Excessive "secrecy," then, seems to be intrinsic to the rhetoric of gambling. The closing of the curtains clearly states the message, "We are here," thus constituting an open challenge to all who stand against the realm of the coffee house. The poetics of secrecy reinforces the symbolic standing of the gamblers in opposition to state laws.

Gambling highlights the dialectic interplay between the different levels of domination and resistance. It reinforces the exclusion of women from the *parea* and the construction of a unisexual order of sexual inequality premised on the assumption that only men are equipped by "nature" with a capacity for *kefi*. And it further generates its own resistance by women who struggle for domestic prosperity (also see Besson 1993). As Mouriani themselves confess, few married men manage to stay for long in gambling. This is mainly due to the strong opposition of their wives. Among those who pursue a gambling "career" are a number of medium landowners, a fisherman, and few of the remaining dependent laborers. More than half of the systematic gamblers in Mouria are bachelors. And I often witnessed quite bitter exchanges between some men who were identified with the values of the household and men who were well known as gamblers. The "householders" argued that gambling destroys families: "The man who gambles is the worst monster to his wife, who is defenseless against him." For the gamblers themselves, however, gambling has nothing to do with the household. As one man who recollected an argument with his wife put it: "This is how I am. You knew it when you married me. You should keep your mind on your work *(doulia)* at home *(spiti)*. You should not be concerned with what I do at the coffee house."

Poka, poker, and a set of variations of poker and dice throwing are the games played in a gambling session. In principle, the player whose turn it is to deal the cards has the right to determine the game they play. If it is a card game, counters, which are provided by the manager, are used rather than money. The opposite is true for dice throwing. The game is always premised on consensus. If a rule is disputed an agreement must be reached before proceeding. While the loser has the right to leave the table at any moment, the winner is usually bound to stay until no one challenges him further. The loser, in other words, is usually expected to bring the game into a balance, *na elthei sta isa, refarei,* and to make his money, *na kanei ta chrimata tou.* Comments on the style of playing or the cards themselves are not made. Nor is any systematic reference to the metaphorical significance of cards.[10]

Proficiency in gambling is less important than knowing how to conduct oneself towards one's fellow players. This point becomes clear if we compare card games with the throwing of *zaria.* A pair of dice are put into a glass and thrown, successively, by the two contestants after the stakes have been decided. The winnings are put on the table and move between the players. Dice throwing may be a side event, taking place either between or even parallel to card games. It may also be the climax and conclusion of a gambling session. In *zaria,* expertise does not count. The two contestants are exposed to an eventuality that they cannot predict or control. *Zaria,* then, points to a core meaning of a gambling session in which two technically different activities are brought together. According to many Mouriani, what is at stake in dice throwing is the determination and courage of the player, his willingness to take risks. The gambler is not afraid of adversities; nor is he lacking in courage. The gambler confronts his *tichi,* luck, as well as his *mira, fate.* Indeed, in *zaria* it is risk rather than luck that is ultimately stressed.[11]

This brings us back to the notion of *kefi.* As we saw, *kefi* underpins a concept of an explicit self-creation, of a self-centered volition, and in this respect it is a notion antithetical to passive destiny. The gambler represents the man who "takes his destiny in his hands," particularly in relation to money as an "external" determinant of identity. The gambler holds a "total agency" (see also Day in this volume), one that is not subjected to money; on the contrary he makes money move around. He directs the flow of money from "within" rather than reacting to "external" flows that dominate him.

What is particularly interesting about gambling is the way it is publicly evaluated. At the conclusion of a particular session, rumors start spreading in the village. Surprisingly, they mainly concern those who have lost and the amount of money lost or owed. Considerably less excitement surrounds those who have won money.[12] In fact, stories about gambling make up a mythological charter of manhood in Mouria. What is commemorated in this folk history of gambling are the personalities of the big risk-takers and losers and the occasions when they lost or came near to an extraordinary loss. One of these stories, which refers to an event that took place in the 1960s, involves two of the men now acknowledged to be "big men" of the village, the one still active in gambling and the other "retired." Allegedly the two men stayed on playing poker during a long gambling session while their co-players dropped out. One won consistently and the other lost a large sum of money. At the climax of the confrontation the one who already owed a record sum challenged his contestant to throw the dice. They agreed to gamble the total of his debt for an olive factory that the losing party owned. Apparently the factory owner won this single round, saved his property, and was credited with the fame of a big *koumartzis*. This story has an interesting message. Actually, there was no winner in this contest. Yet it reached a climax of risk. And most of the credit goes to the man who, despite his big losses, stayed on until his luck turned.

This brings us to the folk meaning of gambling in Mouria. Veteran gamblers insist that *koumari* or *tzogos* is not a profession but a *choui*, a unique and idiosyncratic property of the male character, as well as a *pathos*, a passion. It is subject to the deepest wishes of the male heart, as is *raki*, the alcoholic drink par excellence. *Koumari* is further compared to a *bineliki* (from the Turkish *binek*, to ride, which is metaphorically applied to male homosexuals), a term which often refers to good snacks and sweets. This suggests that *koumari* "sweetens" the heart in the way that other exclusively male habits, such as flirting with women, do. In fact *koumari* has been pointed out to me as a substitute for these male "habits."

Koumari is also described as an extreme expression of spendthrift behavior and generosity, attitudes that are more usually expressed in *kerasma*. The gambler does not take account of the large sums he risks in a single round. He fulfills the "natural" destiny of money: "Money is to be spent." It is interesting to note that the idea of spending money, *xodevo* (and *exodo*, monetary cost), derives from *exodos*, exit, and implies an outward movement, opposite to the inward movement of *eisodima* (income).[13] In some sense, then, money "comes out" in gambling. It is also interesting that spending is referred to as "destroying money," *chalao chrima*. These linguistic uses suggest that consumption, and particularly its more spendthrift forms, involves something more fundamental than a mere technical act of exchange mediated by money.

Money is physically prominent in card playing. It may circulate openly around the table, come and go between players. It is particularly evident in dice throwing, where creased and dirty bank notes are put in front of the players. Its central-ity is further brought out in the folk history of *tzogos*. According to my informants, it is the "rich guys" who brought gambling to Mouria. Apparently, the biggest money lender and his circle of friends were the only systematic players at the beginning of this century. Later, men of this category set up a kind of upper-class club, where dancing was taught and drinks were served.

Today, however, gambling is not an exclusive custom of the upper classes.[14] On the contrary, it is part of a repertoire of masculine practices of the "have-nots" as well as the "haves." The recent economic prosperity of the village, the dramatic in-crease in wages since the war, the direct fueling of the local economy by the state and the Agricultural Bank through a loan system, as well as European Union money and remittances from migrants or men who work in the merchant navy have increased the supply of money in the locality (see also Bennett 1988). Despite this impressive picture, few villagers can really afford the stakes in a card game. Sometimes, the sums played can well exceed one or two months' wages. It is true that playing is adjusted to the agricultural cycle, and most dice confrontations take place in a fertile year. But even under these financially favorable conditions, ambi-tious gamblers have to borrow money in order to keep themselves going.

Borrowing for gambling is suggestive of the symbolic meaning of *tzogos* in general and money in particular. Men who identify more with the values of disin-terested reciprocity and associate closely with the coffee house have an offensive attitude towards debt. For example, they borrow from the Agricultural Bank, but they do not feel morally obliged to repay their debts. Yet the same men are reluc-tant to borrow from individuals. A gambler once stressed to me that he does not borrow from a fellow villager, even when he does not have money to eat. The same man, however, does not hesitate to borrow from anyone if he needs money to gamble. This is customary among gamblers. However, what is even more strik-ing is that these men, who are usually ready to borrow as much as possible from the bank and not pay their loan back, insist that gambling debts are sacred. A proper man is obliged, *ofili*, to repay such a debt. If the debtor is an outsider, he should be paid immediately—one can delay, however, repaying a fellow villager. Accordingly one usually borrows from within to settle an external gambling debt.

Nicos P., a bachelor, is one of the renowned *koumartzides* of the village. He holds a respectable record of fines—sentences "awarded" by the Mytilene Court for illegal gambling. Along with his younger married brother, one of the big sharecroppers of the village, Nicos owns as well as rents more than ninety *modia* of olives. He is naturally regarded as one of the men of good standing in the vil-lage and does not need to do wage labor. Yet during the harvest season, he worked as an unskilled laborer in the local olive factory. When, surprised, I asked him why he had to do so, he explained that he had to repay a large debt from the pre-vious winter's gambling. Nicos could not ask for a bigger share of their joint earnings because gambling should not be mixed with household earnings; nor could he sell part of the patrimony. In his case, wages financed gambling. This suggests that wages and gambling money are directly commensurable sectors of a non-domestic, extra-household sphere of circulation. Family or household property, on the other hand, must not enter the financial cycle of gambling. The money that is used in gambling appears, then, to be a more "economic" form of money that derives from the non-domestic order of wage labor or monetary circulation (loans from the bank), and its spending has not been mediated by women. *Koumartzides* seem to share a view, prominent among the "householders," that the property a woman brings with her at marriage is inviolable. Thus a man from a neighboring village who allegedly "ate" part of his wife's dowry at the card table was stigmatized even by some of his gambling partners.

Gambling, then, represents the extreme form of an anti-savings attitude. There appears to be no purpose in spending one month's income at a gambling table. Money spent in commensal festivity is justifiable in terms of the effect it produces: In the last analysis it maintains male communion and conserves the egalitarian, universalistic, and joyful image of manhood. Gambling, on the other hand, produces an opposite image of the male world: segmented, dark, and tiring. No one in the village was ready to describe gambling as a means of profiting at the expense of another man; in fact some men worried about the ethics of winning the daily wages of those in the same class position. In other words, gambling not only contradicts the requirements of a household-centered ideology, but apparently does not accord with the call for equality in male, unisex association, sharing, and identity. From the point of view of the code of male commensality, gambling, then, appears as an almost futile act of financial destruction. Yet it figures as one of the major avenues for the demonstration of "big manhood."

The Politics of Gambling

In this example of gambling, resistance involves both a fundamentalist opposition and a realist accommodation. These two aspects are combined in a process of constructive and politically effective resistance. In a way, opposition and accommodation could be viewed as two separate stages in a single process. The oppositional meanings of gambling emerge through inversions in the context of coffee house sociality. The accommodational aspect develops when resistant meanings are applied in political negotiation with the state. Let us consider the politics of gambling more closely.

As we saw, gambling provides the context in which men who identify with the values of *kefi* deal with the problem that "raw," "undomesticated" bank and wage money represents. This primarily involves the symbolic confirmation that money exists external to the self. A whole set of symbolic contrasts confirms a big cleavage that separates money from the world of disinterested reciprocity. As we saw, *kefi* represented in the festive and joyful spirit of drunkenness and festivity; "raw" money in the calculating and solemn atmosphere of the gambling session. Lightness and outward orientation is attached to *kefi*; heaviness, darkness, inwardness, seclusion, and isolation to money. This catalogue can be extended to include meanings from other contexts. Interpersonal exchange and the circulation of common substance in the world of men are implicated in *raki* commensality; impersonal exchange, atomization, antagonism, and fragmentation relate to money. And last but not least is the contrast between the equality and autonomy that leads into an expressive individualism symbolized by *kefi* and the submission to the hierarchy of the state and market symbolized by money: a contrast that is especially prominent given the "undomesticated" kind of money used in gambling.

Gambling demonstrates that raw, undomesticated money cannot settle in the world of *kefi*, nor dominate it. Yet asserting the external associations of money is not the end of the symbolic confrontation initiated in gambling. Gambling has a second symbolic function: It is also the setting in which the values of *kefi* override those of money. In gambling, money is emptied of its exchange value; the power of money to mediate in transactions, a power that underlies all its threatening and divisive properties, is set apart. As it is disassociated from the temporal process of exchange, it is, in a certain way, taken outside time. In other words, instead of being acknowledged as a medium of exchange and a powerful crosser of boundaries, it is treated as a mere object, an object of consumption, a point that is confirmed in the prestige advanced to the big loser. The movement of money is inverted as it is deflected and pushed out from the world of the coffee house. From the perspective that sees gambling as an extreme instance of negative reciprocity, money is a burden to be got rid of, an object of filth and denigration. In gambling, it is money that is being contested: The market and state definition of money is inverted and defeated, and economic dependence is symbolically transformed into personal autonomy.

The protagonists in this "destruction" of money are precisely those who stand for the values of disinterested commensality and whose symbolic status is high from the viewpoint of the coffee house: people I would describe as "big-men," to convey their agonistic, performed masculinity. Gambling seems to transform the open character of commensality into an extreme form of non-relatedness. Indeed the gambling table is the most open structure of a male world that is often rather closed to outsiders and newcomers: It brings together men who have transcended membership of the drinking circle (as well as the family) and men who are outsiders.[15] Fellow players, however, do not turn into friends; nor can they practice hospitality, since no one can play the role of the host. They do not seem to relate through ties of interpersonal contest. Loss is not conceived as loss to a particular person, nor does it initiate a new round of gambling with the same contestants. Gambling appears to focus on the absolute singularity of the players who meet on alien territory, since the coffee house is put temporarily outside the community. There they engage primarily not with one another but with money and what it stands for.

Gambling, then, carries a heavy symbolic load. Interpreted from the perspective of the coffee house and in the context of the wider symbolism of money and *raki*, it seems to be a major symbolic gesture of emancipation from economic debt, of defiance of the institutional producers of money; it is an important response to economic dependence, social displacement, and class marginalization. In this capacity, it can become an extreme demonstration of autonomy, expressed in terms of a model of gender relying on *kefi*.

However, the politics of gambling are not exhausted in symbolic empowerment, nor are they restricted to a fundamentalist distancing from the capitalist order of the kind displayed by *yoseba* temporary laborers (see Gill in this volume). Gambling is not just a conceptual laboratory but, indirectly, a "proper" political field close to familiarly instrumental action. These symbolic encounters with money bring about a familiarization with the changing economic order—a side effect of degrading state money and its source (see Verdery 1995). These encounters help establish the possibility of a dialogue with the state, insofar as they provide the symbolic means for pursuing economic demands. These demands rest upon symbolic reclassifications in which the peasants familiarize and personify state banks and the state as a sort of traditional "boss." By bringing to bear the moral sphere of interpersonal contact on problematic economic relations with the state, debts can be subjected to politically effective dispute and morally binding negotiation.

The so-called "regulation of peasant debts" (*rythmisis ton agrotikon chreon*, that is, rescheduling and/or partial annulment) is a good example of the political effectiveness of constructive resistance. The "regulation of peasant debts" is accepted practice in cases of adverse weather or other special conditions that spoil the harvest. But beyond this, a general peasant strategy of avoiding repayment has given rise to the accumulation of unpaid debts to the Agricultural Bank, and these have been subjected to another, more directly political form of debt regulation.

This alternative approach to debt results from a number of factors. On the peasants' side, gambling, among other practices, provides a conceptual framework for equating the loans they get from the Agricultural Bank with wages. If mortgages are seen as subsidies, it seems as if they are part of the moral obligation of the state to support peasant income. After all, it is the peasants who feed the nation. The loan, therefore, is reinterpreted as a form of repayment of peasant labor. It is with their labor that peasants service their debt, not with repayments of interest. Greek peasants' view of the state draws upon a widely shared understanding of the state "as an actual and potential source of rent, privilege and insurance, as well as the embodiment of unwarranted menaces or claims for taxes, obedience or order" (Tsoukalas 1995:208). One cannot be indebted to the state; it is rather the state that is morally indebted to its citizens. This is an obliged rather than an obliging state, and in this sense is therefore perceived as the source of unilateral giving, a form of giving that is not constrained by reciprocity and does not generate the need for a return. The state is there to be harvested as an abundant source, similar to the rich forest and the oil companies that the Huaorani Indians (described in Chapter 3 of this volume) so successfully exploit.

From the point of view of the state, the policy of debt "regulation" has been extended, on a number of occasions and as a measure of last resort, to cases of indebtedness that were not caused by ecological disaster.[16] This policy, which may have been both part of a long-term strategy of social and financial support of the peasants and a means of putting a brake on rural exodus, can also be interpreted as a response to peasants' symbolic claims. Since the late 1970s two major regulations on a national scale have been effected by different governments, one in 1981 and the other in 1989.[17] Both regulations were enacted just before national elections. And in both instances the main principle applied was not the total abolition but the rescheduling of debts. The huge debt that had accumulated because of the multiplying effects of interest was rearranged in the form of a new loan. Thus the interest relation was reproduced in the form of a dialogic relation between the state and its peasant contestants (see Kaplan and Kelly 1994).

In what way was this dialogic encounter beneficial for both sides? In particular, what did the state gain out of these "regulations"? The answer to this question takes us back to the coffee house code of disinterested commensality. As I argued above, in a number of contexts—such as the circle of friends sharing alcoholic drinks in the coffee house—the unilateral gift, that is, giving without the expectation of return, is celebrated as the source of morality (also Papataxiarchis 1991:175–179). This cultural possibility is exploited by officials when they describe the regulation of debts as "gifting" *(charisma ton chreon)*.[18] This interpretation removes the monetary debt from the temporal order of long-standing reciprocities and turns it into an expression of the state's generosity. Thus, a rent (interest) relation, which is extended in time through a prolonged process of repayment and binds the peasant to the state, is symbolically translated into a momentary act of gift giving. In dialogically responding to peasant expectations and adopting the role of unilateral provider, the state, therefore, redeems itself from the constricting and hostile depiction as a demanding Leviathan that uses its immense institutional power to exploit the powerless folk. And, in following the historical example of generous local patrons, it regains its contested legitimacy.

The *charisma* of debts, through which loans become symbolically homologous to gifts of drink offered in a circle of friends, temporarily establishes the state in the role of the generous, and therefore moral, person. The state thus symbolically cleanses itself; it establishes a symbiotic, commensal type of relation with its citizens and regains some legitimacy. The generous state is a friend, "one of us"; it is "our" state. It is in this sense that "our own" state cannot be anything but a spendthrift state. Unilateral giving is therefore a key to understand this paradox.

Notes

1. For a collective review of Greece in the 1980s, see Clogg (1993), and Constas and Stavrou (1995). Also see Mouzelis (1995) and Tsoukalas (1995). I would like to thank my coeditors, Sophie Day and Michael Stewart, as well as Efi Avdela, Alexandra Bakalaki,

Maurice Bloch, Janet Carsten, Peter Loizos, Eleni Papagaroufali, and Maria Phylactou for their comments on earlier drafts of this chapter.

2. The ethnographic material on gambling that is presented in this paper was primarily collected during anthropological fieldwork in north Lesbos from 1979 to 1981. Supplementary material on the macro-social aspects of gambling was provided by further research. My fieldwork was generously supported by the London School of Economics, including the Suntory-Toyota Centre (STICERD), the Central Research Fund of the University of London, and the Wenner Gren Foundation.

3. For example see Herzfeld's (1986) analysis of animal theft in Crete.

4. Male mobility has been a long-standing demographic characteristic of the area (Papataxiarchis 1995) and has contributed to the contestation of the sedentary model (of the "household") promoted by the state.

5. This form of sharing is also different from demand sharing since it is governed by generosity.

6. On the analytic limitations of these binary oppositions see Kahn (1995).

7. In this sense, the practices of disinterested sharing in the coffee house represent what, in the case of the Andalusian bar, Gilmore (1991) describes as the "basic moral order" that transcends individual calculation.

8. Likewise, fishermen retain a nonmonetary sphere of fish distribution.

9. This point is well illustrated in a number of contributions to the volume on money edited by Parry and Bloch 1989; see, for example, Carsten 1989.

10. On gambling in Crete and on the metaphorical significance of cards see Herzfeld (1986:152–162 and 1991:176–187).

11. This contrasts with card playing for money on the occasion of New Year's Eve, when household members can test their luck for the coming year. On this occasion, luck as an aspect of destiny is there to be challenged.

12. According to Herzfeld (1991:179), in Crete "a gambler walks on a social knife-edge. On the one hand, by acknowledging his losses, he shows that he doesn't care and that he denies the permanence of his wealth, such as it is. On the other, serious loss suggests that he is ruining his family." In north Lesbos these two opposed concerns are more clearly defined and kept apart, and the rhetoric of independence from money, as it is premised on the demonstration of loss, is openly juxtaposed to the more conservative concern with the destructive effects that gambling has on the household economy.

13. On the other hand, earning money, *vgazo chrimata*, literally translates as "taking money out."

14. Among nobles in early modern France, the gambling table offered a chance to demonstrate indifference to the loss of wealth and "to show oneself above mercantile calculations"(Dewald 1993:62).

15. The polysemy of gambling, its multivocality, is reminiscent of the ritual beatings of young Palestinian men during the *intifada* (Peteet 1994). Professional gamblers and outsiders linked to the state (e.g., bank officials) engage in gambling in order to win (a confirmation of their dominant position). Local gamblers, on the other hand, are there to lose: This is the path to their empowerment.

16. The regulation of peasant debts is not a recent phenomenon. Historically it can be traced back to the interwar period. See Sakellaropoulos (1992:116, 129).

17. The first regulation was effected according to Decision 334/1981 of the *Nomismatiki Epitropi*, the second according to Decision 1620/1989. On some current problems in agri-

cultural borrowing in Greece see Spathis (1995). For a comparative analysis of the terms and conditions of the borrowing policy of the Agricultural Bank of Greece, see Stamatoukos and Spathis (1990:314–320).

18. The idiom of "gift" is more generally applied in specific ritual occasions for the reinterpretation of "normal" institutionalized payments, such as salaries or wages. For example, at Christmas or Easter, employees in the service sector as well as in industry receive an extra untaxed monetary increment that varies (sometimes it is equal to a month's salary) and is called *to doro* (the gift).

PART FOUR

Writing About Marginality

These concluding chapters take up the challenge implied in the introduction to Part Three: how to discuss people who are multiply disadvantaged and, indeed, often blamed for their own marginality? Stephen Nugent considers whether the use of the concept of marginality has actually brought excluded social groups/societies/peoples into the centers of arguments made on their behalf or whether the concept simply functions as a descriptive marker that serves to confirm "otherness." Nugent shows that the representations of anthropologists concerning the poor and dispossessed have an affinity with politically suspect practices among, for example, nation builders (see Introduction).

Nugent also criticizes the literature on marginality for assuming that "the social reproduction of the subaltern has only two possible trajectories: maintenance (accommodation) and resistance (transformation, with who knows what outcome)." Harris's chapter that follows, which deals with the same ethnographic data about poor frontier peasants in Amazonia (*caboclos*), suggests that avoidance or separation from more powerful neighbors and state officials may be equally important and, indeed, politically effective.

Harris shows that if one takes Nugent's strictures seriously, it is still possible and even desirable to provide detailed accounts of agency alongside political economies (or structures). From Nugent's global perspective, *caboclos* seem not to be opposed to any "center," but Harris provides convincing ethnography of their conflicts with local bosses. He shows that it is possible to enrich our understanding of poor peasant politics through ethnographic description. Indeed, these two perspectives complement each other. Without the ethnography, it is too easy to subsume people who are rarely seen or heard within a larger structural analysis of class and the political economy, where terms of reference derive largely if not exclusively from outsiders' categories. If the terms in which people speak about their own experience are ignored, it becomes easy to attribute similar forms of thought to people simply because they share a common environment. This is misleading, as when poor people are assumed to be the same because they share the same poverty. When self-representations, and associated political or economic practices, are being ignored in favor of outsiders' representations, the anthropologists' role may be to create a forum in which these unfamiliar, discordant voices can be heard.

The interview with an Egyptian doctor, which concludes the volume, operates on a number of levels in this respect. It continues the exploration of "exceptional" individuals from Part Two. The chapter shows how Nisseem's practice, his story, his country are gradually and pleasurably detached from each other and, indeed, by implication, from the historical narrative within which he situates himself. As he constructs an individual, timeless "present" he finds a way to continue living in the village, despite being so different from everyone else. At the same time, the interview format encourages the reader into an active engagement with Nisseem and a gentle interpretation of his position in a way that is similar to the process of watching a cinema verité film. In this sense, Colonna engages with the wider problem of how to discuss the search for happiness among people who refuse many of the more familiar forms of "resistant politics."

9

Verging on the Marginal: Modern Amazonian Peasantries

Stephen Nugent

In an analysis of the implications of the then-recent (1994) election of Fernando Henrique Cardoso as President of Brazil—"Comte's dream of the sociologist-ruler seems to have come true"—Perry Anderson notes how complex the marginality of Brazil is by examining a number of peculiarities. First, while other nations in South America experienced major turbulence in the 1960s–1980s, Brazil's generals succeeded in suppressing opposition and maintained their dictatorship, virtually unchallenged, for two decades. Next, when F. H. Cardoso came to power, other nations in the region had already adopted (or been forced to adopt) neoliberal policies, and Cardoso has had to run to catch up. Third, the modern intellectual and political formation of "the United States of Brazil" drew, through the agency of the University of Sao Paulo, on French scholars (including Lévi-Strauss, Braudel, Foucault, Bastide, Monbeig, Lefort) long before they had achieved international standing (Anderson 1994:5). And finally, against a global backdrop in which such notions as "the working class" are regarded as hopelessly retrograde, "Brazil is the only country in the world to have produced a new working-class party of classical dimensions (Partido Trabalhista, Workers' Party) since the war" (1994:9). In short: "Brazil today has a larger population and gross national product than Yeltsin's Russia. Yet, against all reason, it continues to occupy a curiously marginal position in the contemporary historical consciousness" (1994:3).

These factors, and others, are germane when considering the utility of the notion of marginality as it is employed in Amazonia (which, anthropologically, often serves as a euphemism for Brazil as a whole), for they immediately draw attention to the dynamism of (diverse) externalities, as against the kind of immanence or essentialism with which the marginality concept is often associated. That there are nested versions of marginality (as above) as well as essentialist (e.g., underclass), structuralist (e.g., informal sector), and transformative (e.g., creole elite) variants leads one to question whether the bald concept is itself adequate to the explanatory task to which it has been put. And if, as the example of Brazil indicates, the concept of marginality may be plausibly engaged at the level of global historical consciousness as easily as at the level of an inner city, lumpen car thief—the *malandro*, say (see da Matta 1991)—it may in the end have greater metaphorical than analytic power.

In what follows, I look first at some of the ways in which the marginality concept has been employed generally and, second, at how, in the case of Brazilian Amazonia, the concept is employed in national and regional discourses of identity. My aim is to consider whether the use of the marginality concept has actually brought excluded social groups/ societies/ peoples into the center of arguments claimed on their behalf or whether the concept simply functions as a descriptive marker that serves to confirm otherness.

The Category "Marginal"

Use of the concept *marginal/marginality*, which ostensibly draws attention to the nonnormative, the subaltern, the excluded—appealing anthropological fare—has in fact frequently achieved the opposite effect. Instead of laying the ground for explanations that account for the dynamic relationship between powerful and underpowered social groups (categories, classes, positions), the concept has often (typically) served to reify the excluded as objects and in doing so move them from being structurally marginal—which is a potentially illuminating construction—to being effectively excluded: a sector, culture, domain whose existence is acknowledged but whose affinity with "the center" is denied. For example, the concept of *informal sector*, which appeared in the literature (see Hart 1973; Pearse 1959) as a critique of the received wisdom of a dualism that segregated normative capitalist development from its supposed, chaotic correspondent, was quickly transformed and bowdlerized. Rather than remaining one focus of a wider analysis taking structural exclusion as a central feature of capital accumulation under uneven development (see Bromley and Gerry 1979), the informal sector became a paragon of fetishized marginality. Initially a refutation of the distortions of neocolonialism, the informal sector became essentialized as a new exotic: a bounded system of impoverishment, survival strategies, coping mechanisms, and cultural dysfunction. As traditional objects of anthropological analysis either disappeared or became less plausible as "remote, isolated societies," the bowdlerized notion of informal sector came forth to provide analogues (e.g., peasants in cities, favelados, slum-dwellers). The structured character of formal/informal sector relationships became mere background, and the object of analysis—the margin—came to be treated as thing in and of itself.[1]

A significant precursor of "the informal sector" was "the culture of poverty" thesis, which provides a notorious example of the same kind of slippage—from a structured to an essential reading. Although Oscar Lewis spoke on behalf of the marginal—or, more daringly perhaps, recorded them as they spoke for themselves—his defense of the marginal and subaltern was turned against them: When U.S. policy makers wished to justify reductions in welfare payments to the poor, they could cite culture of poverty arguments to the effect that the poor are so locked into their marginal culture(s) as to be irrecoverable, that marginality/poverty is self-reproducing. Proper attention to the preconditions of such poverty was overwhelmed by demands to deal with consequences of poverty, not causes.[2]

In the emergence of the category "informal sector," as well as the identification of the "culture of poverty," a contradictory effort was being made: On the one hand, there was an attempt to delimit a special kind of social space—that which is occupied by those whose circumstances typically deny them the power or right to authorize their activities, lifestyles, worldviews. On the other hand, once identified, the marginal and subaltern had to be authenticated, they had to be allocated some kind of essentialist marker (Gypsy, druggie, hobo, illegal alien, petty trader—the list is long). As a consequence, the dynamic properties of those relations that enforce the distinction of normative against marginal are frequently reduced, basically, to ethnographic method and the discovery of new analogues of the traditional anthropological object of analysis: someone who is different.

A significant departure from the approach that identifies the marginal and then proceeds to analyze it, while passing over the larger cultural consequences of being so-labeled, is represented in "subaltern studies" such as those associated with Guha (1982, 1983). The version of subaltern studies that has attracted most attention, however, is that which has been appropriated by "postcolonial theory," a version that some might argue actually subverts the critical project: The subaltern becomes an academically valued object of analysis (not dissimilar to the ordinate class of marginal; for a scathing commentary, see Jacoby 1995). But there is a more ambitious and potentially fruitful version, that which—as the editors of this volume argue—does not seek to constitute an inner status or essential identity but shows how so-called subalterns necessarily define themselves in contrast and opposition to a dominant or hegemonic culture and in doing so move toward a revocation of their subaltern status (but see Friedman 1997 for discussion of hyper-valorization of "enlightened creoles"). Marginality in this reading is not so much a cultural category as it is a position within a large, contested cultural domain in which marginality is constantly negotiated and relativized.

This version is represented in a diverse literature (from Gutmanite, to cultural studies, to the anthropology of work; see Calagione, Francis, and Nugent 1992), but the terms of the project (well summed-up by the subtitle of the volume cited above: "Beyond Accommodation and Resistance") are preliminary. "Accommodation" and "resistance" represent a largely reactive characterization. What lies beyond is a different relationship between the normative and subaltern/marginal: if not the consolidation of power by the previously subaltern, at least an agenda-setting role. The EZLN (Zapatista Army of National Liberation) in Chiapas, the Movimento Sem Terra (MST, Landless Peoples Movement) in Brazil, Hawaiian nationalists, and North American Indian casino entrepreneurs all represent considerably more than accommodation and resistance. It seems clear in the cases of both the EZLN and MST, for example, that popular demands exceed the limits of state accommodation or tolerance of resistance. In both cases state repression is the response. The possibilities for movement permitted by the state fall below the demands of the supplicants, and as a consequence, the relationship is one of neither accommodation nor resistance but of unintelligibility, pending a clear political outcome.

Marginal/Subaltern/Hybrid/Creole

Between Park's sketch "The Marginal Man: A Study of the Mulatto Mind" (Linder 1996:154) and the present, the concept of marginality—emerging from a sociological sensibility informed by German romanticism and an explicitly journalistic method (see Linder 1996)—has gone through the three stages sketched above. First, in Park's rendering, the concept referred to an existential condition—"a man on the margin of two cultures and two societies, which never completely interpenetrated and fused" (Park 1928:892, cited in Linder 1996:154). Here the marginal might be characterized as cultural or social product: Given that the city was portrayed by Park as a form of social organism, the marginal represented a specific (and in some respects, explicitly pathological) adaptation to that environment.

Second, and following closely on the culture of poverty thesis, marginality depicted through the informal sector emphasized structure: marginality is not a condition per se but the subordinate partner in uneven development. Against a backdrop provided by dependency theory's assault on modernization theory, the informal sector formulation linked fieldwork case studies with broader historico-theoretical efforts, but the outcome often was resolutely essentialist: The relationship between informal and formal sectors was taken as given, and the major effort went into examining the lifeways of the marginal/informal.[3]

Finally, there is the current Gramscian or post-Gramscian version,[4] in which the marginal is both structurally defined and, vis-à-vis historically "low-rent" symbolic capital, repudiated: The conditions of marginality themselves become the basis for construction of an affirmative, celebratory identity.[5] The celebration of hybrid/creole identity (see Friedman 1997) represents the inversion of Park-era terms of reference (although it is rare to see Park cited as a "hybridity" pioneer) and has led to a significant reconsideration of marginality in light of new nation-/identity-building tendencies evident globally—and across a range from New Social Movements to newly industrialized "Tiger" states.

It is ironic that the issue of marginality in anthropology should be historically bookended by the same term, hybridity.[6] Whereas for Park hybridity was the entry point for the investigation of his version of "the modern problem," hybridity is now a key term in the elaboration of a postmodernist grappling with ways to retire exhausted modernist problematics (see Werbner and Modood 1997). However, not all who write of marginality (in its various forms) currently are confident of the liberating possibilities of a transcendental subalternism. Bourgois, for example, writing about El Barrio—East Harlem, New York, argues that "the street culture of resistance is predicated on the destruction of its participants and the community harboring them. In other words, although street culture emerges out of a personal search for dignity and a rejection of racism and subjugation, it ultimately becomes an active agent in personal degradation and personal ruin" (1995:9).

Bourgois's monograph encapsulates a dilemma that he and other commentators, such as Stephen Steinberg (1995), remark upon with some passion: it may be that it is (sectors of) the social sciences themselves that are marginal, as revealed in their incapacity to deal with the materiality of the lives of those whom they take as subjects. Bourgois writes that "the depth and overwhelming pain and terror of the experience of poverty and racism in the United States needs to be talked about openly and confronted squarely, even if that makes us uncomfortable" (1995:18).

Steinberg, whose volume *The Ethnic Myth* (1991) lucidly documents the way the construction of socioeconomic, ethnic, and cultural marginality in the U.S. was itself integral to modern nation-building, also addresses the frailties of a social science for which marginality is somewhere else or something "different": "So long as social scientists persist in treating the behaviour of the underclass as though it is self-generating and self-explaining, and focusing on agency without regard to structure, we will end up with superficial truths, facile value judgements, and ineffectual policy"(1995:142).

The marginality concept has been employed in various ways to define anthropology's (and other fields') relationship to its objects of analysis, and a persistent tension has existed between marginality as a trait or defining feature and marginality as a structural relationship. In rough terms, from Park to Lewis, discussions of marginality had a strongly centrist agenda in the sense that questions of assimilation were strongly to the fore. In its informal sector version, marginality addressed a broader geopolitical landscape. In its current version, the concept (implicated in postcolonialism, multiculturalism, New Social Movements, and creolization—not to mention Sendero Luminoso, EZLN, MST, or religious/ethnic state-building) is spatially and culturally decentered. Rather than defining a structural relationship, the concept has become an idiom for negotiating the politics of cultural identity.

The Persistently Marginal: The Vicissitudes of Marginality in Amazonia

In what follows, I assume a very limited goal: I look at three levels at which the issue of Amazonian marginality is germane (as an essentialist category; as an expression of regional disarticulation with the nation; as a research domain, literally a branch of the anthropological culture industry). I argue that what counts as marginality in contemporary Brazilian Amazonia[7] is an unnecessarily impoverished way to conceive of the anthropological project as it endeavors to confirm its claims as a modernist discipline that can reflect as usefully on societies that practice anthropology as it can on societies that have traditionally served as objects of scrutiny. In terms of the anthropological literature, Amazonian peasant societies present a particularly severe form of marginality—acknowledged certainly, but relatively ignored.

There are three versions of the marginal in Brazilian Amazonia I would like to discuss in this chapter: 1) the marginal as that category is culturally encoded locally; 2) the marginal as the region relates to the state and the global system; and 3) the marginal as an active category in the research trajectory of anthropological research in the region. The main referent is the so-called *caboclo*, an Amazonian actor whose ambiguous definition exemplifies marginality discourse in the region. Among the variety of definitions provided for *caboclo* are the following: deculturated Indian; *mestiço*; traditional (i.e., not late-modern) frontier colonist; Amazonian peasant; *ribeirinho* (riverside dweller); Amazonian rustic; atomistic veteran of Amazonia's rubber-based belle epoque; lumpen, disenfranchised laborer. This list is not exhaustive but indicates the range of possibility.

In terms of the Amazonianist anthropological literature, the *caboclo* represents a (remote) second-order issue. By comparison with the voluminous ethnographic literature on native peoples (for overviews, see Jackson 1975; Overing 1981; Viveiros de Castro 1996; Carneiro da Cunha 1992), studies of *caboclo* societies are paltry. Wagley's *Amazon Town* ([1953] 1976) remains the standard text [augmented by revisions by his students, see Miller (in Wagley 1976) and others, for example, Pace 1998]. *Amazonian Caboclo Society* (Nugent 1993) and monographs (in Portuguese only) by Furtado, Loureiro, and Esterci, to name but a few—as well as important but poorly disseminated work by Anderson, McGrath, Harris, and others—have endeavored to pull such peoples in from the fringes, but the category *caboclo* remains marginal at best and inchoate at worst.

Part of the explanation for the relegation of the *caboclo* to the margins probably lies in the dynamic of the role of the Indian in Brazilian national discourse and the strong association between the notions of Amazonian society and Indian society. Alcida Ramos has observed (1997) that the Indian represents an insoluble problem to the state: The official view of the Indian is that of "grave inconvenience"; and as the rewritten, 1988 constitution has conferred greater rights on "the Indian" (acknowledging the possibility of a "nations-within-nation" status), the Indian has challenged the tenets of collective individualism according to which Brazil has pressed its syncretic claims: Just as hyphenated Brazilians are anathema to the state (Brazilianness taking precedence over, for example, Japanese-Brazilianness), so must be Indian-Brazilians. And yet, Ramos observes, official discourse requires the presence of the Indian, for the Indian—like the categories "European" and "African"—is necessary for the continuation of the national debate about exactly what it means to be a Brazilian. The assimilation of the Indian would enfeeble the state, and it would destroy the Indian.

From this vantage point, it is not difficult to see that *caboclos* represent a com-
plication: peoples who are marginal in the same way Indians are but who are seen
to lack the cultural/symbolic capital of Indians. They are neither one thing nor
another, neither Indians nor nationals, and their presence does not add to the debate; it detracts from it, for their provenance challenges the racist premises of the
basic terms of debate: They are not "European," "African," or "Indian."

Marginality One

The Portuguese rendering of the term *marginal* is the same as the English and has
vernacular resonance in Amazonian social domains, but it does not necessarily
refer to a relationship (e.g., of dominance/subordination or normal/subaltern). A
marginal in this sense is a chicken thief, dope-smoker, ne'er-do-well, a *Zé
Ninguem* (Joe Nobody; kinless person), a ragged teenager, whose picture shows
up on the crime pages of newspapers, handcuffed to a hospital bed while being
interrogated by a guy who looks like his older brother. A marginal may well be
someone not known locally, a chancer who is clearing land just beyond the
boundaries of the legitimate agrarian landscape, or someone whose entry to the
immediate social landscape is unannounced. Or it may be someone who has
been forcibly excluded from a community because—landless—he could not find
a wife from a landholding family, or because he beat his wife, or because he got
into debt and fell too far behind in his payments.

The point is that marginal in this sense refers to a quality thought to inhere in
an individual. It is a benighted state of (permanent) deviance.[8] A marginal is literally dangerous first; metaphorically dangerous, second. To illustrate: In an estuary[9] island community where I have done research intermittently over the past
few years, there is great stability of membership. Access to the community is afforded only by marriage or by becoming a sharecropper, and two core settlements include the majority of members. On the periphery of the island are
households of squatters who are in no sense marginal but in no sense members
of the island either. They simply do not count. Within the community, marginals
are those who can claim some kind of historical link (generally a kinship or employee connection) but who are marked as drunks, thieves, and/or fighters.

Following a weekly football game, neighbors were commenting on the abilities
of a new goalie who turned out to be a tyro-transvestite. S/he was staying on the
island for a couple of weeks (his/her mother's sister was a permanent resident),
and although s/he was the object of mild ridicule, s/he was not regarded as anything less than a qualified member of the community. It would be hard to describe my neighbors' attitudes toward *travestis* as overly sympathetic, but there
was nothing marginal about this character. Indeed, one of his/her reasons for returning to the island was that s/he found it difficult to cope in his/her parents'
community (interior Pará), where his/her nominated identity was an issue. The
point here is that s/he did not satisfy local criteria for being a marginal, despite

his/her adoption of an identity for which there were neither local analogues nor obvious sympathies.

The moral judgments invoked in attaching marginal status were pragmatic: Those designated marginal were those who, through their persistently antisocial behavior (locally defined in terms of crimes against property and physical safety), adopted the mantle. Those who, despite other transgressions, did not exceed these boundaries received great tolerance. Notoriously, over the years I lived (periodically) on the island, a *filho de criaçao* (adopted child) of a neighbor's house regularly fell prey to dolphin spirits *(boto)* and engaged in (largely self-) destructive acts.[10] In no way did this make him marginal. It made him unusual and different but did not confer sanctions on him, despite the fact that his C.V. would seem to be custom-made for such status.

This category of marginal has been illustrated by negative examples: people who might be assumed to fit the bill, but who, in fact—and perhaps against expectation— do not. Marginals of this level do not constitute a subculture; they are individuals who exist within normal society, perhaps approaching the limits of acceptable behavior.

Marginality Two

The identification of marginal society in Amazonia was achieved in the early decades of this century, following the collapse of the rubber industry, and officially codified in Jose Verissimo's account of *o caboclo indolente* (*the lazy peasant* 1970). What followed the collapse of the rubber industry, according to most accounts, was a period of economic stagnation (1914–1970).[11] Former rubber tappers—and what remained of their decadent overlords in the larger trading centers—became ineffective economic agents, incapable of reconstituting a viable post-rubber society and, unprotected by integration in the global economy, were forced to fall back on a set of livelihoods seriously restricted by "green hell." The extent of marginality, as depicted in the literature, cannot be overstated. The very notion of society lacked cogency. These were people who had drifted so far beyond the measure of normal society that they were, if such be possible, sub-marginal, and the region as a whole became officially marginal, unable to contribute to the nation's mission statement: order and progress. Hence, one finds peasant *inhabitants* or *populations* noted in the literature but not peasant *societies* in Amazonia (a tendency that persists in the 1990s).

The construction of this potent version of marginality drew (and continues to draw) on a vast array of resources. These include not only official versions of the consequences of conquest (beginning with the very identification of Amazonians—analogues of Scythian women archers) and premature conclusions about the prospects for "advanced" societies in the humid neo-tropics,[12] but also evidence precipitated from the accounts provided by Victorian naturalists (such as Bates, Wallace, and Spruce). These naturalists' accounts, in significant part because of the length of time spent in the region, augment a "green hell" image that persists to this day.

The inclusion of Amazonia within the official economic history of the nation has been achieved through incorporating rubber extraction in the list of boom-and-bust industries through which Brazil maintained its integration in the global economy (via sugar, cotton, cocoa, coffee, diverse minerals, etc.). Eventually, growth through dependent development in the post–World War II period lent plausibility to the "giant of Latin America" projections, but this inclusion of rubber-period Amazonia in the narrative of national development is not wholly warranted on several grounds. For one thing, the rubber industry was not a boom industry: For almost a hundred years, Amazonia was the only significant source of rubber *(hevea brasiliensis)*, and during that period, output steadily increased— as did prices, as did demand. The "boom" refers only to the last quarter of the nineteenth century, preceding the transfer of germ-plasm to Southeast Asian plantations. Second, unlike other boom-and-bust entries, rubber production was based neither on a plantation system within which the costs of production could be controlled directly by capital (as in sugar production under slavery, for example) nor on wage labor. In as much as rubber extraction could not be confined to or contained within a plantation system in Amazonia[13] (and still cannot be, economically), there was a nearly hundred-year period during which the rubber industry was lucrative and came to stand for an Amazonia that (very) roughly approximated the large-region, rural oligarchies whose alliances and combinations have long shaped whatever centralized, federal government has been in power. When that industry moved to Southeast Asia, the society with which it had previously been associated became a marginal society, if not a non-society. It did not retain the character of a former regional power except in so far as it has provided leaders of the armed forces with a training ground for career development.

The indices of this level of marginality are not mysterious. First, once the natural monopoly on rubber was lost, Amazonia lost relevance as a potential regional base for national development. Increases in rubber revenue had been achieved not through improvements in productivity but extensively through the growth of a labor force operating over an ever larger area. Demand for rubber in emergent industries (steam, electrical, auto) in the core was not matched in Brazil itself (much less in Amazonia), where ascendancy as an industrial power was delayed for several decades, such that the networks of merchant capital that developed under the rubber regime provided few linkages either nationally or locally back to producers.

Second, although Amazonia had never been part of the system of rural oligarchies according to which centralized state power was achieved, neither was it close enough (by virtue of the restrictions engendered by the dominance of river trade/travel/communication) to centers of economic and political power in Brazil. The rubber industry had in significant respects bypassed Brazil-the-nation. New York and Liverpool were the trade links, such that even if the state shared the proceeds (through taxes, for example), once production and trade declined there was little state infrastructure to be maintained. Under conditions of natural monopoly, where it was the unique provider of an extractive product for which there was rising demand and rising price, the Amazon rubber industry was hardly qualitatively different in 1914 than it had been in 1820. Low productivity was not an issue under conditions of monopoly; but once Southeast Asian rubber entered the market, it became fatal. In a few years, Southeast Asian plantations achieved an increase in output that had taken fifty years to achieve in Amazonia, and they did so under conditions of plantation production that (under a wage regime) easily out-performed Amazonian extractive production. Very shortly after the appearance of Southeast Asian rubber, the Amazonian rubber industry had collapsed.

Third, Amazonia is as exotic a category for most Brazilians as it is for most Europeans and North Americans. It is a repository of possibility (variously regarded as threatened, squandered, retrievable, utopian) at some remove. It harbors, as Ramos's analysis of the hyperreal Indian suggests (1994), both the desirable and the scorned.

This version of marginality that afflicts Amazonia has two faces, one that is addressed (a bit), another that is not (or hardly at all). The addressed version is the agency version: The constituents of Amazonian society, a motley crew of former Indians and miserable immigrants from the Northeast, could not rise to the occasion. Unable to modernize in the face of Southeast Asian competition, they retreated into peasant indolence and livelihoods heavily constrained by an unresilient green hell. The unaddressed version is the structured one: the legatees of the rubber boom were still integrated into local, regional, national, and international trade networks. They enlarged their repertoire of petty commodity activities (through jute, black pepper, cattle, diverse tropical preciosities, fish, forest meat, boats) and became truck drivers, cabbies, sellers of lottery tickets, prostitutes, lawyers, novelists, xenophobes, ethnobiologists, wise forest managers—but they did so without national acknowledgment much less license. Their marginality is expressed both in local/regional terms—overpowered by the extreme natural forces of the *hyleia*, or "green hell"—and in national/external terms—unable to claim full membership in Brazil-the-eighth-largest economy in the world.

Marginality Three

The anthropological version of Amazonian marginality is complicated, not as a consequence of sustained attention to the issues, but as a consequence of the selective choice of appropriate objects of analysis and the narrowness of the anthropological remit.

Although the anthropological literature on Amazonia has historically focused mainly on indigenous societies, the creation of an official neo-Amazonian peasantry[14] opened a new research path in Amazonianist anthropology. And over the past twenty-five to thirty years, a modernization landscape has been added to the natural and social landscapes of Amazonia. A not insignificant feature of this new landscape is a heterogeneous peasantry of *caboclo*, "official," and "spontaneous" Transamazonica fractions.

Around 1970, Amazonia was officially reinvented. It became a desirable frontier that, having long resisted the incorporative efforts of the state, was finally succumbing to the blandishments of modernization. The Transamazonica Highway was the infrastructural centerpiece to a program of barely regulated pillage. The rhetoric of the time emphasized metaphors of marginality ("taking the people without land to the land without people" is the most succinct rendition) and was complemented by jingoistic exhortations ("integrate so that others may not appropriate"—*integrar para nao entregar*).

There are at least two significant ironies in this defeat-of-marginality program. One is that more than half of the territory of Brazilian Amazonia falls either within zones of national security (such as *Calha Norte*) or the Greater Carajas Project (a private state within the state), and it hence could hardly be more official. The second is that those peasants who already occupied the region at the time of reconquest were largely disregarded. In the literature, they are not acknowledged as societies (unless Amerindians awaiting integration into national society via the services of FUNAI—the National Indian Foundation) but mere populations or inhabitants. The marginality that was defeated by the programs associated with and following Transamazonica was a marginality strictly of such programs' making. When the early attempts (1970–1974) to demarcate and distribute plots to official colonists failed to achieve even nominal integration—the stated marker of which was the establishment of an independent, landholding class of small-scale producers—government policy shifted to favor an overtly marginalist program: The advantage afforded by the development of the Amazonian public domain, it was argued, lay in the promotion of cattle ranching and mineral extraction, as well as in infrastructural developments such as a highway system and hydroelectricity (within a program of poles of development). The subsidies available to those with the capital resources to exploit this were unquestionably generous (see Hecht and Cockburn 1989). Since 1970, some 12 percent of the region has been deforested—striking in absolute terms, but more impressive yet in relative terms: Pre-historical Amazonia supported very large populations (Roosevelt 1989), and the region sustained a regime of rubber extraction for almost a hundred years; yet as the result of only a few years of concerted "development," the region bears the marks of serious environmental depredation (extensively documented).

Since 1970, the anthropological remit in Amazonia has changed enormously. Although the central literature on native peoples continues to grow, frontier peasantries, human ecology, ethnobiology, New Social Movements, eco-politics, and tropical forestry have all provided a basis for a redefinition of the scope of Amazonianist anthropology. What is striking, however, is the degree to which the revised (ecophilic) research agenda is not only future-oriented and speculative with regard to *possible Amazonian societies* (utopian or barren), but also blink-ered to *actual non-Indian Amazonian societies*.

The marginalization of historical Amazonian peasantries (here glossed as *cabo-clos* for convenience if not precision)[15] in the current period has several ironies. Not least of these is the fact that the vilified "lazy peasant" of two decades ago may now appear as "the wise forest manager" in the same people's discourse. Subvert-ing that irony, however, is the fact that having served the purpose of demonstrat-ing that non-Amazonians are now sensitive to the virtues of local knowledge, the affirmative peasant is really no less marginal. The wise forest manager may have become an exemplar of alternative management strategies but in doing so—or in being presented as doing so—is in no way licensed autonomy. Enfranchisement is not guaranteed by the convergence of the trajectories of those who live in the for-est/on the river and those who now recognize that such accommodation validates the affirmative claims of the marginal. In fact, it has guaranteed something quite different: *Caboclo* success at accommodating the competing claims of green hell and the market (*açaí* is a case in point) allows the appropriation of the outcome ("green" or "native" Brazil nuts—Ben and Jerry's and Body Shop International, re-spectively) without any serious attention to the local consequences of such arrangements. And it is not hard to see why: The possible negative fallout is almost inconsequential from the point of view of those (consumers in big market soci-eties) who eat niche ice cream or wish to treat their hair exotically.

The point here is that the marginality attributed to Amazonians is not even their own but appears as a consequence of particular kinds of relationships beyond their direct control. The marginality of *o caboclo indolente* is no more nor less than the marginality of "the wise forest manager," regardless of the affirmative qualities at-tached to the latter. The division of academic labor, shaped by a new globalist, eco-logical agenda, has momentarily revealed an integral notion of Amazonian *caboclo* society but has then put it aside with the realization (or, more precisely, claim) that the central issues do not concern carrying capacity, protein capture, "rivers of hunger," polycultural swiddens, and so on—the traditional foci of anthropological and human ecological discourse regarding peasant Amazonia—but biodiversity, commercial prospects for non-timber forest products, global carbon sinks, and sustained-yield tropical forest management (as outlined, for example, by the World Bank Tropical Forest Action Plan), and the like. The resultant marginalization of Amazonian peoples also represents the re-marginalization of the anthropological brief, for the latter has been unable to valorize its object(s) of analysis. As anthro-pology has withered as a significant player in Amazonia, so have its client others.

The essentialist version of marginality in Amazonia has some content: At the local level, there is an agency version. The structural version is apparent as well: Amazonians are (partially and significantly) defined in relation to the construc-tions placed on them by a remote state.

The first two versions of marginality discussed above (what counts as marginal in terms of a local society; the exclusion of the region from the mainstream of national development this century) are, I think, uncontentious. The third is more problematic, for it implicates not just marginals but also those who claim to be experts in identifying marginality, in effect valorizing their own activities in the pursuit of the significantly marginal. The coverage of the Zapatistas in Chiapas (and to a lesser degree, the increased interest in *Movimento Sem Terra* in Brazil) has depended heavily on the redefinition of these groups by external commentators. In the case of both Mexico and Brazil, there is nothing novel about the conditions giving rise to these movements (an institutionalized "revolutionary" party/state; a notoriously skewed distribution of agricultural land), nor are these movements of recent vintage. What accounts significantly for their becoming visibly marginal (as opposed to invisible, lumpen, inchoate) is the value they have as indices of external observers' insights into social movements on the periphery. But to the degree that such movements are mere episodes within a larger politico-historical field, the virtual celebration of their marginality obscures the durability of the structural conditions giving rise to them, and these structural conditions are far from "marginal" in the sense of exceptional. They are normal.

Restating Marginality

One of the organizing themes of this volume is the way in which peoples designated marginal come to define themselves affirmatively in opposition or contrast to a hegemonic culture. At one level, this theme is unproblematic: Given an unambiguous relationship of dominance/subordination, of course the self-construction of the subaltern must refer to limits imposed from outside. But that does not seem to push the issue far enough, and there is implicit in the formulation above the notion that the social reproduction of the subaltern has only two possible trajectories: maintenance (accommodation) and resistance (transformation, with who knows what outcome).

There are four problems with this formulation. The first is that it is not exhaustive of the range of options. There are clear limits, for example, to the tolerance displayed by those who are dominant: The number of countries that acknowledge the ILO (International Labor Organization) protocols concerning nation-within-nation status is rather small. Second, such a characterization of hegemony presumes an abstract notion that is fine heuristically but that holds up less well against the historical record: National liberation and peasant movements in the twentieth century may well have contributed to the defeat of one hegemonic regime after another only to see them replaced by others. To disregard the motor force of the former in order to sustain the durable-hegemony thesis may be to overlook a more complex relationship between the dominant and the subordinate: Rather than marginality being either a structural condition or a reflection of intrinsic shortcomings of the marginal (to summarize, brutally, the two main positions), it might be better to consider marginality as the normative condition and centeredness, material well-being, large symbolic capital bank accounts as the deviant condition, an issue to which I return below. Third, a single, global, and historical model of dominance/subordination confounds the actual record and obscures more than it illuminates: Is subalternity in India really the same as that found in, say, Hawaii (anymore than Chayanov's peasants are analogous with Mexican peasants)? Fourth, and finally, this formulation of marginality purports to include as elements an idealized version of "peoples" that excludes many compelling examples, not least of which is the *caboclo*.

These objections aside, *caboclos* fit the general formulation in every respect other than their being a "people." They are subordinate without question; they position themselves in relationship to a (decreasingly remote: that's modernization) hegemonic culture; they accommodate, and they resist; but they are not outside the system. They are poorly remunerated, marginal, subaltern, but they do not lay claim to autochthony or other independent origins. They cannot do so plausibly. They are refugees from a hegemonic regime that pretends that they are extra-systemic (to the limited degree that they are even acknowledged), but they are not a "people" in the sense of being granted some degree of selective cultural integrity.[16] And arguments advanced concerning the origins of this marginality all contain, to greater or lesser degrees, some plausible elements: geographical-ecological factors, which are hard to ignore (differences between agro-extractive potential on *varzeas* and *terra firme*, for example); the consequences of demographic collapse and haphazard colonization over three or four centuries; the long stability of the rubber industry under a proto-capitalist (merchant capitalist) regime; the diffuseness of regional markets; the distance from national centers of power. As one begins to list these elements, however, two aspects come forward, first—and not terribly surprisingly—the designation "marginal" fits reasonably well from a number of different perspectives; second, however, the hegemony according to which the marginals define themselves is absent.

If it is the case that Amazonian marginality is the normative condition and that official power as represented in centeredness, material well-being, and large symbolic capital accounts lies largely outside the frame, then the idea that subaltern or marginal identity necessarily positions itself—or indeed, in some formulations, defines itself—in relation to a dominant, hegemonic culture loses a lot of force. For one thing, it takes as given the idea that marginality is dependent on hegemony, and although there are plenty of examples to show that this is likely or often the case(most of the chapters in this volume, the revived nations of the former Soviet Union, configurations of political battles in Central Africa—the list is long) it does not follow that the only conditions of existence for marginality depend either on essentialist or structural claims.

Concluding Notes

Using a similar vocabulary, if not always the same conceptual categories, writers on marginality and hybridity in modern anthropology—from Park, say, to Pnina Werbner (1931–1997)—have seized upon a theme that attests (sometimes weakly; at times strongly) to an attempt by anthropology to keep an eye on the way three worlds are related: the worlds of anthropological subject, anthropological object, and of the theoretical field that mediates between the two. This theme has never held center stage (despite several major moments), yet its durability (through various iterations) suggests that it continues to tax the explanatory claims of settled theory.

Since Park wrote, there have been moments when "marginality" represented the convergence of anthropology and cultural critique—the culture of poverty, the informal sector, peasant studies, deviant cultures, subcultures. Although each of these represented attempts to depathologize marginality and to explain it as the outcome of structures and forces beyond the direct control of those labeled as marginal, what is different about the current phase is that the marginality addressed is not simply "contextualized" (although much of the "underclass" literature still attempts to drag the discussion back to essentialist frames of reference) but celebrated. Marginality now is not just reactive (or subordinate), but, as management culture prescribes, it is proactive (incipiently or potentially hegemonic). And it follows that one of the reasons for the upsurge of interest in diasporas, hybridities, marginality, subcultures, and so on is not just that relations between dominant and subordinate cultures have become more complicated, but also that the adequacy of the once progressivist Gramscian model is challenged. Most threatening to the anthropological appropriation of Gramscian or Gramscianesque models is the fact that a more clearly historical approach is required. Although at a fairly abstract level, the formulation, "Oppressed peoples define themselves in contrast and opposition to a dominant or hegemonic culture," goes some way toward mapping the space within which the excluded and the empowered negotiate the terms of their cultural identities; it clearly fails to incorporate all the terms of marginalization and imputes general characteristics to the subaltern/marginal without providing content (e.g., ethnographic), which is hardly unavailable. The *caboclo* example is a minor case in point and probably an extreme example (marginality in the absence of hegemony), but more potent examples are represented by the EZLN, Sendero Luminoso, and the Algerian Armed Islamic Group—the first seeking autonomy from the state, the second seeking the destruction of the state, and the last seeking state power. That there are cultural separations represented in all three appears undeniable, but the prosaic explanatory force of "marginal" does not seem up to the task.

Part of the appeal of the notion of hegemonic regime—and the associated discourses of hybridity, marginality, creolization—is that it connotes both normativity and contestation and seems to provide a dynamic framework within which to consider how historical subjects compete for space within differentiated regimes. It legitimates both normative social force and, to a lesser degree, its dark side. What is does not do, however, is acknowledge that the marginals are no less authentic for falling beyond the normative, and as such, a discussion of marginality intended to bring the marginal back into the frame subverts itself. The marginal is basically the historical subject without the power to define others as marginal. As such, the formulation valorizes the insight of the skeptical observer-critic—who is by definition normative—while continuing to provide a matrix for exclusion. It confirms the divide between those who pontificate and those who genuflect (or do not, as happens to be the case).

Notes

1. There were two dismissals here: first, the other element of the relationship—the informal sector; second, the relationship itself. To insist on the necessity of keeping both in view was to admit to being a theoretical dinosaur in the 1980s and 1990s.

2. Bourgois pushes this discussion further than most in his introduction to *In Search of Respect* (1995). The validation of the structural claims of marginality/culture of poverty theses (in amplified form) entails a dangerous voyeurism. Inadvertently "giving the poor a bad name" is an obligatory risk.

3. In broad stroke terms, dependency theory was refined along several lines, articulation-modes-of-production was one idiom, world systems theory another

4. I am specifically not including in this periodization more recent "hybridity" and other post-postmodernist discussions (see Werbner and Modood 1997), not because they do not provide insight but because I suspect that much of what is offered will eventually have to recognize that much of this ground has been gone over before. The hybridity focus of up-to-date theory in Britain, for example, has significant antecedents in the U.S. (e.g., Park 1928) that are largely unrecognized in Britain for historical reasons: The multiculturalist debate in Britain (of which hybridity-theorizing is a scholarly and policy by-product) is not easily, or directly, comparable to that which prevails in the U.S.. The real circumstances (or differences between circumstances) of racial/ethnic/nationalist discourse that prevail in different polities are not necessarily overcome by a shared theoretical vocabulary.

5. The emergence of queer studies provides an obvious analogue: The essentialized homosexual gets a structural rendering in gay studies. Later emerges queer politics in which the term of abuse gains cachet in part through the willful appropriation and veneration of the previously derided term.

6. This is not to mention the connotations of sterility that the term bears.

7. My generalizations require qualification. I am referring to the lower Amazon region, the state of Pará. Two years in Santarem in the mid-1970s and annual visits to estuary sites since the late 1980s are the fieldwork referents.

8. This is one, essentialist, version. Da Matta has contextualized this sense of marginal in evocative fashion through reference to the *malandro*, a Brazilian jack-the-lad (lower division) who embodies a contradiction that is key to discussions about national identity. Just as carnival is a site of contradiction (a nation celebrates a segment of culture—Afro-Brazilian—that is, in non-ritual parts of the calendar—i.e., most of the year—denigrated), so is the *malandro*, on one side, dismissed as a ridiculous no-hoper (a guy who in the course of stealing a car radio cuts himself so badly that he collapses next to the car) and, on the other side, venerated as having real spirit. Analogously, the term *caboclo*, which has special resonance in Amazonia, is both socially defective and, by virtue of that extreme position, laudable.

9. The "estuary" refers to the confluence of rivers joining the main course of the Amazon near its mouth, but given the dimensions of the "mouth," this is far from precise. I am specifically referring to the Rio Guama, which joins the Amazon River at Belem.

10. These took the form of seizures, speaking in tongues, assaults on property, violence against those trying to prevent him from hurting himself. His parents were said to have been Indians; he witnessed his mother's murder of his drunken father; he was "taken in" by relatives of island inhabitants and eventually sent to the island as a secondhand *filho de criaçao.*

11. This is not to say that 1970 ushered in an era of economic upturn for Amazonia as a whole, but it did mark the beginning of a period in which some people prospered enormously. That the majority of these were not Amazonians is symptomatic of a new phase of marginality.

12. The major revisionist account lies in the work of Roosevelt (1987, 1989, 1991), which is preceded by the incomplete but benchmark work of Lathrap (1968).

13. See Warren Dean (1987) for a comprehensive discussion.

14. A major feature of the early phase of modernization policies in Amazonia was a colonization program intended to relocate landless northeasterners to land-rich Amazonia. Initially closely linked with the construction of the Transamazonica Highway, the settlement program was ended after a few years, only 6,000 of the projected 100,000 immigrant families having been installed within the official scheme.

15. A number of specialists, including Richard Pace and Deborah Lima, have taken umbrage at the usage, and for good reason: the term unquestionably has a pejorative reading; indeed the dominant connotation is highly negative—as may be "peasant," for that matter. That reading, however, is not exclusive. I have argued (Nugent 1997) that the force of the term is contextually and historically variable: In terms of the former, the term connotes affirmation in a local context, whereas in the national context it indicates something quite different; in terms of the latter, the construction of a positive regional *caboclo* identity through the development of cultural capital—icons, novels, popular music, and so on— suggests that it is not necessary to assume that the official reading will endure.

16. Although this is changing. *"Caboclo"* as a category bearing symbolic capital is an emergent feature of contemporary Amazonia. See, for example, Nugent (1997).

10

The Brazilian Floodplains: Where Cholera Does Not Kill *Caboclos*

Mark Harris

The following scene took place on a passenger boat outside a small town on the River Amazon. My fellow travelers and I were sitting amidst a colorful collection of recently made purchases and awaiting the departure of the boat. They had spent the morning selling fish and agricultural produce, and they then bought household items with the money they had earned. They would try to secure the best price from aggressive market traders, perhaps to get credit from bosses, and they never knew if they would have enough money to buy the goods they needed. It was always a tense time. On this occasion, I was seated next to the owner of the boat, Antonio. We were both eating our lunch. When he had finished, he scooped up some water from the river in a calabash dish to wash down his food. I stared in surprise. He saw me observing him and, as if reading my thoughts, told me "cholera does not kill *caboclos*, only upper class people" *(colera não mata o caboclo, so mata a gente fina)*. I was left speechless and unsure how to interpret this bold statement. He had referred to himself as a *caboclo*, a term that is normally highly pejorative (see below; see also Nugent in this volume).[1] I asked him to explain what he meant. He told me that rich people, *os ricos* or *a gente fina*, are physically too weak to fight cholera because they do not drink water from the river; they do not know how to work: This was why they made such a fuss. Instead, they drink filtered or bottled water and eat fish caught, or food processed by, other people. "We, on the other hand," he concluded, "are strong not just because we drink river water but because we produce the food we eat and give generously to our fellow people. Nature helps us to be healthy."

This scene took place in 1992, when there were many cases of cholera around the ports and harbors of various riverine towns in the Brazilian Amazon. The fear of an epidemic prompted municipal authorities to set up a monitoring service and to advise people to boil their drinking water, since they drew it from the river. Despite this advice, Antonio, along with his neighbors and kin, self-consciously constructed an alternative epidemiology of cholera. From this perspective, cholera could not affect *caboclos* because the river literally sustained their lives with food and water. Urban bosses—factory owners, small- and large-scale traders, and politicians, people who had economic and political control over the mechanisms of exchange—had no acquired or natural defenses against such diseases because they did not work with the river.

In this case, an apparent crisis was used to positive effect by people like Antonio to differentiate themselves—peasants—from bosses. People who lived like Antonio were able to avoid infection. Their strength and health derived from the ongoing performance of practices such as drinking untreated water and working as their own boss. This episode, I argue, involves a self-conscious commitment to an oppositional identity.

In order to unravel some of the cultural meanings that lie behind Antonio's comments, and to understand this process of reverse affirmation, I describe the peasants' life on the Amazon floodplain and, in particular, their relations with urban elites. I consider how the peasants' way of life influences the nature of their interaction with bosses. I consider two specific examples: One concerns the exchange of goods for votes at election times and the other, the marketing of fish. The first operates at the level of the community and the second at the level of the individual, as fish are sold to traders in town, who sell on again to consumers. In both cases, peasants are apparently exploited for the gain of the trader or political candidate; but in both cases, peasants also consider that they have made a good bargain. In elections, peasants acquire goods from politicians in exchange for the votes that may secure office. In the market, peasants construct an image of themselves as free, autonomous producers. It is therefore difficult to delineate unambiguously dependency and inequality in such contexts. And so it is with the affirmative identity expressed in the kind of statement made by Antonio. The experience and knowledge among floodplain peasants of their marginal position can also lead to an expression of indifference towards any life outside the present. In fact, Amazonian floodplain peasants combine opposition and indifference in their relationships with bosses and, living in the short term and far away from the centers of power, attempt to avoid or at least limit domination through an anarchic social life.

The Ethnographic Context

Mestiço Amazonians living in riverine areas are often known pejoratively as *caboclos* by local urban elites. When the term is used in the region of Óbidos, it carries connotations of rustic living, laziness, social backwardness, deviousness, and ignorance. Historically the meaning of the term has changed (Lima 1992), and currently it refers to deculturated Amerindians, persons of mixed ancestry, or anybody who lives in rural Brazilian Amazonia (see M. Harris 1998a). The

198   Mark Harris

ethnographic material in English on these people is relatively sparse (see, for example, Wagley [1953] 1976; Lima 1992; Nugent 1993; M. Harris 1996).

Nugent (1993 and Chapter 9 of this volume) uses the phrase "modern or historical peasantries of Amazonia" in an attempt to revise anthropological approaches to the area. The peasantries of the Brazilian Amazon are "reconstituted societies,"[2] a new social formation forged in the interstices of colonial forms of production and organization. By the end of the eighteenth century, aboriginal societies in the lower Amazon had been decimated by disease and slave raids (Sweet 1974; R. L. Anderson 1976; Hemming 1978). A process of miscegenation—actively encouraged by the Portuguese crown (MacLachlan 1973)—African slave imports, and European migration led to the development of a heterogeneous society organized around an export economy, which some authors have claimed is well adapted to the Amazonian environment (e.g., Moran 1974). Historically, the riverine peasantries have been denied the security of land tenure and have been indebted to bosses for most of their lives. At the same time they have accommodated to the unpredictability of the world market, changing their economic orientation in accordance with external demands. These peasantries have followed artisanal methods of production, involving the sale of petty commodities for national and international markets (Nugent 1993; McGrath et al. 1993) and the domestic organization of labor (Lima 1992; M. Harris 1996). They are mostly Catholics (although the numbers of Protestants are slowly increasing in rural areas) and have a tradition of curing with the use of shamanic methods (pajelança), a legacy of their Amerindian past (Galvão 1952).

Nugent (Chapter 9 of this volume) and Slater (1994) emphasize the fluidity and flexibility of Amazonian "identities"; both mention the absence of an integral cultural identity. Despite the lack of a strongly articulated identity, there are nevertheless some Amazonian cultural representations that could be said to be distinct to the riverine peasantry. In this context, Slater's (1994) analysis is particularly helpful. It concerns peasant narratives about the freshwater rose-colored dolphin of the Amazon waterways. These stories tell of the dolphin that can transform itself into a human at will and that lives in an enchanted city of riches at the bottom of the river, where there are washing machines and waiters to serve food. Appearing on land as a typical colonial figure in a white suit, white hat, and black shoes, the dolphin is able to seduce anybody. It can also carry people to the underwater city of unlimited wealth and luxury. Slater argues that the two key elements of these narratives concern enchantment and transformation: The "dolphin stories are concerned far less with setting, than with invalidating, limits" (1994:254) and are thus more about "anarchy" and resistance to control and definition than the creation of an alternative order. According to Slater, these stories have more recently become not only a defiant commentary on "the progressive destruction of the rain forest, . . . an assault on the Dolphin's millennial habitat, but also a way of life that, despite its very real inequities and hardships, displays a coherent and distinctive quality that often impels people to affirm it in the face of onslaughts from without" (1994:215). This chapter attempts to give further ethnographic content to such claims from the realm of everyday life.

An Orientation to the Present in an Amazonian Floodplain Village

The ethnographic focus of this chapter is on the people who live in the small floodplain village of Parú, roughly half a day's journey from Óbidos, a town on the main trunk of the middle lower Amazon, in the state of Pará. They number about 800 and live in one long line of houses, clustered in networks of kinspeople along a thirty kilometer stretch of the river, cut off at either end by tributaries to the Amazon. Currently, they make a living from seasonal economic activities, ranging from agriculture to livestock raising and hunting; the sale of fish dominates their artisanal peasant economy and society. In Parú, agricultural produce—including bitter and sweet manioc, maize, squash, beans and melons—is cultivated mainly for local consumption.

Parú is a village made up of two communities organized around Catholic chapels. Its residents are called Parúaros, a term that expresses a geographical association rather than an ethnic identity. The village is not a homogenous entity, since there is a degree of economic and political differentiation deriving from the ownership of materials, access to the labor of kin, and different family histories. Nevertheless, all 800 people are related through affine, consanguine, or fictive ties, and it is only through these kin ties that people gain access to land and water. Through generally recognized kin links, individuals have usufruct rights to natural resources. As long as the land or water is in use, no other community can lay claim to it; outsiders with no affine links simply have no right of access or use. There is a sense of collective inalienable stewardship or ownership of areas, associated with residential proximity and continued use, the bounds of which are generally agreed upon by neighboring communities.[3]

Marriage to locals in the area allows Parúaros to remain owners/stewards of their communal areas and limits the extent to which outsiders are admitted into the community. About 70 percent of marriages are between people with previous links: geographical (neighbors), affinel (where a sibling has married into the same family), or consanguine (cousin marriage).[4] Despite internal differentiation, it is commonly remarked that "we are all kin here" or "only kin live here." Such phrases suggest an ideology of mutuality and equality among residents, and very real attempts are made to achieve this in practice through various leveling mechanisms that ensure approximate equity in access to resources—for example, choice of spouse, and selection of godparents from within rather than outside of the coresidential group (M. Harris 1996). Although each family and individual experiences dependence, patronage, and exploitation slightly differently, there is a strong tendency to create egalitarian relations around a social group, defined exclusively in terms of who is around at a particular moment in time. Kinship is therefore based in relations of coresidence (see Gow 1991); and affines, adopted children, and distant genealogical kin are easily incorporated into an active network of *parentes* (kin). People with whom there is no contact, such as the dead and those who have moved away permanently, are excluded from the definition of kin.[5]

This orientation to the present characterizes relationships in the dramatic physical environment as well as with kin. The middle reaches of the Amazon River (from Parintins to Santarém) are estimated to have a floodplain forty kilometers across. Between the wet and dry seasons, the height of the river varies from about six to ten meters. As the landmass is immense and flat, the whole area is more or less covered every flood; from one year to the next, people do not know what will be land or water, since erosion and sedimentation occur every flood. In addition, that which is land, lake, and river in the dry season becomes in the wet season one vast mass of water, with houses acting as little islands and the forest half-drowned by the muddy waters. The landscape is in a constant process of redefinition and becoming; there are no fixed boundaries to demarcate discrete pieces of land, forest, house, garden, lake, and stream. In the local perception of landscape, land and water are inseparable; as one person told me, "this river is our land."

Those people who live on the floodplain are continually observing changes in the environment and adjusting their own practices to take advantage of new possibilities. The environment is seen to provide abundant resources, with a range of foods available at different times in the year and affording various delicacies. It is common for people to gorge themselves on whatever fruit or fish is in season. I have argued elsewhere that seasonal change cannot, therefore, be understood as part of a framework of fixed environmental constraints but, to the contrary, is constituted by the movements of people and the rhythmic structure of their social activities (Harris 1998b). Changes in the environment are part of people's activity; people attend continually to the rise and fall of the river, fish migrations, animal movements, soil hardening, plant growth and decay, the winds, rains, and so forth, and they reorganize their own movements in accordance with the fluctuations of the environment.

Lima and de Castro (1996) have used the phrase "privileging of the present" to refer to workings of social memory in a floodplain village in the upper Amazon. These authors demonstrated that on the floodplain there was a remarkable lack of interest in the past, which they related to the changing landscape and the impossibility of encoding memory in stable forms. This is also true of Parú. I would add that little interest is shown in the future because of the impossibility of prediction—no one knows how high or low the flood will be, or how the flood will affect the land. One deals with the present; as I was frequently told, "life is always beginning on the floodplain," or "we live from one harvest to the next."

A continuing concern among villagers with the here and now of their existence—to the exclusion of past and future—is a technique for living in the world that centers on performance: They are, from their own point of view, what they do (Ingold 1993; see also the Introduction to this volume). From this perspective,

villagers are expressing a nonessential identity, one that emerges from the particular character of their relations with each other and the environment. The val-
orization of this way of life persists in the face of outsider prejudice and ridicule
during interactions with powerful outsiders. In this context, villagers affirm their
commitment to the floodplain. Indeed, the present orientation gives peasants the
freedom to be indifferent to change and the formal domination of urban elites.

Political Uses of Living in the Present

In order to assess the political implications of this way of life, further background
on the local economy is needed. Floodplain peasants recognize how much of
their life is determined by forces beyond their immediate environment. Nonetheless, their lives are oriented to the present; floodplain freedom is positively af-
firmed through the severance of relations with bosses. This contradiction forms
the subject of the present chapter. I will discuss two examples: the avoidance of
wage labor and the rejection of class alliances through godparenthood.

Bosses, Traders, and Political Economy

Urban elites are made up of various traders, retailers, politicians, professionals,
and factory owners who are synonymous with the *gente fina*. Bosses exercise control over the flow of money and goods and over exchange. Most belong to a small
number of large families who control most of the important municipal political
offices and own the largest economic institutions in the town, such as retail out-
lets and Brazil nut, jute, and fish processing factories. Some of these families migrated from North Africa (Morocco and Egypt) and Italy at the turn of the century and eventually settled in Óbidos; others claim longer associations in the
area. During the course of this century, these families have built up their enterprises, buying rural produce such as jute, cocoa, and fish and then selling it on to
other firms in larger Amazonian towns. Essentially, bosses have made their
money from trading[6] and used it to gain and maintain political office.

There is a group of traders, however, that is too small-scale to have the resources to seek political office, although they are still a type of boss because they
extend credit and control access to key resources such as fishing equipment.
These people are known as *marreteiros* (middle men, *marreteiras*, women) and
are numerous. They buy items such as fish and agricultural produce on a daily
basis from producers and sell them to local consumers. A few traders have shops
but most set up temporary stalls on the riverfront each day. Most of the fish consumed locally are sold in a specially built market area, where the traders described below operate.

Merchant capital has provided the material context for the development of the
region (Nugent 1993) and linked it to the rest of the world through trade in
Amazonian products. In the absence of any significant and generalized form of

capital, merchant capital and its relations still characterize much of the context of contemporary peasant economy and society. Within this mercantile system, the riverine peasantry has historically been relatively free to organize its own production and labor (Nugent 1993). It is within this space that the way of life, characterized by an orientation to the present, has flourished. At the same time, the reproduction of this life in the floodplain villages is linked to factors that cannot be controlled locally. The sequence of relations includes rural producers, itinerant traders (regatão, see McGrath 1989), large-scale export firms, and businesses such as restaurants in Europe or the United States. Since producers are dependent on bosses for goods, credit, and patronage, they often have little choice but to accept poor terms of exchange. Elites have little interest in owning and developing the means of production but every interest in maintaining political and economic control of the means of exchange and distribution.[7] Long-term debt relationships and exploitation (exploração), derived from the prices attached to commodities, characterize rural experience of the "outside system." Indeed, Parúaros say that exploitation occurs at the point of exchange—the price of whatever they want to sell goes down, whereas the price of what they want to buy goes up.

The survival of the floodplain peasantry depends on just getting on with things. It is their indifferent accommodation to the outside world, combined with their own interest in the present, that have allowed them to reproduce reasonably successfully this century. Though their lives are characterized by struggle and poverty, they have been able to respond to changes in the demands for Amazonian products and to maintain themselves in the absence of a dominant export commodity by falling back on a diverse productive base.

Confirming Freedom (1): Opposition to Wage Labor and Living in Town

For Parúaros there is a clear connection between living on the floodplain, residing with kinspeople, being one's own boss, and owning the products of work. A key aspect of the separation that I have described is the reluctance of Parúaros to sell their labor. Parúaros are unequivocal that they should remain the owners (os donos, masters or mistresses) of their own ability to work (força de trabalho). According to Parúaros, when you are employed (empregado) by a boss (um patrão or um chefe), you lose a vital part of your freedom and never gain just rewards in return. You cannot come and go as you please, or stop to talk and think, or just lie in a hammock if you feel like it.[8] You have to obey and take orders from another man, since it is he who owns the capacity of the paid employee to work. The floodplain peasant values personal autonomy. Work is seen as a creative force applied in daily life that involves producing something new. If the person is no longer in control of its application, as in wage labor, then s/he no longer has proper agency in the world. Those people who only sell or trade products are deemed not to work, since there is no production. Agriculture is said to be the hardest kind of work.

Permanent wage labor and living in the city are considered to be the worst of all possible outcomes. When I asked one man if he had ever been employed, he told me, "No, I have never had to beg for a job, no, my time has not yet arrived, and I am still my own boss and rule what I do each day." Others who associate wage labor with slavery put this even more strongly. As we walked past the Brazil nut and jute factories in Óbidos, one of my closest companions explained to me, "In those places, people are like slaves, employed as though we still had slavery."[9] All factory work is seasonal, and most of the workers live in poor neighborhoods. They lack the riverine resources and kin networks that could keep them out of the factories.

I employ the categories of rural and urban rhetorically, in keeping with the way people talk in the lower Amazon. In practice, there is much movement between these settings, making their boundaries quite fluid. Individuals from rural areas go to school or find temporary work in towns, and there is some permanent migration by families to the town, though very little from Parú. In contrast to the affirmation of floodplain life that I describe, these migrants identified their rural lives as a time of suffering. They saw themselves stepping towards modernity and moving away from a "country-bumpkin" tradition based on oppressive kinship ties. Individual men and women commonly work outside their communities at particular points in the life cycle—after they have learned many of the skills necessary to live in the community, from fishing to preparing food, hunting, looking after children, and knowing how to plant and reap crops. Women tend to leave around the age of twelve, once they have completed the primary school education available in the community school. Men leave around the age of seventeen. A survey of 204 adults (100 men and 104 women) that I conducted showed that 118 (58 percent) had worked outside the community before they had their own house and family, for periods ranging between three months and two years.[10] Once they had married, there would have been significant pressure not to leave. Men engage in factory work (bottling firms, jute processing, food processing), construction work, security patrol, cooking on passenger and trade boats, gardening, loading cattle onto boats and butchering them, painting—basically any form of manual labor that is paid by the day or for each job completed. For women, there are few options. Women tend to work as maids and, if their bosses are willing, they will attend secondary school at the same time.

People said that they worked outside the community to gain experience of the world, to meet new people, and to expand their personal knowledge. The word used to refer to this process is *passear*, literally, to walk or wander around. There is much excitement surrounding this period; it is remembered in positive terms and becomes a source of lively stories. One man told me that he had really enjoyed his *passeio* (literally "trip"); he had seen many interesting things and had come back to Parú quite satisfied. He stated this after telling me he had worked for eight months in a bottling factory in Parintins and for three months in a jute factory in Manaus.

Nobody told me that the primary aim of going away was to make money. Few people, if any, send remittances back to kin while they are away, and no one claims to save any money. Instead money is spent as soon as it is earned—on food, drink, clothes, and sometimes on items such as watches, radios, and tape recorders. Most electronic goods in people's houses are brought back by these young travelers at the end of their *passeio* in Manaus, a free trade zone where many Japanese companies are situated. The items are normally for their personal use.

It was harder for women to make these trips. As the figures show, fewer women make the *passeio* than men, though they still go to see the world. Conditions of work as a maid are not always very attractive. I was told horror stories about men who had demanded sex on a regular basis in the household where the women were employed. The women had to find somewhere else to work or come home. Some of the women were paid nothing for their labor (justified with the argument that they were provided with board and lodging). In contrast to men, some women choose to improve their education by going to secondary school, which explains why the two schoolteachers in Parú were both women.[11] In the sample, 28 percent of women attended secondary school while working as domestics in Óbidos, Oriximiná, or Manaus.

This process of schooling can be seen as the equivalent of men gaining experience of the world. At no point in their lives do men express an interest in secondary school. Mobility, particularly of the upward nature, is more likely for women than men, and education is an important factor in enabling women to marry outside the natal community.

Young people do not come back because they have failed to make money, because this was never the intention. On the contrary, the majority of people leave the community to gain access to experience, commodities, and people whom they would not otherwise meet. They do not consider themselves forced to enter a labor market at a disadvantage.[12] If they were to seek such experience at a later stage in their lives, the political and economic dependency associated with wage labor would be more difficult to endure because adults with their own houses and children are supposed to be autonomous productive beings (see Pine, Chapter 2 of this volume).

There is very little permanent migration of people with established houses and plots of land. I am aware of one family who left in the recent past because one of their children drowned in the flood, and they decided that they did not want to risk the same happening with other children. They subsequently moved to another riverine community, situated on higher land, where they had kin (though they did not have floodplain). Another family left the community because they converted to Seventh Day Adventism and decided it was better to be near other believers. Some individuals as well as families leave the community permanently. They do so first as part of the life cycle, and later they find a spouse in the town or another community nearby. Migration is rarely caused by poverty and lack of resources.

Parúaros return not because they find no opportunities in the towns but because they prefer their own way of life. They talk as we would expect adolescents to talk about their forays into the wider world. They are not adopting strategies to sever links with their floodplain way of life. The movement across the boundaries of types of work and places of residence only serves to reinforce their separation because there are different ways of acting and behaving in each domain. At the same time, the adolescent brings back his or her experiences to enrich life at home, re-domesticating the vitality of the outside world.

Confirming Freedom(2): No Bosses as Godparents

The popular academic representation of godparenthood in Latin America is of "an association that is more political than religious" (Descola 1996:11). The emphasis is on the protection and support sought from a higher status individual by one willing to provide various services in exchange. At the same time, as many studies have shown, godparenthood varies dramatically across Latin America and has a number of constituent parts, which are elaborated or suppressed in different contexts (see, for example, Mintz and Wolf 1968; Gudeman 1971).[13]

Parúaros choose godparents for their children from within the coresidential peer group. Very few people have godparents from a different social class. This choice has political implications, and I suggest that it is linked to the desire to be separate from potential patrons and to create an autonomous sociality.[14] In Parú, godparenthood is limited to baptism and involves a triangular set of relations between the coparents, the godchild, and its parents. Sexual interaction and gossip are prohibited between godparents and godchildren, and indeed one person stated that the same rules of behavior should be observed as between parents and children in general, since the relations are "the same thing as those between parents and children."[15] Respect is central to the relationship, involving the use of formal terms of address between coparents and requests for blessing of godchildren from their godparents. The effect of godparenthood is to transform horizontal ties of kinship, affinity, or neighborly association into formal friendship, creating ties of equality, trust, and respect. In this way, the relations of equality that are implicit in all coresidential ties are emphasized.

Parents normally choose godparents from their childhood friends, regular work partners, or neighbors (these relations often overlap). It was repeatedly stressed that coparents have to get on and like each other for the relationship to work. The most enduring tie is ideally between same-sex coparents *(comadres* or *compadres)*. Each person could have a number of *comadre* or *compadre* relations, which offer networks for work partners, for food distribution, and for sources of information. People avoid godparent ties with rich people because they have little confidence in them. One man said to me, "No one wants a rich person as friend; they always turn against you." Some people said the rich only exploit the poor and never give anything back. One woman told the story of Elinaldo to reinforce her point that bosses had no interest in poor people.

Elinaldo was to be baptized when he was three years old. His father had died, and his mother could not choose a godfather. It had come to the hour of the baptism, and still no one had been found, and so Elinaldo's grandmother persuaded a large cattle owner, who for some reason was present, to be the child's godfather. Following the baptism, the child had virtually no contact with the man: "Why Elinaldo never even asks for blessing from his godfather when he sees him in the street. . . . Although anyone can be a godparent, it is best to choose from people whom you respect and trust, that way they can help you more."

By rejecting elite godparents, Parúaros create a social distance from their bosses. In addition, the value attached to the egalitarian potential of coresidential relations inverts what are seen to be conventional inequalities between patrons and clients that imbue ritual kinship relations with hierarchy.

The Limits of Freedom

Despite the attitude to hierarchy and to bosses that I have described, it is impossible to exclude powerful outsiders all the time. There are occasions when it is to the advantage of Parúaros to engage with and play up the hierarchical nature of relationships. One of the most important examples is the barter for goods at times of political elections.

Bartering for Goods at Election Times

In Óbidos, it is common to offer gifts in return for votes.[16] These gifts range from electricity generators, with a continuous supply of diesel, to satellite dishes for televisions, health posts, schools, hammocks, and T-shirts, all provided with "campaign" money. The patron-client ties sought by politicians are competitive, since their future rests on successful persuasion through "bribes" against opponents. Alliances often depend on a series of negotiations that span a number of elections, and electors tend to be more successful in bartering for goods when they are more crucial to the results.

The politician calculates his support in terms of the percentage of his vote in the municipality. In some cases, a whole area can be persuaded to vote for a single man (there are very few women politicians in the lower Amazon), if a large gift has been made, such as a school or a health post. The density of kin ties makes it conceivable that everybody will vote in similar manner because the senior men involved in negotiations persuade their kin to vote in a particular way. This is how politicians win municipal elections and how rural communities get their basic amenities.

In this context, it is unclear who is dependent on whom or who has the better bargain. It cannot be said that Parúaros are simply being bought out or reinforcing their inferiority and political marginality. Such claims could be made only if politics were understood in terms of formal office-holding and long-term plans. What emerged repeatedly in these data are the different interests of the peasants. Clearly, they have different political goals, as well as different political conceptions, even if populism tries to hide the differences. And Parúaros, among others, are aware of this. They know that political candidates have no real interest in peasants' lives but only in holding office. Parúaros, on the other hand, have no interest in anything other than short-term goals that are suited to the exchange of votes for goods. According to Parúaros, the rich have, so they should give to those poor people who have not. The poor people also say that the votes cast are useless anyway in a corrupt political system that only benefits the rich. Why not get something for nothing? From the point of view of Parúaros and others like them, politics provides for their material reproduction. Nevertheless this particular orientation means that they are unlikely to vote for a party that might serve their long-term rather than short-term interests. Indeed, the low standing of the nationally organized Workers' Party (PT) in rural Amazonia can be explained through the analysis I have offered, since the PT refuses to bribe the villagers (they also do not have the resources), even though they claim to be genuinely committed to the welfare of peasants and workers.

The Marketing of Fish

Traditionally, rural producers have not marketed their own produce directly to consumers. Instead, they sell to middlemen who, in turn, retail to townspeople or transport goods for sale elsewhere.[17] I concentrate on fish because this is the principal item that Parúaros sell, but they also sell cattle, agricultural produce, and game. Nowadays, there is a movement by the fisherpeople's union to encourage people to sell their own fish. Interestingly, this has been resisted by both the traders and the producers. The former would obviously lose their jobs, and the latter are unwilling because it would mean more time spent working. Consumers prefer to buy their food from traders because they think that they are more likely to receive good-quality produce. Rich town-dwellers claim that the only time fisherpeople want to sell their produce is when it is off, when it has been out of water and in the sun too long, so that no trader would buy it.[18]

Fish are sold fresh, salted, or on ice. Fresh fish have been caught the night before and transported on a passenger boat. Normally, larger fish—such as tambaqui or pirarucu—are sold fresh. Salted fish has a longer life and is rarely sold for local consumption. It is mostly sold to the salted fish export company, which consists of a small wooden shack and a large drying area. More and more commonly, fish are caught and stored on ice in a polystyrene box for a few days. This gives more flexibility to the producer, who can control when he markets the fish. In a few cases in Parú, there are specially equipped boats *(geleiras)* with a capacity of four to eight tons and with ice for storage. On these boats a crew of about eight young men work in pairs catching fish; normally, they are related to the owner as either son or nephew. Their catches are often sold to the fish exporting factories, which also sell ice and process the fish.

There is no single strategy for the marketing of fish since the place and manner depends on the season and the type of fish. As described at the beginning of the chapter, people get up in the middle of the night to make the journey downstream to Óbidos and arrive early. Fish can be sold by men or women. As any boat from the interior approaches Óbidos, fish traders will group together and wait for it to dock. These traders descend aggressively upon the boat, anxious to see what is available. A scene of confusion erupts as soon as the boat arrives. There is much heckling over the price, size, and quality of the fish. Prices go up and down depending on market availability, demand, and inflation (which during the time I was conducting fieldwork ran at over 20 percent a month), and the seller of fish rarely has any idea how to compare the price being offered to any other (compare to Astuti, Chapter 4 in this volume, where much is made of individual skill in getting the best price).

There is a good deal of distrust on both sides. Often the first traders to board the boat are the ones who offer the lowest prices, in the knowledge that the new arrivals will not know about higher prices available. Furthermore, they know that the producers want to sell as quickly as possible in order to have money to buy other things. Thus, the knowledge of fisherpeople is confirmed; they see once more that traders are only interested in exploiting poor people. Some fisherpeople will refuse to sell until they get the right deal, but they may be intimidated. In order to obtain a quick sale, they may accede to claims from a trader that prices are low everywhere, that he wants to do his "friend" a favor even though he could buy the same fish more cheaply elsewhere, that the size and quality of the fish are poor. The outcome depends on how quickly the producer wants to get away and how much pressure the trader can exert, as well as on the experience of previous interactions.

It is pertinent to note that the producers believe the mark up price to be 100 percent, meaning that traders get the same amount of money for carrying the fish to their market stall and then selling it as the fisherpeople get for catching the fish and bringing them to market. In reality, the mark up is about 20 percent. The mistaken and exaggerated view of the profit made illustrates how much Parúaros suspect outsiders and, in particular, those who do not work. I put the discrepancy to Parúaros. They replied that I must have been told lies.[19]

The point of selling fish is to raise money to buy important household items, such as cooking oil, salt, sugar, soap, kerosene, and toiletries. These goods are for household consumption. If there is any money left over, it might be used to buy alcohol, clothes, or for the upkeep of fishing or agricultural materials. Very rarely do people actually return with money in their pockets. Saving is therefore a virtually unknown practice. Money is spent as soon as it comes in. People are constantly catching fish in order to come to town to sell their catch and buy daily necessities. This perpetual cycle both confirms and limits their freedom as autonomous producers and consumers who are also dependent and indifferent retailers of their goods.

Conclusion

To conclude, let me return to Antonio's phrase, "cholera does not kill *caboclos*, only upper class people." This bold statement opposes the power of bosses in the everyday lives of floodplain dwellers in Parú. It also distances Parúaros from people with a different way of life. The fact that Antonio reclaims the word *caboclo* and imbues it with a positive significance indicates the importance of this oppositional stance. I have provided some ethnographic context for this position, including material on the unrestricted access to floodplain resources, the organization of subsistence through kinspeople, the avoidance of wage labor, and the rejection of patronage through godparenthood.

I have also portrayed another aspect of this position, which somewhat belies the provocative nature of the phrase, "cholera does not kill *caboclos*." Parúaros are inextricably linked to the regional economic and social system in which they are marginalized and stigmatized. They seek to connect with other parts of this system on their own terms. When they exchange votes for gifts, they appear to get what they want but only at the expense of potential affiliation with other people in similar positions elsewhere in the region. This has led to a form of atomism, where they are mostly concerned with their own local matters. Similarly, the marketing of fish appears to promote their own interests in providing money for everyday needs, but it also reveals the limitations of their freedom as producers, since they cannot enter into exchange relations equally or fairly.

On the other hand, an indifference to, and a positive refusal to entangle themselves in, the outside world afford Parúaros an autonomy not possible for marginal urban proletarians. The "identity" they have as producers who are free to organize their forms and relations of production cannot be separated from the nature of their interaction with bosses. In a sense, what I have identified is a way of life that amounts to "getting on with things in the present," a kind of anarchic mode, that paradoxically gives continuity to their existence. If they were unable to reproduce successfully, the floodplain areas would have been taken over by an agrarian elite of cattle owners and large-scale fishing interests and a small number of waged laborers, displacing the peasantry, as is happening elsewhere in the Amazon (see McGrath et al. 1993). It is the awareness of this possibility that makes what I have described among Parúaros an ideological commitment rather than simply a survival technique. Following Slater's analysis of the dolphin stories as a form of resistance (1994), I am arguing that politics from the peasant perspective in the lower Amazon can be understood as an undertaking, by means of an anarchic sociality oriented towards the present, to avoid control and domination rather than to create an alternative order.

Notes

1. However, since the term is used by some people to describe themselves, we follow the conventions used throughout this volume and write *caboclo*(s).

2. Mintz first applied this term to the Caribbean (Mintz 1974), but it is equally appropriate in the current context.

The fieldwork on which this article is based was carried out during 1992 and 1994 and funded by the Economic and Social Research Council. I am grateful to the British Academy for awarding me a postdoctoral fellowship, which has allowed me to think and write around some of the issues examined here. I am also grateful to my audience at Queen's University of Belfast where an earlier version of this paper was delivered. I wish to thank the editors of this volume for their excellent guidance and suggestions, and Keith Hart, Stephen Nugent, Rita Astuti, and Harvey Whitehouse for their comments.

3. This traditional system of ownership has been challenged recently with the development of large-scale fishing and the invasion of outsiders into these communal areas (see McGrath et al. 1993).

4. Cousin marriage is relatively high—22 percent of marriages in a total of ninety-three unions were between first, second, and third degree cousins.

5. This situation is similar to the Vezo (Astuti, Chapter 4 of this volume and 1995a).

6. Another source of money is an important part of the local economy—cattle ranching. Most people in rural areas have a few head of cattle. These are sometimes overshadowed by the huge ranches of town bosses, who can have many hundreds of cattle on one farm (and they may have many farms). Large-scale cattle ranching is a big threat to peasant communities—it is land extensive and the cattle regularly invade people's gardens and eat the produce.

7. See Gudeman and Rivera (1991) for a theoretical examination of a Latin American economy relevant to my account.

8. The actual phrase used is *ficar sua propria vontade*, which literally means to stay at your own will, or to do as you wish.

9. Slavery was abolished legally in Brazil only in 1889. When I lived in the region, there was much work by unions and the Catholic Church locally against other forms of "slavery," such as debt peonage or patron-client relations. In other words, the discourse of slavery, including tales of torture, is a contemporary concern.

10. These figures do not include people who have only visited kin or friends in towns, but they do include those who have worked for money or goods or gone to school elsewhere.

11. Only the first three years of primary school are available in the two schools in Parú.

12. A large proportion (42 percent) of people does not leave to find work elsewhere. This can be explained with reference to personal preference, parental pressure to remain and work around the house, and responsibility to a spouse and children (i.e., a man may have made a woman pregnant).

13. Gudeman's observations west of Panama city among Spanish speaking peasants are applicable to Parú. He shows that godparenthood and family relationships are "in a relation of complementary opposition; one is concerned primarily with intra-household ties, the other pertains to inter-household links. Families are divided into households; the *compadrazgo* unites these units" (1971:60).

14. Charles Wagley wrote in 1953 that godparenthood in Itá extended links between different kindred. Itá is a small riverside town near the mouth of the River Amazon, not dissimilar to Óbidos, where the kinship circle is quite small. Mainly, he writes, "the *compadrio* system provides a means of cementing relationships between the various social strata of Itá society" ([1953] 1976:157). He claims that people also choose others of the same class and kin circle as godparents for their children and concludes, "between members of the same class, it is a reciprocal relationship of mutual aid; between members of

separate social classes it provides a bridge reinforcing their economic and social relationship by a personal bond validated by the Church and tradition" (1976:159); that is, their marginality is in part reproduced by their unequal commitment to a *compadre* or *comadre*, coparent.

15. There are no marriage restrictions between their kin.

16. This practice is apparently widespread in Latin America, although the anthropological literature is strangely silent about it.

17. See McGrath (1989) for an excellent account of trading in Amazonia.

18. It is not uncommon for producers to sabotage their goods in some way. A jute factory owner told me that numerous bundles of jute in every harvest contain stones and pieces of wood to make them weigh more. Similarly, cocoa pods have been painted in order to appear ripe to buyers. These actions are very much in line with Scott's (1985) analysis.

19. I knew this was not the case because I was able to compare the producer's sale price per kilogram to that of the trader.

11

A Doctor by a Canal:
A Presentation of a Person,
from Nasser to Foucault

Fanny Colonna

In what follows, I set the scene for a dialogue I recorded with an Egyptian village doctor in 1996. I have known Nisseem for many years and had planned to include his testimony in the framework of a research project—not yet complete—on university graduates living in the provinces. The individuals encountered are extremely diverse; they do not all belong to the category of professionals (engineers, doctors, architects)—far from it—nor are they only graduates of the "modern" educational system (i.e., universities conceived along Western lines); there are, among several dozen others, Christian monks and Muslim clerics educated at institutes of theology.[1]

The aim was not to define types, like "the Egyptian peasant," nor to show off a few icons or stars of culture, politics, or saintliness—high-profile figures who are plentiful in Egypt and who regularly appear on the back pages of the national press. In a study that does not purport to be a sample, and that relies on no quotas, their number represents nothing more than the vague contours of a protean "provincial middle class," with diverse beliefs and worldviews.

In the (very recent) interest in the "lives of ordinary people" in the Middle East and North Africa (Burke 1993), the middle classes have not received the same attention as, for example, peasants or women, for obvious reasons: The social sciences traditionally lend themselves more to the study of those whom we have grown accustomed to describing with the unfortunate label of "dominated." And as for the middle classes, unless they were fortunate enough to be Islamists (Kepel 1985), or the bearers of some universalist discourse (Roussillon 1992), they have hardly been represented in their everyday or commonplace character—as intellectuals or the educated (*al-muthaqqafin*, as they are known in Egypt): neither when seen as collective actors nor, before that, as a "futile conscience." So thorough is this lack of representation that the only available ethnography on the subject—admittedly of very high quality—is the contemporary Egyptian novel.[2]

The project to which the conversation with Nisseem belongs strives therefore to fill this gap by "taking intellectuals seriously"—as the Egyptian anthropologist Reem Saad has said—without elitism or aestheticism, and especially without the contempt accorded them by their Western counterparts (or by Arab, Iranian, or Turkish intellectuals living in the West), to the effect that they are incompetent, corrupt, and isolated in a host of ways from their own societies.

The implementation of such a research project necessitated a modified approach, mainly because of the difficulties inherent in an undertaking where, in theory, the researchers and their subjects are interchangeable, though in practice they are separated by belonging to incommensurable historical, political, and social contexts. This relationship of ethnographer and subject led me to try in Egypt a procedure that has seemingly yielded refreshing results elsewhere and that consists in reproducing as faithfully as possible the product of an interaction between the two in a manner fairly close to journalism (Marcus 1993).

For my part, I added to this procedure a more systematic and extensive use of photography, borrowing from a recent documentary trend in France (La Tour 1996). In the course of the project, this use of photography assumed an increasingly important place, parallel to that of the "words" of the conversation. Its use clearly reveals that the photograph constitutes an excellent alternative to an objectivizing commentary on details (Piette 1996)—material ones especially, objects but also gestures—that the analysis either renders insignificant and invisible or that lend themselves to reductionist approaches.

The conversation took place at the outset of my second extended stay in Egypt (1996–1997)—the first was in 1983–1984. During this interval of almost fifteen years, important events and changes, some more visible than others, had a profound impact on the lives of Egyptians and on the appearance of the cities and the countryside alike. Moreover, this time, a new interest in the provinces made me sensitive to things that had totally escaped my first, somewhat kaleidoscopic, impression.

At Cairo airport I noticed the exchange rate had plunged disastrously; monetary relations, however small, between Egyptians and foreigners were far more tense. The city had changed dramatically, gaining in parts a sort of Californian look. Phones had proliferated, and worked. The price of everything, except bread, had soared. It was difficult to distinguish foreign from local goods, except by price. With coastal areas prospering from tourism and "new lands" being cultivated in the interior, the country itself appeared to have grown wider. As for the signs of Islamization, these seemed less conspicuous on my first visit, or perhaps I had become accustomed to them, so familiar have they become even in certain parts of Paris or London.

In the early 1980s, millions of young Egyptians worked in Iraq and the Gulf. The money they earned when remitted transformed the appearance of numerous

Delta villages and towns, replacing traditional dwellings of unbaked brick with more permanent structures, and increasing the number of vehicles. In 1990–1991, the Gulf War put a dramatic end to this manna, and floods of migrant workers awaited repatriation. One outcome of this short-term enrichment was the knowledge that there was no other way of making money than in exile. Since 1991 and the implementation of a structural adjustment policy imposed by the IMF, rural poverty has only been aggravated.

In the second half of the 1980s, Egypt experienced significant social unrest, including the mutiny of security forces, repeated strikes by railway and factory workers, widespread peasant revolts, a number of assassinations and assassination attempts against public figures, and, in the last decade, as in many other countries in the region, a wave of "anti-intellectual terrorism." Egypt is still in a "state of emergency."

For all this, compared to the majority of Arab counties, Egypt remains one of the strongest and most viable, and therefore one of the most attractive, countries for the impressive influx both of tourists (some 4 million a year) and of numerous nationals from neighboring African countries.

In the provinces, home to the rural poor—and especially in Upper Egypt where Nisseem, who is originally from the Delta and who was educated in Cairo, has chosen to live—all that I have described is experienced in a far more acute form. It is still a truly peripheral area—it takes a whole night's train journey to reach Luxor, the first important city. With less cultivable land than the Delta region and relatively light industrialization, the recent, decade-old proliferation of tourist activities only partially compensates for the handicaps of Upper Egypt.

The combination of rapidly growing towns, villages still difficult to reach except by boat, large boats and cruise ships that ply the river, luxurious hotels or small insalubrious dives, asphalt roads and dusty tracks makes for a surprising mix, doubtless capable of seducing and even detaining the traveler. It is in one of these difficult to reach villages that Nisseem settled some twenty years ago to practice medicine, a village that was doubtless isolated.

I accosted him on this occasion with the words, "So, you are still here, even though you could be elsewhere. . . . " Laughing, he replied, "Actually, could I really be elsewhere? . . . " as though his presence in the village unfolded in a kind of (almost) continuous present, without beginning or end. In a world of turmoil, he alone remains unchanged (we shall see that this is not the case and that the village has changed him, though not his determination). One of Nisseem's main preoccupations is the problem of change; it is the decline in people's living conditions, especially those of his patients. But in his account chronological references are rare and, where they do appear, were always prompted by me (I still do not know, except by deduction, exactly when he arrived in the village).

Nisseem is almost fifty but does not look it. He is a pioneer in his "migration to the south," for his generation at least.[3] In fact the image, if not the reality, of the rural doctor existed in Egypt before World War II (Chiffoleau 1995) and is be-

The interview in progress (Fanny Colonna).

coming more common again today, but according to a radically different logic (in those days, to civilize the peasants; in the context of the current crisis, in order to make an easier living). Nisseem's choice is equally remote from both of these.

Nisseem is "a product of his time," as he says himself, that is, of the Nasserist era, in the sense that at any other time it is unlikely he would have had access to the medical profession—and also in the sense of his active response to the Arab socialist project of radical social transformation, of the peasants' condition in particular, as laid out in the 1962 Charter for Social Action.[4] The time he spent at school, then at university, was permeated by a climate of utopia but also by the effective reality of an immense effort at reform and social preparation, to which a very significant portion of Egypt's GNP was devoted until the catastrophic war of 1967.[5] The truly revolutionary character of the early Nasserist phase profoundly altered the image of the medical profession in the country among the privileged classes, as well as among groups targeted by the state: the urban and rural poor. This evolution was faithfully recorded in a number of novels, as it was by the cinema.[6] One is led to believe that the educated youth discovered in these sources material to nourish a dream of participation commensurate with their eagerness.

The project was ambitious—a total, free health service—and, as elsewhere (in Algeria for instance), it very rapidly came up against its own limits: financial, organizational, and social. This was especially the case in the provinces that were far from the capital. The contradictions of the Nasserist regime—popular enthusiasm and the regime's suspicion of anything that resembled spontaneity of the masses, or the elites—are well depicted in the words of one of the characters in a novel by Sonallah Ibrahim (1987:292–293), a doctor posted to Aswan in the extreme south of the Nile valley.

Although Nisseem's story takes place not far from here, his story is a different one. Indeed, he must have encountered the same difficulties and opposition as thousands of young graduates sent to the provinces for civil or military service. The number of doctors grew very rapidly at this time, rising from 17,000 at the time of the Charter to 32,000 in 1977. They faced unhealthy local conditions, empty pharmacies, nonexistent equipment, not to mention complete isolation (Chiffoleau 1996). Like them, but with more patience and determination, Nisseem had to undertake to deal with the difficult conditions (undoubtedly worse twenty years ago, but still bad today) in the area where he found himself during this time: a high birth rate, high infant mortality, endemic diseases, neglect of the handicapped, frequent accidents, illnesses caused by nutritional deficiencies—a situation that might be less visible than it is in Cairo, but one that is serious nonetheless.

In order to achieve his aims, he therefore had to invent and to learn to count on his own means: to choose a site, and not just any site; to build a house from scratch; to define his place in the "medical establishment"; to find and train a nurse—an indispensable but rare element of the set up, being a profession that is locally looked down upon.

The village that he considers "his own," with several thousand inhabitants, is sufficiently set apart from the major tourist venues and has no important archaeological finds in the immediate neighborhood. Tucked away in a sort of cul-de-sac, between a canal and an arid border, it is reached by a narrow path that opens onto a fairly large trail parallel to the canal. This in turn leads to the paved road perpendicular to the river. On the other side of the canal, as far as the eye can see, are fields of sugar cane. Most of the peasants are Muslim, apart from two or three Coptic families. There is a school, several *katatib* (plural of *kuttab*, a Qur'anic school), a mosque, several very small shops, and no services—these are found along the river, at the end of the paved road, some fifteen kilometers away. No seven-seater taxis or minibuses make their way to the agglomeration on a regular basis; one must return to the paved road to find transport, and apart from bicycles, riding on a donkey or a cart or walking are the normal means of transportation. A sign of the times, however, are some fifteen graduates from the village (not counting the primary school teachers), most of whom live there working as professionals: as accountants or as "lawyers," in the local sense of the word—as intermediaries between the population and the legal authorities in various matters.

Upon his arrival, Nisseem built his house on the bank of the canal, at some distance from the agglomeration, which is fairly compact and crowded, in a space that should have been cultivated but that has been since "endowed" with several modern "villas" with white or pastel facades and city-style doors and windows.

Nothing distinguishes his house from the peasants' dwellings: neither the materials used (green, i.e., unbaked, brick) nor the layout, other than the cleanliness of the surroundings and the severe, though elegant, arrangement of the interior. The consultation room is part of the living space, which partly looks onto a tiny patio with climbing plants, which his office bedroom, a room with no openings to the outside, overlooks. A cramped kitchen and, in the middle, a very small bathroom face the patio. At the opposite end, a handsome brick-built staircase leads to a terrace, as in all peasant houses. Unlike his neighbors, he raises neither chickens nor ducks there. There is no furniture, only a small low table and a discreet stereo, of excellent quality nevertheless, as well as quite a few good records. The books—he seems to read a lot—are not visible from the living space. There is a telephone.

Professionally, Nisseem has chosen to practice medicine independently; he is not a government employee and does not depend on any public health organization. He therefore receives neither equipment nor medicine. As a rule, patients come to him and not the reverse, and several hours may pass before anyone knocks on the door, especially in the morning when people are in the fields. For the visitor, this creates a strange feeling of emptiness, of suspended time, which Nisseem says he fills by reading or doing other things, when he has no calls to make in the village or elsewhere.

A few doctors, two it seems, established themselves nearby quite recently, but Nisseem's relations with them, as with colleagues in the neighboring town and other elite persons in the vicinity are very slack. "Before, I was the only one (doctor)," he says, "now there are quite a few, but I practice medicine differently, so I am still working." *Differently* means for very little money, only what he needs to live locally as he attends to the expectations and material and mental possibilities of the people:

> I had been uneasy for a long time with respect to the medical profession: It is powerful, dangerous, and insidious, to a frightening extent. One must be prudent, and at least avoid disturbing people's lives, their ways of seeing. Medicine is manipulative, a power game. I try to take on the role of advisor first and foremost. At the same time, I say everything, if not to the patient, then at least to the family. This is not done here. We must be conscious of our power, not politically, but otherwise.

Without a doubt, this demanding, continuous, and austere disposition would not be possible without the alter ego with whom he has associated himself: a sort of double, both a nurse and a very ceremonial secretary with the attitudes of a butler, who receives the patients, takes care of the house, organizes appointments when there are any, and knows his schedule minute by minute. Like Nisseem, Mahbub is probably a foreigner to the village and most likely a Nubian. Unlike Nisseem, he has established a family in the village and lives with them, a few meters away. That is where Nisseem takes his meals, watches television serials, and talks over village news at the end of the day. That is where he finds a family, so to speak, "foreign" like himself but simultaneously, through Mahbub's wife and children, a link to ordinary life.

Meeting and listening to Nisseem, one feels that he has multiplied the signs of singularity at his own pleasure: In choosing the spot where he lives—extraordinarily beautiful, it must be said—he was drawing closer neither to his family nor to his religious community. He did not seek to become wealthy nor, on the contrary, to "go into the desert"—that is, to a monastery—a choice that has become common among the Coptic intellectual elite, especially among doctors. Detached now from any form of political, religious, social, or cultural militancy, he heals a population on a day-to-day basis that has accepted and respects him without, however, integrating him. In other words, his "formula" has achieved a paradoxical association with two ways of "serving." The medical profession and voluntary poverty, located and legitimized in Egypt since ancient times, are mutually exclusive here: doctors were and still are *muwazzafin* (government employees), that is, wealthy. The destitute who have chosen poverty, including doctors, have chosen a life in the monastery, and it is neither common nor even acceptable, perhaps, to be both simultaneously.

Is this information sufficient to show that in his village, and more generally in the local and national environment, Nisseem is a marginal man? First of all, considering the more thoroughgoing form of integration that he had certainly hoped for, one must recognize that he himself lives apart. This failure, if one may describe it as such, may be attributed to the limits of the people whom he approached, limits that have not receded with time. But one must also see him in context and evaluate people's views of him, in order to appreciate the extent to which this mixture of conscious choice and involuntary determination—everything, ultimately, that he accepts as part of daily life—have made of him, on the local scale of classification, a marginal person: the absence of a household, the virtual absence of any material commodities, and especially of a car—given that not only all his colleagues but also most graduates, and even former emigrants, have one. One must add to this a factor that may be less visible in the villagers' eyes but is certainly very influential in his own view: the financial impossibility of leaving the country, except in very exceptional cases, precisely at a time when one of the Egyptian middle-class status symbols, but also one of their ways of "getting a breath of fresh air," is to go and see what's happening over the borders from time to time. In fact, quite a few people manage this travel through professional networks, and of the "not very rich"—that is, the liberal professions—doctors are certainly among those who travel most.

It is significant, therefore, that in accordance with "the theory of the secret," villagers wonder about the mystery of Nisseem's celibacy, or that of his genealogy (maybe his mother is French?), and that non-Egyptians who frequent the region question his lifestyle—too isolated or too social, depending on the speaker, and even his medical competence.[7] Indeed, it is inevitable that such disregard for ordi-

Nisseem takes his meals at his assistant's home (Fanny Colonna).

nary ways of living arouse suspicion, accusations, or at least a reductionist interpretation. In fact in Egypt, the theme and practice of "the return to the village" is not only a literary motif (Naoum 1991) or a memory of the decades (1930–1950) of social reform (Roussillon 1992). Since the early 1980s, centrifugal tendencies have multiplied among the capital's educated population, pushing them towards the rural fringes of Cairo or the Delta—grouped, as in Fayoum or near Saqqara (by the Pyramids), or isolated (Stauth 1993). The practicalities, the (political, religious, or even selfish) motivations, the duration and effects of these experiences vary enormously from one case to the next; but they all have in common the fact that they feed ambivalent and mostly malicious interpretations, which at their least critical focus on the "virtue" made of "necessity" in this ongoing practice.[8]

Accepting to speak, and especially accepting that his own words be printed, without changing a single one, seems to me to be an important form of *public engagement*, beyond the silent practice of "medicine in the service of the people" (an expression he never uses). To accept this is to run the risk of becoming "a character," which he already is in the ordinary sense of the term. To do so through a narrative in which a biographical trajectory and observations on the state of Egypt today are linked precludes any fictionalization of his "statement": He exposes himself *as a person* (Ion and Péroni 1997) and not as a fictional character. In this way, with the risks that this implies, I think that one of the central points of his text, which functions as a link between personal history and sociohistorical panorama, seems to be what he says of his relation to religion—that of the coun-

Is he a free particle, then? Not really (Fanny Colonna).

try and especially his own. At a moment when, as he emphasizes himself, "religion is at stake at every level"—for the state, Muslims, Copts, and the people of the village—his personal evolution publicly manifests a secularization of voluntary poverty and of the individual in general, which may be his most remarkable singularity, since it implies the renunciation of any institutional or community backing; and in this sense it is clearly symmetrical with his renunciation of assistance from the state medical establishment.

Is he a free particle, then? Not really. Speaking recently of his "only trip to the West," as he says with a laugh, two months in the United States in 1995, he describes how he seriously contemplated departure and how he then made the decision—obvious, so to speak—to return, adding that were he to leave one day, it would be to do "something other than medicine"—as though the ties he has woven in the village are mediated through his care and, conversely, as though his relation to medicine is mediated through the village. It is as if, to use one of his expressions, the whole comprised "a package," one that excludes religious and political motivations. "I am a doctor, that is all," he says. How better to express an attachment, not in a sentimental or even moral sense, but as an extension of his individuality itself (Thevenot 1997). Out of context, his story could initially make one think of a way of being true to oneself, a kind of stubbornness—a little like an old hand still at the factory[9] (and not the asylum) thirty years on—do such really exist? His actual account brings to mind the "last (Egyptian) communist Jew," Shehata Haroun, and it is not by chance that I think of them so naturally together, since my friend speaks mainly of the limits he has come up against, the routes he has been forced to abandon. His words have a full resonance that tell nothing of the future but speak of a life in the present, an existence in the here and now.

A long road from Nasser to this peace. If peace there is.

What Medicine?

N. Every doctor in Egypt, as soon as he graduates, is automatically hired by the state and must work in the civil service for three or four years. What happened is that I did this work during my military service. I was an officer-medic. So I was able to quit afterwards. It was a bit like the civil service. I was in the air force, and I was thinking of coming here. I already owned the land. . . . Here, yes, yes, I already had the plot of land; I had prepared everything. I had the idea of coming anyway.

F.C. Since when?

N. Since—. Already during my military service, it was already becoming clear, and even during my leave, I spent quite a bit of time here in the village.

F.C. You knew the place already?

N. Yes, I already knew the people, through a friend, who is from the village we mentioned, an Egyptologist; through him I got to know this village: it's his village. So we used to come here during college break; when we were still students, we would spend the holidays here. That's how I got to know the village; it was a kind of introduction. And even the plot of land: I bought it from his aunt; his father's sister sold me the land, and so I had already prepared the project almost at the same time. Since I had no means, everyone had advised me, "You have a government job; hold on to your salary; you never know." So I tried to come here, ever since my military service. But my attempts to get posted here met with a certain resistance. It wasn't entirely straightforward. . . .

I found myself at a dead end. I didn't know how things would turn out. I was in a hurry to get here, to start building; so then, I left everything; I packed my bags and then I sent in my letter of resignation. I can't make a fortune, you know; I'm not looking for that, that I'm sure of. But it's true that it surprises me to see other doctors making so much money in no time at all; I can't understand why. I've never understood why. For years, it's true, I took only a pound [one Egyptian pound] for a visit, and they were always house visits: I would go around on a donkey; people made me go miles for nothing. I was in good shape; I was hotheaded, militant at times, and then, little by little, I began to change, from the time when the house was ready—and that took a long time; the building didn't take long, but all the wood, carpentry, electricity, plumbing, and everything else: it took two years before the house was fit to be lived in.

F.C.   Did you draw up the plans, or was it a friend of yours?

N.   No, no, me, building with mud is very easy and the principle is very straightforward.

F.C.   Was Hassan Fathi your inspiration, or not even that?[10]

N.   Friends, who suggested arches for the doors and openings, that's all. They gave me construction forms, nothing more. So, as far as the work is concerned, it took time for things to fall into place. In the meantime, I had a motorbike, so I had started to run errands on the bike; they were still making me travel miles and miles, sure, until the work room was set up properly, and I started to impose a system, really.

F.C.   For people to come themselves?

N.   Yes, and here, in my house, it was two pounds per visit; I was working full time, and little by little, I started to raise the rates a bit. Those who came and who still do are always from the village. It's true that in those days most doctors spent just two to five years here, and then they would go to the city for their internship and specialization, etcetera. Now there are quite a few who have moved in and want to stay. And they create their own system of working hours; even the state is starting to allow them to do that officially. . . .

F.C.   How do you manage to keep up?

N.   There's a kind of seminar held every year in Cairo, but that's not the thing; in any case, we don't yet have an obligatory system. For a long time, I subscribed to a French publication.

F.C.   You mean the *Revue du Praticien* [General Practitioner's Review]?

N.   Yes, that's the one. Then after a while, they changed their system, the *Revue du Praticien*; the subscription is becoming more and more expensive, so I dropped it years ago.

F.C.   Isn't there an Egyptian equivalent?

N.   No, and the other international reviews cost too much; I have to change money. And the mail doesn't come regularly; issues get lost on the way. So for some time now, I've been trying to keep a book of general medicine, the most recent edition when possible; there's also a little American manual which is quite interesting, quite compact, with almost everything. It's renewed; there's a new edition every three or four years. I got the last two that way; my brother sends them to me. And then sometimes foreign doctors pass through here. I know one or two who come to Egypt regularly; they love it; the country really interests them; they come here regularly, and there's a chance that they might know things, details.

F.C.   Americans, French, English?

N.   An American, especially; I've had a few contacts with the French, but not many. It's true that this place is like a spot people pass through, and sometimes I even have tourists visiting because they're dying of cold; they need a doctor, and the village people bring them back here. Internal medicine is not a problem, because here there are mainly chronic diseases, things you see all the time. I haven't ever been able to visit Europe; the only place I've visited in the West is the U.S., thanks to my brother, two years ago; I was mainly in New York. And I also went to visit relatives who live in Texas. A package deal, for two months.

F.C.   What would you say of your relation to the public health system, and with medical graduates in general?

N.   I barely know any personally, only two doctors, one gynecologist and an orthopedic surgeon, but I know the second one because of Mahbub, who had metal plates put in because of a motorbike accident. So that's how the two of us got in touch; and with the gynecologist, it's been much longer.

F.C.   Do you send her patients?

N.   I send her patients; sometimes I bring cases back with me, because they're emergencies, problems with a delivery, something like that. . . . And that's how we got to know each other. What happened afterwards is that Mahbub's wife, for her delivery, it was a cesarean, and it was also at her house. Since then we've had very regular professional contact.

       Of course, there's the doctor from the village I told you about. . . .

F.C.   What would you say, in terms of your own practice, of their relations, of their way of listening to people's needs?

N.   I would say that in the doctor/money, patient/doctor equation, he acts like a classical doctor.

F.C.   And if he's a very good doctor, attentive, etcetera, isn't it normal that he should be well paid?

N.   Well, let's say that as far as practice goes, his scientific level: perfect.

F.C.   And the sense of responsibility, etcetera?

N.   He doesn't give a damn about people's conditions; he doesn't mind writing a prescription for fifty or sixty pounds for someone who doesn't have a penny.

F.C.   So they don't go to him for treatment?

N.   He always deals with it in terms of, "Oh, I do what has to be done." I'm not so sure he's right.

F.C.   Especially that the money goes to his brother [the pharmacist].

N.   No, no, on that point they actually disagree. No, the brother disagrees completely on that count. We talk about that a lot together.

F.C.   Oh really, with the brother who's a pharmacist?

N.   Yes, because, like all pharmacists in Egypt, people go to him directly; they ask him for advice directly, without going through a doctor. That's done very frequently and it works; it saves many lives. But I mean, my problem with other doctors is that a lot of doctors know me by name, but I'm still a strange specimen.

F.C.   Why?

"The Big Idea of Sharing the Lives of Others"

N.   Because I'm a doctor who doesn't make any money. You know, at the beginning I had started with many people from the village; I spent a lot of time; now it's changed: I took a few steps back; I was pushed away—both at once. How can I explain? I'm a stranger, that's all; I'm not from the village; I'm not from the families, the clans. Someone from a village one kilometer away is a stranger.

F.C.   Yes, but in a sense it's easier to discuss an abortion with a stranger than with—.

N.   When I was in secondary school, I went through two political initiation courses in the Mit Ghanem zone, on the famous National Charter.[11]

F.C.   What year was that?

N.   In 1966–1967.

F.C.   Before the "catastrophe."[12]

N.   It was just before the catastrophe, only just, and also I had my final exams just after. As for political education, I was never gifted, not really. At university we had a lot of activities until 1973. I'm a product of that period, that's all. My father was a teacher; we were not from a rich family; we were a bourgeois family with a business in a little Delta village. My father, when his father was still alive, had his business, a small business. Also, if there hadn't been Nasser's system I don't know where we would be. There were two of us boys studying medicine; if we had had to pay, we couldn't have done it.

F.C.   And as for that, that path which opened up, is it still open?

N.   It's open, yes and no, because even in my day, for instance, we had to buy books, especially in the first year, medical textbooks, anatomy manuals, and things like that, foreign books, English, and expensive. So even then there had to be a minimum purchasing power. But actually at the time in Egypt the market was limited, but everyone had access to this market everywhere. It was well leveled. The little citizen had an honest, direct dream, simple and easy. It wasn't a problem, and that's what I still hold dear from that time, right up until today. Sadat started to open things up. Despite certain advantages that came to the country, all the people who left for the Gulf, who brought back money; even in the villages, everyone had money, and it always scared me a bit; I saw it as a kind of danger. We don't have the means to live an American dream, but despite all this we're going ahead. We're still being pushed; we've chosen a market economy, and for a while now we've really been seeing the [negative] results. . . .

For me the political side was always a question of personal conditions, not at all of militancy. My choice to come and live here in this way was stimulated by the big idea of sharing others' lives.

I came across it [this idea] in Cairo during the two last years of my studies, through the Little Brothers of Jesus.

F.C. Are you Catholic?

N.   No, I was born a Copt.

F.C. Do you go to church?

N.   I'm not really keen on that, frankly; as far as mass goes, I only go to Catholic mass from time to time. There are two [Little Brothers of Jesus] in a primary school run by a Catholic association of Upper Egypt. One is a carpenter, and a long time ago he spent ten years in Marrakech. So we got here at the same time. The idea of sharing.

It's true that I've always had quite a strange status [in the fraternity], but I participate in their reunions every two years. Now there's an Egyptian brother, he comes from Minya. . . .

"I'm a Stranger, Not a Relative"

N.   At one time, I thought I had to take the whole package, but I think I'm not as religious as all that. After all these years I've discovered that my real place is as a doctor, that's all. Everything else is not possible; I don't adhere; I'm not a relative. I'm Christian.

F.C. But they [the peasants] know about that.

N.   They know about it, yes, but—.

F.C. Are there any Christians around here?

N.   In the village, they're confined; they have their little corner; they're there; they're from the village, but they have their little corner. It's calm; there's no problem, just formalities, of kindness, protocol, funerals, weddings; their lives are completely separate just about everywhere, and it wasn't very convenient for them. And where do I fit in? The adults whom I called "uncle," and the old men whom I called "grandfather," they liked that; it was a little game, but ultimately, seriously, it wasn't comfortable.

F.C. How long ago did you discover that?

N.   Oh, I took a few punches.

F.C. Like?

N.   It was little by little; but it happened to me several times; for instance, there's a problem; I give my opinion, and I get the answer: Yes, you're quite right, what you say is quite correct, but that's not our way of doing things. And after that, twice, I had real problems with someone from the village. Yes, I said real, real problems: I'm all alone, and I go and ask these people, who I consider family, and who consider me family, and I was running around; they didn't know what to do, they were—I had embarrassed them. I was friends with a young man, about my age; we used to spend evenings together, with others, quite long evenings, regularly; we would talk about everything. And then one fine day, I found out that he was telling Security[13] everything. A few months after, I was with him and Mahbub and said that at so-and-so's, we had seen someone who the police were after, a fundamentalist or whatever, from Aramant, the relative of someone from Security; and all at once, I saw this man jump up: "Who is he, what's his name?" And at that point I understood. All that time I couldn't see it, and I'm sure that he doesn't realize. Now he's not here; he's in the Gulf.

So I withdrew. I would, for instance, go to all the funerals; every time there was something, I would go along with everybody else. And then little by little I withdrew, and there was no problem, because if Mahbub doesn't go to a funeral, people will get upset; but I heard it said that, "Oh, so what, we don't have to do him favors in return," and it's true, so there's no problem. I went into my shell; I have to say I feel a lot better; my status is clearer: I'm a doctor. I don't deny that they trust me; I mean, in that domain I have a lot of friendly relations with my clients, my patients, even a sort of complicity. They come to my house; I'm a doctor; things are much clearer, much more real I think. The women come alone. I am the midwife; I don't know how many children I've delivered in this village; I'm sure the women prefer me as a midwife, although we have specialists now, and even so, you see all these people who keep coming. But things are much clearer, and much more real, I think.

"Although we have specialists now, I'm sure the women prefer me as a midwife" (Fanny Colonna).

Nasser and the Middle-Class Dream

N.   At the time when I came here, it wasn't done for a doctor from a city in the north to come settle in a village of the south. Now all the young doctors have no choice; if they want to practice medicine, they have to go to the countryside, as far away as possible. As soon as they're established, they dig themselves a hole, as soon as possible, otherwise they have no chance. The Nasserist dream is about that, in a sense: that a simple, middle-class life should be within everyone's reach. Now it's beyond the means of the majority; one has to have money. . . .

"Although we have specialists now, I'm sure the women prefer me as a midwife" (Fanny Colonna).

We tried a little bit to count those in the village who are educated, who have really reached positions which change and disrupt their previous status. In the whole village, there are about fifteen, fifteen to seventeen; that's a lot. But careful, we didn't count those who are teachers, because they're really squashed. They work in education and come back with very low salaries and lives, very tight and restricted, which means that the change is not obvious.

Still, there is a small change, that's for sure, in the way they try to fix up their house.

F.C.   And the way they see their children's future?

N.   Oh, not all of them, it depends; their conditions were so stifling that they let things go; let's say that they are repeating their own history. It's only one or two of the four or five brothers who received an education, the girls just a little bit and *yallah;* they married them off very young. So for them it's still a very slow transition, but many of that big pile [the fifteen] are the products of the advantages of the Nasser period.

F.C.   That's something I've understood since I came here; it's less obvious in Cairo. Even in the Delta it's less obvious; the situation is very complex. . . .

The Egypt of Our Childhood

N.   In my childhood, there was an Italian family, the Dipietros, who worked in a cotton-cleaning factory, and the two Dipietro children were in school with me. The eldest, Mario, was in my class until the end of school. There was another one, of Yugoslav origin but of Greek nationality, who was there with his wife and children; they taught French in Egyptian schools. There were only those two, but on the other side of the Nile, there was Zifta, where there were people like that. When I got here, there was a Greek wine seller in 1979.

F.C.   I think there were quite a few Greeks?

N.   Throughout Egypt, but much more so in the Delta; it was more visible; there were Greeks, Armenians, Italians. The Italians were royalists; the Jews are yet another phenomenon, but we didn't really see them during my generation; we were still children. In Alexandria, the French-speaking Jews who all had Swiss passports left later; there were quite a few Italians, also, Italian Jews, but we didn't see that, our parents did. The few Jews we met later, they were rare phenomena. The person we were talking about the other day, his father was an Egyptian Jew, extreme left-wing, and he "hung on" in Egypt, until 1960. . . .

       I know a few intellectuals. This woman told me a little of her father's story: it was a family of good old Jews allied to the old court in Istanbul; the men converted to Islam, but the women stayed Jewish, so the children became Jews; and then later on they came to Egypt. They passed through Egypt, and at that point, they took root; they're Oriental Jews, most probably Sephardim. The father left in the 60s, around the middle of the 1960s? He lasted a long time in Egypt. There's only one who stayed until he died, the famous Shehata. You know, we saw from a distance the end of a couple of things. Yet we lived in a fairly quiet Egypt, fairly Egyptian, Durrell's Egypt; because what's happening now is not like before, in the sense that there's no longer that way of living peacefully and quietly; people are much more tense, even in my village.

F.C.   You mean they're xenophobes, in that sense for example?

N.   There is a cultural xenophobia; that's very much the fashion now.

F.C.   Who makes that difference in that attitude towards people?

N.   "People are all right," I mean, "foreigners are all right; we work with them; it's OK, but not their way of talking, right—not their ideas, not their lifestyle": this way of talking is really getting big; it's taking on crazy proportions. But, even among Egyptians, we've lost quite a lot of that humorous side, and it's a question of race; everyone is now in a racial category [he is speaking of Muslim clerics and their efforts toward the Christians]. It's a question of justice, but careful, I've heard this several times; for a long time, it was the done thing to preach to someone because he wasn't praying, he was drinking and all the rest of it, and one of the things that the sheikh said most often was, "Why don't you pray, are you a Christian? *Inta Nasrani?*" *Nasrani* (Christian) is an insult for them. You see all this exists.

Muslims, Christians, and Jews

N. And so in Sadat's time, it has to be said that he's the one who started this whole way of talking, because he started a war [against the Copts]. One day, he started yelling in Parliament, and Patriarch Shenouda, well, Shenouda, he exiled him in the desert! Sadat locked him up in a monastery.

F.C. What? Really?

N. Of course, there's a problem; you see, after the decrees of Khatt-i Hamayuni,[14] once the community chooses a patriarch, the patriarch is recognized by the state; [he] becomes almost a state employee; and Sadat said: "As president, I decree the appointment of this gentleman to the head of the Coptic church, so I can remove him, good-bye; he's not the head anymore." [Jurists] took months and months to explain to him this wasn't possible. The state no longer recognizes him as a state official, fine. But he's still the head of the church; whatever you do, he has to die; he can't step down, that's how it is, that's the law in our church.

F.C. It's a canon law problem.

N. Yes, it's canon law; you can't touch anything; Shenouda even formed a committee of bishops to replace himself immediately, and he was only returned to his post after Sadat's death, by Mubarak. The secularist experience in Egypt is not as old as all that. . . .

With the Islamists, there are two trends, one trend that says: "Oh no, no problem; they're people of the country; they have the right to citizenship and everything"; because at one point when there was the issue of Shari'a or no Shari'a,[15] the Christians yelled: "What about us, what do we have to do with the Shari'a?" As far as I am concerned, the question is a bit silly: Whether it's positive law or whatever law, do we have a Christian law? There is none. Positive or not, that's not the most important point, especially since Shari'a recognizes special status for those of other religions; in that case, their own law takes precedence, and that's what happens for family law and all the rest; we have a separate law. . . . [16]

Jews are such a strange phenomenon for the people of Egypt that it's a shock; here they don't know Jews, they know Israel.

F.C.   They've heard about Moses, though? [laughter]

N.   It has nothing to do with it, that has nothing to do with it, no, no, no! That's something that even in Cairo [one hears] very easily, "He's a Jew." And, no, and no, because when I hear my mother and my aunt talking about the Jewish neighbors, whoever was a seamstress or whatever, they were always [described as] strange creatures, like in the stories of the Jews in Europe at the turn of the century, always the same stories, the same kind of thing. The Christians too are anti-Jewish. They tell old anti-Jewish stories, really classical nineteenth century anti-Semitism.

       But it was always around with us; it's still around; it's really no fun. I met a French Jewish woman; she told me, "I'm Egyptian; once my father had got to France, he refused to say a single word in French; yet he spoke French; until his death, he spoke only the Cairene dialect, at home and with everyone in the street." He didn't want to know about this [his Jewishness]; he said he was Egyptian and that he would die as an Egyptian. For her this was very, very powerful, and very difficult.

F.C.   That's what Curiel used to say. . . . [17]

N.   Curiel too, although he was not as rooted in Egypt: his father had just arrived. See, in Algeria for instance, who talks about Franz Fanon?[18] They've just written a book on his life, I heard, I think in the States. But you see, who talks about him?

F.C.   Yes they do; people talk about him quite a lot; first of all in Algiers there's an avenue named after him, a big avenue which starts at the National Library; he's more or less taught at university, even in Arabic. There are textbooks about him, in Arabic.

"In Egypt, Religion Is Important at Every Level"

N.   But it's true; it has to be said that in Egypt, there's a sort of tolerance; the Christians are protected by the state. . . .

       We don't pay the *dhimmi* tax,[19] since we serve in the army, and if we do pay the *dhimmi* tax, we don't do military service.

F.C.   Are the Christians citizens? Do they vote?

N.   Everything, everything, everything; yes, no problem.

F.C.   Except access to certain positions?

N.   Yes, it's always been like that, even under Nasser. Under Nasser the religious discourse did not exist; with Sadat, we started talking about it; Sadat himself talked about it all the time, and with Mubarak, it's a small, slow procedure, calm; no one does anything against the Shari'a.

F.C.   There's also the idea of not doing anything that would be against the national consensus?

N.   And also, a lawyer can complain about the law to the Constitutional Council, because the clauses of the law are against the Shari'a; that is how they attacked some of the laws on women and divorce and all the rest. So it was necessary to revise some details of that law, and it's done on a very regular basis against this or that law which does not conform to the Shari'a; and they let it happen. It's the Constitution; that's clear; there's no doubt; if the mufti makes a decision on something, and there's a law against it, they'll immediately go to Parliament to change it, which was never done before; our mufti, Doctor Tantawi, never went that far. He became Sheikh of Al-Azhar; he's quite open; he was clear on two problems: the interest rate of banks at a certain point; he said that if the banks take interest rates from people, and don't give them anything on that, I'm against it.[20] Because they earn money through that; so they have to give that gain back to people. If you put money in the bank with the *niyya*, that is, the intention of investing, that's normal. Why not? Economic machines do the calculations and the rest, so it's normal that people should receive the gain. And he was clear on that. He wrote a whole series of articles in *Al-Ahram*[21] to explain the whole story from A to Z. It was war; Al-Azhar had a fit, not officially, but little articles here and there; they couldn't touch him.

      The second thing was girls' circumcision; well, that was a lot easier because it's neither Sunna[22] nor part of Islamic tradition, so no problem finding in the sources that it's not Qur'anic. But the sheikh, the former Sheikh of Al-Azhar who just passed away, said one day that the Prophet said something or other about *khitan*;[23] then that was it, no one mentioned it anymore, and everyone was really sick of the story, which had been so big at one point, after the CNN film. CNN had aired a film where they showed the excision of a girl from Cairo; at first it was a big scandal—how can they do something like that?—then journalists started to say, "Why make such a big deal of a tradition which has almost disappeared in Egypt?"

F.C. And is it done in the village?

N.   You bet! Regularly, more than 80 percent of Egyptian women are circumcised, everywhere, even in the city.

F.C. Who does that, doctors?

N.   There are doctors who do it, otherwise midwives and everyone. Except that the journalists say, "Oh, that's impossible; it's a scandal for Egypt, an insult! How can they show that," etcetera, and then, "Oh well, it's disappearing anyway." They took a month in *Al-Ahram* to start publishing the articles by doctors, sociologists, and little by little it blew up: According to the most conservative statistics, at least 70 percent [of families practice girls' circumcision]. They showed studies, research, saying that the number is much greater than that and that it is a real scandal and a real problem.

Oh, that's the problem that I've always had here with quite a few foreigners, especially women, militant feminists. The first question they ask is, "What about circumcision?" Careful, there's nothing you can do about it; it's so old and deeply rooted in this Nile valley that nothing can be done; it's a Nilotic tradition that started at the source of the Nile and then moved north.

It's a scandal because it's linked to the West, to the modern world; it's starting to disappear, and we know that at least two generations of educated women are needed before it will disappear; in my own family, my aunts were circumcised, on my mother's side; it never happened in my [father's] family, because already my grandmother had been to school, an American school especially for girls. Already her own mother was the daughter of a priest; it was an educated environment at the end of the last century. They were educated in the home; it was another lifestyle. It's true; it's disappearing now in a sense, but now the minister of health has issued a decree: When the Sheikh of Al-Azhar said it's a Muslim tradition and everything, they had to do it. [The health administration] set up one day a week in hospitals when parents bring their daughter to have her circumcised by a doctor inside the hospital, where at least it's possible to avoid the whole drama of infections, of girls dying. And then one fine day the Sheikh at Al-Azhar upped and died, and a successor, the mufti Tantawi, was against circumcision; he asked the doctors and everything and said that it wasn't a Muslim tradition, so people can do it or not; it's up to them; but because medicine says it's harmful, it's better not do it. As soon as he was promoted to Sheikh of Al-Azhar, in a week, the minister of health issued a decree, forbidding completely and absolutely that any doctor have anything to do with the whole business, privately or in a public clinic and everything. Now there are cases before the courts against this decree. There's a professor at the university of gynecology who's at the head of the brigade *in favor of* circumcision; I have an article by him; it's an anthology—how to use positive science—that's the kind of debate going on in Egypt.

"Ultimately, the Two Communities Don't Recognize Each Other"

F.C. What do you think of what your Patriarch Shenouda said, "Really, the monks' story could never have happened here?"[24]

N. It has to be said that the Islamists, even the moderates who are in the medical syndicates, the engineers' syndicates and all, they're everywhere; they're very powerful.

F.C. Yes, and so?

Nisseem's assistant, Mahbub, an outsider to the region (Fanny Colonna).

N.   And they're very, very kind to the Christians.

F.C.   Even to the actively religious?

N.   That's different.

F.C.   And those who don't proselytize? The Trappists didn't proselytize [having taken a vow of silence].

N.   We don't have that image of the European cleric as a colonialist; it's completely dissociated from the history of the English occupation; that was an occupation, not a mission; there were no English missions, but there were French and Italian ones.

F.C.   There were Methodists, weren't there?

N.   No, the Protestant missionaries were mainly American, and a few Germans; the English didn't give a damn. We don't have that problem of [seeing] *rumi, al-kafir* ["enemy Christian blasphemers"] as if they were figures from hell; that phenomenon doesn't exist in Egypt. For the Muslims in Egypt, the Copts are a fact, ever since the beginning; they didn't pose a problem; even when there were attacks on Christians, it was simply to destabilize the state; they weren't really a problem.

Still, it has to be said that among the Islamists there are several trends. At one point, there were one or two big sheikhs who had even given an ultimatum: to convert or leave the country. But despite everything, you don't find that stereotypical identification [of Christian and colonizer]. This doesn't mean that the Copts, some of whom have money and power— Their attitude from the national point of view [is unclear]; they were the first to back the Westerners; they're still on that side, the West is Christianity.[25] I mean, in Egypt the question of religion can be found at every level, and, at every level, it has its own completely different game.

Copts are the indigenous people, the country's people; they've been here forever. But there is a real problem, which is that ultimately the two communities don't recognize each other; they only recognize each other from the outside [i.e., as strangers]. In a village, there's a certain tradition; otherwise it's total ignorance; it's true you know. In Egypt, you find very, very few Copts who know anything about Islam.

F.C. And how many Muslims who know anything about the Copts?

N. A few; it's the same, not more than that. The separation is there.

F.C. Aren't you saying that it's a future Lebanon?

N. I mean, if you take the history of Egypt as told by the chroniclers, a quiet reading of Ibn Iyas and Jabarti, you see clearly that the presence of Copts is tolerated, but in their place.[26]

F.C. As *dhimmis*.[27]

N. *Dhimmis.* Starting from the well-known Ottoman decree recognizing the citizenship of the subjects of the different churches in the Empire, which was applied in Egypt, a Coptic, a Greek, and a Syrian church were recognized. Only the Middle East has had this experience, and this with the state's secularizing trend which has dominated until now, and which continues to dominate; but if something is happening, that is de-secularization; care is always taken that a Christian doesn't occupy a key post within the army—because there emerges the problem, the famous story that a Muslim cannot obey a non-Muslim. It's back on the table; it's been said as something people don't question; what's happening within the state is that Christians are being pushed into the background more and more; they're not allowed key posts, not any more. At one point in the municipalities and everything, you could have Copts in the administration; it was fine. For example, for ministers, Boutros Boutros Ghali: Sadat had made him minister of foreign affairs, and afterwards he realized that it was a bit much, a country that says it's Muslim but has a Christian minister of foreign affairs. He appointed a Muslim minister of foreign affairs, and Boutros Ghali was made secretary of state for foreign affairs.

Anyway, the Copts always say they're being persecuted; they're always complaining about it, but at the same time they don't know the stakes. Here, for instance, the young people studying at Al-Azhar, in their Shari'a courses there's something about *qisas*, if there's a murder. Well, if someone kills, he gets killed; but then there's "something notable": a Muslim will not be executed if he has killed a non-Muslim.[28]

"I am a doctor, that is all" (Fanny Colonna).

Ultimately—I took some time to understand this—I can't be equal. The fact of being Christian means that one is not the same. When it comes to justice, that is sacred; but listen, as a Christian, I should not act as if I were an equal, especially in the power stakes. A Copt is safe in a village, as a protected minority, protected even by the sheikhs. They have every right, as long as they don't cross certain borders.

Notes

1. The editors are grateful to Pascale Ghazaleh for the translation of the article and to Maria Phylactou for her green-fingered pruning. The research was funded by the Middle Eastern Ford Foundation. The editors have cut the interview in parts, represented by dots at the end of sections, thus . . . , and inserted occasional explanations in square brackets. The complete text will appear in French under the author's name at a later date.

2. See the evolution from the paternalistic hero of *Um Hashem's Lantern* in the 1940s, highlighted by Berque (1967), to the young communist practitioner of Sherif Hetata (1982) or the militant feminist Nawal El-Saadawi (1925).

3. This is a reference to the cult novel of the seventies, *Season of Migration to the North*, by the Sudanese author Al-Tayeb Salih. The interest of this book, for our purpose, beside its immense literary quality, is its ability to set the scene for a recurrent topos, in North Africa as well, according to which every migration of this type hides an unavowable *secret*.

4. The National Charter of 1962: the important doctrinal text of Gamal Abdel-Nasser, which laid the foundations of his socialist policy.

5. The defeat of the Egyptian army by Israel in 1967, which was consolidated, among other things, by the occupation of Sinai and the Suez Canal. Nasser then announced his resignation, which the Parliament and the people refused. He died in 1970.

6. See endnote 2.

7. Another allusion to *The Season of Migration to the North;* see endnote 3.

8. See also Ghosh (1994:119ff, 287).

9. In the original, *un vieil établi,* that is, a graduate "68er" still choosing to work in a factory. See Leenhart (1972).

10. An Egyptian architect, famous in the 1970s and 1980s for his original views on the architectural vernacular and building with mud.

11. See endnote 4.

12. The defeat of the Egyptian army by Israel in 1967. See endnote 5.

13. The Security Forces.

14. The *Khatt-i Hamayuni* of the mid–nineteenth century, also known as the Tanzimat, were decisive reforms imposed on the whole of the Ottoman Empire.

15. The Shari'a is the religious law of the Qur'an and the Tradition (Sunna).

16. Each religion is allowed its own civil law code, as was the case throughout the Ottoman empire.

17. Henri Curiel was a leading comrade of the Communist Party, exiled to France in 1951. See Gilles Perrault, *Un Homme à Part* (1984).

18. A doctor from the Antilles, the co-theorist of the Algerian revolution, who died in 1961 at the age of forty.

19. The *dhimmi* tax was paid, before the Tanzimat (reforms), by the people of the Book, the two other revealed religions.

20. Al-Azhar university is a thousand-year-old Islamic institution that has set up branches, first in important medium-sized, then in secondary, towns.

21. Egypt's main daily paper.

22. The tradition codified after the death of the Prophet, as important a source as the Qur'an.

23. *Khitan* is the circumcision of boys and the excision of girls.

24. Reference to the abduction of seven Trappist monks in Algeria in 1996.

25. The Copts have been presumed to side with "the West" since Napoleonic times.

26. Ibn Iyas and Jabarti are Egyptian chroniclers of the sixteenth and nineteenth centuries.

27. Those who are "protected," "dependents."

28. *Qisas* refers to the death penalty and the principle of retaliation.

References

Abegglen, J. C. 1973. *Management and Worker*. Tokyo: Kodansha.

Abu-Lughod, L. 1990. "The romance of resistance: Tracing transformations of power through Bedouin women." *American Ethnologist* 17:41–55.

Alexander, K. C. 1968. *Social Mobility in Kerala*. Poona: Deccan College.

Althusser, L. 1971. *Lenin and Philosophy, and Other Essays*. London: New Left Books.

Anderson, P. 1994. "The dark side of Brazilian conviviality." *London Review of Books* 24:3–8.

Anderson, R. L. 1976. "Following Curupira: Colonization and migration in Para, 1758 to 1930." Unpublished Ph.D. dissertation, University of California–Davis.

Anderson, S. 1992. "Engenhos na várzea." In *Amazonia: A Fronteira Agrícola 20 Anos Depois, ed.* P. Lena and A. E. de Oliveira. Belém: MPEG.

Aoki H. 1989. *Yoseba Rodosha no Sei to Shi* [The life and death of the yoseba worker]. Tokyo: Akashi Shoten.

Astuti, R. 1995a. *People of the Sea: Identity and Descent Among the Vezo of Madagascar*. Cambridge: Cambridge University Press.

_____. 1995b. "'The Vezo are not a kind of people': Identity, difference, and 'ethnicity' among a fishing people of western Madagascar." *American Ethnologist* 22:464–482.

Bahr, H. M. 1973. *Skid Row: An Introduction to Disaffiliation*. New York: Oxford University Press.

Balbus, I. 1982. *Marxism and Domination: A Neo-Hegelian, Feminist, Psychoanalytical Theory of Sexual, Political, and Technological Liberation*. Princeton: Princeton University Press.

Balée, W. 1994. *Footprints of the Forest. Ka'apor Ethnobotany: The Historical Ecology of Plant Utilization by an Amazonian People*. New York: Columbia University Press.

Bates, H. 1964. *The Naturalist on the River Amazon*. London: John Murray.

Bellier, I. 1991. *El Temblor y la Luna: Ensayo Sobre las Relaciones Entre las Mujeres y los Hombres Mai Huna*. Quito: Abya Yala.

Bennett, D. 1988. "'The poor have much more money': Changing socio-economic relations in a Greek village." *Journal of Modern Greek Studies* 6:217–243.

Berger, J., and J. Mohr. 1982. *Une Autre Façon de Raconter*. Paris: Maspéro.

Berque, J. 1967. *L'Egypte, Impérialisme et Révolution*. Paris: Gallimard.

Besson, J. 1993. "Reputation and respectability reconsidered: A new perspective on Afro-Caribbean peasant women." In *Women and Change in the Caribbean, ed.* J. Momsen. Bloomington: Indiana University Press.

Bird-David, N. 1990. "The giving environment: Another perspective on the economic system of gatherer-hunters." *Current Anthropology* 31:183–196.

_____. 1992. "Beyond 'the hunting and gathering mode of subsistence': Culture-sensitive observations on the Nayaka and other modern hunter-gatherers." *Man*, 27(1):19–44.

Bloch, M. 1975. "Property and the end of affinity." In *Marxist Analyses and Social Anthropology*, ed. M. Bloch. London: Malaby Press.

_____. 1977. "The past and the present in the present." *Man*, n.s., 12:278–292.

_____. 1982. "Death, women, and power." In *Death and the Regeneration of Life*, ed. M. Bloch and J. Parry. Cambridge: Cambridge University Press.

_____. 1986. *From Blessing to Violence: History and Ideology in the Circumcision Ritual of the Merina of Madagascar.* Cambridge: Cambridge University Press.

_____. 1989. *Ritual, History, and Power.* London: Athlone Press.

_____. 1992a. *Prey into Hunter: The Politics of Religious Experience.* Cambridge: Cambridge University Press.

_____. 1992b. "What goes without saying: The conceptualization of Zafimaniry society." In *Conceptualizing Society*, ed. A. Kuper. London: Routledge.

Bohannan, P., and G. Dalton, eds. 1962. *Markets in Africa.* Evanston: Northwestern University Press.

Bouquet, M. 1993. *Reclaiming English Kinship: Portuguese Refractions of British Kinship Theory.* Manchester: Manchester University Press.

Bourdieu, P. 1977. *Outline of a Theory of Practice.* Cambridge: Cambridge University Press.

Bourgois, P. 1995. *In Search of Respect: Selling Crack in El Barrio.* Cambridge: Cambridge University Press.

Bremen, J. 1994. *Wage Hunters and Gatherers: Search for Work in the Urban and Rural Economy of South Gujarat.* Delhi: Oxford University Press.

Brenneis, D., and F. Myers. 1984. *Dangerous Words: Language and Politics in the Pacific.* New York: New York University Press.

Breznay, I. 1932. *Eger a XVIII században* (Eger in the eighteenth century). Eger: n.p.

Bromley, R., and C. Gerry, eds. 1979. *Casual Work and Poverty in Third World Cities.* Chichester and New York: John Wiley and Sons.

Burawoy, M. 1986. *The Politics of Production.* London: Verso.

Burke, E., III. 1993. *Struggle and Survival in the Modern Middle East.* New York and London: Tauris.

Buzás, E. 1983. "Egy cigány telep felszámolása" (Winding up a Gypsy settlement). In *Roma, Válogatás a cigányokkal kapcsolatos sajtótermékekből* (Roma, a selection of the treatment of Gypsies in the media). Budapest: Népművelési Intézet.

Calagione, J., D. Francis, and D. Nugent, eds. 1992. *Workers' Expressions: Beyond Accommodation and Resistance.* Albany: SUNY Press.

Carneiro da Cunha, M. 1992. *A Historia dos Indios no Brasil.* Sao Paulo: Ed. Schwarz.

Carrier, J. 1992. "Emerging alienation in production: A Maussian history." *Man*, n.s., 27:539–558.

_____. 1997. "Introduction." In *Meanings of the Market: The Free Market in Western Culture*, ed. J.G. Carrier. Oxford and New York: Berg.

Carsten, J. 1989. "Cooking money: Gender and the symbolic transformation of means of exchange in a Malay fishing community." In *Money and the Morality of Exchange*, ed. J. Parry and M. Bloch. Cambridge: Cambridge University Press.

Carsten, J., and S. Hugh-Jones, eds. 1995. *About the House: Lévi-Strauss and Beyond.* Cambridge: Cambridge University Press.

Chalmers, N. 1989. *Industrial Relations in Japan: The Peripheral Workforce.* London and New York: Routledge.

Chiffoleau, S. 1995. "La réforme sociale par l'hygiène: Une formule pour médicaliser les campagnes." In *Entre Réforme Sociale et Mouvement National, Identité et Modernisation en Egypte (1882–1962)*, ed. A. Roussillon. Cairo: CEDEJ.

_____. 1996. "Un médecin au service du peuple: Changer le mythe en réalité." *Nasser: 25 Ans* (Special issue of *Peuples Méditerranéens*) 74–75:229–247.

Cleary, D. 1993. "After the frontier: Problems with political economy in the modern Brazilian Amazon." *Journal of Latin American Studies* 25:331–349.

Clogg, R., ed. 1993. *Greece 1981–1993: The Populist Decade.* New York: St. Martin's Press.

Comaroff, J. 1985. *Body of Power, Spirit of Resistance.* Chicago: University of Chicago Press.

Constas, D., and T. Stavrou, eds. 1995. *Greece Prepares for the Twenty-First Century.* Baltimore: The John Hopkins University Press.

da Matta, R. 1991. *Carnivals, Rogues, and Heroes.* Notre Dame: University of Notre Dame Press.

Day, S. 1990. "Prostitute women and the ideology of work in London." In *AIDS and Culture: The Global Pandemic*, ed. D. A. Feldman. New York: Praeger.

_____. 1994. "L'argent et l'esprit d'enterprise chez les prostituées à Londres." *Terrain* 23:99–114.

_____. 1996. "The law and the market: Rhetorics of exclusion and inclusion among London prostitutes." In *Inside and Outside the Law*, ed. O. Harris. London: Routledge.

Day, S., H. Ward, and L. Perrotta. 1993. "Prostitution and risk of HIV: Male partners of female prostitutes." *British Medical Journal* 307:359–361.

Dean, W. 1987. *Brazil and the Struggle for Rubber: A Study in Environmental History.* Cambridge: Cambridge University Press.

de Heusch, L., 1966. *A la découverte des Tsiganes: Une expedition de reconnaissance (1961)*, Bruxelles: Ed. de L'Institut de Soc. de L'Université Libre.

de la Tour, E. 1996. *Si Bleu Si Calme: La Prison Intérieure.* 16mm film aired on Arte, 4 March 1997.

de Pina-Cabral, J. 1986. *Sons of Adam, Daughters of Eve: The Peasant Worldview of the Alto Minho.* Oxford: Clarendon Press.

Deleuze, G. 1994. *Difference and Repetition.* London: Athlone Press.

Deleuze, G., and F. Guattari. 1986. *Nomadology: The War Machine.* New York: Semiotext(e).

_____. 1987. *A Thousand Plateaus: Capitalism and Schizophrenia.* London: Athlone.

Descola, Ph. 1993. "Les affinités sélectives: Alliance, guerre et prédation dans l'ensemble jivaro." *L'Homme* 33:171–190.

_____. 1994. *In the Society of Nature: A Native Ecology in Amazonia.* Cambridge: Cambridge University Press.

_____. 1996. *The Spears of Twilight: Life and Death in the Amazon.* London: Thames and Hudson.

DeVos, G., and H. Wagatsuma. 1967. *Japan's Invisible Race: Caste in Culture and Personality.* Berkeley: University of California Press.

Dewald, J. 1993. "The ruling class in the marketplace: Nobles and money in early modern France." In *The Culture of the Market: Historical Essays*, ed. T. Haskell and R. Teichgraeber. Cambridge: Cambridge University Press.

Dilley, R. 1992. "Introduction." In *Contesting Markets: Analyses of Ideology, Discourse, and Practice*, ed. R. Dilley. Edinburgh: Edinburgh University Press.

Dobrowolski, K. 1966. "Tradycjna rodzina chłopska w południowej Polsce na przełomie XIX i XXw" (The traditional peasant family in the south of Poland at the turn of the century). In *Studia Na Życiem Społecznym i Kultura* (Studies of social life and culture). Warsaw: Polska Akademia Nauk.

Doi, T. 1973. *The Anatomy of Dependence.* Trans. John Bester. Tokyo and New York: Kodansha International.

Dongó Beszámoló. 1984. *Beszámoló a Dongó Közösségben élő cigánylakosság helyzetéről* (Report on the conditions of Gypsies living in the community of Dongó). Dongó: n.p.

Dubisch, J. 1986. "Culture enters through the kitchen: Women, food, and social boundaries in rural Greece." In *Gender and Power in Rural Greece,* ed. J. Dubisch. Princeton: Princeton University Press.

Dumont, L. 1959. "Structural definition of a folk deity of Tamil Nadu: Aiyanar, the Lord." *Contributions to Indian Sociology* 3:75–87.

Egypt Human Development Report. 1996. Cairo: Institute of National Planning.

Engels, F. 1972. *The Origin of the Family, Private Property, and the State.* New York: Pathfinder Press.

Esterci, N. 1987. *Conflito no Araguaia.* Petropolois: Ed. Vozes.

Farag, I. 1991. "Intellectuel et muthaqqaf: Champ sémantique, champ conceptuel et champ historique." In *Etudes Politiques du Monde Arabe* (Dossier du CEDEJ), 151–163. Cairo: Cahiers du CEDEJ.

Feeley-Harnik, G. 1978. "Divine kingship and the meaning of history among the Sakalava (Madagascar)." *Man,* n.s., 13:402–417.

Fél, E., and T. Hofer. 1969. *Proper Peasants: Traditional Life in a Hungarian Village.* Chicago: Aldine Publishing Co.

Forray, K., and A. Hegedűs. 1985. *Az együttélés rejtett szabályai: Egy cigány csoport sikerének mértéke és ára egy iskolában* (The hidden rules of co-habitation: The degree and cost of a Gypsy group's successes in a school). Budapest: Országos Pedagógiai Intézet.

Fowler, E. 1996. *San'ya Blues: Laboring Life in Contemporary Tokyo.* Ithaca and London: Cornell University Press.

Friedman, J. 1997. "Global crises, the struggle for cultural identity intellectual porkbarrelling: Cosmopolitans versus locals, ethnics and nationals in an era of de-hegemonisation." In *Debating Cultural Hybridity: Multicultural Identities and the Politics of Anti-Racism,* ed. P. Werbner and T. Modood. London and Atlantic Highlands: Zed.

Fuller, C. J. 1976. *The Nayars Today.* Cambridge: Cambridge University Press.

———. 1988. "The Hindu pantheon and the legitimation of hierarchy." *Man,* n.s., 23:19–39.

———. 1992. *The Camphor Flame: Popular Hinduism and Society in India.* Princeton: Princeton University Press.

Funamoto, S. 1985. *Damatte Notarejinu-na* (Do not be silent and die in the gutter). Tokyo: Renga Shobo Shinsha.

Furtado, L. 1987. *Curralistas e Redeiros de Maruda.* Belem: MPEG.

Galvão, E. 1952. "The religion of an Amazon community: A study in culture change." Unpublished Ph.D. dissertation, Columbia University.

Geertz, C. 1973. "Deep play: Notes on the Balinese cockfight." In *The Interpretation of Cultures: Selected Essays.* New York: Basic Books.

———. 1980. *Negara: The Theatre State in Nineteenth-Century Bali.* Princeton: Princeton University Press.

Gell, A. 1982. "The market wheel: Symbolic aspects of an Indian tribal market." *Man*, n.s., 17:470–491.

Ghosh, A. 1994. *Un Infidèle en Egypte*. Paris: Seuil. English translation, 1994. *In an Antique Land*. London: Granta.

Gibson, T. 1986. *Sacrifice and Sharing in the Philippine Highlands: Religion and Society among the Buid of Mindoro*. London: Athlone Press.

———. 1988. "Meat sharing as a political ritual: Forms of transaction versus models of subsistence." In *Hunters and Gatherers*. Vol. 2, *Property, Power, and Ideology*, ed. T. Ingold, D. Riches, and J. Woodburn. Oxford: Berg.

Gill, T. 1996. Men of uncertainty: The social organization of day labourers in contemporary Japan." Unpublished Ph.D. dissertation, University of London.

Gilliat-Smith, B. 1963. "An eighteenth-century Hungarian document." *Journal of the Gypsy Lore Society*, 3d ser., 43, no. 3–4:129–131.

Gilmore, D. 1991. "Commodity, comity, community: Male exchange in rural Andalusia." *Ethnology* 30:17–30.

Gluckman, M. 1963. "Rituals of rebellion in south east Africa." In *Order and Rebellion in Tribal Africa*. London: Cohen and West.

Gold, A G. 1994. "Sexuality, fertility, and erotic imagination in Rajasthani women's songs." In *Listen to the Heron's Words: Reimagining Gender and Kinship in North India*, ed. G.G. Raheja and A. G. Gold. Berkeley and Los Angeles: University of California Press.

Gough, E. K. 1959. "The Nayars and the definition of marriage." *The Journal of the Royal Anthropological Institute* 89:23–34.

———. 1970. "Pālakkara: Social and religious change in central Kerala." In *Change and Continuity in India's Villages*, ed. K. Kshwaran. New York: Columbia University Press.

Gow, P. 1991. *Of Mixed Blood: Kinship and History in Peruvian Amazon*. Oxford: Clarendon Press.

Grandidier, A. 1971. *Souvenirs de voyages d'Alfred Grandidier 1865–1870* (d'après son manuscrit inédit de 1916). Association malgache d'archéologie. Documents anciens sur Madagascar, VI. Antananarivo.

Grandidier, A., and G. Grandidier. 1908–1928. *Ethnographie de Madagascar*. 4 vols. Part of *Histoire physique, naturelle et politique de Madagascar*. Paris: n.p.

Gropper, R. 1975. *Gypsies in the City: Culture Patterns and Survival*. Princeton: Darwin Press.

Gudeman, S., and A. Rivera. 1991. *Conversations in Columbia: The Domestic Economy in Life and Text*. Cambridge: Cambridge University Press.

Gudeman, S. 1971. *The Compadrazgo as a Reflection of the Spiritual and Natural. Proceedings of the Royal Anthropological Institute*. London: Royal Anthropological Institute.

Guha, R. 1982. "On some aspects of the historiography of Colonial India." In *Subaltern Studies*, ed. R. Guha. Vol.1. Delhi: Oxford University Press.

Guha, R., ed. 1983. *Subaltern Studies*. Vol. 2. Delhi: Oxford University Press.

Guss, D. 1989. *To Weave and to Sing: Art, Symbolism, and Narrative in the South American Rain Forest*. Berkeley: University of California Press.

Guy, W. 1975. "Ways of looking at Rom: The case of Czechoslovakia." In *Gypsies, Tinkers, and Other Travellers*, ed. F. Rehfisch. London: Academic Press.

Hannerz, U. 1969. *Soulside: Inquiries into Ghetto Culture and Community*. New York and London: Columbia University Press.

Haqqi, Y. 1944. "La Lanterne d'Oum Hachem." In *Choc*. Paris: Nouvelles.

Harris, M. 1996. "People of the Amazon floodplain: Kinship, work, and sharing in a Cabo-clo community, near Óbidos, Pará, Brazil." Unpublished Ph.D. dissertation, University of London.

_____. 1998a. "What it means to be caboclo: Some notes on the construction of Amazon-ian caboclo society as an anthropological object." *Critique of Anthropology* 18, no. 1:83–95.

_____. 1998b. "The rhythm of life on the Amazon floodplain: Seasonality and sociality in a caboclo village" *Journal of Royal Anthropological Institute (Incorporating Man)*4:1–18

Harris, O. 1980. "The power of signs: Gender, culture, and the wild in the Bolivian Andes." In *Nature, Culture, and Gender*, ed. C. P. MacCormack and M. Strathern. Cambridge: Cambridge University Press.

_____. "Households as natural units." In *Of Marriage and the Market: Women's Subordi-nation in International Perspective*, ed. K. Young et al. London: CSE Books.

Hart, K. 1973. "Informal income opportunities and urban employment in Ghana." *Journal of Modern African Studies* 2:61–89.

Hecht, S., and A. Cockburn. 1989. *Fate of the Forest: Developers, Destroyers, and Defenders of the Amazon*. New York and London: Verso.

Heelas, P., and P. Morris, eds. 1992. *The Values of the Enterprise Culture: The Moral Debate*. London: Routledge.

Hemming, J. 1976. *Red Gold: The Conquest of the Brazilian Indians*. London: Macmillan.

Hendry, J. 1989. *Understanding Japanese Society*. London: Routledge.

Herzfeld, M. 1986. *The Poetics of Manhood: Contest and Identity in a Cretan Mountain Vil-lage*. Princeton: Princeton University Press.

_____. 1987. *Anthropology Through the Looking Glass: Critical Ethnography in the Mar-gins of Europe*. Cambridge: Cambridge University Press.

_____. 1991. *A Place in History: Social and Monumental Time in a Cretan Town*. Prince-ton: Princeton University Press.

Hetata, S. 1982. *The Eye with an Iron Lid* (novel). London: Onyx Press.

Higa-san Iko-shu Henshu I'inkai [editorial committee for a posthumous collection of Mr. Higa's writings]. 1993. *Aru Nojuku Rodosha no Sei to Shi: Uchinanchu Higa-san no Iko Kara* (The life and death of a certain homeless worker: Posthumous excerpts from the writings of Mr. Higa, Uchinanchu). Fukuoka: Ashi Shobo.

Hirschman, A. O. 1982. "Rival interpretations of market society: Civilizing, destructive or feeble?" *Journal of Economic Literature* 20:1463–1484.

Hochschild, A. R. 1997. *The Time Bind: When Work Becomes Home and Home Becomes Work*. New York: Metropolitan Books.

Howe, L. 1990. *Being Unemployed in Northern Ireland: An Ethnographic Study*. Cambridge: Cambridge University Press.

_____. 1998. "Scrounger, worker, beggarman cheat: The dynamics of unemployment and the politics of resistance in Belfast." *Journal of the Royal Anthropological Institute*, n.s., Vol. 4, no. 3:531–550.

Hugh-Jones, S. 1979. *From the Milk River: Spatial and Temporal Processes in Northwest Amazonia*. Cambridge: Cambridge University Press.

_____. 1993. "Clear descent or ambiguous houses? A re-examination of Tukanoan social organisation." *L'Homme* 33:95–119.

_____. 1995. "Inside-out and back-to-front: The androgynous house in northwest Ama-zonia." In *About the House: Lévi-Strauss and Beyond*, ed. J. Carsten and S. Hugh-Jones. Cambridge: Cambridge University Press.

Hungarian Statistical Pocketbook. 1984. Budapest: Magyar Statisztikai Hivatal.

Ibrahim, S. [1966] 1986. *Cette Odeur-là* (novel). Trans. R. Jacquemond. Arles: Actes Sud.

_____. [1976] 1987. *Etoile d'Aout* (novel). Trans. J-F Fourcade. Paris: Sindbad.

_____. 1993. *Les Années de Zeth* (novel). Trans. R. Jacquemond. Arles: Actes Sud.

Ifunke no Kai. 1991. *Ifunke: Aru Ainu no Shi* (Ifunke: The death of an Ainu). Tokyo: Sairyusha.

Ingold, T. 1991. "Notes on the foraging mode of production." In *Hunters and Gatherers.* Vol. 1, *History, Social Change, and Evolution,* ed. T. Ingold, D. Riches, and J. Woodburn. Oxford: Berg.

_____. 1993. "The art of translation in a continuous world." In *Beyond Boundaries,* ed. G. Palsson. Oxford: Berg.

_____. 1996. "Hunting and gathering as ways of perceiving the environment." In *Redefining Nature: Ecology, Culture, and Domestication,* ed. R. Ellen and K. Fukui. Oxford: Berg

Ion, J., and M. Péroni, eds. 1997. *Engagement Public et Exposition de la Personne.* La Tour d'Aigues: Editions de l'Aube.

Jackson, J. 1975. "Recent ethnography of indigenous northern lowland South America." *Annual Review of Anthropology* 4:307–340.

Jacoby, R. 1995. "Marginal returns: The trouble with post-colonial theory." *Lingua Franca* (September/October):30–37.

Joseph, I. 1997. "Les vocabulaires de l'engagement." In *Engagement Publique et Exposition de la Personne,* ed. J. Ion and M. Péroni. La Tour d'Aigues. Editions de l'Aube.

Journet, N. 1995. *La Paix des Jardins.* Paris: Institut d'Ethnologie, Musée de l'Homme.

Kahn, J. 1995. *Culture, Multiculture, Postculture.* London: Sage Publications.

Kaplan, M., and J. D. Kelly. 1994. "Rethinking resistance: Dialogics of disaffection in colonial Fiji." *American Ethnologist* 21:123–151.

Kepel, G. 1985. *Muslim Extremism in Egypt: The Prophet and Pharaoh.* Trans. Jon Rothschild. Berkeley: University of California Press.

Kirzner, I. 1973. *Competition and Entrepreneurship.* Chicago: University of Chicago Press.

Koechlin, B. 1975. "Les Vezo du sud-ouest de Madagascar: Contribution a l'étude de l'ecosysteme de semi-nomades marins." *Cahiers de l'Homme* 15. Paris: Mouton.

Kondo, D. 1990. *Crafting Selves: Power, Gender, and Discourses of Identity in a Japanese Workplace.* London: University of Chicago Press.

Lan, D. 1985. *Guns and Rain: Guerrillas and Spirit Mediums in Zimbabwe.* London: James Currey.

Lathrap, D. 1968. "The 'hunting' economies of the tropical forest zone of South America: An attempt at historical perspective." In *Man the Hunter,* ed. R. Lee and I. DeVore. Chicago: Aldine.

La Tour, E. de la. 1996. Si Bleu Si Calme: La Prison Intérieure. 16mm film aired on Arte, 4 March 1997.

Lea, V. 1992. "Mebengokre (Kayapó) onomastics: A facet of houses as total social facts in central Brazil." *Man,* n.s., 27:129–153.

_____. 1995. "The houses of the Mebengokre (Kayapó) of Central Brazil: A new door on their social organization." In *About the House: Lévi-Strauss and Beyond,* ed. J. Carsten and S. Hugh-Jones. Cambridge: Cambridge University Press.

Leenhart, R. 1972. *L' Établi.* Paris: Editions de Minuit.

Leupp, G. P. 1992. *Servants, Shophands, and Laborers in the Cities of Tokugawa Japan.* Princeton: Princeton University Press.

Lévi-Strauss, C. 1968. "The concept of 'primitiveness.'" In *Man the Hunter*, ed. R. Lee and I. DeVore. Chicago: Aldine.

Lewis, O. 1966. "The culture of poverty." *Scientific American* 210 (October):10–25.

_____. (1965) 1968. *La Vida: A Puerto Rican Family in the Culture of Poetry.* 2d ed. New York: Knopf.

Liebow, E. 1967. *Tally's Corner.* Boston: Little, Brown.

Lima, D. 1992. "The social category 'caboclo': History, social organisation, identity, and outsiders' social classification of the rural population of an Amazonian region." Unpublished Ph.D. dissertation, University of Cambridge.

Lima, D., and E. de Castro. 1996. História e memória social no médio Solimões." Paper delivered to ABA conference. Salvador, Brazil, April 1996.

Linder, R. 1996. Reprint. *The Reportage of Urban Culture*, trans. A. Morris. Cambridge: Cambridge University Press, 1990.

Loizos, P., and E. Papataxiarchis. 1991. "Introduction: gender and kinship in marriage and alternative contexts." In *Contested Identities: Gender and Kinship in Modern Greece*, ed. P. Loizos and E. Papataxiarchis. Princeton: Princeton University Press.

Loureiro, V. 1985. *Os Parceiros Do Mar.* Belém: CNPq/MPEG.

MacLachlan, C. 1973. "The Indian directorate: Forced labour acculturation in Portuguese America (1757–1799)." In *Colonial Roots of Modern Brazil: Papers of the Newberry Library Conference*, ed. D. Alden. Berkeley: University of California Press.

MacLean, N. 1984. "Is gambling 'bisnis'? The economic and political functions of gambling in the Jimi valley." *Social Analysis* 16:44–59.

Macpherson, C. B. 1962. *The Political Theory of Possessive Individualism: Hobbes to Locke.* Oxford: Clarendon Press.

Marcus, G. ed. 1993. *Perilous States: Conversations on Culture, Politics, and Nation.* Chicago and London: University of Chicago Press.

Marikandia, M. 1991. Contribution à la connaissance des Vezo du Sud-Ouest de Madagascar: Histoire et société de l'espace littoral au Fiherena au XVIII et au XIX siècles. Thèse de Troisiéme cycle, Université de Paris I, Pantheon-Sorbonne.

Marx, K., and F. Engels. 1958. *Selected Works.* Vol. 1. Moscow: Progress Publishers.

Mavrogordatos, G. 1983. *Stillborn Republic: Social Coalitions and Party Strategies in Greece 1922–1936.* Berkeley: University of California Press.

McGrath, D. 1989. "The Paraense traders: Small-scale, long distance trade in the Brazilian Amazon." Unpublished Ph.D. dissertation, University of Wisconsin–Madison.

McGrath, D. et al. 1993. "Fisheries and the evolution of resource management on the lower Amazonia várzea." *Human Ecology* 21:167–196.

Meillassoux, C. 1973. "On the mode of production of the hunting band." In *French Perspectives in African Studies: A Collection of Translated Essays*, ed. P. Alexandre. Oxford: University Press for the International African Institute.

Menget, P. et al. 1985. "Guerre, société et vision du monde dans les basses terres de l'Amérique du Sud." *Journal de la Société des Américanistes* 71.

Miller, D. 1994. *Modernity, an Ethnographic Approach: Dualism and Mass-Consumption in Trinidad.* Oxford: Berg.

Mintz, S. 1974. *Caribbean Transformations.* Chicago: Aldine.

Mintz, S., and E. Wolf. 1968. "An analysis of ritual co-parenthood (compadrazgo)." In *Marriage, Family, and Residence*, ed. P. Bohannan and J. Middleton. New York: Natural History Press.

Mitchell, W. E. 1988. "The defeat of hierarchy: Gambling as exchange in a Sepik society." *American Ethnologist* 15:638–657.

Moffat, M. 1979. *An Untouchable Community in South India: Structure and Consensus*. Princeton: Princeton University Press.

Moran, E. 1974. "The adaptive system of the Amazonian caboclo." In *Man In the Amazon*, ed. C. Wagley. New York: Columbia University Press.

Morris, B. 1982. "Economy, affinity, and inter-cultural pressure: Notes around Hill Pardaram group structure." Man, n.s., 17:452–461.

Mouzelis, N. 1995. "Greece in the twenty-first century: institutions and political culture." In *Greece Prepares for the Twenty-First Century*, ed. D. Constas and T. Stavrou. Baltimore: Johns Hopkins University Press.

Murray, H. 1984. "Time in the streets." *Human Organization* 43:154–161.

Myers, F. 1986. *Pintupi Country, Pintupi Self: Sentiment, Place, and Politics among Western Desert Australian Aborigines*. Washington D.C.: Smithsonian Press.

Nakane, C. 1970. *Japanese Society*. London: Weidenfeld and Nicolson.

Namihira, E. 1977. "Hare, Ke, and Kegare: The structure of Japanese folk belief." Unpublished Ph.D. dissertation, University of Texas–Austin.

Naoum, N. 1991. *Retour au Temple* (novel). Trans. R. Jacquemond. Arles: Actes Sud.

Netting, R., R. Wilk, and E. Arnould, eds. 1984. *Households: Comparative and Historical Studies of the Domestic Group*. Berkeley: University of California Press.

Nugent, S. 1993. *Amazonian Caboclo Society: An Essay on Invisibility and Peasant Economy*. Oxford and Providence: Berg.

_____. 1997. "At play in the fields of culture." *Critique of Anthropology* 17:3–51.

Okely, J. 1975. "Gypsy women: Models in conflict." In *Perceiving Women*, ed. S. Ardener. London: Malaby.

_____. 1983. *The Traveller Gypsies*. Cambridge: Cambridge University Press.

Oldenburg, V. 1990. "Lifestyle as resistance: The case of the courtesans of Lucknow, India." *Feminist Studies* 16:259–287.

Ong, A. 1987. *Spirits of Resistance and Capitalist Discipline: Factory Women in Malaysia*. Albany: State University of New York Press.

Ortner, S. 1995 "Resistance and the problem of ethnographic refusal." *Comparative Studies in Society and History* 37:73–93.

Orwell, G. [1933] 1986. *Down and Out in Paris and London*. London: Penguin Books.

Overing, J. 1981. "Review article: Amazonian anthropology." *Journal of Latin American Studies*. 13:151–164.

_____. 1992. "Wandering in the market and the forest." In *Contesting Markets: Analyses of Ideology, Discourse, and Practice*, ed. R. Dilley. Edinburgh: Edinburgh University Press.

Pace, R. 1998. *The Struggle for Amazon Town: Gurupá Revisited*. Boulder, Colo.: Lynne Rienner Publishers.

Papataxiarchis, E. 1991. "Friends of the heart: Male commensal solidarity, gender, and kinship in Aegean Greece." In *Contested Identities: Gender and Kinship in Modern Greece*, ed. P. Loizos and E. Papataxiarchis. Princeton: Princeton University Press.

_____. 1992. "O kosmos tou kafeneiou" (The world of the coffee house). In *Tavtotites kai Fylo sti Synchroni Elladha* (Gender identities in modern Greece), ed. E. Papataxiarchis and T. Paradellis. Athens: Kastaniotis Publications.

_____. 1994. "Emotions et stratégies d'autonomie en Grèce égéenne." *Terrain* 23:5–20.

_____. 1995. "Male mobility and matrifocality in the Aegean Basin." In *Brothers and Others: Essays in Honour of John Peristiany,* ed. J. Pitt-Rivers et al. Paris and Athens: Museé de l'homme and EKKE.

Park, R. 1913. "The marginal man: A study of the mulatto mind." N.p.

_____. 1928. "Human migration and the marginal man." *American Journal of Sociology* 33:881–893.

_____. 1931. "The mentality of racial hybrids." *American Journal of Sociology* 36:534–551.

Parker, C. H. 1920. *The Casual Labourer and Other Essays.* New York: Harcourt, Brace and Howe.

Parker, E., ed. 1985. *The Amazon Caboclo: Historical and Contemporary Perspectives.* Vol. 32, *Studies in Third World Societies.* Virginia: College of William and Mary.

Parry, J., and M. Bloch, eds. 1989. *Money and the Morality of Exchange.* Cambridge: Cambridge University Press.

Pateman, C. 1988. *The Sexual Contract.* Stanford: Stanford University Press.

Pearse, A. 1959. "Some characteristics of urbanization in the city of Rio de Janeiro." In *Urbanization in Latin America,* ed. P. M. Hauser. New York: UNESCO.

Perlman, J. E. 1976. *The Myth of Marginality: Urban Poverty and Politics in Rio De Janerio.* Berkeley: University of California Press.

Perrault, G. 1984. *Un Homme à Part.* Barrault Press.

Peteet, J. 1994. "Male gender and rituals of resistance in the Palestinian intifada: A cultural politics of violence." *American Ethnologist* 21:1–49.

Peterson, N. 1993. "Demand sharing: Reciprocity and the pressure for generosity among foragers." *American Anthropologist* 95:60–74

Piette, A. 1996. *Ethnographie de l'Action: L'Observations des Détails.* Paris: A. M. Métaillé.

Pillai, S. T. 1993. *Scavenger's Son.* Oxford: Heinemann.

Pine, F. 1988. "Kinship, marriage, and social change in a Polish highland village." Unpublished Ph.D. dissertation, University of London.

_____. 1993. "The cows and the pigs are his, the eggs are mine: women's labour and entrepreneurial activities in rural Poland." In *Socialism: Ideals, Ideologies, and Local Practice,* ed. C. Hann. London: Routledge.

_____. 1994. "Maintenir l' economie domestique: travail, argent et éthique dans les montagnes polonaises." *Terrain* 23:81–98.

_____. 1996. "Naming the house and naming the land: Kinship and social groups in the Polish highlands." *Journal of the Royal Anthropological Institute (Incorporating Man)* 2:443–459.

_____. 1997. "Pilfering culture: Górale identity in post-socialist Poland." *Paragraph* 20, no. 1 (Spring). [Special issue: *Changing Cultural Identities in Europe,* ed. D. Forgacs.]

_____. 1998. "Dealing with fragmentation: The consequences of privatisation for rural women in central and southern Poland." In *Surviving Post-Socialism: Local Strategies and Regional Responses in Post-Socialist Eastern Europe and the Former Soviet Union,* ed. S. Bridger and F. Pine. London: Routledge.

Prakash, G. 1990. *Bonded Histories: Genealogies of Labor Servitude in Colonial India.* Cambridge: Cambridge University Press.

Ramos, A. 1991. "Hall of mirrors." *Critique of Anthropology* 11, no. 2:155–169.
_____. 1994. "The hyperreal Indian. " *Critique of Anthropology* 14:153–171
_____. 1997. "Indigenous organisation in Brazil: A conversation with Alcida Ramos." Paper given at American Anthropological Association annual meeting, Washington D.C.
Réger, Z. 1990. *Útak a nyelvhez* (Routes to language). Budapest: Akadémiaikiadó.
Rehfisch, F., ed. 1975. *Gypsies, Tinkers, and Other Travellers.* London: Academic Press.
Rival, L. 1992. "Social transformations and the impact of formal schooling on the Huaorani of Amazonian Ecuador." Unpublished Ph.D. dissertation, University of London.
_____. 1993. "The growth of family trees: Huaorani conceptualization of nature and society." *Man,* n.s., 28:35–52.
_____. 1996a. *Hijos del Sol, Padres del Jaguar, los Huaorani Hoy.* Quito: Abya Yala.
_____. 1996b. "Blowpipes and spears: The social significance of Huaorani technological choices." In *Nature and Society: Anthropological Perspectives,* ed. P. Descola and G. Palsson. London: Routledge.
_____. 1998a. "Domestication as a historical and symbolic process: Wild gardens and cultivated forests in the Ecuadorian Amazon." In *Principles of Historical Ecology,* ed. W. Balée. New York: Columbia University Press.
_____. 1998b. "Introductory essay on South American hunters-and-gatherers." In *The Cambridge Encyclopedia of Hunters and Gatherers,* ed. R. Lee and R. Daly. Cambridge and New York: Cambridge University Press.
_____. In press/a. "Androgynous parents and guest children: The Huaorani comrade." *Journal of the Royal Anthropological Institute (Incorporating Man)* Vol. 5, no. 4.
_____. In press/b. "Marginality with a difference: How the Huaorani remain autonomous, preserve their sharing relations, and naturalize outside economic powers." In *Hunters and Gatherers in the Modern Context: Conflict, Resistance, and Self-Determination,* ed. M. Biesele and P. Schweitzer. Providence, R.I.: Berghan Books of Providence.
_____. Forthcoming. *Trekking Through History: Ecology and Society in the Ecuadorian Amazon.* New York: Columbia University Press.
Roosevelt, A. 1987. "Chiefdoms in the Amazon and Orinoco." In *Chiefdoms in the Americas,* ed. R. D. Drennan and C. A. Uribe. New York and London: University Presses of America.
_____. 1989. "Natural resource management in Amazonia before the conquest." In *Resource Management in Amazonia: Indigenous and Folk Strategies,* ed. D. A. Posey and W. Balée. (*Advances in Economic Botany* 7) New York: New York Botanical Society.
_____. 1991. *Moundbuilders of the Amazon: Geophysical Archaeology on Marajó Island.* New York and London: Academic Press.
_____. 1993. "The rise and fall of the Amazon chiefdoms." *La Remontée de l'Amazone.* (Special Issue) *L'Homme* 33:231–254.
Roussillon, A. 1990. "Intellectuels en crise dans l'Egypte contemporaine." In *Intellectuels et Militants dans l'Islam Contemporain,* ed. G. Kepel. Paris: Seuil.
_____. 1992. *Entre Réforme Sociale et Mouvement National: Identité et Modernisation en Egypte (1882–1962).* Cairo: CEDEJ.
Sahlins, M. 1968. "La première société d' abondance." *Les Temps Modernes* 268:641–680.
_____. 1965. "On the sociology of primitive exchange." In *The Relevance of Models for Social Anthropology,* ed. M. Banton. London: Tavistock.
Saito, H. 1994. *Kankoku-kei Nihon-jin: Maria Onma no Kiseki o Otte* (A South Korean Japanese: Tracing the trajectory of Maria Onma). Tokyo: Sairyusha.

Sakellaropoulos, T. 1992. "I metapolemiki agrotiki politiki" (The post-war agricultural policy). In *Oikonomia kai Politiki sti Synchroni Elladha* (Economy and politics in modern Greece), ed. T. Sakellaropoulos. Athens: Pliroforisi.

Schneider, D. 1968. Reprint. *American Kinship: A Cultural Account.* Chicago: Chicago University Press.

Scott, J. 1985. *Weapons of the Weak: Everyday Forms of Peasant Resistance.* New Haven: Yale University Press.

_____. 1990. *Domination and the Arts of Resistance: Hidden Transcripts.* New Haven: Yale University Press.

Sibley, D. 1995. *Geographies of Exclusion: Society and Difference in the West.* London: Routledge.

Simmel, G. 1955. *Conflict and the Web of Group Affiliations.* Glencoe, Ill.: The Free Press.

Slater, C. 1994. *Dance of the Dolphin.* Chicago: Chicago University Press.

Spathis, P. 1995. *Agrotiki Pisti kai Synetairismoi* (Agricultural credit and cooperatives). Athens: ISEM.

Spruce, R. 1970. *Notes of a Botanist on the Amazon and Andes.* New York and London: Johnson Reprint Co.

Stamatoukos, J., and P. Spathis. 1990. *Agrotiki Pisti* (Agricultural credit). Athens: Agricultural Bank of Greece.

Stauth, G. 1993. "Return to the village: Patterns of spiritual, social, and spatial relocations of Egyptian intellectuals in the 1980s and 1990s." Working paper no. 193, Sociology of Development Research Centre, Bielefeld.

Steinberg, S. 1991. *The Ethnic Myth: Race, Ethnicity, and Class in America.* Boston:Beacon Press.

_____. 1995. *Turning Back: The Retreat from Racial Justice in American Thought and Policy.* Boston: Beacon Books.

Stevens, C. 1997. *On the Margins of Japanese Society.* London: Routledge.

Stewart, M. 1993. "Gypsies, the work ethic and Hungarian society." In *Socialism: Ideals, Ideologies, and Local Practice,* ed. C. Hann. London: Routledge.

_____. 1997. *The Time of the Gypsies.* Boulder, Colo.: Westview.

Stoler, A. 1986. "Plantation politics and protest on Sumatra's east coast." *Journal of Peasant Studies* 13:24–43.

Strathern, M. 1988. *The Gender of the Gift: Problems with Women and Problems with Society in Melanesia.* Berkeley: California University Press.

Sweet, D. 1974. "A rich realm of nature destroyed: The middle Amazon valley, 1640–1750." Unpublished Ph.D. dissertation, University of Wisconsin.

Tawfiq Ibrahim, Hasanayn. 1994. "La violence politique en Egypte." In *Le Phénomène de la Violence Politique: Perspectives Comparatistes et Paradigme Egyptien,* ed. B. Dupret. Cairo: Dossiers du CEDEJ.

Thapan, M. 1995. "Images of the body and sexuality in women's narratives on oppression in the home." *Economic and Political Weekly,* 28 October.

Thevenot, L. 1997. "Pragmatique de la Connaissance." In *Sociologie et Connaissance: Nouvelles approches cognitifs,* ed. A. Bornex, R. Bouvier, and P. Pharo. Paris: Editions CNRS.

Thomas, N. 1991. *Entangled Objects: Exchange, Material Culture, and Colonialism in the Pacific.* Cambridge, Mass.: Harvard University Press.

Tooker, D. E. 1996. "Putting the mandala in its place: A practice-based approach to the spatialization of power on the Southeast Asian 'periphery'—the case of the Akha." *The Journal of Asian Studies* 55, no. 2:323–358.

Tsoukalas, C. 1995. "Free riders in wonderland; or, of Greeks in Greece." In *Greece Prepares for the Twenty-First Century*, ed. D. Constas and T. Stavrou. Baltimore: John Hopkins University Press.

Turner, V. 1974. *Dramas, Fields, and Metaphors: Symbolic Action in Human Society*. Ithaca: Cornell University Press.

Uchiyamada, Y. 1995. "Sacred grove *(kaavu)*: Ancestral land of 'landless agricultural labourers' in Kerala, India." Unpublished Ph.D. dissertation, University of London.

_____. 1997a. "Ancestor spirits and land reforms: Contradictory discourses and practices on rights on land in South India." *IDRI Occasional Paper* 1.

_____. 1997b. "Identity and 'twisted' debt relationships in Kerala, India." *IDRI Occasional Paper* 2.

_____. 1998. "'The grove is our temple.' Contested representations of Kaavu in Kerala, South India." In *The Social Life of Trees*, ed. L. Rival. Oxford: Berg.

_____. Forthcoming. "Soil, self, resistance: Late-modernity and spirit possession in Kerala." *Purusartha* 21 [Special issue: *Possession in South Asia: Self, Territory, and Borders*, ed. J. Assayag and G. Tarabout.] Paris: Ecole des Hautes Etudes en Sciences Sociales.

Verdery, K. 1995. "'Caritas' and the reconceptualisation of money in Romania." *Anthropology Today* 11:3–7.

Verissimo, J. 1970. *Estudos Amazônicos*, Coleção Amazônica. Serie Jose Verissimo. Belem: UFPa.

Viswambharan, R. 1996. "Striikalkkumaatiyam" (Women only). *Mangalam* 27, no. 23:25.

Viveiros de Castro, E. 1992. *From the Enemy's Point of View: Humanity and Divinity in an Amazonian Society*. Chicago: Chicago University Press.

_____. 1996a. "Images of nature and society in Amazonian ethnology." *Annual Review of Anthropology* 25:179–200.

_____. 1996b. "Cosmological deixis and Amerindian perspectivism: A view from Amazonia." *Journal of the Royal Anthropological Institute (Incorporating Man)* 2:115–144.

Vogel, E. F. 1979. *Japan as Number One: Lessons for America*. Cambridge, Mass.: Harvard University Press.

Wagley, C. [1953] 1976. *Amazon Town: A Study of Man in the Tropics*. New York: Macmillan.

Wallace, A. 1989. *A Narrative of Travels on the Amazon and Rio Negro*. London: Ward, Lock and Co.

Ward, H., S. Day, J. Mezzone, L. Dunlop, C. Donegan, S. Farrar, L. Whitaker, J. R. W. Harris, and D. L. Miller. 1993. "Prostitution and risk of HIV: Female prostitutes in London." *British Medical Journal* 307:56–58.

Ward, H., and S. Day. 1997. "Health care and regulation: New perspectives." In *Rethinking Prostitution*, ed. G. Scambler and A. Scambler. London: Routledge.

Wasserfall, R. 1990. "Bargaining for gender identity: Love, sex, and money in an Israeli Moshav." *Ethnology* 29:327–340.

Wedel, J., ed. 1992. *The Unplanned Society: Poland During and After Communism*. New York: Columbia University Press.

Werbner, P., and T. Modood, eds. 1997. *Debating Cultural Hybridity: Multi-cultural Identities and the Politics of Anti-Racism*. London and New Jersey: Zed Books.

Whitten, N. 1985. *Sicuanga Runa: The Other Side of Development in Amazonian Ecuador*. Urbana: University of Illinois Press.

Williams, P. 1984. *Marriage Tsigane: Une Cérémonie de fiançaille chez les Rom de Paris*. Paris: L'Harmattan, Selaf.

Williams, R. 1912. *The Liverpool Docks Problem*. Liverpool: Northern Publishing Co.

Willis, P. 1977. *Learning to Labour: How Working Class Kids Get Working Class Jobs*. Aldershot: Ashgate.

Wiseman, J. O. 1970. *Stations of the Lost: The Treatment of Skid Row Alcoholics*. New York: Prentice-Hall.

Woodburn, J. 1968. "Discussions, Part II." In *Man the Hunter*, ed. R. B. Lee and I. DeVore. Chicago: Aldine.

_____. 1979. "Minimal politics: The political organisation of the Hadza of Tanzania. In *Politics in Leadership: A Comparative Perspective*, ed. P. Cohen and W. Shack. Oxford: Clarendon Press.

_____. 1981. "Egalitarian Societies." *Man*, n.s., 17:31–51.

_____. 1982. "Social dimensions of death in four African hunting and gathering societies." In *Death and the Regeneration of Life*, ed. M. Bloch and J. Parry. Cambridge: Cambridge University Press.

_____. 1988. "African hunter-gatherer social organisation: Is it best understood as a product of encapsulation?" In *Hunters and Gatherers. Vol. 1, History, Social Change, and Evolution*, ed. T. Ingold, D. Riches, and J. Woodburn. Oxford: Berg.

_____. 1997. "Indigenous discrimination: The ideological basis for local discrimination against hunter-gatherer minorities in sub-Saharan Africa." *Ethnic and Racial Studies* 20, no.2 (April):45–61.

_____. 1998 "Sharing is not a form of exchange": An analysis of property sharing in immediate return hunter-gatherer societies." In *Property Relations: Renewing the Anthropological Tradition*, ed. C. M. Hann. Cambridge: Cambridge University Press.

Yanagisako, S. 1979. "Family and household: The analysis of domestic groups." *Annual Review of Anthropology* 8:161–205.

_____. 1987. "Mixed metaphors: Native and anthropological models of gender and kinship domains." In *Gender and Kinship: Essays Towards a Unified Analysis*, ed. J. Collier and S. Yanagisako. Stanford: Stanford University Press.

Yanagisako, S., and J. Collier. 1995. "Naturalizing power." In *Naturalizing Power: Essays in Feminist Cultural Analysis*, ed. S Yanagisako and J. Collier. London: Routledge.

Yokoyama, G. [1899] 1985. *Nippon no Kaso Shakai* (Japan's lower class society). Tokyo: Iwanami Shoten [Kyobunkan].

Yoshino, I. R., and S. Murakoshi. 1977. *The Invisible Visible Minority: Japan's Burakumin*. Osaka: Buraku Liberation Institute.

Zimmer, L., ed. 1987. "Gambling with cards in Melanesia and Australia." *Oceania* 58:1–59.

Zoubeida, S. 1993. "Naji: An Iraqi country doctor." In *Struggle and Survival in the Modern Middle East*, ed. Edmund Burke III. New York and London: Tauris.

About the Editors
and Contributors

Rita Astuti is a lecturer in anthropology at the London School of Economics and Political Science. She is the author of *The People of the Sea* (1995) and is currently engaged in a research project on infant cognition in Madagascar.

Fanny Colonna is Directeur de Recherche at the Centre Nationale de la Recherche Scientifique. She has worked for many years in North Africa, notably Algeria. Among her books is *Etre Marginal au Maghreb* (with Z. Daoud, 1991).

Sophie Day is a senior lecturer in anthropology at Goldsmiths College, London, and is also a senior research fellow at Imperial College, London, where her research into sexually transmitted infections and sex work is supported by the Wellcome Trust.

Tom Gill is a fellow of the Institute for Cultural and Human Research at Kyoto Bunkyo University, Japan. He is writing a book about the *yoseba*.

Mark Harris holds a post-doctoral fellowship awarded by the British Academy at the University of Manchester. He is working on a manuscript with the title *Confident Men: The Identity of an Amazonian Peasantry.*

Stephen Nugent is reader in anthropology at Goldsmith's College, London, and is author of *Big Mouth: The Amazon Speaks* (1990) and *Amazonian Caboclo Society: An Essay on Invisibility and Peasant Economy* (1993).

Evthymios Papataxiarchis is associate professor in the Department of Social Anthropology at the University of the Aegean, Greece. He is the coeditor (with Peter Loizos) of *Contested Identities: Gender and Kinship in Modern Greece* (1991).

Frances Pine is lecturer in anthropology at the University of Cambridge and is the coeditor (with Sue Bridger) of *Surviving Post-Socialism: Local Strategies and Regional Responses in Post-Socialist Eastern Europe and the Former Soviet Union* (1996).

Laura Rival is lecturer in the Department of Anthropology at the University of Kent at Canterbury. She is preparing a monograph titled, *Trekking Through History: The Huaorani of Amazonian Ecuador.*

Michael Stewart is a lecturer in anthropology at University College, London, and is the author of *The Time of the Gypsies* (1997). He is currently writing a book about the Gypsy Holocaust.

Yasushi Uchiyamada is a senior researcher at the Foundation for Advanced Studies on International Development, Tokyo. He is the author of various articles on untouchables in South India.

Index

Abortion, 17, 106, 149. *See also* Children; Household

Abundance, 12–13, 63, 70–75, 77
 and denial of labor, 4
 of money, 164
 sources of, 78(n5), 139–140, 172, 200
 symbolic construction of, 1, 74–75
 See also Economy

Adoption, forced, 27, 33–34

Aesthetics
 and pleasure, 93
 and politics, 20
 See also Style

Age. *See* Time, and aging

Agriculture, 48, 50–51, 160

Alcohol, 125, 134(n6). *See also* Gender

Althusser, Louis, 10, 43(n13)

Amazon
 invention of, 189
 rubber industry in, 187–188

Ancestors. *See* Authority, of ancestors

Anderson, Perry, 179

Australian Aborigines. *See* Hunters and gatherers

Autarky, 62, 67
 and flight, 26, 68–69,
 See also Abundance

Authority
 of ancestors, 86–87
 avoidance of, 3, 9, 16, 37–42, 52, 85, 129, 140
 imposition of, 86

Autonomy. *See* Freedom

Avoidance
 of debts, 8, 125
 of friendship, 151, 225–226
 of leaders, 42

of money, 164
of obligations, 75, 81, 85–86, 89, 105–106, 130–131, 146–147, 151, 205–206
of power, 217 *See also* Authority, avoidance of; Bachelors; Labor, devaluation of; Single women

Bachelors
 in Egypt, 216–219, 220
 in Greece, 166–167, 170
 in Japanese *yoseba*, 122–123, 127
 in Poland, 56
 See also Gender; Household; Marriage; Single women

Bandits. *See* Tricksters

Banks. *See* Borrowing

Bloch, Maurice, 2, 8, 10–11, 21, 58–59

Body
 symbolic division of human, 148
 transformed, 151–52

Borrowing, 126, 161, 169, 172–173

Bosses, 201
 relation of marginal people to, 48–49, 50, 52, 101, 105, 112–113, 130, 133(n30), 134(n10), 169, 205–206, 208–209

Boundaries
 of caste, 96–100, 109, 111
 geographical, 48
 between inside and outside, 28–29, 45–46, 50, 51, 54–55, 59, 68–69, 120, 131, 148, 170–171, 199
 between living and dead, 86–87
 transgression of, 40–41, 97–98, 105, 107, 111–112, 113, 114–115, 144, 150–153, 204–205

Motherhood, 148–150, 152. *See also*
Children; Household; Kinship;
Pregnancy; Single women
Muslims. *See* Islam
Myers, Fred, 11
Myth, 67–68, 107, 116(n5), 198

Names, 51
multiple, 9, 41, 122, 142–143
See also Labeling
Nasser, Gamal Abdel, 226–227
Nationalist discourse, and construction of
marginality, 21–22, 186–188

Okely, Judith, 24(n18)
Ortner, Sherry, 19
Outcaste status, 29, 120

Park, Robert, 182, 194(n4)
Perlman, Janice, 22–23(n4)
Piaroa (Amazon), 78(n3)
Planning. *See* Economy
Podhale. *See* Poland
Poland
difference of Gorale from other
peasants, 46
Gorale farmers of, 4, 15, 22, 25–26,
45–60
history of marginality in, 48–51, 53–55
Policing, of marginals, 30, 141
Political economy
and ethnography, 177
of modern Brazil, 179–180, 184–185,
186–188, 189, 198–199, 201–205
of modern Egypt, 213–214, 215–216
of modern Greece, 158, 159–161, 169
Politics
aesthetic dimension of, 13, 19, 20
and authority, 42, 85–86
and electoral bribery as
accommodation, 206–207
populist, 19–20, 173, 224–225
of the present orientation, 2–3, 18–20,
114–115, 154–155, 172–173, 207
of protest, 52, 159, 161, 181–182, 183,
191–192, 211(n18)
and resistance, 18–19, 159, 170, 172–173

Pollution, 97, 99, 106, 121
Poverty
and marginality, 5–7, 98–100
and rhetoric of undeserving poor, 6
Predation, prey/predator relationship, 26,
67, 77. *See also* Violence
Pregnancy, 16–17
difficulties with, 148–149, 152
without a man, 151
See also Abortion; Children;
Motherhood
Present
privileging of, 200
See also Abundance; Identity, created in
the present; Politics; Present
orientation; Time
Present orientation, 2–3, 123–127, 199–201
achievement of, 151–153
as feature of mainstream, 22(n2)
as ideology, 10–14, 16, 25
limits to, 14, 16–17, 46, 59, 83, 86–87,
138, 144
origins of, 5–10, 62, 77
pleasures of, 89–91, 92–94, 118
politics of, 18–22, 155
as "realism," 126, 209
state attempts to subvert, 126
Private, and public, 14–15, 16, 28, 144, 146,
156(n9)
Proletarians, 160
and culture of poverty, 6
Prostitutes. *See* India; United Kingdom
Prostitution
as business, 139–144
likened to day labor, 133(n6)
in marriage, 110–111, 155(n1)
See also Sex, as work

Reciprocity
denial of, 12, 64, 161–162, 165, 173,
175(n18)
and gambling, 159
between husbands and wives, 65–66,
78(n6)
See also Exchange; Generosity; Sharing
Religion
and anti-clericalism, 52